DATE DUE

~~JE 3 0 94~~ FE 8 02			
~~DE 2 3 '94~~			
~~OC 1 6 '98~~			
~~NO 3 00~~			
~~NO2 2 00~~			

DEMCO 38-296

GENOCIDE IN IRAQ

PREVIOUSLY PUBLISHED REPORTS ON IRAQ AVAILABLE FROM HUMAN RIGHTS WATCH

The Anfal Campaign in Iraqi Kurdistan: The Destruction of Koreme
Hidden Death: Land Mines and Civilian Casualties in Iraqi Kurdistan
Endless Torment: The 1991 Uprising in Iraq and its Aftermath
Unquiet Graves: The Search for the Disappeared in Iraqi Kurdistan
Needless Deaths in the Gulf War: Civilian Casualties During the Air Campaign and Violations of the Laws of War
Human Rights in Iraq

GENOCIDE IN IRAQ

THE ANFAL CAMPAIGN AGAINST THE KURDS

A Middle East Watch Report

Human Rights Watch

New York • Washington • Los Angeles • London

Library of Congress Card Catalog Number: 93-79064
ISBN: 1-56432-108-8

Cover photo shows Kurdish widows at newly exhumed mass grave site.
● Susan Meiselas, Magnum Photos, Inc.

Middle East Watch
Middle East Watch was founded in 1989 to establish and promote observance of internationally recognized human rights in the Middle East. The chair of Middle East Watch is Gary Sick and the vice chairs are Lisa Anderson and Bruce Rabb. Andrew Whitley is the executive director; Eric Goldstein is the research director; Virginia N. Sherry and Aziz Abu Hamad are associate directors; Suzanne Howard is the associate.

A PETITION

In the Name of God, the Merciful, the Compassionate

The Venerable Chief and Leader, the Honorable Saddam Hussein (May God Protect Him), President of the Republic and Head of the Honorable Revolutionary Command Council:

Struggling Comrade, I greet you. And I present myself to you as a devoted citizen.

I implore you in the name of Ba'athist Justice to hear my plight, which has deprived me of sleep night and day. For I lost all hope and when I had no one left to turn to except yourselves, I came to you with my problem, which may be of some concern to you.

Sir:

I, the undersigned, Assi Mustafa Ahmad, who returned as a prisoner of war on August 24, 1990, am a reserve soldier born in 1955. I participated in the Glorious Battle of Saddam's Qadissiyat in the Sector of Al-Shoush and was taken prisoner on March 27, 1982. I remained a prisoner until the day that the decision to exchange prisoners of war was issued. Then I returned to the homeland and kissed the soil of the Beloved Motherland and knelt in front of the portrait of our Victorious Leader and President Saddam Hussein. In my heart I felt a tremendous longing to return to my family. They would delight in seeing me, and I would delight in seeing them, and we would all be caught up in an overwhelming joy that could not be described.

However, I found my home completely empty. My wife and my kids were not there. What a catastrophe! What a horror! I was told that the whole family had fallen into the hands of the Anfal forces in the Anfal operation conducted in the Northern Region, under the leadership of Comrade Ali Hassan al-Majid. I know nothing of their fate. They are:

1. Azimah Ali Ahmad, born 1955/ My wife.
2. Jarou Assi Mustafa, born 1979/ My daughter.
3. Faraydoun Assi Mustafa, born 1981/ My son.
4. Rukhoush Assi Mustafa, born 1982/ My son.

I have thus come to you with this petition, hoping that you would take pity on me and inform me of their fate. May God grant you success and protect you. You have my thanks and respect.

[signature]
Former Prisoner of War
Reserve Soldier/Assi Mustafa Ahmad
Without home or shelter in Suleimaniyeh/
Chamchamal/Bekas Quarter/
Haji Ibrahim Mosque   October 4, 1990

THE REPLY

In the Name of God, the Merciful, the Compassionate

Republic of Iraq
Bureau of the Presidency

Reference No.: Sh Ayn/B/4/16565

Date: October 29, 1990

Mr. Assi Mustafa Ahmad
Suleimaniyah Governorate
Chamchamal District
Bekas Quarter
Haji Ibrahim Mosque

With regard to your petition dated October 4, 1990. Your wife and children were lost during the Anfal Operations that took place in the Northern Region in 1988.

Yours truly,

[signature]
Saadoun Ilwan Muslih
Chief, Bureau of the Presidency

TABLE OF CONTENTS

LIST OF MAPS

PREFACE & ACKNOWLEDGEMENTS

Occasionally, opportunity can grow out of tragedy. For Middle East Watch, the opportunity to carry out human rights research in northern Iraq for the first time opened up unexpectedly, in the wake of the tumultuous, heart-wrenching events of early 1991 familiar to most readers from their television sets. As Iraqi government troops fell back in the face of advancing allied troops and Kurdish *peshmerga* fighters, returning along with civilian refugees from the Turkish and Iranian borders, it became evident that Baghdad's long-standing ban on access to the Kurdish region by independent investigators had been broken -- by force majeure. How long the window of opportunity would stay open no one could predict.

The debilitating uncertainty remains. For the Iraqi Kurds, their future as an often-threatened minority as well as their lives are at risk. As of this writing, a severe economic squeeze, resulting from a combination of UN sanctions against Iraq and an internal blockade imposed by government forces, threatens to produce mass starvation among the 3.5 million inhabitants of the Kurdish rebel-controlled enclave. Government troops massed along a ceasefire line could easily reconquer the region before the West had a chance to come to the Kurds' aid.

For Middle East Watch, a driving consideration over the past two years has been whether time would permit adequate research to be conducted to obtain reliable information that could both convince international public opinion and, later, satisfy a court of law. Although interim reports have previously been released about the Anfal[1], with the

---

[1] *Hidden Death: Land Mines and Civilian Casualties in Iraqi Kurdistan* (October 1992; pp 67); *Unquiet Graves: The Search for the Disappeared in Iraqi Kurdistan* (February 1992; pp 41); and *The Anfal Campaign in Iraqi Kurdistan: The Destruction of Koreme* (January 1993; pp 116). The two latter reports were published jointly with Physicians for Human Rights. *Human Rights in Iraq*, a Middle East Watch report published in February 1990, contained a long chapter on the government's repression of the Kurds; it is available from Yale University Press (New Haven, 1990).

xi

publication of this book, the first objective has been accomplished. Although there is persuasive evidence that virtually all are dead, whether the fate of the many tens of thousands of Kurdish civilians "disappeared" by government forces during 1988 can be definitively settled anytime soon remains to be seen. Much depends on the future course of internal Iraqi politics.

Allegations about enormous abuses against the Kurds by government security forces had been circulating in the West for years before the events of 1991; Kurdish rebels had spoken of 4,000 destroyed villages and an estimated 182,000 disappeared persons during 1988 alone. The phenomenon of the Anfal, the official military codename used by the government in its public pronouncements and internal memoranda, was well known inside Iraq, especially in the Kurdish region. As all the horrific details have emerged, this name has seared itself into popular consciousness -- much as the Nazi German Holocaust did with its survivors. The parallels are apt, and often chillingly close.

Fragmented by their mountainous geography, their own political fractiousness, and the divide-and-rule policies of regional governments, at the time, few Kurds appreciated the highly organized and comprehensive nature of the Anfal. And for obvious reasons, prior to October 1991, when Kurdish rebel leaders unexpectedly found themselves temporary masters of much of their traditional lands, there were few hard facts for external organizations to rely upon.

In its February 1990 report, *Human Rights in Iraq*, Middle East Watch reconstructed what took place from exile sources, with what in retrospect turned out to be a high degree of accuracy. Even so, some of the larger claims made by the Kurds seemed too fantastic to credit. As it transpires, this has been a humbling, learning process for all those foreigners who followed Kurdish affairs from abroad. Western reporters, relief workers, human rights organizations and other visitors to Iraqi Kurdistan have come to realize that the overall scale of the suffering inflicted on the Kurds by their government was by no means exaggerated.

With this latest report, painstakingly compiled over eighteen months, Middle East Watch believes it can now demonstrate convincingly a deliberate intent on the part of the government of President Saddam Hussein to destroy, through mass murder, part of Iraq's Kurdish

minority. The Kurds are indisputably a distinct ethnic group[2], separate
from the majority Arab population of Iraq, and they were targeted during
the Anfal as Kurds. Two government instruments -- the October 1987
national census and the declaration of "prohibited areas", covering more
and more of the Kurdish countryside like a crazy-patterned quilt -- were
institutional foundations of this policy. These instruments were
implemented against the background of nearly two decades of
government-directed "Arabization", in which mixed-race districts, or else
lands that Baghdad regarded as desirable or strategically important, saw
their Kurdish population diluted by Arab migrant farmers provided with
ample incentives to relocate, and guarded by government troops.

The Kurds bear arms as a matter of course, and have regularly
resorted to them when thwarted in their demands for greater political
and cultural autonomy. Indeed, the Anfal cannot be understood without
an awareness of the half century of Kurdish armed struggle against the
central government of Iraq, through various political regimes. In the
early 1970s, the Ba'athists, still uncertain about their hold on power, went
much further than their predecessors in recognizing those demands --
offering a substantial degree of self-government and recognizing the
Kurds' separate identity in a new Provisional Constitution. That
constitution is still in force, and Baghdad still maintains the fiction that
"its" autonomous region, with its own Kurdish administration, is in force.
This puppet administration sits in government-controlled Kirkuk, and
regularly denounces the "foreign-backed usurpers" in the Kurdish rebel-
run territory.

The logic of the Anfal, however, cannot be divorced either from
the Iran-Iraq War. After 1986, both the Patriotic Union of Kurdistan
(PUK) and the Kurdistan Democratic Party (KDP), the two major parties,
received support from the Iranian government and sometimes took part
in joint military raids against Iraqi government positions; the KDP also
had a rear base inside Iran. That Baghdad was entitled to engage in
counterinsurgency action, to wrest control over Iraq's northeast border
region and much of the mountainous interior from rebels, is undisputed.
What Middle East Watch contends is that, in doing so, the central
government went much further than was required to restore its authority

---

[2] Anthropologically, they are an Indo-European people, speaking a language
that is related to Persian, albeit with a large admixture of Arabic and Turkish,
varying according to the countries they inhabit.

through legitimate military action. In the process, Saddam Hussein's regime committed a panoply of war crimes, together with crimes against humanity and genocide.

While many readers will be familiar with the attack on Halabja, in March 1988, in which up to 5,000 Kurdish civilians died -- the incident caused a brief international furor -- they may be surprised to learn that the first use of poison gas against the Kurds by the central government occurred eleven months earlier. All told, Middle East Watch has recorded forty separate attacks on Kurdish targets, some of them involving multiple sorties over several days, between April 1987 and August 1988. Each of these attacks were war crimes, involving the use of a banned weapon; the fact that noncombatants were often the victims added to the offence.

By our estimate, in Anfal at least 50,000 and possibly as many as 100,000 persons, many of them women and children, were killed out of hand between February and September 1988. Their deaths did not come in the heat of battle -- "collateral damage" in the military euphemism. Nor were they acts of aberration by individual commanders whose excesses passed unnoticed, or unpunished, by their superiors. Rather, these Kurds were systematically put to death in large numbers on the orders of the central government in Baghdad -- days, sometimes weeks, after being rounded-up in villages marked for destruction or else while fleeing from army assaults in "prohibited areas".

While a minority had been combatants, or else served as a "backing force" for the rebel parties, the vast majority of the dead were noncombatants whose death resulted from the fact that they inhabited districts declared off-limits by the Iraqi government. Underlining the deliberate, preplanned nature of the Anfal, those responsible for their murder by firing squad were usually members of élite security units unconnected to the forces responsible for the Kurds' capture; in other words, while one hand would sweep, the other would dispose of what the regime considered to be the "garbage".

Two experienced field researchers, Jemera Rone and Joost Hiltermann, assisted for part of the time by a junior researcher, spent six months in northern Iraq between April and September 1992, gathering testimonial information about the Anfal (see separate Note on Methodology). Previously, one 12-year old boy, Taymour Abdullah Ahmad, had been the only known survivor of many accounts that Kurds -- men, women and children -- had been trucked southward to the Arab heartland of Iraq in large numbers, and then disappeared. It was assumed they had all been summarily executed, but there was no proof. During their assignment, the Middle East Watch team found and interviewed another seven survivors of mass executions recalled in convincing detail; five of them had been taken away and shot during the six-month-long military campaign, two shortly afterward.

To reach the point whereby we could safely assert these conclusions, without fear of contradiction, has not been easy. A division of Human Rights Watch, Middle East Watch has already devoted more resources to this ambitious project than any other undertaking in its parent organization's fifteen-year history. For those individuals and foundations that have generously supported work on the Kurds Project, we are deeply grateful. The publication of this book is a landmark. But, the end is not yet in sight. Only when those responsible -- both the government as a whole and the individuals who masterminded and carried out the Anfal -- are brought to justice will the work end.

In the absence of an international criminal court with jurisdiction to try those responsible for the grave crimes enumerated above, three options present themselves. The first is an Iraqi national court. Under present circumstances, with President Saddam Hussein and the Ba'ath Party still in power, it is almost inconceivable that this course will be realized. Second, there is the prospect of an ad hoc international tribunal, charged by the United Nations Security Council with hearing some or all of the above offences, on the basis of evidence to be gathered by a special commission of inquiry. While such a proposal has been tabled at the Security Council by the Clinton Administration, its realization is fraught with uncertainty, subject to the fluctuating politics of the major powers at the United Nations.

Last, there is the International Court of Justice (ICJ) at The Hague, the World Court. Part of the UN system, the ICJ's raison d'être is to resolve disputes between nations over breaches of international agreements and treaties; in the case of the Iraqi Kurds, the relevant treaty is the 1951 Convention on the Prevention and Punishment of the Crime of Genocide, to which Iraq and a further 107 states are parties. Importantly, Iraq has also accepted the jurisdiction of the ICJ to hear cases of genocide brought against itself by other state parties with similar standing. In Middle East Watch's judgement, this is potentially the most fruitful channel through which to achieve justice for the Anfal.

Pursuing this option does not involve abandoning the other courses of action; indeed, they could complement each other well, as the ICJ is empowered to adjudicate only state, not individual, responsibility. But, contrary to popular misconceptions, the ICJ can be of practical benefit to the Iraqi Kurds -- by, for instance, ordering provisional measures of protection (a state party or parties to the Genocide Convention would be acting in effect on behalf of the Kurds), or by demanding that the government pay damages, or reparations, to the victims.

To date, only Bosnia and Herzegovina has ever brought a case against another state under the Genocide Convention. The ICJ swiftly granted provisional protective measures, in March 1993, but has yet to rule on the substance of the complaint. Bringing a full-fledged case against Iraq, on behalf of the Kurds, will thus be a momentous event in international human rights law; one that it will be imperative to win, and to win on strong legal and factual grounds. The judgement will breathe life into the moribund Genocide Convention, strengthen respect for international law, and give pause to tyrannical regimes around the world tempted to undertake similar actions against a minority people.

How, then, has the evidence been gathered, and why is Middle East Watch confident that a successful action can be brought against the Iraqi government?

It was in late 1991 -- a month after the Iraqi Kurdistan Front, a coalition of seven parties, had established its authority in the rebel enclave -- that we decided to send our second mission to the region (an earlier mission had produced an authoritative survey of the endemic problem of landmines, a serious hindrance to the resettlement of refugees). This mission -- a joint venture with Physicians for Human Rights (PHR), who had already carried out groundbreaking work on Iraq's use of chemical gas in 1988 during the Final Anfal -- would enter Iraqi Kurdistan from Turkey. Its purpose was to examine the scale of the phenomenon of mass graves then being discovered by the Kurds in various locations. The ten-day mission exhumed several mass graves in and around the major Kurdish cities of Erbil and Suleimaniyeh, containing victims of the *Amn*, the main internal security force. The team left just as a deadline for the renewal of Operation Provide Comfort -- the Turkey-based allied protection operation -- expired (Ankara renewed permission at the eleventh hour).

During the unsuccessful March 1991 uprising, huge quantities of Iraqi government records were captured, when local Kurds stormed the secret police buildings that dominated every town and city. Much was burned or destroyed in the haste, confusion and panic that marked those days. The Kurds were mostly seeking references to themselves, to discover how much they had been infiltrated; few were thinking about the Anfal -- despite the fact that it had ended barely eighteen months earlier. Obtaining access to these official records became a Holy Grail for researchers: to have the opportunity to speak to survivors of human rights violations, dig up the bones of those who did not survive, and then read the official account of what took place -- all while the regime that carried out these outrages was still in power -- was unique in the annals of human rights research.

Together with the Iraqi writer Kanan Makiya[3] and Peter Galbraith of the U.S. Senate Foreign Relations Committee, Middle East Watch discussed with the Kurdish parties holding these documents their transfer to the United States, for safekeeping and analysis. Uncertainty surrounded the subject: Exactly how much had the Kurds seized; how useful would the documents turn out to be; where were the caches; and how could the logistical and diplomatic hurdles to getting them out of the country be overcome? Several visits to the region were required before all the arrangements could be made. In May 1992, some fourteen tons of documents were finally transferred to the U.S., at the initiative of Middle East Watch; at all times, the material remained under our control. On arrival, the Senate Foreign Relations Committee took charge of the documents, entrusting them to a safe location where they have been examined by a team led by Middle East Watch (see Methodology section for a description of how the work has been conducted.)

Primarily records of the *Mudiriyat al-Amn al-Ameh* (General Security Directorate), the *Mudiriyat al-Istikhbarat al-Askariyeh al-Ameh* (General Military Intelligence Directorate), and, to a lesser extent, the Ba'ath Party these documents represent a key ingredient in the understanding of the logic, and realization, of the Anfal. Spanning the years from the early 1960s to 1991, they will be crucial in the building of

---

[3] Makiya is the author, under his pseudonym, Samir al-Khalil, of *Republic of Fear: The Inside Story of Saddam Hussein's Iraq* (New York: Pantheon Books, 1990), and *Cruelty and Silence: War, Tyranny, Uprising and the Arab World* (New York: W.W. Norton, 1993).

a legal case against the Iraqi government. Between April 1992 and April 1993, Middle East Watch took oral testimony from over 350 eyewitnesses or survivors of Anfal-related actions by the authorities; this information forms the heart of our understanding of the government's behavior. Even on the basis of a partial examination, the documents have filled in many gaps, corroborating testimonial accounts and proving the witnesses' general reliability.

From the material examined to date, it is evident that detailed records had been kept of all Kurds rounded-up, then sorted out and dispatched, either to their deaths or to prison or resettlement camps. When the overlord of Anfal, Ali Hassan al-Majid, who was subsequently promoted to Defense Minister, met with Kurdish leaders in May 1991 for abortive peace negotiations, he knew what he was talking about. Faced with the Kurds' demands for an explanation as to what had happened to the disappeared -- a number they put at 182,000 -- he exploded that the total number (killed in the Anfal) "could not have been more than 100,000." It was a telling order of magnitude, not to mention an admission of guilt.

Somewhere in a Baghdad archive there exists, almost certainly, a complete dossier of the missing Kurds: some may still be alive, five years after their capture. But, in our view, the vast majority probably ended up in remote mass graves such as those described in this report. Middle East Watch calls on the Iraqi authorities to provide a full accounting of those they abducted so that relatives can mourn their dead and resume their lives.

Gradually it became clear from our field research that although the Anfal -- when most disappearances took place -- had lasted only six months, the main campaign of village destruction and forcible relocation of hundreds of thousands of persons inhabiting the "prohibited areas" had covered a two-year span, from March 1987 to April 1989. This coincided with the period during which al-Majid held extraordinary powers of life-and-death, as secretary of the Ba'ath Party's Northern Bureau. The campaign was the culmination of twenty-five years of Arabization, mass deportations and the destruction of villages.

We also learned about variations in government actions during different phases of the campaign. In the Final Anfal during late August 1988, after the ceasefire in the Iran-Iraq War, we encountered one of the few known cases in which government troops massacred male villagers on the spot. (Elsewhere male villagers disappeared en masse and are presumed to have been executed in clandestine locations.) The remote former village of Koreme, in Dohuk governorate, had been identified in February 1992 as containing a mass grave. A second forensic anthropological team, again in conjunction with PHR, drawing on the expertise of Latin American researchers, was sent to the region in May 1992. After a month's fieldwork at Koreme and other sites, their findings -- a detailed case study of the fate of Anfal victims from one region -- were published in January 1993.

After a break during the winter of 1992/1993, field research for this report resumed in March 1993, enabling gaps in our knowledge to be filled in. However, much remains to be done before all the answers are given to the tragedy that befell the Kurds. In the absence of disclosures from Baghdad, there is a need, for instance, to come up with a more precise estimate of the number of disappeared. Some, but by no means all, of the killing sites are known; extensive research work needs to be conducted in areas of Iraq that remain under government control.

But time does not stand still, and the Ba'athist regime's threat to the Kurdish enclave remains as potent as ever. Behind a military cordon running diagonally across northern Iraq -- a cordon that has sealed off supplies of food, fuel, medicine and other essentials to the Kurds for the past two years -- the government has massed its troops. All that apparently holds them back is the threat of retaliation from the American, British and French aircraft that daily patrol the region of Iraq north of the 36th parallel. Every six months the ritual of seeking Ankara's permission for the continuation of Operation Provide Comfort is reenacted. Until now it has always been granted; but, given Turkish negative sentiment toward the Kurds, whether in Turkey itself or across the Iraqi border, it is unlikely that Turkey will allow the Western allies to maintain their protective shield over the budding proto-state indefinitely.

Based on the evidence contained in this report, Middle East Watch urges the international community to recognize that genocide occurred in the mountainous region of northern Iraq during 1988. The legal obligations to act on the basis of this information, to punish its perpetrators and prevent its recurrence, are undeniable. These could be pursued either through the International Court of Justice or through the U.N. Security Council. The Security Council is required under the Genocide Convention to prevent genocidal action; moreover, in July 1993, the Council had before it a draft U.S. proposal to establish a commission of enquiry into Iraqi war crimes and genocide. For this purpose, the U.S. government, and other states with relevant information, should disclose what knowledge they have about the Anfal.

Continued protection for the Kurds is essential, if the strong threat of reprisals from the Baghdad authorities is not to be realized. But in the process of safeguarding the status quo one should not lose sight of the imperative that the Iraqi government provide a full, public accounting of all those taken into the hands of its forces before, during and after the Anfal. While it would be unrealistic to expect President Saddam Hussein to put himself and his closest aides and relatives on trial, a successor government in Baghdad should not shirk from its responsibility to carry out a thoroughgoing investigation of these enormous crimes, and prosecute all those involved -- to the full extent of the law.

The Iraqi Kurds must be permitted to live in peace and security, free to speak their language, practice their customs and associate as Kurds. The killings, deportations, and widespread village clearances detailed in the following pages must not be allowed to happen again.

* * *

This report was written by George Black, a writer on human rights and other international issues.[4] However, bringing it to fruition was a collaborative effort involving Mr. Black, Joost Hiltermann, the Kurds' Project director at Middle East Watch, and Jemera Rone, counsel at Human Rights Watch, the parent organization.

Overall editorial responsibility for the report lies with Andrew Whitley, executive director of Middle East Watch. Shorsh Resool, a researcher with Middle East Watch, contributed to the editing process and made important suggestions and corrections. Suzanne Howard was responsible for preparing the manuscript for publication. Document translation was handled by a number of persons.

Field researchers were Dr. Hiltermann and Ms. Rone, assisted by Mostafa Khezri, a consultant to Middle East Watch. Their field work in 1992 and 1993 represents the heart of the information presented in the

---

[4] Mr. Black's most recent book, *Black Hands of Beijing*, (John Wiley & Sons, New York, 1993) is a history of the Chinese democracy movement since 1976, co-authored with Robin Munro of Asia Watch.

following pages. The tireless work of our Kurdish interpreters in helping obtain this information is appreciated. Middle East Watch also extends its thanks to the Kurdistan Human Rights Organization in Iraqi Kurdistan, including its branches in Erbil, Suleimaniyeh and Dohuk; the Committee to Defend Anfal Victims' Rights in Suleimaniyeh; and a number of doctors, lawyers and other professionals in Iraqi Kurdistan, who must remain anonymous for their own safety. Special recognition is due to Mr. Resool, for his pioneering work, under arduous conditions, on the Anfal campaign in 1988-89, prior to joining the staff of Middle East Watch.

Forensic research referred to in this report was conducted by joint Middle East Watch/Physicians for Human Rights (PHR) teams led, in December 1991, by Eric Stover, and, in May-June 1992, by Ken Anderson. Mr. Stover is executive director of PHR; Mr. Anderson is director of Human Rights Watch's Arms Project. Dr. Clyde Snow, a distinguished forensic anthropologist, headed the scientific teams in both of these missions and participated in another visit to Iraqi Kurdistan, in February 1992.

Legal research on the standards by which the Ba'ath regime should be judged on its actions in Iraqi Kurdistan, from 1987-89, was undertaken by Professor Lori Damrosch of Columbia University's Law School. Keith Highet of Curtis, Mallet et al provided expert advice, as did Kenneth Roth, acting executive director of Human Rights Watch.

Peter Galbraith, then senior advisor to the U.S. Senate Foreign Relations Committee, and Ambassador Charles Dunbar, formerly of the U.S. Department of State, also deserve Middle East Watch's warm thanks for the unstinting assistance they provided to this large undertaking.

Finally, Middle East Watch wishes to thank Susan Meiselas for her enthusiasm, and commitment, to a subject and people she has come to know well. Her photographs and video recordings have been of great benefit.

Andrew Whitley
Executive Director
Middle East Watch
New York

A NOTE ON METHODOLOGY

THE METHODOLOGICAL APPROACH
TO
DOCUMENTARY, TESTIMONIAL AND FORENSIC EVIDENCE
USED IN THIS REPORT

TESTIMONIAL EVIDENCE

To a large measure this report is based on testimonies obtained in Iraqi Kurdistan from eyewitnesses to (and often victims of) Anfal-related abuses. Two Middle East Watch researchers and an assistant spent a total of six months in the Kurdish areas on three separate missions between April 1992 and April 1993, conducting approximately 350 in-depth interviews. The methodology they used in obtaining this testimonial evidence is described below.

Prior to its first mission in April 1992, the research team designed a questionnaire on the basis of our understanding of Anfal, still limited at that time, and following discussions with regional experts and statisticians. This questionnaire was constructed with a view to facilitating the tabulation and quantification of data concerning the forced displacement and/or disappearance of Kurds during Anfal.

The team tested the questionnaire through a small number of interviews shortly after its arrival in the area, and immediately determined that the questions did not take account of a number of factors, including specific historical events that are instrumental to understanding the circumstances that surrounded Anfal, as well as the methodical nature of the operation. The team then revised the questionnaire drastically and began its research, only making minor adjustments to the basic design in the weeks that followed.

The purpose of the research was to find out as much as possible about Anfal and about the people who were said to have disappeared during and after the operation. The research population was divided into three groups: (1) direct eyewitnesses to Anfal-related abuses; (2) persons active in (para-)military units, either Kurdish guerrillas (*peshmerga*), former military officers, or leaders (*mustashars*) of the pro-government

Kurdish militias; and (3) staff of local and international non-governmental organizations and officials of the local Kurdish administration, all of whom were intimately familiar with the situation on the ground before, during and after Anfal.

Because of the particular nature of Iraqi policy vis-a-vis rural Kurds in the 1980s, most eyewitnesses to Anfal were to be found in the large housing complexes (*mujamma'at*) in the valleys of northern Iraq. After the Iraqi government withdrew from a large part of the Kurdish region at the end of October 1991, villagers in some areas began returning to their destroyed villages to farm the lands and, sometimes, to rebuild their homes. The research team visited as many of the complexes as possible, as well as some of the (partially rebuilt) villages. In all cases, the operative question was: "Where can we find the Anfals?" (*Anfalakan*, in Kurdish). Local residents would then guide the team to a house where Anfalakan were said to be living, and some initial questioning was done to ascertain that the people were indeed "Anfals" and not persons who had been relocated there from their villages during earlier stages of village destruction and had not been affected directly by Anfal. This method had a snowball effect: one family of Anfalakan would lead the team to another, until the team felt it had exhaustively covered a particular geographic area of Anfal.

Essentially, the team obtained eyewitness testimonies in three different ways: (1) by visiting places of residence randomly and asking for Anfalakan (the most frequent method); (2) by pursuing specific leads; and (3) occasionally, by responding to unsolicited requests to be interviewed. In the beginning, the sole criterion employed in deciding whether or not a person should be interviewed was whether the person was present in a military-demarcated area during Anfal and had lost relatives as a result of the campaign. In later stages of the research, when clear patterns had started to emerge, the search was more specifically for persons from certain Anfal areas, i.e., those about which the team had insufficient data, or those where particularly egregious abuses, like chemical weapons attacks, had taken place. In addition, a number of interviews were conducted at that time with people who had been in Anfal areas during Anfal but whose families had managed to escape unhurt, as well as with people who had experienced various forms of human rights abuses in the periods immediately preceding and following Anfal (1987 and 1989).

The team specifically sought out one sub-population of eyewitnesses: those who had been arrested in Anfal and taken to mass execution sites (then and now in areas that are controlled by the Iraqi government) from where they had managed to escape and return to safety. The testimonies of these execution survivors have proven crucial in the effort of Middle East Watch to provide evidence that the vast majority of those detained during Anfal, whose fate is officially said to be unknown, were actually killed. The team was able to locate seven such Anfal survivors, as well as one person who had survived an execution three months after Anfal. Some of these survivors did not want their identities to be known because, they said, they feared future government reprisal. One of the eight, Taymour, had already been interviewed by local Kurdish television, as well as by foreign journalists on numerous occasions. A second one, Hussein, had given testimony to the UN Special Rapporteur on Iraq, Mr. Max van der Stoel, during the latter's visit to the area earlier in 1992. Four were located through local *peshmerga* commanders who had heard of their stories. The remaining two were found through the testimony of one of the survivors who had been in the same group as them at the time of the execution.

Invariably, respondents were eager to tell the team what had happened to them. In almost all cases, these people had not been interviewed about their experiences before. All freely gave their names, and only some requested that their identities be concealed for publication. Apart from the small number of persons who requested that their names be changed, all names referred to in this report are genuine. The team taped most interviews on audio-cassette and took photographs (slides) of the respondents afterwards. In the case of important interviews, the team asked the respondent's permission to videotape either highlights or a full second interview (as in the case of some of the execution survivors). The team traveled with one or more Kurdish interpreters at all times. These persons were asked to provide literal translations from English to Kurdish (Surani or Kurmanji dialects) and back. In addition, some interviews were conducted by team members directly in English or in Arabic.

In virtually all cases, the team interviewed a single person at a time, although close relatives were often present during the interview. The questions covered the following topics:

1. Personal history before Anfal (personal status, family members, property, occupation, religious and tribal affiliations, etc.)

2. Information concerning the village in which the person was living before Anfal (location, size of population, main tribe, main economic activity, availability of goverment services and facilities, etc.)

3. Military activity in and around the village before Anfal, and government policies affecting the inhabitants (presence of *peshmerga*, government attacks, administrative and economic blockade, casualties, 1987 population census, etc.)

4. Events during Anfal (nature of government attack, circumstances of arrest, route of transport, selection process, conditions of detention, casualties, circumstances of release, etc.)

5. Living conditions after Anfal and attempts, if any, to locate missing relatives.

Usually, topics 1 and 2 followed a fairly strict question-and-answer format, while topics 3, 4 and 5 allowed for greater flexibility: the person was asked to recount events as he or she remembered them, and the team would (a) only ask questions for clarification about specific dates, locations or identities; or (b) pursue at some length a narrative of particular interest to the project; or (c) probe any contradictions that might appear in the testimony, or between the testimony and a previous one.

Due to the high incidence of illiteracy in rural Kurdistan, as well as the local population's particular way of marking time, the team encountered considerable difficulty in its attempts to establish exact dates for specific events, or particular chronologies, on the basis of interviews with individual villagers. Dates would often be related to religious feasts, for example. On the whole, though, after numerous interviews, the team was satisfied that it had obtained an accurate picture of the separate stages of Anfal and the events that transpired within these stages. Some of these dates have subsequently been substantiated in documents captured by the Kurds from the Iraqi intelligence agencies during the March 1991 uprising.

Generally, the team determined the accuracy of individual accounts by virtue of their internal consistency, their general consistency with the overall patterns that emerged during the project, including with other types of evidence, and their specific consistency with a follow-up interview conducted, in a few cases, with the same respondent. In the case of all interviews, the team tried to obtain supporting evidence. This included personal documents that were in the possession of the respondents (for example, "movement permits" and administrative orders), or an inspection of the site described (e.g. a prison, or a village that had been subjected to a chemical attack). As a result of this procedure, a small number of interviews, or segments thereof, were discarded or left unused, either because the testimony was not deemed to be reliable or sufficient supporting evidence was not immediately available.

* * *

DOCUMENTARY EVIDENCE

In the March 1991 popular uprising in northern Iraq, Kurdish civilians and members of the Kurdish political parties stormed and took control of offices of the Iraqi government and its agencies, including the various intelligence agencies. Several of these buildings were heavily damaged, or even burned to the ground, but others survived unscathed. The Kurds thus came into possession of the inventories of many of these facilities. Matters taken include large quantities of documents, logs and registers, as well as audiotapes, videotapes, films and photographs.

In the days before the uprising was crushed by advancing Iraqi troops, the Kurdish parties succeeded in removing the majority of the documents they had captured from the towns to strongholds in the mountains. In the spring of 1992, one of the two largest parties, the Patriotic Union of Kurdistan (PUK), agreed to a tripartite arrangement in which Middle East Watch and the U.S. Senate Foreign Relations Committee were the other two partners. Under this arrangement, the PUK agreed to send the documents in its possession to the United States for research and analysis; the Senate Foreign Relations Committee agreed to turn the documents into official records of the U.S. Congress and store them in the facilities of the U.S. National Archives; and Middle East Watch agreed to conduct research on the documents for human rights purposes, including the pursuit of a genocide case before the International Court of Justice at The Hague.

The PUK cache consists of fourteen tons of documents contained in 847 boxes. The total number of pages has been estimated at over four million. In May 1992, the PUK placed these documents in the temporary custody of Middle East Watch and they were then flown, in the presence of the director of Middle East Watch, to the United States. In Washington, D.C., the documents were then handed over to the U.S. National Archives and placed in its storage facilities, while remaining under the joint custody of the PUK and Middle East Watch.

At the end of October 1992, a Middle East Watch-led team of researchers began the task of screening, cataloguing, and analyzing these documents. Important documents were pulled out, photocopied and translated, and a number of these have been included in this report. The United Nations Special Rapporteur on Iraq, Mr. Max van der Stoel, has also made use of some of the documents found by Middle East Watch, in his report to the U.N. Human Rights Commission in March 1993.

The vast majority of the documents are from two main locations: Suleimaniyeh governorate and its districts; and Erbil governorate and its districts, especially the *qadha* of Shaqlawa. Almost all hail from the offices of Iraq's General Security Directorate (*Mudiriyat al-Amn al-Ameh*) in these locations, with a smattering of documents belonging to the General Military Intelligence Directorate (*Mudiriyat al-Istikhbarat al-Askariyeh al-Ameh*) and the Ba'ath Party. Generally, the documents are either file folders or pages tied together with shoelaces between two hard covers. There are also a number of bound ledgers. Due to the conditions that prevailed at the time of the uprising, especially in Suleimaniyeh, a number of the documents have completely fallen apart, and individual pages have been burned, trampled upon, muddied, or, in many cases, torn. The majority of the documents are in good order, however.

All documents, handwritten or typewritten, are in good and legible Arabic. They cover a wide variety of subjects that can most easily be divided into three main categories:

(1) administrative matters concerning agency staff: salaries, vacations, promotions, gun permits, disciplinary actions, etc.

(2) Personal information: These are files containing information on agency staff, ordinary citizens, or suspected members of Kurdish resistance parties. They include secret background checks, as well as records of investigations and interrogations. A number of files contain

virtual life histories, some concluding with execution orders and death certificates.

(3) Reports on events in the area, and policy statements: These two types of documents are often mixed in together, and include reports on *Amn* and military actions undertaken against the *peshmerga*; reports on *peshmerga* activity in a particular area; and official orders and instructions that are being passed on down through the ranks.

Although the three categories generally appear separately in the documents, it does happen that a copy of an important order concerning the government's policy vis-a-vis the Kurds will appear in a person's secret file. Sometimes, evidence of abuse is either fragmentary and embedded in a larger text that outwardly seems innocuous, or phrased in such euphemistic terms that an untrained eye would have difficulty in recognizing it. The task of the Middle East Watch-led team, then, has essentially been to sift through these tons of documents in search of hidden nuggets.

* * *

FORENSIC EVIDENCE

A team of forensic investigators was sent by Middle East Watch and Physicians for Human Rights to Iraqi Kurdistan in May-June 1992. The team consisted of forensic investigators trained in forensic anthropology, archeology, and law, who had carried out exhumations of graves in several countries, including Argentina, Chile, El Salvador and Guatemala. It carried out exhumations of graves at three sites in Iraqi Kurdistan: at the village of Koreme, the village of Birjinni, and the cemetery of a complex of Anfal survivors outside the city of Erbil.

In its investigations, the team followed internationally accepted standards set forth in the United Nations "Model Protocol for a Legal Investigation of Extra-Legal, Arbitrary and Summary Executions" (the "Minnesota Protocol").[1] The full results of the team's investigations are

---

[1] *Manual on the Effective Prevention and Investigation of Extra-Legal, Arbitrary and Summary Executions*, 1991.

found in Middle East Watch and Physicians for Human Rights, *The Anfal Campaign in Iraqi Kurdistan: The Destruction of Koreme*, January 1993, and its methodology at each site is described below.

Koreme Site:
    The team undertook the exhumation of a mass grave at the destroyed village of Koreme containing the skeletal remains of twenty-six men and boys, all of whom had died by gunfire at close range in a line indicating execution by firing squad. The team archaeologist directed the survey of the destroyed village, mapping the village as it stood before destruction, using standard archeological survey techniques; in addition, the team archeologist directed the collection and mapping of cartridge casings to determine the pattern of weapons firing at the execution site. The team's lead anthropologist directed the exhumation of the gravesite at Koreme, using standard exhumation techniques to preserve the skeletons and other artifacts. Investigations were carried out at the morgue at Dohuk General Hospital to determine the number of different individuals in the grave; sex, age, and other identifying marks; and manner of death. The team's lawyers directed interviews with survivors and other villagers to give a narrative of events corroborated by scientific evidence.

Birjinni Site:
    The team carried out archeological surveys and exhumations of graves at the destroyed village of Birjinni which, according to surviving villagers, had been bombed in August 1988 with chemical weapons. The team archeologist carried out standard surveys of the ruined village. The forensic anthropologists exhumed the graves of persons reported to have died from inhalation of chemical agents. The team's lawyers conducted interviews with surviving villagers to obtain their account of events. In addition, the team took soil and other samples from the craters where chemical weapons were reported to have impacted. In 1993, the British Ministry of Defense chemical weapons laboratory at Porton Down reported discovering degradation products of mustard gas and nerve agents in samples taken from these sites. This is the first instance of a chemical weapons attack being proved on the basis of chemical residues left behind at the impact site.

Erbil Site:
    The team undertook exhumations at the graveyard of a complex where survivors of the Anfal were taken. The gravesite was surveyed by the archeological team in order to make determinations of the ratio of adult and child graves in the cemetery. The forensic scientists exhumed three children's graves, one of them reported to have been made by a survivor from the village of Koreme and containing his infant sister. The exhumation of that grave corroborated his account, and contained the skeletal remains of a girl about one-year old, with evidence of malnutrition.

———

GENOCIDE IN IRAQ

Iraq and Iraqi Kurdistan

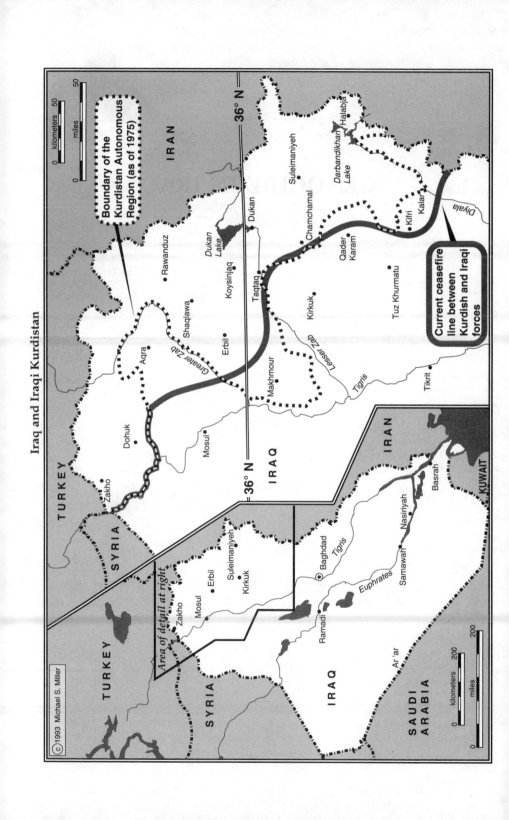

© 1993 Michael S. Miller

Boundary of the Kurdistan Autonomous Region (as of 1975)

Current ceasefire line between Kurdish and Iraqi forces

TURKEY

SYRIA

IRAN

Zakho

Dohuk

Aqra

Shaqlawa

Erbil

Greater Zab

Mosul

Rawanduz

Koysinjaq

Dukan Lake

Dukan

Taqtaq

Makhmour

Lesser Zab

Kirkuk

Chamchamal

Qader Karam

Suleimaniyeh

Darbandikhan Lake

Halabja

Kalar

Kifri

Diyala

Tuz Khurmatu

Tigris

Tikrit

IRAQ

36° N

36° N

IRAN

0 kilometers 50

0 miles 50

Area of detail at right

TURKEY

SYRIA

Zakho

Mosul

Erbil

Kirkuk

Suleimaniyeh

Tigris

Baghdad

Ramadi

Euphrates

Samawah

Nasiriyah

Basrah

IRAN

KUWAIT

SAUDI ARABIA

IRAQ

Ar 'ar

0 kilometers 200

0 miles 200

INTRODUCTION

This report is a narrative account of a campaign of extermination against the Kurds of northern Iraq. It is the product of over a year and a half of research, during which a team of Middle East Watch researchers has analyzed several tons of captured Iraqi government documents and carried out field interviews with more than 350 witnesses, most of them survivors of the 1988 campaign known as Anfal. It concludes that in that year the Iraqi regime committed the crime of genocide.

Anfal--"the Spoils"--is the name of the eighth *sura* of the Koran. It is also the name given by the Iraqis to a series of military actions which lasted from February 23 until September 6, 1988. While it is impossible to understand the Anfal campaign without reference to the final phase of the 1980-1988 Iran-Iraq War, Anfal was not merely a function of that war. Rather, the winding-up of the conflict on Iraq's terms was the immediate historical circumstance that gave Baghdad the opportunity to bring to a climax its longstanding efforts to bring the Kurds to heel. For the Iraqi regime's anti-Kurdish drive dated back some fifteen years or more, well before the outbreak of hostilities between Iran and Iraq.

Anfal was also the most vivid expression of the "special powers" granted to Ali Hassan al-Majid, a cousin of President Saddam Hussein and secretary general of the Northern Bureau of Iraq's Ba'ath Arab Socialist Party. From March 29, 1987 until April 23, 1989, al-Majid was granted power that was equivalent, in Northern Iraq, to that of the President himself, with authority over all agencies of the state. Al-Majid, who is known to this day to Kurds as "Ali Anfal" or "Ali Chemical," was the overlord of the Kurdish genocide. Under his command, the central actors in Anfal were the First and Fifth Corps of the regular Iraqi Army, the General Security Directorate (*Mudiriyat al-Amn al-Ameh*) and Military Intelligence (*Istikhbarat*). The pro-government Kurdish militia known as the National Defense Battalions, or *jahsh*, assisted in important auxiliary tasks.[1] But the integrated resources of the entire military, security and

---

[1] A derisive Kurdish term for the National Defense Battalions, the word *jahsh* means "donkey foals."

3

civilian apparatus of the Iraqi state were deployed, in al-Majid's words, "to solve the Kurdish problem and slaughter the saboteurs."[2]

The campaigns of 1987-1989 were characterized by the following gross violations of human rights:

• mass summary executions and mass disappearance of many tens of thousands of non-combatants, including large numbers of women and children, and sometimes the entire population of villages;

• the widespread use of chemical weapons, including mustard gas and the nerve agent GB, or Sarin, against the town of Halabja as well as dozens of Kurdish villages, killing many thousands of people, mainly women and children;

• the wholesale destruction of some 2,000 villages, which are described in government documents as having been "burned," "destroyed," "demolished" and "purified," as well as at least a dozen larger towns and administrative centers (*nahyas* and *qadhas*);

• the wholesale destruction of civilian objects by Army engineers, including all schools, mosques, wells and other non-residential structures in the targeted villages, and a number of electricity substations;

• looting of civilian property and farm animals on a vast scale by army troops and pro-government militia;

• arbitrary arrest of all villagers captured in designated "prohibited areas" (*manateq al-mahdoureh*), despite the fact that these were their own homes and lands;

• arbitrary jailing and warehousing for months, in conditions of extreme deprivation, of tens of thousands of women, children and elderly people, without judicial order or any cause other than their presumed sympathies for the Kurdish opposition. Many hundreds of them were allowed to die of malnutrition and disease;

---

2 "Saboteurs" is the term commonly applied by the Iraqi regime to the Kurdish *peshmerga* guerrillas and their civilian sympathizers.

• forced displacement of hundreds of thousands of villagers upon the demolition of their homes, their release from jail or return from exile; these civilians were trucked into areas of Kurdistan far from their homes and dumped there by the army with only minimal governmental compensation or none at all for their destroyed property, or any provision for relief, housing, clothing or food, and forbidden to return to their villages of origin on pain of death. In these conditions, many died within a year of their forced displacement;

• destruction of the rural Kurdish economy and infrastructure.

Like Nazi Germany, the Iraqi regime concealed its actions in euphemisms. Where Nazi officials spoke of "executive measures," "special actions" and "resettlement in the east," Ba'athist bureaucrats spoke of "collective measures," "return to the national ranks" and "resettlement in the south." But beneath the euphemisms, Iraq's crimes against the Kurds amount to genocide, the "intent to destroy, in whole or in part, a national, ethnical, racial or religious group, as such."[3]

＊ ＊ ＊

The campaigns of 1987-1989 are rooted deep in the history of the Iraqi Kurds. Since the earliest days of Iraqi independence, the country's Kurds--who today number more than four million--have fought either for independence or for meaningful autonomy. But they have never achieved the results they desired.

In 1970, the Ba'ath Party, anxious to secure its precarious hold on power, did offer the Kurds a considerable measure of self-rule, far greater than that allowed in neighboring Syria, Iran or Turkey. But the regime defined the Kurdistan Autonomous Region in such a way as deliberately to exclude the vast oil wealth that lies beneath the fringes of the Kurdish lands. The Autonomous Region, rejected by the Kurds and imposed unilaterally by Baghdad in 1974, comprised the three northern governorates of Erbil, Suleimaniyeh and Dohuk. Covering some 14,000

---

[3] As defined in the Convention on the Prevention and Punishment of the Crime of Genocide (hereinafter the Genocide Convention), 78 UNTS 277, approved by GA Res. 2670 on December 9, 1948, entered into force January 12, 1951.

square miles -- roughly the combined area of Massachusetts, Connecticut and Rhode Island -- this was only half the territory that the Kurds considered rightfully theirs. Even so, the Autonomous Region had real economic significance, since it accounted for fully half the agricultural output of a largely desert country that is sorely deficient in domestic food production.

In the wake of the autonomy decree, the Ba'ath Party embarked on the "Arabization" of the oil-producing areas of Kirkuk and Khanaqin and other parts of the north, evicting Kurdish farmers and replacing them with poor Arab tribesmen from the south. Northern Iraq did not remain at peace for long. In 1974, the long-simmering Kurdish revolt flared up once more under the leadership of the legendary fighter Mullah Mustafa Barzani, who was supported this time by the governments of Iran, Israel, and the United States. But the revolt collapsed precipitately in 1975, when Iraq and Iran concluded a border agreement and the Shah withdrew his support from Barzani's Kurdistan Democratic Party (KDP). After the KDP fled into Iran, tens of thousands of villagers from the Barzani tribe were forcibly removed from their homes and relocated to barren sites in the desert south of Iraq. Here, without any form of assistance, they had to rebuild their lives from scratch.

In the mid and late 1970s, the regime again moved against the Kurds, forcibly evacuating at least a quarter of a million people from Iraq's borders with Iran and Turkey, destroying their villages to create a cordon sanitaire along these sensitive frontiers. Most of the displaced Kurds were relocated into *mujamma'at*, crude new settlements located on the main highways in army-controlled areas of Iraqi Kurdistan. The word literally means "amalgamations" or "collectivities." In their propaganda, the Iraqis commonly refer to them as "modern villages"; in this report, they are generally described as "complexes." Until 1987, villagers relocated to the complexes were generally paid some nominal cash compensation, but were forbidden to move back to their homes.

After 1980, and the beginning of the eight-year Iran-Iraq War, many Iraqi garrisons in Kurdistan were abandoned or reduced in size, and their troops transferred to the front. In the vacuum that was left, the Kurdish *peshmerga*--"those who face death"--once more began to thrive. The KDP, now led by one of Barzani's sons, Mas'oud, had revived its alliance with Teheran, and in 1983 KDP units aided Iranian troops in their capture of the border town of Haj Omran. Retribution was swift: in a lightning operation against the complexes that housed the relocated

Barzanis, Iraqi troops abducted between five and eight thousand males aged twelve or over. None of them have ever been seen again, and it is believed that after being held prisoner for several months, they were all killed. In many respects, the 1983 Barzani operation foreshadowed the techniques that would be used on a much larger scale during the Anfal campaign. And the absence of any international outcry over this act of mass murder, despite Kurdish efforts to press the matter with the United Nations and Western governments, must have emboldened Baghdad to believe that it could get away with an even larger operation without any adverse reaction. In these calculations, the Ba'ath Party was correct.

Even more worrisome to Baghdad was the growing closeness between the Iranians and the KDP's major Kurdish rival, Jalal Talabani's Patriotic Union of Kurdistan (PUK). The Ba'ath regime had conducted more than a year of negotiations with the PUK between 1983-1985, but in the end these talks failed to bear fruit, and full-scale fighting resumed. In late 1986 Talabani's party concluded a formal political and military agreement with Teheran.

By this time the Iraqi regime's authority over the North had dwindled to control of the cities, towns, complexes and main highways. Elsewhere, the *peshmerga* forces could rely on a deep-rooted base of local support. Seeking refuge from the army, thousands of Kurdish draft-dodgers and deserters found new homes in the countryside. Villagers learned to live with a harsh economic blockade and stringent food rationing, punctuated by artillery shelling, aerial bombardment and punitive forays by the Army and the paramilitary *jahsh*. In response, the rural Kurds built air-raid shelters in front of their homes and spent much of their time in hiding in the caves and ravines that honeycomb the northern Iraqi countryside. For all the grimness of this existence, by 1987 the mountainous interior of Iraqi Kurdistan was effectively liberated territory. This the Ba'ath Party regarded as an intolerable situation.

* * *

With the granting of emergency powers to al-Majid in March 1987, the intermittent counterinsurgency against the Kurds became a campaign of destruction. As Raul Hilberg observes in his monumental history of the Holocaust:

A destruction process has an inherent pattern. There is only one way in which a scattered group can effectively be destroyed. Three steps are organic in the operation:

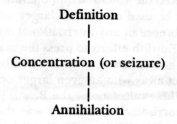

Definition

Concentration (or seizure)

Annihilation

This is the invariant structure of the basic process, for no group can be killed without a concentration or seizure of the victims, and no victims can be segregated before the perpetrator knows who belongs to the group.[4]

The Kurdish genocide of 1987-1989, with the Anfal campaign as its centerpiece, fits Hilberg's paradigm to perfection.

* * *

In the first three months after assuming his post as secretary general of the Ba'ath Party's Northern Bureau, Ali Hassan al-Majid began the process of definition of the group that would be targeted by Anfal, and vastly expanded the range of repressive activities against all rural Kurds. He decreed that "saboteurs" would lose their property rights, suspended the legal rights of all the residents of prohibited villages, and began ordering the execution of first-degree relatives of "saboteurs" and of wounded civilians whose hostility to the regime had been determined by the intelligence services.

In June 1987, al-Majid issued two successive sets of standing orders that were to govern the conduct of the security forces through the Anfal campaign and beyond. These orders were based on the simple axiom on which the regime now operated: in the "prohibited" rural areas,

---

[4] Raul Hilberg, *The Destruction of the European Jews* (New York: Holmes and Meier, 1985 student edition), p.267.

all resident Kurds were coterminous with the *peshmerga* insurgents, and they would be dealt with accordingly.

The first of al-Majid's directives bans all human existence in the prohibited areas, to be applied through a shoot-to-kill policy. The second, numbered SF/4008, dated June 20, 1987, modifies and expands upon these orders. It constitutes a bald incitement to mass murder, spelled out in the most chilling detail. In clause 4, army commanders are ordered "to carry out random bombardments, using artillery, helicopters and aircraft, at all times of the day or night, in order to kill the largest number of persons present in these prohibited zones." In clause 5, al-Majid orders that, "All persons captured in those villages shall be detained and interrogated by the security services and those between the ages of 15 and 70 shall be executed after any useful information has been obtained from them, of which we should be duly notified."

Even as this legal and bureaucratic structure was being set in place, the Iraqi regime became the first in history to attack its own civilian population with chemical weapons. On April 15, 1987, Iraqi aircraft dropped poison gas on the KDP headquarters at Zewa Shkan, close to the Turkish border in Dohuk governorate, and the PUK headquarters in the twin villages of Sergalou and Bergalou, in the governorate of Suleimaniyeh. The following afternoon, they dropped chemicals on the undefended civilian villages of Sheikh Wasan and Balisan, killing well over a hundred people, most of them women and children. Scores of other victims of the attack were abducted from their hospital beds in the city of Erbil, where they had been taken for treatment of their burns and blindness. They have never been seen again. These incidents were the first of at least forty documented chemical attacks on Kurdish targets over the succeeding eighteen months. They were also the first sign of the regime's new readiness to kill large numbers of Kurdish women and children indiscriminately.

Within a week of the mid-April chemical weapons attacks, al-Majid's forces were ready to embark upon what he described as a three-stage program of village clearances or collectivization. The first ran from April 21 to May 20; the second from May 21 to June 20. More than 700 villages were burned and bulldozed, most of them along the main highways in government-controlled areas. The third phase of the operation, however, was suspended; with Iraqi forces still committed to the war front, the resources required for such a huge operation were not available.   But the goals of the third stage would eventually be accomplished by Anfal.

In terms of defining the target group for destruction, no single administrative step was more important to the Iraqi regime than the national census of October 17, 1987. Now that the springtime village clearances had created a virtual buffer strip between the government and the *peshmerga*-controlled zones, the Ba'ath Party offered the inhabitants of the prohibited areas an ultimatum: either they could "return to the national ranks"--in other words, abandon their homes and livelihoods and accept compulsory relocation in a squalid camp under the eye of the security forces; or they could lose their Iraqi citizenship and be regarded as military deserters. The second option was tantamount to a death sentence, since the census legislation made those who refused to be counted subject to an August 1987 decree of the ruling Revolutionary Command Council, imposing the death penalty on deserters.

In the period leading up to the census, al-Majid refined the target group further. He ordered his intelligence officials to prepare detailed case-by-case dossiers of "saboteurs'" families who were still living in the government-controlled areas. When these dossiers were complete, countless women, children and elderly people were forcibly transferred to the rural areas to share the fate of their *peshmerga* relatives. This case-by-case, family-by-family sifting of the population was to become a characteristic feature of the decisions made during the Anfal period about who should live and who should die.

Last, but not without significance, the census gave those who registered only two alternatives when it came to declaring their nationality. One could either be Arab or Kurdish--a stipulation that was to have the direst consequences for other minority groups, such as the Yezidis, Assyrians and Chaldean Christians who continued to live in the Kurdish areas.[5]

* * *

The Anfal campaign began four months after the census, with a massive military assault on the PUK headquarters at Sergalou-Bergalou on the night of February 23, 1988. Anfal would have eight stages in all, seven of them directed at areas under the control of the PUK. The KDP-

---

[5] While the Yezidis, a syncretic religious sect, are ethnic Kurds, the Assyrians and Chaldeans are a distinct ancient people in their own right.

controlled areas in the northwest of Iraqi Kurdistan, which the regime regarded as a lesser threat, were the target of the Final Anfal operation in late August and early September, 1988.

The Iraqi authorities did nothing to hide the campaign from public view. On the contrary, as each phase of the operation triumphed, its successes were trumpeted with the same propaganda fanfare that attended the victorious battles in the Iran-Iraq War. Even today, Anfal is celebrated in the official Iraqi media. The fifth anniversary in 1993 of the fall of Sergalou and Bergalou on March 19, 1988 was the subject of banner headlines.

Iraqi troops tore through rural Kurdistan with the motion of a gigantic windshield wiper, sweeping first clockwise, then counterclockwise, through one after another of the "prohibited areas." The First Anfal, centered on the siege of the PUK headquarters, took more than three weeks. Subsequent phases of the campaign were generally shorter, with a brief pause between each as army units moved on to the next target. The Second Anfal, in the Qara Dagh region, lasted from March 22 to April 1, 1988; the Third, covering the hilly plain known as Germian, took from April 7 to April 20; the Fourth, in the valley of the Lesser Zab river, was the shortest of all, lasting only from May 3 to May 8.

Only in the Fifth Anfal, which began on May 15 in the mountainous region northeast of Erbil, did the troops have any real difficulty in meeting their objectives. Encountering fierce resistance in difficult terrain from the last of the PUK *peshmerga*, the regime called a temporary halt to the offensive on June 7. On orders from the Office of the Presidency (indicating the personal supervisory role that Saddam Hussein himself played in Anfal), the operation was renewed twice in July and August, with these actions denominated Anfal VI and Anfal VII. Eventually, on August 26, the last PUK-controlled area was declared "cleansed of saboteurs."

By this time, Iran had accepted Iraq's terms for a ceasefire to end the war, freeing up large numbers of Iraqi troops to carry the Anfal operation into the Badinan area of northern Iraqi Kurdistan. The Final Anfal began at first light on August 25, and was over in a matter of days. On September 6, 1988, the Iraqi regime made its de facto declaration of victory by announcing a general amnesty for all Kurds. (Ali Hassan al-Majid later told aides that he had opposed the amnesty, but had gone along with it as a loyal party man.)

Each stage of Anfal followed roughly the same pattern. It characteristically began with chemical attacks from the air on both civilian and *peshmerga* targets, accompanied by a military blitz against PUK or KDP military bases and fortified positions. The deadly cocktail of mustard and nerve gases was much more lethal against civilians than against the *peshmerga*, some of whom had acquired gas masks and other rudimentary defenses. In the village of Sayw Senan (Second Anfal), more than eighty civilians died; in Goktapa (Fourth Anfal), the death toll was more than 150; in Wara (Fifth Anfal) it was thirty-seven. In the largest chemical attack of all, the March 16 bombing of the Kurdish town of Halabja, between 3,200 and 5,000 residents died. As a city, Halabja was not technically part of Anfal--the raid was carried out in reprisal for its capture by *peshmerga* supported by Iranian Revolutionary Guards--but it was very much part of the Kurdish genocide.

After the initial assault, ground troops and *jahsh* enveloped the target area from all sides, destroying all human habitation in their path, looting household possessions and farm animals and setting fire to homes, before calling in demolition crews to finish the job. As the destruction proceeded, so did Hilberg's phase of the "concentration" or "seizure" of the target group. Convoys of army trucks stood by to transport the villagers to nearby holding centers and transit camps, while the *jahsh* combed the hillsides to track down anyone who had escaped. (Some members of the militia, an asset of dubious reliability to the regime, also saved thousands of lives by spiriting people away to safety or helping them across army lines.) Secret police combed the towns, cities and complexes to hunt down Anfal fugitives, and in several cases lured them out of hiding with false offers of amnesty and a "return to the national ranks"--a promise that now concealed a more sinister meaning.

* * *

To this point, Anfal had many of the characteristics of a counterinsurgency campaign, albeit an unusually savage one. And captured Iraqi documents suggest that during the initial combat phase, counterinsurgency goals were uppermost in the minds of the troops and their commanding officers. To be sure, Iraq--like any other sovereign nation--had legitimate interests in combating insurgency. But the fact that Anfal was, by the narrowest definition, a counterinsurgency, does nothing to diminish the fact that it was also an act of genocide. There is nothing mutually exclusive about counterinsurgency and genocide. Indeed, one may be the instrument used to consummate the other. Article I of the Genocide Convention affirms that "genocide, whether committed in time of peace or in time of war, is a crime under international law." Summarily executing noncombatant or captured members of an ethnical-national group as such is not a legitimate wartime or counterinsurgency measure, regardless of the nature of the conflict.

In addition to this argument of principle, many features of Anfal far transcend the realm of counterinsurgency. These include, first of all, the simple facts of what happened after the military goals of the operation had been accomplished:

• the mass murder and disappearance of many tens of thousands of non-combatants--50,000 by the most conservative estimate, and possibly twice that number;

• the use of chemical weapons against non-combatants in dozens of locations, killing thousands and terrifying many more into abandoning their homes;

• the near-total destruction of family and community assets and infrastructure, including the entire agricultural mainstay of the rural Kurdish economy;

• the literal abandonment, in punishing conditions, of thousands of women, children and elderly people, resulting in the deaths of many hundreds. Those who survived did so largely due to the clandestine help of nearby Kurdish townspeople.

Second, there is the matter of how Anfal was organized as a bureaucratic enterprise. Viewed as a counterinsurgency, each episode of Anfal had a distinct beginning and an end, and its conduct was in the hands of the regular army and the *jahsh* militia. But these agencies were quickly phased out of the picture, and the captured civilians were transferred to an entirely separate bureaucracy for processing and final disposal. Separate institutions were involved--such as *Amn*, *Istikhbarat*, the Popular Army (a type of home guard) and the Ba'ath Party itself. And the infrastructure of prison camps and death convoys was physically remote from the combat theater, lying well outside the Kurdistan Autonomous Region. Tellingly, the killings were not in any sense concurrent with the counterinsurgency: the detainees were murdered several days or even weeks after the armed forces had secured their goals.

Finally, there is the question of intent, which goes to the heart of the notion of genocide. Documentary materials captured from the Iraqi intelligence agencies demonstrate with great clarity that the mass killings, disappearances and forced relocations associated with Anfal and the other anti-Kurdish campaigns of 1987-1989 were planned in coherent fashion. While power over these campaigns was highly centralized, their success depended on the orchestration of the efforts of a large number of agencies and institutions at the local, regional and national level, from the Office of the Presidency of the Republic on down to the lowliest *jahsh* unit.

The official at the center of this great bureaucratic web, of course, was Ali Hassan al-Majid, and in him the question of intent is apparent on a second, extremely important level. A number of audiotapes were made of meetings between al-Majid and his aides from 1987 to 1989. These tapes were examined by four independent experts, to establish their authenticity and to confirm that the principal speaker was al-Majid. Al-Majid was known to have a distinctive, high-pitched voice and the regional accent of his Tikrit district origins; both these features were recognized without hesitation by those Iraqis consulted by Middle East Watch. As a public figure who frequently appears on radio and television in Iraq[6], his voice is well known to many Iraqis. One Iraqi consulted on this subject pointed out that the principal speaker on the many hours of recordings in Middle East Watch's possession spoke with authority and used obscene language. In contrast, he said: "Others in those meetings were courteous and respectful with fearful tones, especially when they addressed al-Majid himself." Al-Majid, two experts noted, was often referred to by his familiar nickname, "Abu Hassan."

The tapes contain evidence of a bitter racial animus against the Kurds on the part of the man who, above any other, plotted their destruction. "Why should I let them live there like donkeys who don't know anything?" al-Majid asks in one meeting. "What did we ever get

---

[6] Al-Majid has served variously over the past five years as Secretary General of the Ba'ath Party's Northern Bureau, Interior Minister, Governor of Iraqi-occupied Kuwait in 1990 and, as Defense Minister.

from them?" On another occasion, speaking in the same vein: "I said probably we will find some good ones among [the Kurds]...but we didn't, never." And elsewhere, "I will smash their heads. These kind of dogs, we will crush their heads." And again, "Take good care of them? No, I will bury them with bulldozers."

Loyalty to the regime offered no protection from al-Majid's campaigns. Nor did membership in the pro-government *jahsh*. Al-Majid even boasted of threatening militia leaders with chemical weapons if they refused to evacuate their villages. Ethnicity and physical location were all that mattered, and these factors became coterminous when the mass killings took place in 1988.

The 1987 village clearances were wholly directed at government-controlled areas, and thus had nothing whatever to do with counterinsurgency. If the former residents of these areas refused to accept government-assigned housing in a *mujamma'a*, and took refuge instead in a *peshmerga*-controlled area -- as many did -- they too were liable to be killed during Anfal. The same applied to other smaller minorities. In the October 1987 census, many Assyrian and Chaldean Christians -- an Aramaic-speaking people of ancient origin -- refused the government's demands that they designate themselves either as Arabs or Kurds. Those who declined to be Arabs were automatically treated as Kurds. And, during the Final Anfal in Dohuk governorate, where most Christians were concentrated, they were in fact dealt with by the regime even more severely than their Kurdish neighbors. Those few Turkomans, a Turkic-speaking minority, who fought with the Kurdish *peshmerga* were not spared, because they too were deemed to have become Kurds.

Almost continuously for the previous two decades, the Ba'ath-led government had engaged in a campaign of Arabization of Kurdish regions. The armed resistance this inspired was Kurdish in character and composition. In 1988, the rebels and all those deemed to be sympathizers were therefore treated as Kurds who had to be wiped out, once and for all. Whether they were combatants or not was immaterial; as far as the government was concerned they were all "bad Kurds", who had not come over to the side of the government.

* * *

To pursue Hilberg's paradigm a little further, once the concentration and seizure was complete, the annihilation could begin. The target group had already been defined with care. Now came the definition of the second, concentric circle within the group: those who were actually to be killed.

At one level, this was a straightforward matter. Under the terms of al-Majid's June 1987 directives, death was the automatic penalty for any male of an age to bear arms who was found in an Anfal area.[7] At the same time, no one was supposed to go before an Anfal firing squad without first having his or her case individually examined. There is a great deal of documentary evidence to support this view, beginning with a presidential order of October 15, 1987--two days before the census--that "the names of persons who are to be subjected to a general/blanket judgment must not be listed collectively. Rather, refer to them or treat them in your correspondence on an individual basis." The effects of this order are reflected in the lists that the Army and *Amn* compiled of Kurds arrested during Anfal, which note each person's name, sex, age, place of residence and place of capture.

The processing of the detainees took place in a network of camps and prisons. The first temporary holding centers were in operation, under the control of military intelligence as early as March 15, 1988; by about the end of that month, the mass disappearances had begun in earnest, peaking in mid-April and early May. Most of the detainees went to a place called Topzawa, a Popular Army camp on the outskirts of Kirkuk--the city where Ali Hassan al-Majid had his headquarters. Some went to the Popular Army barracks in Tikrit. Women and children were trucked on from Topzawa to a separate camp in the town of Dibs; between 6,000 and 8,000 elderly detainees were taken to the abandoned prison of Nugra Salman in the southern desert, where hundreds of them died of neglect, starvation and disease. Badinan prisoners from the Final Anfal went through a separate but parallel system, with most being detained in the huge army fort at Dohuk and the women and children being transferred later to a prison camp in Salamiyeh on the Tigris River close to Mosul.

The majority of the women, children and elderly people were released from the camps after the September 6 amnesty. But none of the

---

[7] Rural Kurdish men carry personal weapons as matter of tradition, regardless of their politics.

Anfal men were released. Middle East Watch's presumption, based on the testimony of a number of survivors from the Third and bloodiest Anfal, is that they went in large groups before firing squads and were interred secretly outside the Kurdish areas. During the Final Anfal in Badinan, in at least two cases groups of men were executed on the spot after capture by military officers carrying out instructions from their commanders.

The locations of at least three mass gravesites have been pinpointed through the testimony of survivors. One is near the north bank of the Euphrates River, close to the town of Ramadi and adjacent to a complex housing Iranian Kurds forcibly displaced in the early stages of the Iran-Iraq War. Another is in the vicinity of the archaeological site of Al-Hadhar (Hatra), south of Mosul. A third is in the desert outside the town of Samawah. At least two other mass graves are believed to exist on Hamrin Mountain, one between Kirkuk and Tikrit and the other west of Tuz Khurmatu.[8]

While the camp system is evocative of one dimension of the Nazi genocide, the range of execution methods described by Kurdish survivors is uncannily reminiscent of another--the activities of the *Einsatzkommandos*, or mobile killing units, in the Nazi-occupied lands of Eastern Europe. Each of the standard operating techniques used by the *Einsatzkommandos* is documented in the Kurdish case. Some groups of prisoners were lined up, shot from the front and dragged into pre-dug mass graves; others were shoved roughly into trenches and machinegunned where they stood; others were made to lie down in pairs, sardine-style, next to mounds of fresh corpses, before being killed; others were tied together, made to stand on the lip of the pit, and shot in the back so that they would fall forward into it--a method that was presumably more efficient from the point of view of the killers. Bulldozers then pushed earth or sand loosely over the heaps of corpses. Some of the gravesites contained dozens of separate pits, and obviously contained the bodies of thousands of victims. Circumstantial evidence suggests that the executioners were uniformed members of the Ba'ath Party, or perhaps of Iraq's General Security Directorate (*Amn*).

By the most conservative estimates, 50,000 rural Kurds died during Anfal. While males from approximately fourteen to fifty were

---

[8] Other mass graves have been found elsewhere in Kurdish-controlled territory, containing the remains of *Amn* executions before, during and after the Anfal period.

routinely killed en masse, a number of questions surround the selection criteria that were used to order the murder of younger children and entire families.

Many thousands of women and children perished, but subject to extreme regional variations, with most being residents of two distinct "clusters" that were affected by the Third and Fourth Anfals. Abuses by zealous local field commanders may explain why women and children were rounded up, rather than being allowed to slip away. But they cannot adequately explain the later patterns of disappearance, since the detainees were promptly transferred alive out of army custody, segregated from their husbands and fathers in processing centers elsewhere, and then killed in cold blood after a period in detention. The place of surrender, more than place of residence, seems to have been one consideration in deciding who lived and who died. *Amn* documents indicate that another factor may have been whether the troops encountered armed resistance in a given area--which indeed was the case in most, but not all, of the areas marked by the killing of women and children. A third criterion may have been the perceived "political stance" of detainees, although it is hard to see how this could have been applied to children.

Whatever the precise reasons, it is clear from captured Iraqi documents that the intelligence agencies scrutinized at least some cases individually, and even appealed to the highest authority if they were in doubt about the fate of a particular individual. This suggests that the annihilation process was governed, at least in principle, by rigid bureaucratic norms. But all the evidence suggests that the purpose of these norms was not to rule on a particular person's guilt or innocence of specific charges, but merely to establish whether an individual belonged to the target group that was to be "Anfalized," i.e. Kurds in areas outside government control. At the same time, survivor testimony repeatedly indicates that the rulebook was only adhered to casually in practice. The physical segregation of detainees from Anfal areas by age and sex, as well as the selection of those to be exterminated, was a crude affair, conducted without any meaningful prior process of interrogation or evaluation.

* * *

Although Anfal as a military campaign ended with the general amnesty of September 6, 1988, its logic did not. Those who were released from prisons such as Nugra Salman, Dibs and Salamiyeh, as well as those who returned from exile under the amnesty, were relocated to complexes with no compensation and no means of support. Civilians who tried to help them were hunted down by *Amn*. The *mujamma'at* that awaited the survivors of the Final Anfal in Badinan were places of residence in name alone; the *Anfalakan* were merely dumped on the barren earth of the Erbil plain with no infrastructure other than a perimeter fence and military guard towers. Here, hundreds perished from disease, exposure, hunger or malnutrition, and the after-effects of exposure to chemical weapons. Several hundreds more--non-Muslim Yezidis, Assyrians and Chaldeans, including many women and children-- were abducted from the camps and disappeared, collateral victims of the Kurdish genocide. Their particular crime was to have remained in the prohibited majority Kurdish areas after community leaders declined to accept the regime's classification of them as Arabs in the 1987 census.

The regime had no intention of allowing the amnestied Kurds to exercise their full civil rights as Iraqi citizens. They were to be deprived of political rights and employment opportunities until *Amn* certified their loyalty to the regime. They were to sign written pledges that they would remain in the *mujamma'at* to which they had been assigned--on pain of death. They were to understand that the prohibited areas remained off limits and were often sown with landmines to discourage resettlement; directive SF/4008, and in particular clause 5, with its order to kill all adult males, would remain in force and would be carried out to the letter.

Arrests and executions continued, some of the latter even involving prisoners who were alive, in detention, at the time of the amnesty. Middle East Watch has documented three cases of mass executions in late 1988; in one of them, 180 people were put to death. Documents from one local branch of *Amn* list another eighty-seven executions in the first eight months of 1989, one of them a man accused of "teaching the Kurdish language in Latin script."

The few hundred Kurdish villages that had come through Anfal unscathed as a result of their pro-government sympathies had no guarantees of lasting survival, and dozens more were burned and bulldozed in late 1988 and 1989. Army engineers even destroyed the large Kurdish town of Qala Dizeh (population 70,000) and declared its environs a "prohibited area," removing the last significant population center close to the Iranian border.

Killing, torture and scorched-earth policies continued, in other words, to be a matter of daily routine in Iraqi Kurdistan, as they always had been under the rule of the Ba'ath Arab Socialist Party. But the Kurdish problem, in al-Majid's words, had been solved; the "saboteurs" had been slaughtered. Since 1975, some 4,000 Kurdish villages had been destroyed; at least 50,000 rural Kurds had died in Anfal alone, and very possibly twice that number; half of Iraq's productive farmland had been laid waste. All told, the total number of Kurds killed over the decade since the Barzani men were taken from their homes is well into six figures.

By April 23, 1989, the Ba'ath Party felt that it had accomplished its goals, for on that date it revoked the special powers that had been granted to Ali Hassan al-Majid two years earlier. At a ceremony to greet his successor, the supreme commander of Anfal made it clear that "the exceptional situation is over."

To use the language of the Genocide Convention, the regime's aim had been to *destroy the group* (Iraqi Kurds) *in part*, and it had done so. Intent and act had been combined, resulting in the consummated crime of genocide. And with this, Ali Hassan al-Majid was free to move on to other tasks demanding his special talents--first as governor of occupied Kuwait and, then, in 1993, as Iraq's Minister of Defense.

The Anfal Campaigns: February - September, 1988

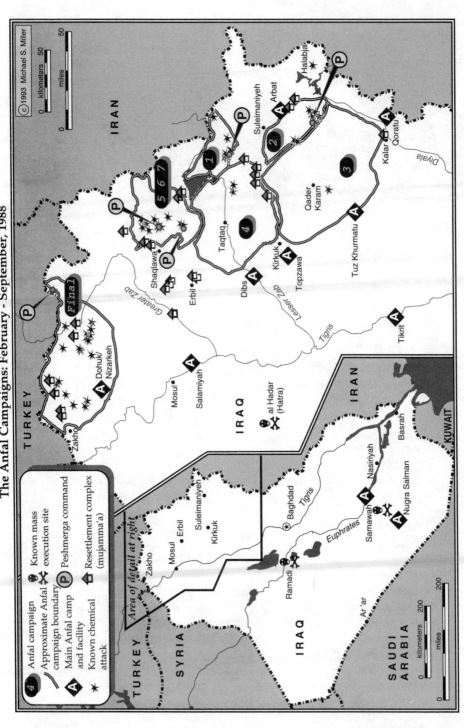

1
BA'ATHIS AND KURDS

"Black are his colors, black pavilion,
His spear, his shield, his horse, his armor, plumes,
And jetty feathers menace death and hell--
Without respect of sex, degree or age,
He razeth all his foes with fire and sword.
      *-- Christopher Marlowe, **Tamburlaine the***
      ***Great, Part One** (IV,i)*

"Each era is different. Everything changes. But Saddam
Hussein is worse than Tamburlaine of 600 years ago."
      -- Abd-al-Qader Abdullah Askari of Goktapa,
      site of chemical weapons attack, May 3,
      1988.

It is a land of spring flowers and waving fields of wheat, of
rushing streams and sudden perilous gorges, of hidden caves and barren
rock faces. Above all, it is a land where the rhythm of life is defined by
the relationship between the people and the mountains. One range after
another, the peaks stretch in all directions as far as the eye can travel, the
highest of them capped year-round by snow. "Level the mounts," so the
old saying goes, "and in a day the Kurds would be no more."

The Kurds have inhabited these mountains for thousands of
years. "The territories designated since the 12th Century as Kurdistan,"
says one scholar, "were inhabited since the most distant antiquity and
constitute one of the very first settlements of human civilization. Jarmo,
in the valley of Chamchamal, at present in Iraq, is the most ancient
village of the Middle East. Here, four thousand years before our era,
man already cultivated diverse grains (wheat, barley, lentils, peas, etc.),
plucked fruits (olives, almonds, pistachios, figs), raised sheep and goats."[1]

Yet for all their antiquity, the Kurds have never been able to
form an independent political entity of their own in modern times. From

---

[1] P.J. Braidwood, *Prehistoric Investigation in Iraqi Kurdistan* (Chicago, 1960).

the 16th to the early 20th centuries, their territories formed part of the Ottoman and Persian empires. With the collapse of the Ottoman empire after World War One, the Kurds were to be granted their independence under the 1920 Treaty of Sèvres. But that promise evaporated as the nationalist movement of Kamal Ataturk seized control of the Kurdish lands in eastern Turkey and the Kurds saw their mountain homeland divided once more among four newly created states--Turkey, Syria, Iraq and the Soviet Union, and one ancient land--Iran, or Persia as it was then known.

Each of these states has balked at assimilating its Kurdish minority, and each of the Kurdish groups has rebelled against the authority of its new central government. Of these traditions of rebellion, none has been more persistent than that of the Iraqi Kurds.[2] There are larger Kurdish populations--some ten to fifteen million Kurds live in Turkey and seven million in Iran, compared to just four million in Iraq.[3] Yet a number of factors set the Iraqi Kurds apart from their neighbors. They were proportionately the largest ethnic minority in the region, at least until the 1980s, accounting for fully 23 percent of the total Iraqi population[4]. The proportion of Kurds in Turkey may now be fractionally higher, but this is not a consequence of normal demographic trends. The relative decline of the Iraqi Kurdish population is a political matter. Hundreds of thousands have fled into exile; tens of thousands more have been killed, above all in 1988, in the course of the six-and-a-half month long campaign of extermination known as Anfal.

---

[2] The definitive work on the Kurds is Martin Van Bruinessen, *Agha, Shaikh and State: The Social and Political Structures of Kurdistan* (London: Zed Books, 1992). For a general historical and cultural overview, see Mehrdad R. Izady, *The Kurds: A Concise Handbook* (Washington, D.C.: Crane Russak, 1992). A useful brief summary is David McDowall, "The Kurdish question: a historical review," in Philip G. Kreyenbroek and Stefan Sperl, eds., *The Kurds: A Contemporary Overview* (London and New York: Routledge, 1992), especially pp.24-30.

[3] Izady, op cit, p.117, gives the following figures: Turkey 13.65 million, Iran 6.6 million, Iraq 4.4 million.

[4] According to Izady, loc cit, Kurds made up fully 25 percent of the Iraqi population in 1980, compared to 21.3 percent in Turkey. By 1990, he estimated the figures were 23.5 percent and 24.1 percent respectively. Other estimates are much lower, putting the Kurds at only 16 or 17 percent of the Iraqi population.

The Iraqi Kurds have also been the victims of an accident of geography, for vast oil reserves were discovered in the 20th century on the fringes of their ancestral lands. The Kurds have repeatedly challenged the government in Baghdad for control of these areas--especially the ethnically mixed city of Kirkuk. And it is this contest for natural resources and power, as much as any consideration of ideology or deep-rooted ethnic animus, which underlies the brutal treatment of the Kurds by the ruling Arab Ba'ath Socialist Party.

Since the 1920s, the Iraqi Kurds have staged one revolt after another against the central authorities. Most of these rebellions had their nerve center in a remote area of northeastern Iraq called the Barzan valley, which lies close to the Iranian and Turkish borders on the banks of the Greater Zab river. From the early 1940s to the mid-1970s, the idea of Kurdish rebellion was inseparable from the name of a charismatic tribal leader from that valley, Mullah Mustafa Barzani.

Barzani's only real success came in 1946, when Iraqi and Iranian Kurds joined forces to found the Mahabad Republic. But the Mahabad experiment lasted only a year before it was crushed, and Barzani fled to the Soviet Union with several thousand fighters in a celebrated "long march."[5] After the overthrow of the Iraqi monarchy in 1958, the Kurds encountered a familiar pattern under each of the regimes that followed: first a period of negotiations that invariably failed to satisfy Kurdish demands for autonomy, and then, when the talks broke down, renewed outbreaks of violence.[6] Rural villages were bombed and burned and

---

[5] The Kurds, however, unlike other national liberation movements, were never able to count on consistent Soviet support.

[6] Since the revolution of July 14, 1958, there have been four regimes in Baghdad: the military government of Abd al-Karim Qasem and the "Free Officers" (1958-1963); the first regime of the Ba'ath Arab Socialist Party (February-November 1963); the governments of the Arif brothers and Abd al-Rahman al-Bazzaz (1963-1968); and the second Ba'ath regime (1968 to the present). Saddam Hussein, one of the leaders of the July 1968 coup, has been President of Iraq since 1979. The best general work on the period is Marion Farouk-Sluglett and Peter Sluglett, *Iraq Since 1958: From Revolution to Dictatorship* (London: I.B. Tauris, 1990). Other useful studies include Phebe Marr, *The Modern History of Iraq* (Boulder: Westview Press, 1985) and CARDRI (Committee against Repression and for Democratic Rights in Iraq), *Saddam's Iraq: Revolution or Reaction?* (London: Zed Books, 1986).

Kurdish fighters hunted down relentlessly. The name that they adopted expressed accurately the condition of their existence. They called themselves *peshmerga*--"those who face death."

* * *

In 1988, during the final six months of Iraq's eight-year long war with Iran, something terrible occurred in the mountains of northern Iraq. At least metaphorically, the regime of Saddam Hussein did "level the mounts," in the sense of razing thousands of villages, destroying the traditional rural economy and infrastructure of Iraqi Kurdistan and killing many tens of thousands of its inhabitants.

The outside world has long known of two isolated episodes of abuse of the Iraqi Kurds in 1988. In both instances, it was the proximity of the victims to international borders, and thus to the foreign media, that accounted for the news leaking out. In the first, the March 16 poison gas attack on the Kurdish city of Halabja, near the border with Iran, the Iranian authorities made it their business to show off the site to the international press within a few days of the bombing. Even so, the illusion has long persisted, fostered initially by reports from the U.S. intelligence community, which "tilted" strongly toward Baghdad during the 1980-1988 Iran-Iraq War, that both sides were responsible for the chemical attack on Halabja.[7] This is false: The testimony of survivors

---

[7] Books on the Iran-Iraq War have routinely echoed the unsubstantiated report that both sides had used chemical weapons in Halabja. This notion originated in a study for the U.S. Army War College: Stephen C. Pelletiere, Douglas V. Johnson II and Leif R. Rosenberger, *Iraqi Power and U.S. Security in the Middle East* (Carlisle Barracks, PA: Strategic Studies Institute, U.S. Army War College, 1990). It is repeated in a later book by Pelletiere, a former U.S. intelligence officer, *The Iran-Iraq War: Chaos in a Vacuum* (New York: Praeger, 1992). This strongly pro-Iraqi work comments, "On May 23 (sic), in fighting over the town, gas was used by both sides. As a result scores (sic) of Iraqi Kurdish civilians were killed. It is now fairly certain that Iranian gas killed the Kurds." (pp.136-137)

The supposed factual basis for this conclusion is that the Halabja victims had blue lips, characteristic of the effects of cyanide gas--which Iraq was not believed to possess. Cyanide gas, a metabolic poison, would indeed produce blue lips, but they are far from being a specific indicator of its use. Nerve agents, which are acetylcholinesterase inhibitors that cause respiratory paralysis, would also turn

establishes beyond reasonable doubt that Halabja was an Iraqi action, launched in response to the brief capture of the city by Iraqi *peshmerga* assisted by Iranian Revolutionary Guards (*pasdaran*). The thousands who died, virtually all of them civilians, were victims of the Iraqi regime.[8]

The second well-publicized event was the mass exodus of at least 65,000, and perhaps as many as 80,000, Iraqi Kurdish refugees from the northern mountains of the Badinan area into the Turkish borderlands, during the final days of August.[9] The reason for their flight was later conclusively demonstrated to have been a further series of chemical weapons attacks by the Iraqi armed forces.[10] Since World War One, the use of poison gas in warfare has been regarded as a special kind of abomination. Chemical weapons were banned by the Geneva Protocol of 1925, to which Iraq is a party, and many countries subsequently destroyed

------

victims' lips blue. Middle East Watch interview with Dr. Howard Hu, Harvard School of Public Health, May 13, 1993. On Iraq's proven use of nerve agents against the Kurds during Anfal, see below footnote 10.

[8] The Kurdish researcher Shorsh Resool, author of a study of the destruction of Kurdish villages (*Destruction of a Nation*, privately published, April, 1990), has assembled a list of the names of some 3,200 people who died in the Halabja attack. More impressionistic estimates have ranged as high as 7,000 (see below p.108).

[9] The most frequently cited figure of 65,000 derives from Peter W. Galbraith and Christopher Van Hollen, Jr., "Chemical Weapons Use in Kurdistan: Iraq's Final Offensive," staff report to the U.S. Senate Committee on Foreign Relations, September 21, 1988. Tens of thousands also sought refuge in Iran, either fleeing directly from Iraq or else after passing through Turkey.

[10] See Galbraith and Van Hollen, op cit. The February 1989 report by Physicians for Human Rights, "Winds of Death: Iraq's Use of Poison Gas Against its Kurdish Population," concluded that the injuries of refugees examined in Turkey were consistent with exposure to sulfur mustard (yperite). However, PHR noted, "Eyewitness accounts of deaths beginning within minutes of exposure...cannot be explained by mustard gas alone." The mystery was laid to rest in April 1993, when research on soil samples from the village of Birjinni, the site of a 1988 chemical weapons attack, showed the presence of trace elements of the nerve agent GB, also known as Sarin. See PHR-Human Rights Watch, "Scientific First: Soil Samples Taken from Bomb Craters in Northern Iraq Reveal Nerve Gas--Even Four Years Later," April 29, 1993.

their stockpiles. While Iraq, and to a lesser extent Iran, had broken the battlefield taboo on many occasions since 1983, the Halabja and Badinan attacks marked a new level of inhumanity, as the first documented instances of a government employing chemical weapons against its own civilian population.

Yet Halabja and Badinan are merely two pieces in a much larger jigsaw puzzle, and they formed part of a concerted offensive against the Kurds that lasted from March 1987 until May 1989. In the judgment of Middle East Watch, the Iraqi campaign against the Kurds during that period amounted to genocide, under the terms of the Genocide Convention.[11]

Middle East Watch has reached this conclusion after over eighteen months of research. Our methodology has had three distinct and complementary elements. The first was an extensive series of field interviews with Kurdish survivors. Between April and September 1992, Middle East Watch researchers interviewed in depth some 300 people in Iraqi Kurdistan and spoke to hundreds of others about their experiences. Most had been directly affected by the violence; many had lost members of their immediate families. In March and April 1993, an additional fifty interviews sought to deal with the questions that remained unanswered.

The second dimension of Middle East Watch's Iraqi Kurdistan project was a series of forensic examinations of mass gravesites, under the supervision of the distinguished forensic anthropologist Dr. Clyde Collins Snow. Dr. Snow's first preliminary trip, to the Erbil and Suleimaniyeh areas, was in December 1991. On two subsequent visits, Dr. Snow's team exhumed a number of graves, in particular a site containing the bodies of twenty-six men and teenage boys executed by the Iraqi Army in late

---

[11] Convention on the Prevention and Punishment of the Crime of Genocide, 78 UNTS 277, approved by General Assembly resolution 2670 on December 9, 1948, entered into force January 12, 1951. The convention defines genocide as "acts committed with intent to destroy, in whole or in part, a national, ethnical, racial or religious group, as such." For a general discussion of the issues, as well as a series of case studies, see Frank Chalk and Kurt Jonassohn, *The History and Sociology of Genocide: Analyses and Case Studies* (New Haven: Yale University Press, 1990), and Helen Fein, ed., *Genocide Watch* (New Haven: Yale University Press, 1992).

August 1988 on the outskirts of the village of Koreme, in the Badinan area.[12]

The third, and most ambitious, strand in our research has been the study of captured Iraqi intelligence archives. During 1991 and early 1992, through a variety of sources, Middle East Watch had assembled a modest file of official Iraqi documents that described aspects of the regime's policy toward the Kurds. For the most part, these had been seized from Iraqi government buildings during the aborted Kurdish uprising of March 1991. Then, in May 1992, Middle East Watch secured permission to examine and analyse 847 boxes of Iraqi government materials that had been captured during the *intifada* by the Patriotic Union of Kurdistan (PUK), one of the two main parties in Iraqi Kurdistan. Through an arrangement between the PUK and the U.S. Senate Foreign Relations Committee, the documents became Congressional Records of the Committee.[13] Analysis of the documents began on October 22, 1992, and in many cases it has been possible to match documentary evidence about specific villages or campaigns with testimonial material from the same locations.

As Raul Hilberg notes in his history of the Holocaust, "There are not many ways in which a modern society can, in short order, kill a large number of people living in its midst. This is an efficiency problem of the greatest dimensions..."[14] The trove of captured documents demonstrates in astonishing breadth and detail how the Iraqi state bureaucracy organized the Kurdish genocide. Some of these documents were seized during the uprising by the citizens of the Kurdish city of Suleimaniyeh and later stuffed haphazardly into stout plastic flour sacks. Others, piled first into tea boxes and then wrapped in sacks stamped

---

[12] The findings of these missions are contained in two Middle East Watch-Physicians for Human Rights reports: *Unquiet Graves: The Search for the Disappeared in Iraqi Kurdistan*, February 1992, and *The Anfal Campaign in Iraqi Kurdistan: The Destruction of Koreme*, January 1993.

[13] While the U.S. Defense Department has helped to expedite the research of the documents by assigning technical staff to the Iraqi Kurdistan project, Middle East Watch and the PUK jointly retain full control over the archive.

[14] Raul Hilberg, *The Destruction of the European Jews* (New York: Holmes and Meier, 1985), p.8.

"PUK Shaqlawa," were taken from the offices of Iraq's General Security Directorate (*Mudiriyat al-Amn al-Ameh*), commonly known as *Amn*, in Erbil and the northern resort town of Shaqlawa.[15] The contents of these boxes are often charred as a result of the March 1991 fighting, in which many government buildings were torched. Some are wrinkled, partly shredded and almost illegible after prolonged exposure to moisture. The documents are crammed into bulging ring-back letter files or bound together loosely with staples, string, laces or pins. Hand-written ledgers are covered with flowered wallpaper, kept clean with sheets of transparent plastic. Sometimes their Arabic titles are lettered in ornate psychedelic script with a variety of colored felt-tip pens, by bored or whimsical clerks with the right security clearance. One police binder is neatly bound in Christmas wrapping paper from Great Britain that shows a red-breasted robin singing cheerfully among sprigs of holly.

Between them, the documents show in compelling detail how the Iraqi security bureaucracy tackled the "efficiency problem" of razing thousands of Kurdish villages from the map and murdering tens of thousands of their inhabitants. There are smoking guns here, in the form of signed government decrees ordering summary mass execution. Yet equally telling in their own way are the thousands upon thousands of pages of field intelligence notes, scribbled annotations of telephone conversations, minutes of meetings, arrest warrants, deportation orders, notes on the burning of a particular village, casualty lists from chemical attacks, lists of the family members of "saboteurs," phone surveillance logs, food ration restrictions, interrogation statements and salutes to victorious military units. Between them these are, so to speak, the innumerable tiny pixels that together make up the picture of the Kurdish genocide.

* * *

---

[15] *Amn*, whose technical functions are roughly equivalent to those of the U.S. Federal Bureau of Investigation, originated in the mid-1960s in a secret unit of the Ba'ath Party known as *al-Jihaz al-Khas*, the "special apparatus." Its code name was *Jihaz Haneen*, the "instrument of yearning." Saddam Hussein personally supervised the restructuring of the secret police that gave *Amn* its present name and functions in 1973. See Samir al-Khalil, op. cit., pp.5-6, 12-13. (Al-Khalil was the pseudonym formerly adopted by the Iraqi writer Kanan Makiya.)

For those who survived the slaughter, the experience can be summed up in a single word: *al-Anfal*. The word is religious in origin; it is the name of the eighth *sura*, or chapter, of the Koran. According to the Iraqi writer Kanan Makiya, whose May 1992 article in *Harper's Magazine* was the first written journalistic treatment of the Anfal campaign, the eighth *sura* is "the seventy-five-verse revelation that came to the Prophet Mohammed in the wake of the first great battle of the new Muslim faith at Badr (A.D. 624). It was in the village of Badr, located in what is now the Saudi province of Hejaz, that a group of Muslims numbering 319 routed nearly 1,000 Meccan unbelievers. The battle was seen by the first Muslims as vindication of their new faith; the victory, the result of a direct intervention by God."[16]

In this *sura*, the Arabic word 'al-Anfal' means 'spoils,' as in the spoils of battle. It begins, "They will question thee concerning the spoils. Say: 'The spoils belong to God and the Messenger; so fear you God, and set things right between you, and obey you God and his Messenger, if you are believers."

The *sura* continues with the revelation of God's will to the angels:

"I am with you; so confirm the believers. I shall cast into the unbelievers' hearts terror; so smite above the necks, and smite every finger of them!" That, because they had made a breach with God and with His Messenger; and whosoever makes a breach with God and with His Messenger, surely God is terrible in His retribution.

---

[16] The Iraqi regime may have selected this *sura* to legitimize its war on the Kurds by invoking a battle between two regular armies, and against a numerically stronger adversary. Makiya's article, "The Anfal: Uncovering an Iraqi campaign to exterminate the Kurds," (*Harper's Magazine*, May 1992, pp.53-61), is an extract from his book, *Cruelty and Silence: War, Tyranny, Uprising and the Arab World* (New York: Norton, 1993). Makiya's visit to northern Iraq also formed the basis for a report by the British film-maker Gwynne Roberts, "Saddam's Killing Fields," broadcast on BBC TV in January 1992 and PBS *Frontline*, March 31, 1992.

Two other overviews of the Anfal campaign have been published: Raymond Bonner, "Always Remember," (*The New Yorker*, September 28, 1992, pp.46-51, 54-58 and 63-65); and Judith Miller, "Iraq Accused: A Case of Genocide," (*The New York Times Magazine*), January 3, 1993, pp.12-17, 28, 31-33, 36). Miller's article deals in some detail with the progress of Middle East Watch's Iraqi Kurdistan documents project.

That for you; therefore taste it; and that the chastisement
of the Fire is for the unbelievers."[17]

Although Saddam Hussein has often chosen in recent years to
wrap his campaigns in religious language and iconography, Ba'athist Iraq
is a militantly secular state. The victims of the 1988 Anfal campaign, the
Kurds of northern Iraq, are for the most part Sunni Muslims. During
Anfal, every mosque in the Kurdish villages that were targeted for
destruction was flattened by the Iraqi Army Corps of Engineers, using
bulldozers and dynamite.

* * *

KURDISH AUTONOMY AND ARABIZATION

Yet for all its horror, it would be wrong to say that Anfal was
entirely unprecedented, for terrible atrocities had been visited on the
Kurds by the Ba'ath Party on many occasions in the past. Ironically,
when Iraqi Kurds are asked if they can recall a period of stable peace,
they speak first of the early years of the second Ba'ath Party regime, after
the coup of July 1968. The radical pan-Arabist ideology on which the
party had been founded was hostile to the non-Arab Kurds, who are
culturally and linguistically related to the Persians. Yet the new Iraqi
regime made a priority of achieving a durable settlement with the Kurds.
The Ba'ath was not lacking in pragmatism. The party was weak
when it came to office, and it had no desire to contend with a
troublesome insurgency. Pan-Arabist rhetoric was therefore played down
after 1968, in favor of a new effort to forge a single unified Iraqi identity,
one in which the Kurds would be accepted as partners--if not exactly
equal ones. The modern nation-state of Iraq had been an artificial
creation of the League of Nations in the 1920s, when the former
southern *vilayat* of the Ottoman Empire were subdivided into mandate
territories administered by Britain and France. Iraq's boundaries,
incorporating the *vilayet* of Mosul, reflected British interest in achieving
control over that region's known oil resources.

---

[17] A.J. Arberry (trans.), *The Koran Interpreted* (New York: Collier Books,
Macmillan Publishing Co., 1955), p.198.

It was oil that proved to be the Achilles' heel of the autonomy package that was offered to the Kurds by Saddam Hussein, the Revolutionary Command Council member in charge of Kurdish affairs. On paper the Manifesto of March 11, 1970 was promising. It recognized the legitimacy of Kurdish nationalism and guaranteed Kurdish participation in government and Kurdish language-teaching in schools.[18] But it reserved judgment on the territorial extent of "Kurdistan," pending a new census. Such a census would surely have shown a solid Kurdish majority in the city of Kirkuk and the surrounding oilfields, as well as in the secondary oil-bearing area of Khanaqin, south of the city of Suleimaniyeh. But no census was scheduled until 1977, by which time the autonomy deal was dead.[19]

As before, Kurdish ideals were hostage to larger political forces. In April 1972, the Ba'ath regime signed a 15-year friendship treaty with the Soviet Union; two months later it nationalized the Iraq Petroleum Company; and with the October 1973 Arab-Israeli war, Iraq's oil revenues soared tenfold.[20] In June of that year, with Ba'ath-Kurdish relations already souring, the legendary guerrilla leader Mullah Mustafa Barzani laid formal claim to the Kirkuk oilfields. Baghdad interpreted this as a virtual declaration of war, and in March 1974 unilaterally decreed an autonomy statute.

The new statute was a far cry from the 1970 Manifesto, and its definition of the Kurdish autonomous area explicitly excluded the oil-rich areas of Kirkuk, Khanaqin and Jabal Sinjar. In tandem with the 1970-

---

[18] Indeed, the July 1970 Provisional Constitution stated that "The People of Iraq is formed of two principal nationalities, the Arab nationality and the Kurdish nationality. This Constitution shall recognize the national rights of the Kurdish people and the legitimate rights of all minorities within the unity of Iraq." The Iraqi government's view of the autonomy issue is set forth in *Settlement of the Kurdish Problem in Iraq* (Baghdad: Ath-Thawra Publications, c.1974).

[19] Again, interestingly, it was a census that defined the geographical extent of the 1988 Anfal operation. See below pp. 84-90. See also the comments of Ali Hassan al-Majid on the size of the Arab population in Kurdistan, appendix A, p.353.

[20] According to Farouk-Sluglett and Sluglett (op cit p.172), Iraqi oil revenues, a mere $575 million in 1972, rose to $1.84 billion in 1973 and $5.7 billion in 1974.

1974 autonomy process, the Iraqi regime carried out a comprehensive administrative reform, in which the country's sixteen provinces, or governorates, were renamed and in some cases had their boundaries altered. The old province of Kirkuk was split up into two. The area around the city itself was now to be named al-Ta'mim ("nationalization") and its boundaries redrawn to give an Arab majority. A new, smaller province, to be known as Salah al Din, included the city of Tikrit and the nearby village of al-Ouja, Saddam Hussein's birthplace. Clearly the parallel between Saddam and the legendary mediaeval warrior, known in the West as Saladin, was anything but accidental (although, ironically, Saladin was himself a Kurd, and like many of his kin had initially hired himself out to Arab armies).[21] Baghdad gave the Kurds two weeks to accept its terms[22]; Barzani responded with a renewal of his dormant armed revolt.

In the belief that they have no lasting friends, Kurdish leaders have long made alliances of convenience with outsiders, and Barzani assumed that foreign support would allow his fight to prosper. Horrified by Iraq's new alignment with the Soviet Union, the Israeli government and the U.S. Central Intelligence Agency trained senior KDP leaders and kept Barzani generously supplied with intelligence and arms, including heavy weaponry. The Shah of Iran, meanwhile, provided an indispensable rearguard territory as well as logistical support.

With this help, the *peshmerga* resisted the Iraqi assault for a year, although more than a hundred thousand refugees fled to Iran and the Kurdish towns of Zakho and Qala Dizeh were heavily damaged by aerial bombing.

But Barzani grossly overestimated the commitment of outsiders to his cause. In March 1975, the Shah and Saddam Hussein signed the Algiers Agreement, which surprised most observers by putting an end--at

---

[21] The Israeli scholar Amatzia Baram, in his fascinating book *Culture, History and Ideology in the Formation of Ba'thist Iraq, 1968-89* (New York: St. Martin's Press, 1991), pp.61-62, shows how much of this administrative reform illustrated the party's desire to relate Iraq's modern history to the glories of antiquity. Most strikingly, the province of Diwaniya was renamed Qadissiya--after the decisive battle between the Arab and Persian armies in A.D. 635. The Iran-Iraq War of 1980-1988, it should be noted, was officially referred to as "Saddam's Qadissiyah."

[22] This was, as McDowall (*op cit*) puts it, "autonomy by ultimatum."

least for the time being--to the long-standing quarrel between the two countries. Iraq granted Iran shared access to the disputed Shatt al-Arab waterway; as a quid pro quo, the Shah abruptly withdrew his military and logistical support from the Iraqi Kurds. Within a week, Barzani's revolt had collapsed. Its leader, a broken man, was soon dead. "Covert action should not be confused with missionary work," was Dr. Henry Kissinger's famous remark on the affair.

In the eyes of the Ba'ath Party, Barzani's collaboration with Iran, the United States and Israel marked the Kurds down as Fifth Columnists. "Those who have sold themselves to the foreigner will not escape punishment," said Saddam Hussein, who at this point was deputy chairman of Iraq's Revolutionary Command Council, and the official responsible for internal security matters.[23]   That attitude colored Ba'ath dealings with the Kurds for the next two decades. Its culmination was the campaign known as Anfal.

* * *

With the collapse of the Barzani Revolution, as Kurds call it, the Iraqi regime shifted its anti-Kurdish activities into a higher gear. The traditional concerns of counterinsurgency planners now gave way to the more ambitious goal of physically redrawing the map of northern Iraq. This meant removing rebellious Kurds from their ancestral lands and resettling them in new areas under the strict military control of the Baghdad authorities.

In 1975 the Iraqi government embarked on a sweeping campaign to "Arabize" the areas that had been excluded from Kurdistan under the

---

[23] Speech of September 24, 1973, in Saddam Husain, *On Current Events in Iraq* (London: Longman, 1977), pp.17-18, cited in al-Khalil, *Republic of Fear.* There is also some evidence that the Ba'ath Party harbored a general racial hostility against the Kurds for their kinship with the Persians. According to al-Khalil, for example (op cit p.17), the Iraqi government publishing house Dar al-Hurriyya circulated a pamphlet in 1981 entitled *Three Whom God Should Not Have Created: Persians, Jews and Flies* and written by Saddam Hussein's father-in-law, Khairallah Tulfah, a former governor of Baghdad. According to Tulfah, Persians are "animals God created in the shape of humans"; Jews are a "mixture of the dirt and leftovers of diverse peoples"; and flies are a trifling creation "whom we do not understand God's purpose in creating."

offer of autonomy--an effort that had first begun in 1963. Hundreds of
Kurdish villages were destroyed during the mid-1970s in the northern
governorates of Nineveh and Dohuk, and about 150 more in the
governorate of Diyala, the southernmost spur of Iraqi Kurdistan, where
there were also significant oil deposits.[24] Restrictions were imposed,
and maintained over the years that followed, on the employment and
residence of Kurds in the Kirkuk area.[25] Arab tribespeople from
southern Iraq were enticed to move to the north with government
benefits and offers of housing. Uprooted Kurdish farmers were sent to
new homes in rudimentary government-controlled camps along the main
highways.

Some were forcibly relocated to the flat and desolate landscapes
of southern Iraq, including thousands of refugees from the Barzani tribal
areas who returned from Iran in late 1975 under a general amnesty.
Once moved, they had no hope of resuming their traditional farming
activities: "The houses that the government had allocated for the Kurds
in those areas were about one kilometer away from each other," recalled
one returning refugee. "They told me I should stay there and become a
farmer, but we could not farm there: it was all desert."[26] In November
1975, an Iraqi official acknowledged that some 50,000 Kurds had been

---

[24] A helpful guide to the scale of these village clearances is Resool,
Destruction of a Nation, op.cit. Resool's figures, which Middle East Watch regards
as highly reliable, list 369 villages destroyed or depopulated in the northern part
of Iraqi Kurdistan, and another 154 in Diyala governorate.

[25] For example, a directive from the headquarters of the General Security
Directorate (*Amn*), dated May 4, 1985 and coded K3/34478, expresses concerns
about Kurdish migration to the city of Kirkuk. The document orders that no
changes of residence in the governorate of Al-Ta'mim (Kirkuk) will be allowed
"until the Northern Affairs Committee [of the Revolutionary Command Council
and security circles have given their opinion. This is in order to carry out a
secret investigation of the person and the reasons for his taking up residence in
the above-mentioned governorate."

[26] Middle East Watch interview, Qushtapa complex, May 3, 1992.

deported to the southern districts of Nasiriya and Diwaniya, although the true figure was almost certainly higher.[27]

This reference to "houses" is a little misleading, for the new quarters were primitive in the extreme. The relocated Kurds were simply driven south in convoys of trucks, dumped in the middle of nowhere and left to their own resources. "This is to prevent you from going to Mustafa [Barzani] or Iran," one villager remembers being told by a soldier.[28] Many people died of heat and starvation; the remainder survived at first in "shades"--crude shelters fashioned from branches and thatch, or rugs strung on a framework of poles. In time they managed to build mud houses with the money that the men earned as day-laborers in the nearest town.

In 1977-1978, under the terms of the 1975 Algiers Agreement, Iraq began to clear a *cordon sanitaire* along its northern borders. At first, a former Iraqi military officer told Middle East Watch, this no-man's land extended five kilometers (3.1 miles) into Iraq; later, it was extended to ten kilometers, then to fifteen, and finally to thirty (18.6 miles). The governorate of Suleimaniyeh, which shares a long mountainous border with Iran, was the worst affected, and estimates of the number of villages destroyed during this first wave of border clearances run as high as 500, the great majority of them in Sulemaniyeh.[29] Again, official Iraqi statements convey some minimal sense of the numbers involved: the Ba'ath Party newspaper *Al-Thawra* admitted that 28,000 families (as many as 200,000 people) had been deported from the border zone in just two

---

[27] Reported in *The Times* (London), November 27, 1975, as cited in Martin van Bruinessen, "The Kurds Between Iran and Iraq," *Middle East Report*, July-August 1986, p.27.

[28] Middle East Watch interview, Qushtapa complex, May 4, 1992.

[29] Resool (op cit) gives the following figures: 336 villages destroyed in Suleimaniyeh (26 in 1977 and 310 in 1978); 120 in Erbil governorate (79 in 1977 and 41 in 1978); and the remainder scattered in the governorates of Dohuk and Diyala. Additional testimony gathered by Middle East Watch speaks of 124 villages destroyed around the town of Qala Dizeh; and of 260-265 villages destroyed in the entire governorate of Sulemainiyeh.

months during the summer of 1978.[30] Deportees say that they were
given five days to gather up their possessions and leave their homes;
when that deadline had expired the army demolition crews moved in.

This was no haphazard operation. A new bureaucratic
infrastructure was set up in August 1979 to handle these forced mass
relocations, in the form of the Revolutionary Command Council's
Committee for Northern Affairs, headed by Saddam Hussein.
(Reportedly, a "Special Investigation Committee" (*Hay'at al-tahqiq al-
khaseh*) was also set up at this time, charged with identifying potential
peshmerga and authorized to order the death penalty without consulting
Baghdad.)[31]

Saddam Hussein's committee now began systematically to redraw
the map of Iraqi Kurdistan, and the border clearances of the late 1970's
marked the first large-scale introduction of the *mujamma'a*, or "complex"
system of Kurdish resettlement camps.[32] The *mujamma'at* (plural) were
crudely built collective villages, located near large towns or along the
main highways in areas controlled by the Iraqi Army. Sometimes the
Kurds received some nominal compensation for their confiscated lands,
although the amounts offered were usually derisory. They could also
apply for loans from the government's Real Estate Bank in order to build
a home in the complexes; but they were forbidden to return to their
ancestral lands.

After the start of the war with Iran, which began with the Iraqi
invasion of September 22, 1980, Baghdad's campaign against the Kurds

---

[30] *Al-Thawra*, September 18, 1978, cited in Van Bruinessen, op cit p.24.

[31] The Northern Affairs Committee is the source of numerous Iraqi
government documents that Middle East Watch has examined. It is also referred
to (as the "Higher Committee for Northern Affairs") by al-Khalil, in *Republic of
Fear*, p.24. The Kirkuk-based Special Investigations Committee, according to a
former Iraqi military intelligence officer interviewed by Middle East Watch,
consisted of four members--one each from the Ba'ath Party, the General Security
Directorate (*Amn*), Military Intelligence (*Istikhbarat*) and the foreign intelligence
organization (*Mukhabarat*).

[32] Other resettlement camps--*Urdugakan* in Kurdish, or *Mu'askarat* in Arabic,
had been built during the 1975 Arabization campaign to house newly arrived
Sunni Arabs from the south. This was especially true of areas on the plain north
of Dohuk that was formerly occupied by the Kurdish Sleivani tribe.

faltered.   Army garrisons in Iraqi Kurdistan were progressively abandoned or reduced, their troops transferred to the Iranian front; into the vacuum moved the resurgent *peshmerga*. Villages in the north began to offer refuge to large numbers of Kurdish draft dodgers and army deserters.   Increasing stretches of the countryside effectively became liberated territory.

In these early years of the Iran-Iraq war, it was the KDP--now commanded by Mullah Mustafa Barzani's sons, the half-brothers Mas'oud and Idris--that was the main object of Baghdad's attention.[33]   Since 1975, the KDP had been based at Karaj, outside Teheran. The Iraqi regime's hostility only grew when it learned that the Kurdish group was now allying itself quite as readily with Iran's new clerical rulers as it had with the Shah.

The villagers who had been removed from the Barzan valley in 1975 spent nearly five years in their new quarters in the southern governorate of Diwaniya.   But in 1980 army trucks, East German-supplied IFAs, rolled up outside their desert encampment and told them they were to be relocated again.   For most, the new destination was Qushtapa, a new resettlement complex a half-hour drive to the south of the Kurdish city of Erbil.   Some were taken to Baharka, north of Erbil, and others to the *mujamma'at* of Diyana and Harir, some way to the northeast. There was no permanent housing in these complexes, nothing but tents, but the villagers were relieved at first to be breathing the air of Kurdistan once more.

But in the last week of July 1983, the residents of Qushtapa became aware of unusual military movements. Fighter planes screamed overhead, making for the Iranian border. Troop convoys could be seen on the paved highway that bisected the camp, headed in the same direction. Listening to Teheran radio, the Barzanis learned that the strategic border garrison town of Haj Omran had fallen to an Iranian assault. What they did not know at first was that the KDP had effectively acted as scouts and guides for the Iranian forces.

The reprisals began in the early hours of July 30. "We were all asleep when the soldiers surrounded the complex at 3:00 a.m.," said one

---

[33] Idris died of a heart attack in 1987; Mas'oud Barzani remains the supreme leader of the KDP.

Barzani woman who was living in Qushtapa at the time.[34] "Then, before dawn, as people were getting dressed and getting ready to go to work, all the soldiers at once charged through the complex. They captured the men walking on the street and even took an old man who was mentally deranged and was usually left tied up. They took the religious man who went to the mosque to call for prayers. They were breaking down doors and entering the houses searching for our men. They looked inside the chicken coops, water tanks, refrigerators, everywhere, and took all the men over the age of thirteen. The women cried and clutched the Koran and begged the soldiers not to take their men away."

"I tried to hold on to my youngest son, who was small and very sick," added another of the "Barzani widows," as the women are now known. "I pleaded with them, 'You took the other three, please let me have this one.' They just told me, 'If you say anything else, we'll shoot you,' and then hit me in the chest with a rifle butt. They took the boy. He was in the fifth grade."

Between five and eight thousand Barzani men from Qushtapa and other other camps were loaded into large buses and driven off toward the south. They have never been seen again, and to this day the widows show visitors to the Qushtapa camp framed photographs of their husbands, sons and brothers, begging for information about their fate.[35] For almost a year after the raid the Qushtapa camp was sealed.

---

[34] Middle East Watch interview, Qushtapa, May 4, 1992.

[35] There is some evidence that the Barzani men were kept alive in captivity for at least a year before eventually being killed. One *Mukhabarat* file contains a sequence of thirty-nine presidential decrees issued in 1983, numbered 998 to 1036, listing individuals who have been sentenced to death in "cases of a special nature." Later correspondence is appended, and one handwritten comment asks "Are any of the above-mentioned persons who have been sentenced to death in our custody?" The reply, also handwritten and dated April 9, 1985, says "None of the above-mentioned persons who have been sentenced to death are in our custody, *with the exception of the Barzani group who were living in our area prior to their detention.*" [emphasis added]

According to a surviving Barzani tribesman interviewed by Middle East Watch in Salah al-Din on March 18, 1993, some of the Barzani women and children were again rounded up by government officials in 1986, trucked to the Turkish border and ordered to leave the country. After remaining on the border for

Electrical power was cut off; the women were not allowed to leave, even to shop, and townspeople of Erbil smuggled in food secretly at night. "Now that your men are gone, why don't you come and stay with us?" one woman who remained behind recalls being taunted by *Amn* agents.

In a 1983 speech, President Saddam Hussein left little doubt what had happened to the Barzanis. "They betrayed the country and they betrayed the covenant," he said, "and we meted out a stern punishment to them and they went to hell."[36] The seizure and presumed mass killing of the Barzani men was the direct precursor of what would be repeated on a much larger scale five years later, during the campaign known as Anfal.

* * *

EXPLOITING KURDISH DIVISIONS

The Barzani half-brothers' KDP, however, was not the only source of *peshmerga* resistance to the regime. Divisions within the Kurdish movement had deep roots, which were as much historical and tribal as doctrinal. The Barzan Valley's claim to leadership of the movement had long been couched in religious and mystical terms. This uncompromising attitude made the Barzanis bitter enemies among a number of neighboring tribes such as the Surchi and Zebari.[37] Mullah Mustafa Barzani's charismatic, not to say high-handed, style of leadership had also

---

some time, they returned to Qushtapa and it appears that no further action was taken against them. A series of proposed measures against the surviving Barzanis, including stripping them of their Iraqi citizenship, are detailed in *Istikhbarat* correspondence from January 1986, reporting a ruling by the Northern Affairs Committee of the Revolutionary Command Council. NAC letter no.6740, classified "confidential and personal" and dated January 16, 1986.

[36] *Al-Iraq*, September 13, 1983.

[37] See, for example, Van Bruinessen, *Agha, Shaikh and State*, pages 28, 231-232.

produced a steady stream of rivals within his party. And after the debacle of 1975 these conflicts erupted into the open.

The power of the Barzani half-brothers--or the "offspring of treason," as the Ba'ath regime now took to calling them--was quickly challenged by Jalal Talabani. Formerly a lieutenant of the elder Barzani and a member of the KDP politburo, Talabani had long been critical of the "feudal" style of the tribally-based organization and now proposed to supplant it with a secular leftist movement rooted among urban intellectuals. In 1976, Talabani made the break formal with the creation of his Patriotic Union of Kurdistan (PUK), and two years later open warfare broke out between the two rival groups. The bitter schism would plague them until the final two years of the Iran-Iraq War.

Other groups complicated the picture still further. In 1979 another of Mullah Mustafa's former senior aides, Mahmoud Osman, joined forces with a breakaway group of *peshmerga* from the PUK to form the Kurdistan Socialist Party. In the same year, the Iraqi Communist Party also took up arms against the Baghdad regime and set up its headquarters to the north of the city of Suleimaniyeh, in the same valley as the PUK.[38] A clear geographical division quickly emerged. The KDP remained the dominant force in the mountain areas of Badinan in the far north, while the PUK held sway to the east and south of the Greater Zab river. (Other, smaller groups operated locally under suffrance of the two main *peshmerga* organizations.) This divide was linguistic as well as cultural: to the north and west of the river, the principal Kurdish dialect is Kurmanji; to the south, it is Sorani.[39]

Hampered in its ability to solve the Kurdish problem by force, the Iraqi regime leavened its repressive policies with a calculated attempt at divide-and-rule. This in turn had two dimensions: first, to play on the

---

[38] For general background, see Farouk-Sluglett and Sluglett, pp.187-190, and Van Bruinessen, *Agha, Shaikh and State*, pp.31-32 and 34-36. The picture was further complicated by the presence in these areas of a number of smaller groups, including Iranian organizations such as the KDP-Iran and Komala, who were conducting guerrilla war against the regime in Teheran from Iraqi soil.

[39] Kurdish is a member of the Iranian language group, and has many dialects in addition to Sorani and Kurmanji. See Van Bruinessen, *Agha, Shaikh and State*, pp.21-22, citing D.N. MacKenzie, "The Origins of Kurdish," *Transactions of the Philological Society*, 1961, pp.68-86.

acrimonious divisions between the leading Kurdish parties; and second, to recruit as many Kurds as possible into tribally-based pro-government paramilitary groups.

Baghdad's best opportunity to drive a wedge between the KDP and the PUK came with what was, on the face of it, a menacing development in the Iran-Iraq War. Talabani had bitterly opposed the Barzanis' decision to facilitate Iran's Haj Omran offensive in July 1983, and in September of that year he grew even more alarmed when further Iranian attacks penetrated the border area around the town of Penjwin-- uncomfortably close to the PUK's own strongholds in Suleimaniyeh governorate.[40] Talabani vowed that his troops would fight side-by-side with the Ba'ath Party to expel the invaders from Iraqi soil. Seizing the opportunity, Saddam Hussein offered the PUK leader a renewed commitment to Kurdish autonomy, hoping to win his seasoned guerrilla army permanently over to Baghdad's side. Almost a decade later, one member of the PUK team that negotiated with the Iraqi regime recalled clearly the words of Tariq Aziz, a member of the Revolutionary Command Council and later Iraq's Foreign Minister. "He told us, 'If you help us, we will never forget it. But if you oppose us, we will never forget it. And after the [Iran-Iraq] war is over, we will destroy you and all your villages completely."[41] It was not an empty threat.

The negotiations dragged on inconclusively for more than a year before they finally broke down in January 1985. While there were a number of reasons for the collapse of the talks, none was more important than Talabani's reported reiteration of Mullah Mustafa Barzani's unacceptable demand that the Kirkuk and Khanaqin regions, with their oilfields, be considered part of Kurdistan.[42] But although Saddam Hussein failed to cement a lasting alliance with Talabani, he could take

---

[40] By now Iraq had used chemical weapons a number of times against Iranian troops, but it is probable that the Penjwin offensive marked their first use on Iraqi soil. See Anthony H. Cordesman and Abraham R. Wagner, *The Lessons of Modern War, Volume II: The Iran-Iraq War* (London and Boulder: Mansell-Westview, 1990), p.514, and generally pp.506-518.

[41] Middle East Watch interview with Naywshirwan Mustafa Amin, Washington, D.C., May 2, 1993.

[42] Marr, op cit, p.307.

satisfaction in the fact that the PUK-KDP rift was now deeper and more bitter than ever.

Tribal loyalties in much of Iraqi Kurdistan have loosened somewhat during the modern era. Where they remain strong, however, they have offered fertile soil for successive regimes to recruit militias in the drive to undermine Kurdish solidarity. Known officially under Saddam Hussein as the Command of the National Defense Battalions (*Qiyadet Jahafel al-Difa' al-Watani*), these paramilitary bands have long been derided by other Kurds as *jahsh*, or "donkey foals."[43]

The *jahsh* have existed in some form since at least the early 1960s, but their role has been expanded several times since. In principle, each tribal group was supposed to produce its contingent of *jahsh* as a demonstration of loyalty to the regime; each unit's commander enjoyed the title of *mustashar* (consultant or advisor). If tribal leaders did not agree to cooperate in forming *jahsh* units, then *Amn* threats would often be persuasive.[44]

The ordinary *jahsh* came under the operational command of military intelligence (*Istikhbarat*) in the final stages of the Iran-Iraq War and during the Anfal campaign. But there were also two élite forces of pro-government Kurds. The *Quwat al-Taware'* (Emergency Forces) carried out intelligence and counter-terrorism activities in the cities under the control of the Ba'ath Party. The *Mafarez Khaseh*, meanwhile, or "special units" of Kurdish agents, were formed by hard-core collaborators and were an official part of *Amn*. All of these groups were heavily indoctrinated by the regime against their fellow Kurds. In an introductory seminar, one former *jahsh* commander recalled, military

---

[43] The epithet is in such common everyday use that it has lost much of its pejorative force in the process. In the Kurmanji-speaking areas of the north, the Kurdish paramilitaries are also referred to as *chatta*--brigands or bandits.

[44] One former *mustashar* described a 1987 conversation with the head of *Amn* in Suleimaniyeh, a colonel by the name of Khalaf. "He told me that I must carry a gun for the government. He pressured me to join. He told me, 'You did not participate in the [Iran-Iraq] war; you must now become a *mustashar*.' He then told me, 'If you don't join, your identification card may be revoked.'" The later implications of this threat turned out to be very grave, since during Anfal the correct identification card could be a matter of life or death. Middle East Watch interview, Suleimaniyeh, May 12, 1992.

intelligence officers told the assembled *mustashars* that the *peshmerga* were neither Kurds nor Iraqis; under Islamic law, they were "infidels and shall be treated as such."[45]

The duties of the rank-and-file *jahsh* were broadly akin to those of similar militias in other parts of the world.[46] Poorly equipped with light weapons, they maintained road blocks, patrolled the countryside, did advance scouting work for the regular army, searched villages for army deserters and draft dodgers, and handed over suspected *peshmerga* to the authorities. For obvious reasons the regime never fully trusted the *jahsh's* loyalties. Even though *jahsh* members were largely recruited from complexes, towns and villages under government control (Zakho, for instance, is said to have had as many as 5,000 *jahsh*), their units were frequently rotated to prevent local sympathies from developing. *Mustashars* knew that the regime was wary of any illicit contacts they might have with *peshmerga* commanders in the vicinity, and *Amn* files that Middle East Watch has examined contain extensive surveillance dossiers on *jahsh* leaders.

The early years of the war against Iran made it apparent that Kurdish conscripts made reluctant soldiers, and on a number of occasions groups of Kurds were released from military service and inducted into the *jahsh* instead. If an adult male Kurd had connections to his local *mustashar*, he would pull every possible string to evade military service and serve in the *jahsh* instead.

Many of the *mustashars* found their new role appealing. Some were nobodies, elevated by the government to positions of real power. Others were traditional tribal leaders who discovered that the rich opportunities for graft as a *mustashar* more than made up for their declining influence among the local Kurds. In addition to his fixed

---

[45] In general, Islamic law does not apply in Iraq, a secular state--although some elements of Islamic law have been incorporated into areas such as family law. However, like the Anfal operation itself, this was an entirely characteristic attempt by the Ba'ath regime to legitimize its campaigns by wrapping them in the language of religion.

[46] There are obvious parallels, for example, with Guatemala and Peru. See Americas Watch, *Civil Patrols in Guatemala*, (August 1986) and *Peru Under Fire: Human Rights Since the Return of Democracy* (New Haven: Yale University Press, 1992).

salary, the *mustashar* was entitled to a small monthly cash payment for each man nominally under his command. Yet it was a common practice for many of these men--even the vast majority in some cases--to avoid active duty. On paper, the regime had, at the peak of their numbers, 250,000 Kurdish foot-soldiers at its disposal; in practice, only a fraction of that number genuinely bore arms. In exchange for a signed *jahsh* ID that would protect them from military service, these Kurdish men were quite content for the *mustashar* to pocket their salary as well as his own. At 85 dinars ($255) a month for each paper soldier, it was easy for a canny *mustashar* to amass a fortune. The brothers Omar and Hussein Surchi, for example, parlayed their earnings into a contracting and construction business that made them the richest men in Kurdistan.

While the government was prepared to tolerate practices like this for the sake of a *mustashar's* fealty, it acted ruthlessly toward any show of independence. Several witnesses told Middle East Watch the story of a *mustashar* named Ja'far Mustafa, who was executed in 1986 for insubordination. The man was reportedly a fervent partisan of the Ba'ath regime, but would only agree to head up a *jahsh* contingent on condition that he be allowed to remain in his home area in the northern mountains of Badinan. In 1986 the order came through for Ja'far Mustafa's transfer, and he refused to move. During the standoff his defiance of Saddam Hussein was the talk of Iraqi Kurdistan. But after a week he was executed in Baghdad, and his body then returned from the capital to his home, near the northern town of Mangesh, where it was publicly hanged for the second time. The two villages that he owned--Besifki and Dergijneek--were burned to the ground some time later.[47]

* * *

1985-1987: OPEN WAR

After the collapse of the Ba'ath-PUK talks in January 1985, the Iraqi regime found its control of Kurdistan eroding once more. The war

---

[47] According to a dossier of destroyed villages compiled by the Kurdistan Reconstruction and Development Society (KURDS), Upper and Lower Besifki were destroyed in 1987 and Dergijneek in 1988. Both were in the *nahya* of Al-Doski.

with Iran, calculated to bring a swift victory, was dragging on interminably with heavy casualties on both sides. Although the government had built a chain of small forts and larger fortresses throughout the Kurdish countryside, it was simply not feasible to keep large numbers of troops pinned down there. Several dozen Kurdish settlements, mainly in PUK-controlled areas near the Iranian border, were burned in piecemeal fashion in the mid-1980s, and their inhabitants resettled in *mujamma'at*. But hundreds of other ancient villages--perhaps as many as 2,000--tried to integrate the counterinsurgency war into the rhythms of their daily lives. In the process, their communities were transformed.

The biggest threat to civilian morale came from shelling. The Iraqi Army had divided up Kurdistan according to a grid pattern and placed heavy artillery at regular intervals with a range of up to twenty-five miles. The guns pounded around the clock, and it was impossible to predict which targets would be hit on any given day. Routine farm work became a potentially lethal game of chance; sleep patterns were disrupted; the constant uncertainty shredded everyone's nerves.

Helicopters regularly dropped troops and *jahsh* into the villages to search for draft dodgers, deserters and suspected *peshmerga*. A steady stream of captured Kurds were taken away and executed. Others died in the frequent attacks by Soviet-supplied government MIGs and Sukhoi fighter-bombers.

Since the time of the first Ba'ath regime in 1963, Kurdish villagers had learned to protect themselves against aerial attack by building primitive shelters outside their homes. Now the pace of shelter construction accelerated, their design becoming more elaborate. Many were virtual underground rooms, high enough to stand up in, covered with wooden planks or corrugated iron sheeting and layers of dirt, stones and branches. The more sophisticated had twisting entrance tunnels to protect the occupants against shrapnel and blast. Many whole villages moved into nearby caves and rock overhangs and came to lead a virtual nocturnal existence, emerging to tend their animals and fields only when darkness fell.

Hamlets of three or four houses and small towns of three or four thousand people practiced an enforced self-sufficiency. Many villages elected their own five-person councils (*majlis al-sha'ab* in Arabic, or *anjuman* in Kurdish). As the government withdrew its rudimentary public services from rural areas, *peshmerga* teachers arrived to staff the abandoned schools and itinerant *peshmerga* paramedics tried to make up for the clinics that had been closed. In most cases, the villages had never had electricity or piped water, and in this sense the regime's ability to inflict additional hardship was limited. As before, the Kurds drew their water from rivers, springs and underground streams,[48] and the more prosperous took their electrical power from private generators. Commerce depended on smuggling. Knowing every goat-path in the surrounding hills, the villagers learned to evade the government roadblocks that tried to enforce a blockade on foodstuffs to *peshmerga*-controlled areas. Only women were allowed past these checkpoints. Sometimes younger boys could slip through with the help of a bribe, but it was a risky business, and some were arrested and disappeared on suspicion of aiding the *peshmerga*.

By now the practical distinction between *peshmerga* and ordinary civilians had blurred. In principle at least, active *peshmerga* received a salary from the organization to which they belonged and served duty rotas of 15-20 days at a time, with equal spells at home to work their lands. But many of the military-age men (and even some of the women) were also armed and organized into a so-called Civil Defense Force (*hezi bergri milli* or *hezi peshjiri*), whose main task was to defend their villages and hold off the army until *peshmerga* reinforcements could arrive. Light arms could be bought without much difficulty from the *jahsh* and it was common for households to have more than one weapon.

The *peshmerga*, meanwhile, tried to keep the regime off balance with their mixture of fixed and mobile forces. Hundreds of the smallest guerrilla units, or *mafrazeh*, roamed the countryside. In mountainous areas, a *mafrazeh* could be as small as five men; in the villages, fifteen was the minimum number needed for successful defense. Above the *mafrazeh* was the *kird*, and above the *kird* the *teep*, which the Kurds thought of as their equivalent of an army division.[49]

By the beginning of 1987, the only parts of Iraqi Kurdistan over which Baghdad exercised effective control were the cities, larger towns,

---

[48] Some villages had developed relatively sophisticated water-supply and irrigation systems, channeling rivers to their homes through mud-brick covered trenches called *karez*.

[49] Middle East Watch interview with Naywshirwan Mustafa Amin, Washington, D.C., May 2, 1993.

complexes and paved highways. Authority over the rural areas was roughly divided between the KDP in the north and the PUK in the south. While the regime had long vilified the KDP as the "offspring of treason," it now saw ominous signs that the PUK, too, was acting as the military and political surrogate of a foreign power with which Iraq was at war. Talabani's group would henceforth be known officially as *Umala Iran*-- "agents of Iran"--a term reportedly coined by Saddam Hussein himself.[50]

Insulting though it may have been, the phrase was grounded in fact, for since the latter part of 1986 Iranian-PUK collaboration had been a reality. While the KDP had long enjoyed access to Iranian sanctuaries, the PUK now felt that it had no alternative but to do likewise. In landlocked Kurdistan, the struggle could never succeed without help from a friendly neighbor. "There was no way for food and supplies to reach us, no help for our wounded, no roads out of the territory that we had liberated," claimed Naywshirwan Mustafa Amin, who was deputy commander of the PUK at the time. "Iran was our window to the world."

In October 1986, the PUK and the Iranian government concluded a sweeping accord on economic, political and military cooperation. Both parties agreed that they would press the fight against the Iraqi regime until Saddam Hussein was toppled, and both promised to make no unilateral deals with Baghdad.[51] If either party faced a serious military threat, the other would open a second front to relieve the pressure; Iran agreed to provide the PUK with arms, financial support and medical aid, while foreswearing the right to impose an Islamic regime in Baghdad.[52] The results of the accord were apparent almost at once,

---

[50] The tendency to describe the regime's opponents with insulting epithets was very common. One 17-year-old who was executed by the regime was described in an official *Amn* document, ordering the Suleimaniyeh morgue to dispose of his body, as a "fire-worshipper"--a derogatory reference to the ancient Iranian religion of Zoroastrianism.

[51] This was another in the long line of broken promises to the Kurds, who were certainly not consulted in July 1988 when Teheran accepted the UN ceasefire resolution in the middle of the Anfal campaign.

[52] Middle East Watch interview with Naywshirwan Mustafa Amin, Washington D.C., May 2, 1993.

on October 10, when a group of Iranian Revolutionary Guards, or *pasdaran* accompanied by Kurdish *peshmerga*, struck at the Kirkuk oilfields, deep inside Iraqi territory. At the same time, to Baghdad's evident fury, the Iranians brokered a unity agreement between the PUK and the KDP, putting an end to their longstanding rivalry.

The Teheran accords brought a radical shift in the attitude of the Iraqi regime. Despite having the upper hand in the war against Iran, the security situation within its own borders had slipped badly. Since the resumption of the war with the PUK in 1985, Kurdish affairs had been overseen by Muhammad Hamza al-Zubeidi, head of the Northern Bureau of the Ba'ath Party Organization. After a full-scale security review of the region, al-Zubeidi had reportedly been ordered to bring the situation under control within six months; when that period elapsed there was a six-month extension. But still the situation continued to deteriorate, and in early 1987 Baghdad decided on harsher measures. From now on, all those who still lived and farmed in the Kurdish mountains would be considered as active enemies of the state by virtue of nothing more than their ethnicity and their physical presence in their ancestral homeland.

2
PRELUDE TO ANFAL

"I will confute those vile geographers
That make a triple region of the world,
Excluding regions which I mean to trace,
And with this pen reduce them to a map,
Calling the provinces, cities, and towns
After my name...
— *Marlowe, **Tamburlaine the Great**, Part One (IV, iv)*

All of the tendencies that had been implicit in earlier phases of Iraq's war on the Kurds reached their culmination in 1987-1988 with the endgame of the Iran-Iraq War and the campaign known as al-Anfal. In the captured Iraqi documents that are now being studied by Middle East Watch, the term crops up with great frequency: villages are "purified" in the course of "the Heroic Anfal Operation"; the reason for the flight of villagers into neighboring countries is given as "Anfal"; an "Anfal" oilfield is inaugurated and a special "Anfal Section" of the Ba'ath Arab Socialist Party created in commemoration of the event; one of the government contractors hired to work on the drainage of Iraq's southern marshes is the "Anfal Company."[1] It is evident from the documents, and from the supporting testimony of those who survived Anfal, that the resources of the Iraqi state were deployed and coordinated on a massive level to assure the success of the operation.

"Anfal" was the name given to a concerted series of military offensives, eight in all, conducted in six distinct geographical areas between late February and early September, 1988. Overall command of the operation was in the hands of the Northern Bureau of the Ba'ath Party

---

[1] The marshes have been the object of a vast engineering scheme designed to bring the rebellious south under the control of the central government in Baghdad. The regime's treatment of the Shi'a inhabitants of the south, including the *Ma'dan*, or Marsh Arabs, is detailed in the Middle East Watch report, "Current Human Rights Conditions among the Iraqi Shi'a," March 1993.

51

Organization, based in the city of Kirkuk and headed, after March 1987, by the "Struggling Comrade" Ali Hassan al-Majid.[2]   Kurdish villagers who survived the events of 1988 routinely refer to al-Majid as "Ali Anfal" or "Ali Chemical."

Al-Majid's appointment was highly significant for a number of reasons. Until 1987, military policy against the *peshmerga* had been set by the First and Fifth Corps of the Iraqi Army, based in Kirkuk and Erbil respectively. Now, however, the Ba'ath Party itself assumed direct charge of all aspects of policy toward the Kurds. Al-Majid's command also made the settlement of the Kurdish problem the concern of Iraq's innermost circle of power--the close network of family ties centered on the city of Tikrit and the personal patronage of President Saddam Hussein.

Saddam's father, whom he never knew, was a member of Tikrit's al-Majid family, and Ali Hassan al-Majid was the Iraqi president's cousin.[3] Al-Majid, who was born in 1941, had humble origins, and first made his reputation in 1968--as a mere sergeant--as the bodyguard to Hammad Shihab al-Tikriti, commander of the Baghdad army garrison and one of the ringleaders of the Ba'ath coup in July of that year. Al-Majid rose quickly in the Tikrit circle and in 1979 played an important role in the purge of the party leadership. During the 1983-1985 negotiations between the regime and the PUK, Saddam Hussein appointed his cousin to head *Amn*.

Even by the standards of the Ba'ath security apparatus, al-Majid had a particular reputation for brutality. According to the (admittedly subjective) account of one former *mustashar* who had frequent dealings with him, "He is more of a risk-taker than Saddam Hussein, and he has no respect for people. It was very difficult to work with him. He was stupid,

---

[2] The Northern Bureau is one of four regional bureaus of the Ba'ath, and is quite separate from the Northern Affairs Committee of the Revolutionary Command Council. Other party bureaus have responsibility for the South, the Center, and the capital city of Baghdad. This division of Iraq into security zones is mirrored by the four-bureau organization of *Amn* and military intelligence (*Istikhbarat*).

[3] The family tree is shown in Simon Henderson, *Instant Empire: Saddam Hussein's Ambition for Iraq* (San Francisco: Mercury House, 1991), p.87. Other notable cousins of Saddam's include the former Defense Minister Adnan Khairallah, who died in a helicopter crash in 1989, and Hussein Kamel Majid, Minister of Industry and Military Industry.

and only carrying out Saddam Hussein's orders. In the past, he used to be a police sergeant; today he is Minister of Defense. Saddam Hussein, by contrast, is 'a snake with deadly poison.' He pretends to be weak, but at any chance he will use his poison....In tough cases, in which he needs people without a heart, he calls upon Ali Hassan al-Majid."[4]

The main military thrust of Anfal was carried by regular troops of the the First and Fifth Corps, backed up by units from other corps as they became available from the Iranian front.[5] The elite Republican Guards took part in the first phase of Anfal; other units which saw action included the Special Forces (*Quwat al-Khaseh*), commando forces (*Maghawir*) and Emergency Forces (*Quwat al-Taware'*)--the Ba'ath Party-controlled urban counterterrorism squads. Finally, a wide range of support activities-- entering population centers ahead of regular army units, burning and looting villages, tracking down fleeing villagers and organizing their surrender--were handled by the Kurdish paramilitary *jahsh*.

But the logic of Ali Hassan al-Majid's campaign against the Kurds went far beyond the six-month long military campaign. From a human-rights perspective, the machinery of genocide was set in motion by al-Majid's appointment in March 1987 and its wheels continued to turn until April 1989. Within weeks of al-Majid's arrival in Kirkuk, it was apparent that the Iraqi government had decided to settle its Kurdish problem once

---

[4] Middle East Watch interview with former *mustashar*, Zakho, September 1, 1992. In 1989 al-Majid was appointed as Minister of the Interior, and then, after the August 1990 invasion, as governor of Kuwait. He is now Iraq's Defense Minister, and continues to be implicated in actions of the grossest brutality. According to an eyewitness, Majid personally shot to death some 25-30 detainees in Basra Prison on April 3 or 4, 1991. The dead included six children. See Middle East Watch, "Current Human Rights Conditions Among the Iraqi Shi'a," March 5, 1993.

[5] The Iraqi Army has seven regular corps in all. The term "special forces" requires some explanation. In the U.S. armed forces and others built on the U.S. model, these are light infantry forces designed to conduct irregular missions such as guerrilla warfare and covert operations. Iraq's special forces, by contrast, are mobile elite infantry units, armed with the best available weapons and often supported by tank battalions. Growing out of the Iran-Iraq War, they have been compared to the German *Stosstruppen* of World War One. See "Iraqi Order of Battle: Ground Troops," in *Desert Shield Factbook* (Bloomington, IN: GDW, 1991), pp.50-59.

and for all, and that the resources of the state would be used in a coordinated fashion to achieve this goal. A sustained pattern of decrees, directives and actions by the security forces leaves no doubt that the intent of the Iraqi government was to destroy definitively the armed organizations of the Kurdish resistance and to eradicate all remaining human settlements in areas that were disputed or under *peshmerga* control--with the exception of those inhabited by the minority of tribes whose loyalty to Baghdad was indisputable. If anything stood in the way of these goals in 1987, it was logistical shortcomings--above all, the fact that a large proportion of the troops and materiel that would be required for Anfal were still tied down on the Iranian war front.

***

It was Iraq that launched the war in 1980, and Iraq that maintained the initiative for much of the eight years that the conflict lasted.[6] Nonetheless, the Iranians did succeed in putting Iraq on the defensive on a number of occasions. In July 1983, Iranian troops had seized the important border garrison town of Haj Omran, east of the town of Rawanduz. But the highpoint of the war from Iran's point of view was its Val Fajr 8 offensive of February 1986; this included a surprise attack that seized the marshy Fao peninsula, thereby blocking Iraq's access to the Persian Gulf.

Fresh from its success in Fao, which inflicted huge losses on the Iraqi Army (and reinforced the U.S. "tilt" toward Baghdad), Iran reopened its second front in the north, in the rugged mountains of Iraqi Kurdistan. For more than six years, the Iraqi regime had ceded de facto control over

---

[6] The basic texts on the war include Edgar O'Ballance, *The Gulf War* (London: Brassey's, 1988); Dilip Hiro, *The Longest War: The Iran-Iraq Military Conflict* (New York: Routledge, 1991); Shahram Chubin and Charles Tripp, *Iran and Iraq at War* (Boulder: Westview Press, second revised edn., 1991); and Cordesman and Wagner, *The Lessons of Modern War, Volume II*. Most of these books share the defect of neglecting the temporary revival of Iran's fortunes in the final year and a half of the war--without which it is difficult to understand the relationship between the first Gulf War and the Anfal campaign. A useful corrective is Richard Jupa and James Dingeman, *Gulf Wars: How Iraq Won the First and Lost the Second. Will There Be a Third?* (Cambria, CA: 3W Publications, c.1991), pp.1-9.

much of the rural north to the *peshmerga*; now foreign troops threatened to occupy more and more border territory, diverting much-needed forces from the southern front around Basra. As the October 1986 raid by Iranian *pasdaran* suggested to nervous Iraqi officials, the vital Kirkuk oilfields, almost a hundred miles from the border, were no longer immune.

There is debate among scholars as to the precise threat that Iraq faced from Iran at this late stage of the war. Certainly, Iran's huge Karbala 5 offensive against Basra's Fish Lake in January 1987 marked its final use of the "human wave" tactic of hurling tens of thousands of troops--most of them poorly trained *basij*[7]--against fixed enemy targets. The resulting casualty levels were simply not sustainable, as Teheran now acknowledged. On February 12, Iranian troops returned to the Haj Omran area with a small offensive codenamed Fatah 4--although some believe that this was less a real attack than a diversionary action for propaganda purposes.[8] But three weeks later, on March 4, a new and more alarming Iranian assault, this one codenamed Karbala 7, managed to penetrate eight miles into Iraqi territory east of Rawanduz with a joint military force which this time included *peshmerga* of the KDP and the PUK. The Iraqi regime was infuriated by these renewed signs of collusion, particularly since they now involved both rival Kurdish parties.[9] On March 13, in a rare interview with a foreign reporter, Iraqi cabinet minister Hashim Hassan al-'Aqrawi commented, "The Iranians are trying to use these people to carry out dirty missions, and since they know the geography of the area and its ins and outs, the Iranians use them merely as guides for the Khomeini Guards and

---

[7] The *basij*, or Mobilization Unit, were virtually untrained volunteers under *pasdaran* supervision. They were integral to Iran's conception of an "Islamic warfare" that depended more on faith than on technology and conventional military skills. See Chubin and Tripp, *Iran and Iraq at War*, pp.42-49.

[8] See, for example, Cordesman and Wagner, *op cit*, p.257.

[9] The KDP and PUK eventually reached formal military and political agreements to collaborate in November 1987, and in 1988 formed the Iraqi Kurdistan Front. Five smaller parties later joined the Front.

the Iranian forces." The Kurds--or at least Talabani's PUK--even began to talk openly of dismembering the Iraqi state.[10]

On March 14 or 15, Saddam Hussein presided over a five-hour meeting of the Armed Forces General Command. Ali Hassan al-Majid was also reportedly in attendance. Any outsider's account of what took place in such a secretive meeting must be highly speculative, but according to at least two accounts, the Iraqi president told his senior officers that he feared a "defeat by attrition."[11] On March 18, the Revolutionary Command Council and the Ba'ath Party's Regional Command jointly decided to appoint al-Majid, the president's cousin, as Secretary General of the Northern Bureau of the Ba'ath Party Organization. His predecessors, Sa'adi Mahdi Saleh and Muhammad Hamza al-Zubeidi, had allowed the Kurdish problem to fester for too long; al-Majid would not repeat their mistakes.

In essence, the disagreements among scholars of the Iran-Iraq War are academic--at least as far as the Kurds are concerned. Saddam Hussein may indeed have foreseen a slow defeat as a result of Baghdad's existing policies; alternatively, he may have seen Iran's stalled Fish Lake offensive in January as a turning point in Iraq's favor, and an opportunity to press home his advantage. Either way, it is apparent that he decided that exceptional measures were necessary to settle the Kurdish problem, that troublesome sideshow of the Iran-Iraq conflict, once and for all.

Ali Hassan al-Majid's extraordinary new powers--equivalent in the Autonomous Region to those of the president himself--came into effect with decree no. 160 of the Revolutionary Command Council, dated March 29, 1987. Al-Majid was to "represent the Regional Command of the Party and the Revolutionary Command Council in the execution of their policies for the whole of the Northern Region, including the Kurdistan Autonomous Region, for the purpose of protecting security and order, safeguarding stability, and applying autonomous rule in the region." The decree went on to explain that, "Comrade al-Majid's decisions shall be mandatory for all

---

[10] According to comments by Naywshirwan Mustafa Amin in an April 1987 interview with *Le Monde*, one option under consideration by the PUK was "the severance of Iraq into a number of small states: Shi'a, Kurdish and Sunni." Cited in Baram, *op. cit.*, p.127.

[11] Cordesman and Wagner, *op. cit.*, pp.259-260. O'Ballance also echoes this view, but provides less detail.

state agencies, be they military, civilian and security." His fiat would apply "particularly in relation to matters that are the domain of the National Security Council and the Northern Affairs Committee." A second order by Saddam Hussein, issued on April 20, 1987, gave al-Majid the additional authority to set the budget of the Northern Affairs Committee.

Al-Majid's "decisions and directives" were to be obeyed without question by all intelligence agencies--including military intelligence (*Istikhbarat*)--and by all domestic security forces; by the Popular Army Command (*Qiyadat al-Jaysh al-Sha'abi*); and by all military commands in the northern region. Decree 160 and its riders leave no room for doubt: simply put, Ali Hassan al-Majid was to be the supreme commander, the overlord, of all aspects of Anfal.

* * *

Almost a year would pass before that campaign began. But within weeks of al-Majid's appointment, the *logic* of Anfal was fully apparent. Its legal framework was set in place; new standing orders were issued to the security forces; and a two-month wave of military attacks, village destruction and forced relocations was unleashed--a rough draft, as it were, of the larger campaign ahead. "I gave myself two years to end the activity of the saboteurs," al-Majid later told his aides.[12] And with the first warm days of spring and the melting of the snow in the mountains, al-Majid embarked on his brutal three-stage process of "village collectivization"--in other words, the wholesale destruction of hundreds of Kurdish farming villages and the relocation of their residents into *mujamma'at*.

Even his top military commanders were shocked by the brutality of what he had in mind. He later confided to aides:

> When we made the decision to destroy and collectivize the villages and draw a dividing line between us and the saboteurs, the first one to express his doubts to me and before the President was [former Fifth Corps commander] Tali'a al-Durri. The first one who alarmed me was Tali'a al-Durri. To this day the impact of Tali'a is evident. He didn't destroy all the villages that I asked him to at that

---

[12] Audiotape of a conversation between Ali Hassan al-Majid and unnamed Ba'ath Party aides, January 22, 1989.

time. And this is the longest-standing member of the
Ba'ath Party. What about the other people then? How
were we to convince them to solve the Kurdish problem
and slaughter the saboteurs?[13]

The timetable for the three phases of al-Majid's campaign is clearly
spelled out in a number of official documents, notably including a letter
from the General Staff of the *jahsh* to the command of the Fifth Army
Corps, dated April 13, 1987. This appears to be in response to a verbal
order from the Fifth Corps commander concerning "final obligations in
winding up [illegible] procedures for the termination of sabotage in the
Northern Region, [and] the manner and the priorities of implementing the
evacuation and demolition of security-prohibited villages." The first phase
of the operation would begin on April 21 and end on May 20; the second
would start immediately on May 21 and continue until June 20.[14]
Military and security maps were "redlined," with clear boundaries drawn to
denote areas "prohibited for security reasons." *Amn* set up a special
"prohibited villages committee" to oversee the forbidden areas. Within the
zones designated for phases one and two, the order was clear and explicit:
"All prohibited villages will be destroyed."[15]

A former military intelligence (*Istikhbarat*) officer who later crossed
over to the PUK told Middle East Watch of a meeting in Kirkuk that
spring, attended by the governors of Erbil, Kirkuk, Dohuk and
Suleimaniyeh, the commanders of the First and Fifth Army Corps,
divisional military commanders and senior Ba'ath Party officials. Ali
Hassan al-Majid, speaking in characteristically irascible tones, gave orders
that "no house was to be left standing" in the Kurdish villages on the Erbil
plain. Only Arab villages would be spared.[16] At a later meeting in Erbil,

---

[13] Ibid. For the full text, see appendix A, pp.351-352.

[14] Special National Defense Forces General Staff (Operations) to Fifth Corps
Command, Erbil: letter no. 28/573, dated April 13, 1987 and classified "Top Secret
and Confidential." The town of Makhmour lies some thirty-five miles southwest
of Erbil.

[15] Minutes of Shaqlawa Security Committee meeting, April 4, 1987.

[16] Middle East Watch interview, Zakho, June 24, 1992.

the witness heard al-Majid repeat these orders, and back them up with a personal threat: "I will come and observe," he said, "and if I find any house intact, I will hold the section commander responsible." After receiving these orders, the former *Istikhbarat* officer said, "I got two IFAs [East German-built military trucks] full of explosives from a warehouse in Erbil. I commandeered 200 bulldozers from civilians of Erbil--by force, with no payment. We started destroying mud villages with bulldozers, and dynamiting the cement structures. We used military engineers for this." The troops went in at dawn; wells were filled in and electricity supplies torn out, leaving only the poles standing. After the engineering work was completed, *Istikhbarat* would inspect the affected villages by helicopter. If any structure was found to be still standing, the sectional commander would be ordered to return and finish the job, and would risk disciplinary action. It was an extraordinarily thorough enterprise, and the evidence is visible all over Iraqi Kurdistan, with many villages not so much demolished as pulverized.

No farming of any sort was to continue in the destroyed areas. Government aircraft would conduct regular overflights to detect any unauthorized farming, and local security committees would be held responsible for any violations. Stringent restrictions were imposed on all grain sales in the Kurdish areas, as well as on agricultural trade across governorate boundaries.

Al-Majid also reportedly issued specific rules of engagement at the Erbil meeting. The army should only open fire in cases of active resistance, he ordered. But if resistance were encountered, the entire village population was to be killed in reprisal. In the event, there was no resistance, since the villages selected for the 1987 clearances were on or near the main roads and under government control. Only during Phase III of the campaign would the troops venture into *peshmerga*-held territory.

* * *

THE CHEMICAL THRESHOLD

Even before the first stage of the village clearances got underway, the Iraqi regime had crossed a new barrier in its war against the Kurds. Throughout the early weeks of al-Majid's rule, the *peshmerga*--and in particular the PUK--kept up a steady rhythm of military actions. In early

April the PUK launched its most ambitious drive to date in the Jafati Valley, which runs southeast from Dukan Lake. The valley was home to the PUK's national headquarters, and thousands of *peshmerga* congregated there for the assault. In a matter of hours they had overrun dozens of small military posts and taken hundreds of prisoners.

The government's response was not long in coming. "Our leadership received information that the Iraqis were going to use chemical weapons," said a PUK *peshmerga* who fought in this campaign:

> They issued instructions on what to do in case of a chemical attack. We were instructed to put wet cloths on our faces, to light fires, or to go to places located above the point of impact. In the beginning, the government used chemical artillery shells. This was in the Jafati and Shahrbazar valleys [on April 15], one or two nights after our victory. We didn't realize they were chemicals. The sound was not as loud as the ordinary shelling, and we smelled rotten apples and garlic.... Uncounted numbers of shells fell on us, but they had little effect.[17]

This was not the case the following day, however, in the villages of Balisan and Sheikh Wasan. These two settlements lie scarcely a mile and a half apart, in a steep-sided valley south of the town of Rawanduz. The Balisan valley was home to the PUK's third *malband*, or regional command.[18] Yet few *peshmerga* were present on the afternoon of April 16, since most had been taking part in the military action in the Jafati

---

[17] Middle East Watch interview, Choman, March 23, 1993. There was also reportedly a chemical attack on April 15, 1987 on the KDP headquarters in Zewa, a largely depopulated area close to the Turkish border.

[18] The PUK had four *malbands* altogether. The first, based in the Qara Dagh mountains, was responsible for political and military affairs in the governorate of Suleimaniyeh. The second, in the Jafati Valley, was in charge of operations in Kirkuk (al-Ta'mim). The third and fourth, based in the Balisan Valley and the adjoining Smaquli Valley, shared responsibility for the PUK's work in Erbil. Later, the third and fourth *malbands* were merged; under the PUK-KDP unity agreements, a new fourth malband was opened in Zewa, the KDP headquarters on the Turkish border, to handle operations in the governorate of Dohuk.

valley, on the far side of Dukan Lake. Instead, their families would be made to suffer the repercussions.

Balisan itself was a sizeable village, which until April 1987 had some 250 households (about 1,750 people)[19] of the Khoshnaw tribe, as well as four mosques, a primary school and an intermediate school. As the crow flies, it lay some twelve miles east of the town of Shaqlawa; Sheikh Wasan, a smaller settlement of about 150 houses, lay nestled in the hills a little way to the northeast. The valley was long-time *peshmerga* country; the Barzani movement had controlled it from 1961-74, and the PUK, through its third *malband*, since the outbreak of the war with Iran in 1980. Since about 1983, the Balisan Valley had been a "prohibited area," with government checkpoints attempting with only partial success to prevent the entry of foodstuffs and supplies. Food rations had been suspended, and government teachers withdrawn from the schools. Iraqi aircraft made frequent harassment attacks, to which the villagers responded by hiding away in deep, dark caves in the surrounding mountains. But ground troops had never managed to penetrate the valley.

In the drizzly late afternoon of April 16, the villagers had returned home from the fields and were preparing dinner when they heard the drone of aircraft approaching. Some stayed put in their houses; others made it as far as their air-raid shelters before the planes, a dozen of them, came in sight, wheeling low over the two villages to unload their bombs. There were a number of muffled explosions.

Until this moment no government had ever used chemical weapons against its own civilian population. But the plummeting enlistment rate among Iranian volunteers over the previous year, when poison gas was widely used on the battlefield, was vivid testimony to the Iraqi government of the power of this forbidden weapon to instil terror. More gruesome yet was the decision to record the event on videotape.

The Iraqi regime had long conducted its record-keeping in meticulous fashion. (Those in neighboring countries say, only half-

---

[19] Population figures for Balisan and Sheikh Wasan are derived from Resool's dossier of destroyed villages, although villagers interviewed by Middle East Watch suggested that Balisan may have been even larger, with perhaps as many as 525 households. Officials of the United Nations High Commissioner for Refugees assume an average household size of seven persons in Kurdish villages.

jokingly, that the Iraqis are the "Prussians of the Middle East.")[20] From the grandest decree to the most trivial matter, all the business of the security forces was recorded in letters and telegrams, dated, numbered and rubber-stamped on receipt. Even when an original command carried a high security classification, abundant numbers of handwritten or typed copies were later prepared, to be handed down the chain of command and filed, the writers apparently confident that prying eyes would never see these secrets. In the mid-1980s, the Iraqi security services developed a fascination for video technology as a valuable new form of record-keeping. The actions of the security forces were now to be routinely documented on tape: village clearances, executions of captured *peshmerga*, even chemical weapons attacks on civilians.

The official videotape of the Balisan Valley bombing, reportedly made by a member of the *jahsh*, shows towering columns and broad, drifting clouds of white, gray and pinkish smoke. A cool evening breeze was blowing off the mountains, and it brought strange smells--pleasant ones at first, suggestive of roses and flowers, or, to others, apples and garlic. Other witnesses still say there was the less attractive odor of insecticide. But then, said one elderly woman from Balisan, "It was all dark, covered with darkness, we could not see anything, and were not able to see each other. It was like fog. And then everyone became blind." Some vomited. Faces turned black; people experienced painful swellings under the arms, and women under their breasts. Later, a yellow watery discharge would ooze from the eyes and nose. Many of those who survived suffered severe vision disturbances, or total blindness, for up to a month. In Sheikh Wasan, survivors watched as a woman staggered around blindly, clutching her dead child, and not realizing it was dead. Some villagers ran into the mountains and died there. Others, who had been closer to the place of impact of the bombs, died where they stood.[21] One witness, a *peshmerga*, told Middle

---

[20] Not coincidentally, the Iraqi intelligence agencies were mainly equipped and trained by their East German equivalents. It may well be that the files of the former *Staatssicherheitsdienst* (Stasi) will shed further light on this relationship.

[21] The symptoms described by villagers are generally consistent with the effects of mustard gas--although reports that some victims died immediately suggest that nerve agents may also have been used, since mustard gas, even in high concentrations, is not usually lethal for at least half an hour. See Physicians for Human Rights, *loc. cit.*.

East Watch that a second attack followed an hour later, this one conducted by a fleet of helicopters.[22]

The few fighters who had been at home when the raid occurred were taken by the PUK for treatment in Iran, fearing that they would not survive a visit to an Iraqi hospital. (The presence of *peshmerga* in the village is, one should add, quite irrelevant from a legal point of view. By their very nature, chemical weapons make no distinction between civilian and military targets, and their use is outlawed under any circumstances.)[23]

The following morning, ground troops and *jahsh* entered Balisan, looted the villagers' deserted homes and razed them to the ground. The same day, or perhaps a day later--having presumably left sufficient time for the gas to dissipate--army engineers dynamited and bulldozed Sheikh Wasan. But the surviving inhabitants had already fled during the night of the attack. Some made their way to the city of Suleimaniyeh, and a few to Shaqlawa. But most headed southeast, to the town of Raniya, where there was a hospital. They were helped on their way by people from neighboring villages, some of which--including Barukawa, Beiro, Kaniberd and Tutma-- had also suffered from the effects of the windborne gas.

The people of Beiro sent tractor-drawn carts to Sheikh Wasan, and ten of these vehicles, each carrying fifty or sixty people, left for Raniya. At the complex of Seruchawa, just outside the town, the tractors stopped to bury the bodies of fifty people who were already dead. The refugees who reached Raniya spent one night there. Local doctors washed their wounds and gave them eye-drops, but these did nothing to ease the effects of the gas on their vision. The refugees spent a restless night, and the hospital at Raniya was full of the sound of weeping.

---

[22] Middle East Watch interview, Erbil, March 16, 1993.

[23] In an interesting, if indirect confirmation of the May 16 attack, an undated handwritten note from *Amn* Shaqlawa also mentions that sixteen Iranian Revolutionary Guards (*pasdaran*) were present during a bombing raid on the villages of Balisan, Sheikh Wasan and Tutma. The *pasdaran* are reported to have "made fires which saved their lives"--a reference which cannot conceivably apply to anything but an attempted defense against poison gas. A separate *Amn* Shaqlawa document in the same file, dated May 20, 1987, notes that three members of the PUK Politburo are reported to have been injured by gas during "the latest military attacks in Kurdistan."

The next morning, agents from *Amn* --and some witnesses say also from military intelligence (*Istikhbarat*)-- arrived at the hospital. They ordered everyone out of bed and into a number of waiting Nissan Coasters that were parked outside.[24] These would take them to the city of Erbil for medical care, the villagers were told; however, they were warned later that day that they would only be given treatment if they told the doctors that their injuries were the result of an attack by *Iranian* airplanes.[25]

At about 9:00 that morning, exhausted and bedraggled people in Kurdish dress began to stream into the emergency room of the Republic Hospital in Erbil. One witness counted four packed coasters, each with twenty-one seats, and seven other vehicles--both cars and pickup trucks. Others placed the number of arrivals at perhaps 200, of all ages, men, women and children. They were all unarmed civilians. Four were dead on arrival. The survivors arriving from Ranya told the doctors that they had been attacked with chemical weapons. Despite their burns, their blindness and other, more superficial injuries, those who had survived the journey from the Balisan Valley were generally still able to walk, although some were unconscious.

Even with the assistance of doctors who rushed across from the nearby Maternity and Pediatric Hospital, the facilities were not sufficient to deal with such a large-scale emergency. There were far from enough beds to deal with so many victims; many of the patients were laid on the floors, and the occupants of three of the four coasters were obliged to wait in the parking lot while the preliminary triage was done and the first treatment carried out. On examination, the doctors found that the victims' eyes were dried out and glued shut. Having some rudimentary notion of how to treat chemical victims, they applied eye drops, washed their burns and administered injections of atropine, a powerful antidote to nerve agents.

The doctors had been at work on their patients for about an hour when the head of the local branch office of *Amn* arrived, an officer by the name of Hassan Naduri. The staff of the Erbil Republic Hospital, and especially the municipal morgue which was attached to it, had a great deal of prior and subsequent experience of *Amn*. The city housed not only the

---

[24] These workhorse vehicles are ubiquitous in Iraq. They are commonly known simply as "coasters," and are referred to by that name throughout this text.

[25] Middle East Watch interview, Balisan, April 30, 1992.

municipal office of the secret police agency, but also *Amn's* headquarters for the Erbil governorate and its operational command for the entire "autonomous region" of Iraqi Kurdistan. For several years the Republic Hospital morgue had received a steady flow of corpses from both *Amn* offices. Hospital records examined by Middle East Watch give details of approximately 500 bodies received from *Amn* between 1968-1987-- although there is no reason to suppose that this was more than a very incomplete record.

These deaths were recorded in the form of letters of transmittal from *Amn*, and the agency's bureaucracy appears to have been scrupulously efficient. Two copies of each letter of transmittal were sent to the morgue; the doctor on duty was required to sign one of these and then return it to *Amn*. Hospital staff also kept a second, secret ledger of their own, entitled "Record Book of Armed Dead People from Erbil." This covered a three-year period beginning in June 1987; the final entry was dated June 25, 1990. The entries were cross-referenced to the number of the relevant *Amn* transmittal letter. In interviews with Middle East Watch, hospital staff also estimated that they made out some 300 death certificates, on orders from *Amn*, for named individuals whose bodies were never made available to them. This practice began in 1987.

There appears to have been no single standard procedure: Corpses arrived at the Erbil morgue in a number of different ways. Sometimes the staff would receive a telephone call from *Amn*, often in the middle of the night, telling them that they should prepare to receive the body or bodies of "executed saboteurs" and ordering them to issue death certificates. Individual hospital porters were hand-picked for the task of handling the bodies, presumably because they enjoyed the trust of the *Amn* agents. On some occasions the corpses arrived in pickup trucks or station wagons, covered with blankets. At other times, hospital ambulances would be summoned to collect the bodies from the *Amn* headquarters in Einkawa, a Christian suburb of Erbil, or from a nearby military base. Although some showed signs of having been beaten to death, most appeared to have been executed by firing squads; they had multiple gunshot wounds, sometimes as many as thirty, and had their hands and upper arms bound behind them, as if they had been tied standing to a post.[26] The eyes were blindfolded with articles of clothing such as a Kurdish cummerbund or headscarf. The bodies had been stripped of their wristwatches, IDs and other personal possessions.

However the bodies arrived, the entire operation was shrouded in secrecy, and morgue staff were ordered (under threat of death) neither to contact the relatives of the deceased nor to divulge their names to anyone else in the hospital. Doctors on duty in the morgue were not allowed to touch or examine the bodies; their duty was merely to furnish death certificates. If the cadavers arrived during daylight hours, the entire area around the morgue would be cordoned off by *Amn* guards and other hospital personnel warned away from the area. *Amn* personnel would even take charge of the morgue's freezer facilities until municipal employees arrived to take the corpses away for secret burial in the paupers' section of the Erbil cemetery. If an especially large number of corpses was involved, a bulldozer would be commandeered from a local private contractor to dig a mass grave. The morgue staff were forbidden to wash the bodies or otherwise prepare them for burial facing Mecca, as Islamic ritual demands. "Dogs have no relation to Islam," an *Amn* officer told one employee.[27]

When Hassan Naduri arrived at the Republic Hospital on the morning of April 17, 1987, every doctor in the hospital was busy dealing with the emergency. The officer was accompanied by two other *Amn* agents; a large number of guards also remained outside in the hospital courtyard. According to some witnesses, Hassan Naduri was accompanied by Ibrahim Zangana, the governor of Erbil, and by a local Ba'ath Party

---

[26] This is consistent with the procedures of an Iraqi firing squad, as recorded on a videotape that has been viewed by Middle East Watch. Five prisoners in Kurdish clothes are blindfolded, tied to posts and machinegunned with almost luxurious excess by a line of troops with AK-47s. The firing continues long after it is obvious that the prisoners are dead. Even then, a uniformed officer delivers the coup de grace to each man with a pistol. There is a pause. Finally, another officer moves down the line, discharging his pistol into the fallen bodies. This particular execution was carried out in a public square in front of a large crowd, and was greeted with applause from party and security dignitaries in the front row.

[27] This account is based on Middle East Watch interviews in Erbil, April 23-25, 1992.

official known only by his first name, Abd-al-Mon'em. The *Amn* officers
questioned the hospital guards, demanding to know where the new patients
were from and who the doctors were who were treating them. They then
repeated these questions to the medical personnel, and demanded to know
what treatment was being given. With these questions answered, Capt.
Naduri telephoned *Amn* headquarters for instructions. After hanging up,
he ordered that all treatment cease immediately. He told the doctors to
remove the dressings from their patients' wounds. The doctors asked why.
The captain responded that he had received orders from his superiors to
transfer all the patients to the city's Military Hospital. At first, the hospital
staff demurred, but the three *Amn* agents drew their pistols and ordered
them to stop what they were doing at once. Otherwise they would be taken
off to *Amn* headquarters themselves.

After a second phone call, this time ostensibly to the Military
Hospital, a number of ambulances or trucks arrived and took the patients
away, together with those who had remained, for a full hour now, in the
three parked coasters. Later that day, the doctors telephoned the Military
Hospital to check on the condition of their patients. But they had never
arrived there, and the doctors never saw any of the survivors of the Balisan
Valley chemical attack again. They heard later that loaded military
ambulances had been seen driving off in the direction of Makhmour, to the
southwest of Erbil.

In fact, a handful of survivors told Middle East Watch, the Balisan
Valley victims were taken to a former police station that was now an *Amn*
detention center, a stark white cement building in the Arab quarter of the
city, near the Baiz casino. There was a chaotic scene on arrival, as *Amn*
agents attempted to sort out the detainees by age and sex, and in the
confusion several people managed to escape. At least one woman fled
leaving her children behind. Those who remained were thrown into locked
cells, guarded by uniformed agents--some dressed all in green and others
all in blue. Here they were held for several days with neither food,
blankets nor medical attention.

Hamoud Sa'id Ahmad is an employee of the municipal morgue
attached to Erbil's Republic Hospital, a dignified middle-aged man who has
made the pilgrimage to Mecca. Over the next few days, he was summoned
on a number of occasions to the *Amn* jail in the city's Teirawa quarter and
ordered to pick up bodies and prepare them for burial. Over a three-day
period he counted sixty-four bodies. Arriving to collect them, he saw other
prisoners wandering around in the prison courtyard building. Some had

a clear fluid oozing from their mouths; others had dark, burn-like marks on their bodies, especially on the throat and hands. He saw men, women and children in detention, including several nursing babies in their mothers' arms. The bodies, kept in a separate locked cell, bore similar marks. None showed any signs of gunshot wounds. Most of the dead appeared to be children and elderly people. An *Amn* official told Ahmad that "they are saboteurs, all saboteurs we attacked with chemical weapons." An ambulance driver told Ahmad that he recognized one of the dead as a Republic Hospital employee from Sheikh Wasan.

Family members waiting outside the jail for news said that the detainees were being held as hostages, to compel their *peshmerga* relatives to surrender. On the last of his three visits, Ahmad saw two large buses pull up outside the prison, their windows sealed with cloths. Later in the day, a female prisoner managed to whisper to him, "Do you know what the buses were doing here? They took all the men away, to the south, like the Barzanis [in 1983]." The men were never seen alive again.[28]

After the mass disappearance of the men, the surviving women and children were taken out during the night and driven off in the direction of Khalifan, three hours to the northeast of Erbil. At a place called Alana, they were dumped in an open plain, on the banks of a river, and left to fend for themselves. They were reunited here with the Balisan Valley villagers who had fled to Suleimaniyeh. These people reported that they had been detained there in a converted hospital that was guarded by *Amn* agents and off limits to civilians. (There is no independent account of what happened to their menfolk, some of whom also disappeared.)

At Alana, the mother who had escaped from the *Amn* jail in Erbil was reunited with her children. She recognized families from the villages of Kaniberd and Tutma, as well as from Sheikh Wasan and Balisan, who told her that many children had died in this place of hunger, thirst and exposure. (With the exception of a few villages, the entire Balisan Valley had been evacuated in terror: Ironically, as we shall see, their flight may

---

[28] The bodies of those who died in custody were exhumed from the Erbil cemetery in September 1991, and reburied in a ceremony that was recorded on videotape. In the course of later exhumations Hamoud Sa'id Ahmad discovered the body of his own brother, who was killed by *Amn* in a separate incident in April 1988. Ahmad was interviewed by Middle East Watch in Erbil, April 25, 1992. For additional detail, see Middle East Watch/Physicians for Human Rights, *Unquiet Graves: The Search for the Disappeared in Iraqi Kurdistan*, February 1992.

have saved thousands of lives during the following year's Anfal campaign.) Eventually, sympathetic Kurdish residents of the town of Khalifan took some of the survivors into their homes--"in their arms and on their backs"-- and cared for them until they regained their health and strength. Other survivors ended up in the squalid government complex of Seruchawa, where so many of their fellow villagers had fled on the night of the chemical attack. When the elderly *mullah* of Balisan went to Ba'ath Party officials at Seruchawa to plead for an improvement in conditions in the complex, he was told contemptuously, "You're not human beings."[29]

* * *

On the basis of interviews with four survivors, and with a number of medical and morgue personnel in Erbil, it is possible to give a rough estimate of the numbers who died as a result of the chemical bombing of Balisan, Sheikh Wasan and neighboring villages.

• Twenty-four deaths in Balisan, as a direct result of exposure to chemical weapons; these people were buried in a mass grave in the village;

• 103 deaths in Sheikh Wasan, including about fifty buried in a mass grave in the complex of Seruchawa. The dead included thirty-three children aged under four, another twenty-eight aged 5-14, and nine elderly people, aged 60-85;[30]

• Eight or nine deaths in the hospital at Raniya;

• Four dead on arrival at the Erbil Emergency Hospital;

• Between sixty-four and 142 deaths in the *Amn* detention center in Erbil, of untreated injuries sustained in the chemical bombing, aggravated by starvation and neglect. These included two elderly women

---

[29] Middle East Watch interview with Sheikh Qader Sa'id Ibrahim Balisani, Balisan, April 30, 1992.

[30] A handwritten list of 103 dead and forty-eight injured villagers was given to Middle East Watch in 1992 by the Inspection Committee of Oppressed Kurds, a human rights group in Erbil.

named Selma Mustafa Hamid and Adila Shinko, and a nine-year old girl, Howsat Abdullah Khidr;

• Two busloads of adult men and teenage boys, disappeared from the *Amn* detention center in Erbil and presumed by Middle East Watch to have been executed later. A number of witnesses place the number at between seventy and seventy-six: twenty-two men from Balisan, fifty from Sheikh Wasan and four from other nearby villages. Among these were Muhammad Ibrahim Khidr, aged eighteen, and Mohsen Ibrahim Khidr, aged twelve, the two youngest sons of the *mullah* of Balisan;

• "Many children" dumped on the barren plain near Khalifan.

Allowing for some overlap, Middle East Watch calculates that at least 225, and perhaps as many as 400, civilians from the Balisan Valley died as a direct or indirect result of the Iraqi air force's chemical attack on their villages on April 16, 1987.

The Sheikh Wasan and Balisan attacks are significant for a number of reasons. First, they are the earliest fully documented account of chemical attacks on civilians by the Iraqi regime. Second, they offer concrete evidence of the security forces' intent, on the orders of higher authority, to disappear and murder large numbers of civilian non-combatants from areas of conflict in Iraqi Kurdistan. In this sense, like the mass abduction of the Barzani men in 1983, the Balisan Valley disappearances directly prefigure Anfal--although with the crucial difference that women and children were directly targeted. Similarly, the treatment of those who survived the actual bombing, in particular their separation by age and sex, their illegal confinement without food or medical care, and the dumping of women and children in barren areas far from their homes, foreshadowed many of the techniques that were employed on a much vaster scale during the 1988 campaign. The Balisan Valley episode also illustrates the central role that would be played in the extermination campaign by the General Security Directorate--*Amn*. The events at Erbil's Republic Hospital additionally constitute the gravest possible violation of medical neutrality.

* * *

The regime was far from finished with these rebellious valleys, however. Amidst the thousands of pages of secret Iraqi intelligence reports on air-raids and village burnings, Middle East Watch researchers discovered one that contained an intriguing detail. It is a brief report from *Amn* Erbil, dated June 11, 1987, on a recent airstrike on five villages in the Malakan Valley, a few miles to the east of Balisan and Sheikh Wasan. In the course of the attack, it noted, "thirty persons lost their eyesight." Two of the victims were named. Here was an unmistakable fingerprint, for there is only one kind of weapon that characteristically causes blindness, and that is poison gas.[31]   During a subsequent field-trip to Iraqi Kurdistan, it proved possible to interview one of the blinded survivors--one of many occasions on which a precise match could be made between documentary and testimonial evidence.

The man's name was Kamal, and he was living in Choman, a destroyed town on the road from Rawanduz to Iran.[32]   An active *peshmerga*, Kamal had already experienced chemical warfare in the Jafati Valley, and his account of the April 15 attack there is included above at pp.59-61. Hearing the news of the devastating attack on the Balisan Valley the next day, he rushed back to his family in the nearby village of Upper Bileh.   He found that they had taken refuge in some caves in the mountains. It was bitterly cold, and Kamal persuaded them to return cautiously to their homes.

At 6:00 a.m on May 27, his wife woke him to warn him that the village was under attack.

> "We knew it was chemicals because the sound [of the explosions] was not loud. There were many bombs. I told my family that it wasn't a chemical attack because I didn't want to scare them, but they knew what it was. So we began burning the branches we had stored for animal feed, and they made a very strong fire. We also soaked

---

[31] *Amn* Erbil governorate to *Amn* Shaqlawa, letter no. Sh Sh/4947, dated June 11, 1987, and classified secret. Exposure to mustard gas causes prolonged temporary blindness or vision impairment, and dozens of survivors interviewed by Middle East Watch described being blind for at least a month after a chemical attack.

[32] Middle East Watch interview, Choman, March 23, 1993.

cloths and headscarves at the spring. My aged father was
there. The attack was so intense that we were unable to
leave the village; that was why we lit the fires. There was
a separate spring for the women, and I told everyone, men
and women, to jump into the water. The attack lasted
until 10:00 a.m., and I sent my brother to the *malband* to
get medical help. By sunset the situation was getting
worse. Several people had gone blind.

After sunset we crossed the stream and moved to a rocky
area outside the village. Our situation was very bad. We
had all been affected by the chemicals. We had trouble
seeing and we were short of breath. We had nosebleeds
and fainting spells. We sent someone to the surrounding
villages to fetch water, and I offered to pay them whatever
they asked for. But the villagers were afraid to come,
thinking that the chemicals were contagious. But people
from Kandour village, who are very brave people, came to
bring us milk.[33]

In the meantime, my brother and a companion had
reached the *malband*, but on the way back they collapsed
because they had lost their sight. People from other
villages sent mules to bring them back. They were
carrying some medicine and eyedrops provided by the
malband. When morning came, no one had died, but
things were very bad. The third *malband* sent us a doctor
and money to buy horses that could carry us to Iran. The
women with us were in a terrible state, and we had to
spoon-feed them. The small children were hardly
breathing. We went to Malakan, where it was colder. We
thought it would be better because of the fresh air. Then
we reached the Sewaka area. There were people there
who raised animals and they took pity on us. They wept
a lot and gave us food. Next morning we left for Warta.

---

[33] Kandour is one of the five villages named in the *Amn* report on the May
27 attack. The others are Malakan, Talinan and Upper and Lower Bileh.

We had to cover our faces because the bright light hurt us like needles stuck into our eyes."[34]

On the third night, the caravan of survivors reached the lower slopes of Qandil Mountain, a towering peak of almost 12,000 feet on the Iranian border south of Haj Omran. Once they reached Iran, they were given medical care. All of them lived through the ordeal but one--Kamal's eighteen-month old nephew.

* * *

THE SPRING 1987 CAMPAIGN:
VILLAGE DESTRUCTION AND RESETTLEMENT

Five days after the Balisan Valley chemical attack, the infantry troops and bulldozers went to work on hundreds of villages in Iraqi Kurdistan. According to Resool's authoritative survey, the army obliterated at least 703 Kurdish villages from the map during the campaigns of 1987. Of these, 219 were in the Erbil area; 122 in the hilly plain known as Germian, to the southeast of Kirkuk; and 320 in various districts of the governorate of Suleimaniyeh. Badinan, too was hit, although less severely, with the Kurdistan Reconstruction and Development Society (KURDS), a local relief agency, listing fifty villages that were destroyed in Dohuk governorate. Most of the villages destroyed during Ali Hassan al-Majid's "first and second phases" lay along the main roads and were under government control. Their removal had the effect of physically severing the *peshmerga*-controlled rural areas from the rest of the country.

For destruction on this scale, the Iraqi state had to deploy vast resources. Yet there were important differences between the village clearances of spring 1987 and the Anfal campaign of the following year. The most important concerned the treatment of residents of the villages destroyed by the army. The 1987 campaign offered them clear, if unpalatable alternatives; Anfal did not.

The inhabitants of Narin, for example, a village in the *nahya* of Qara Tapa in the southern part of Germian, were relocated in 1987 to the

---

[34] The symptoms described by Kamal are entirely consistent with exposure to mustard gas.

Ramadi area, in central Iraq.[32] The villagers of nearby Zerdow were warned that their turn was next. They left their homes and moved in with relatives in nearby towns or villages. Some were resettled in the newly opened complex of Benaslawa, six miles from Erbil on the site of an old Kurdish village. They were not punished otherwise, although Zerdow itself was razed to the ground with bulldozers a few days later. One family interviewed by Middle East Watch lost its livestock, furniture and food stores in the destruction of Zerdow, but was paid compensation of 1,000 dinars ($3,000 at the then-official exchange rate). Later, the family was able to build a house in Benaslawa with a 4,500 dinar loan from the state Real Estate Bank.

This was a typical pattern. The villagers were not physically harmed; some token compensation was paid, although it might be withheld if a family refused to accept relocation in the towns or complexes; there was some advance notice of the regime's intent to destroy the village (even if this was not always respected in practice). The villagers of Qishlagh Kon, for example, in the Germian *nahya* of Qader Karam, were told by soldiers that they had fifteen days to evacuate; in fact, the army moved in and razed their homes well before the expiry of this deadline. According to one man from this village, army troops swept through the area populated by the Kurdish Zangana tribe in April 1987, bulldozing and dynamiting between seventy and one hundred villages along the main road, spread out over three adjacent *nahyas*--Qader Karam, Qara Hassan and Qara Hanjir.[33]

Many of the villagers were offered an explicit choice by the soldiers or *jahsh*. "Go to the saboteurs or join the government," was the message delivered to one Qader Karam village of the Jabari tribe. No neutrality was to be allowed, and a person's physical location would henceforth be taken as proof of their political affiliation. Coming over to the government's side was spoken of as "returning to the national ranks," a phrase that appears in official documents with increasing frequency from early 1987 onward. Previous political loyalties were irrelevant to this new drawing of battle lines, and so was the size of the settlement. Several *nahyas*

---

[32]   There are two basic administrative divisions within each Iraqi governorate: the *qadha* and the smaller *nahya*. The *nahya* of Qara Tapa belongs to the *qadha* of Kifri. The examples of Narin and Zerdow are drawn from a Middle East Watch interview, Benaslawa complex, July 7, 1992.

[33] Middle East Watch interview, Suleimaniyeh, July 23, 1992.

were cleared of their population and/or destroyed during the spring 1987 campaign, including Naujul, Qaradagh, Qara Hanjir, Koks and Sengaw. Shwan followed in September. In the northernmost governorate of Dohuk, the *nahya* of Kani Masi was evacuated and destroyed, apparently in retaliation for a six-day takeover by KDP forces. Some of these *nahyas* were towns of several thousand people.

Even a strong *jahsh* presence offered no protection, if the town lay within a designated area of army operations. As Ali Hassan al-Majid later told a meeting of senior Ba'ath Party officials, "I told the *mustashars* that the *jahsh* might say that they liked their villages and would not leave. I said I cannot let your villages stay because I will attack them with chemical weapons. And then you and your family will die."[34]

For all the scale of the destruction, it is apparent from one batch of official Iraqi files, found in the *Amn* offices in Erbil and Shaqlawa, that the regime was far from satisfied with the "first stage" of its village clearance program. A watchful, almost apprehensive tone creeps into many government documents from this period. Among the questions put to people surrendering to the authorities from *peshmerga*-controlled areas was one that asked, "How are the people affected economically and psychologically by the elimination of the villages and other policies?"[35]

On April 20, *Amn* Erbil warns its branches that the new campaign of village destruction may provoke demonstrations to mark the 14th anniversary of the bombing of Qala Dizeh on the 24th. On the same day the Erbil Security Committee, presided over by Governor Ibrahim Zangana, warns that "saboteurs" may attack government installations as a reprisal against the deportation of villagers from the "prohibited areas" (*manateq al-mahdoureh*). On April 22, Governor Zangana predicts that the PUK may even try to bring in the International Committee of the Red Cross to observe the clearances. Three days later, on April 25, *Amn* Erbil issues an alert warning of *peshmerga* reprisal raids on Arab villages; it also complains that government forces destroying the village of Freez have come under attack from "saboteurs" and that air-cover has failed to materialize as requested. By May 20, the director of *Amn* Shaqlawa is

---

34 Audiotape of a meeting between Ali Hassan al-Majid and senior Ba'ath Party officials, Kirkuk, May 26, 1988.

35 June 1987 statement by a "returnee to the national ranks," found in *Amn* files.

complaining to Erbil that the "saboteurs" have been able to exploit the unpopularity of the campaign; in particular he expresses irritation that no complexes have been made ready for the villagers who are to be relocated, and that many of them have been obliged to remain in the open air, exposed to the elements.[36]

***

EARLY USES OF AL-MAJID'S SPECIAL POWERS

In these early months of Ali Hassan al-Majid's rule, the Ba'ath Party tightened the noose around the population of rural Kurdistan through a series of sweeping decrees and administrative orders.[37]

---

[36] Since few villages were destroyed in the Shaqlawa area at this time, other than those in the Balisan Valley, it is possible that this may refer to the dumping of the survivors of the chemical attack, at Alana. See above p.68-69.

[37] The power structure of the Ba'ath Party is complex, and a full grasp of the chain of command in the anti-Kurdish campaigns depends on understanding the nuances that distinguish several overlapping bodies. As one national branch of the Ba'ath Arab Socialist Party, the Iraqi Ba'ath has a Regional Command--of which Ali Hassan al-Majid had been a member since 1986. Within Iraq, the highest executive body is formally the Revolutionary Command Council, which did not include al-Majid--although in practice ultimate power is wielded by Saddam Hussein himself and a largely Tikrit-based group of loyalists from the military and security sectors, many of them related to the president. Al-Majid is a key member of this fraternity.

The RCC in turn has a number of regionally based committees, including its Northern Affairs Committee. Saddam Hussein was secretary of this committee at the time of the 1970 autonomy manifesto. In 1987-1988, the post was held by Taher Tawfiq, who, as an RCC member, was thus technically al-Majid's superior-- although the temporary special powers granted to al-Majid under decree 160 superseded this. Al-Majid himself was Secretary General of the Ba'ath Party Northern Bureau; to complicate matters further, the Northern Bureau *Command* was a parallel but separate entity, under Taher Tawfiq. The Northern Bureau and Northern Bureau Command are clearly distinguished where necessary in the text.

• On April 6, all "saboteurs" lost their property rights. "By the authority vested in us by the Revolutionary Command Council's decree number 160 of March 29, 1987," writes al-Majid himself, "we have decided to authorize the chairmen of the security committees [*Ru'asa' al-Lijan al-Amniyeh*] in the northern governorates to confiscate the real and personal property of the saboteurs, provided that their properties are liquidated within one month of the date of issuance of the confiscation decree."[38]

• On April 10, al-Majid suspended the legal rights of the residents of villages prohibited for security reasons. "His Excellency has given instructions not to hear cases brought by the population of security-prohibited villages," writes deputy secretary Radhi Hassan Salman of the Northern Bureau Command, "and likewise those brought by the saboteurs, no matter what their character, as well as to freeze all claims submitted previously."[39]

• On May 1, al-Majid began to order the execution of first-degree relatives of "saboteurs." It had long been the policy of the regime to detain and punish the families of active Kurdish *peshmerga*, often by destroying their homes. But al-Majid now ordered their physical elimination, at least on an occasional exemplary basis. These orders evidently remained in force throughout the Anfal campaign and for some time afterwards. For example, a handwritten note dated November 20, 1989, signed "Security Chief, Interrogating Officer," and originating in *Amn* headquarters in the city of Suleimaniyeh, gives details of a case in which an Iraqi citizen has petitioned the authorities for news about his disappeared parents and brother.

The security chief's letter informs the unnamed recipient (who is addressed only as "Your Excellency,") that the missing parents, Qoron Ahmad and his wife Na'ima Abd-al-Rahman, were "liquidated" in Baghdad on May 19, 1987. Their son, Hushyar Ahmad, "a member of the group of Iranian saboteurs," was executed by hanging on July 12, 1987 by order of the Revolutionary Court (*mahkamat al-thawrah*). What is significant here is the reason for the killing of the man's parents. It was ordered, the document explains, "in compliance with the order from the Struggling

---

[38] Northern Bureau letter S Sh/18/2396, April 6, 1987.

[39] Northern Bureau Command letter no. 1/2713, April 10, 1987.

Comrade Ali Hassan al-Majid, member of the Regional Command [of the Ba'ath Party] that was relayed to us by letter no. 106309 of the Security Directorate of the Autonomous Region, marked 'Secret and to be Opened Personally,' and dated May 1, 1987, regarding the liquidation of first-degree relatives of criminals."

Another letter on *Amn* Suleimaniyeh letterhead, numbered S-T: 21308, dated September 16, 1989 and classified "Top Secret," describes the public execution by firing squad of five "criminals" with a "connection to the internal organizations of the agents of Iran." The execution had been carried out on October 24, 1987 in the presence of intelligence and Ba'ath Party officials.[40] Some time afterwards, "it was decided that three families of the criminals...should be executed in a discreet manner." The authority for their execution was given by letter number 6806, dated December 12, 1987, from the Northern Bureau Command.

• Wounded civilians could now also be executed, according to a hand-written communication (no. 3324) of May 14 from the Security Director of the city of Halabja, in southeastern Iraqi Kurdistan, to *Amn* Suleimaniyeh. This note gives details of an operation against the city's Kani Ashqan neighborhood, and makes reference to a cable (no. 945), dated the previous day, from the Command of the Fifth Army Corps. "It was by order of the Commander of the First Army Corps, on the recommendation of Comrade Ali Hassan al-Majid, to execute the wounded civilians after confirming their hostility to the authorities with the Party Organization, the Security and

---

[40] The principle of collective implication in executions, including an insistence that party members form part of the firing squads, is a well-established element of Ba'ath Party rule. The most notorious example of this was the televised purge of two dozen senior Ba'ath officials and military officers, including several members of the Revolutionary Command Council, in July 1979--a month after Saddam Hussein had assumed the presidency. In front of a roomful of their peers, the condemned men make ritual confessions on charges of treason in front of a roomful of their peers and are then whisked away to be killed. A tearful Saddam implores--and thus effectively orders--other senior Ba'athis to take part in the execution squad. See al-Khalil, *Republic of Fear*, pp.70-72. Also Chibli Malat, "Obstacles to Democratization in Iraq: A Reading of Post-Revolutionary Iraqi History through the Gulf War," unpublished paper, 1992--which differs from al-Khalil in other important respects about the nature of the Ba'ath's exercise of power.

Police Departments and the Intelligence Center, and to utilize backhoes and bulldozers to raze the neighborhood of Kani Ashqan."[41]

* * *

ORDERS FOR MASS KILLING

The full extent of the Iraqi regime's intentions, however, are spelled out with brutal clarity in two directives issued by al-Majid's office in June 1987. Both documents lay out, in the most explicit detail, a prohibition on all human life in designated areas of the Kurdish countryside, covering more than 1,000 villages, to be applied through a shoot-to-kill order for which no subsequent higher authorization is required.

The first is a personal directive, numbered 28/3650, signed by Ali Hassan al-Majid himself and dated June 3, 1987. Addressed to a number of civilian and military agencies, including the Commanders of the First, Second and Fifth Army Corps, the Security Directorate (*Amn*) of the Autonomous Region, the *Istikhbarat* and *Mukhabarat*, it states the following:

> 1. It is totally prohibited for any foodstuffs or persons or machinery to reach the villages that have been prohibited for security reasons that are included in the second stage of collecting the villages. Anyone who so desires is permitted to return to the national ranks. It is not allowed for relatives to contact them except with the knowledge of the security agencies.
>
> 2. The presence of the people from relocated areas who are from villages prohibited for security reasons included

---

[41] This exemplary collective punishment, according to a former resident interviewed by Middle East Watch in Halabja on June 11, 1992, was meted out in retaliation for an anti-government demonstration. Some 1,500 homes were reportedly destroyed.

in the first stage until June 21, 1987, is prohibited for the areas included in the second stage.[42]

3. Concerning the harvest: after the conclusion of winter, which must end before July 15, farming will not be authorized in [the area] during the coming winter and summer seasons, starting this year.

4. It is prohibited to take cattle to pasture within these areas.

5. *Within their jurisdiction, the armed forces must kill any human being or animal present within these areas. They are totally prohibited.* (emphasis added)

6. The persons who are to be included in the relocation to the complexes will be notified of this decision, and they will bear full responsibility if they violate it.

These orders were evidently relayed later to the lower echelons in the chain of command. They are repeated word for word, for example, in a letter (no. 4754), dated June 8, 1987, from *Amn* Erbil to all its departments and local offices.

Three days after al-Majid's directive, on June 6, Radhi Hassan Salman, deputy secretary of the Northern Bureau Command, issued a series of general instructions to all army corps commanders, "aimed at ending the long line of traitors from the Barzani and Talabani clans and the Communist Party, who have joined ranks with the Iranian invader enemy with a view to enabling it to acquire territory belonging to the cherished homeland." Salman ordered increased combat readiness, improved intelligence and a heightened state of alert among all units, while

---

[42] By now it appears that the two phases originally envisioned (April 21-May 20 and May 21-June 20) have been collapsed into one single operation. In this order, the "second stage" is clearly intended to begin on June 21.

at the same time betraying a certain anxiety about renewed *peshmerga* attacks designed "to cut the chain of command."[43]

The most important document of all, however, was issued on June 20, 1987. Issued by the Northern Bureau Command over Ali Hassan al-Majid's signature, and additionally stamped with the seal of the RCC's Northern Affairs Committee, this directive, coded SF/4008, amended and expanded the June 3 instructions in a number of very important ways--including a direct incitement to pillage, in clear violation of the rules of war, and the baldest possible statement of a policy of mass murder, ordered by the highest levels of the Iraqi regime. From the repeated references to it in official documents throughout 1988, it is apparent that directive 4008 remained in force as the standing orders for the Iraqi armed forces and security services during the Anfal campaign and beyond. For example, a letter from *Amn* Suleimaniyeh, dated October 29, 1988, makes reference to the directive as the basis for "the execution of 19 accused, executed by this directorate because of their presence in the security-prohibited villages."

It is quite apparent that al-Majid's demand for the summary killing of people arrested in the prohibited areas caused some consternation among those who were charged with carrying out his orders. Throughout 1987 and 1988, high-level Iraqi officials issued a steady stream of ill-tempered clarifications of clause 5 of directive SF/4008--the paragraph that concerns executions. "The security agencies should *not* trouble us with queries about clause 5," complains a Northern Bureau letter of December 1987; "the wording is self-explanatory and requires no higher authority."[44] Instructions from *Amn* Erbil, dated November 22, 1988, insist that clause 5 must be "implemented without exception."

The full text of directive SF/4008 reads:

---

[43] Northern Bureau Command letter reference no. 28/3726, dated June 6, 1987 and classified "highly confidential and personal." This document is reproduced in the "Report on the situation of human rights in Iraq, prepared by Mr. Max Van der Stoel, Special Rapporteur of the Commission on Human Rights, in accordance with Commission resolution 1992/71," February 19, 1993, p.77.

[44] Northern Bureau Command directive no. 855, classified "confidential and personal for addressee only," December 29, 1987.

June 20, 1987

From: Northern Bureau Command
To: First Corps Command, Second Corps Command, Fifth Corps
        Command[45]

Subject: *Procedure to deal with the villages that are prohibited*
                   for security reasons

In view of the fact that the officially announced deadline for the amalgamation of these villages expires on June 21, 1987, we have decided that the following action should be taken with effect from June 22, 1987:

1. All the villages in which subversives, agents of Iran and similar traitors to Iraq are still to be found shall be regarded as out of bounds for security reasons;

2. They shall be regarded as operational zones that are strictly out of bounds to all persons and animals and in which the troops can open fire at will, without any restrictions, unless otherwise instructed by our Bureau;

3. Travel to and from these zones, as well as all agricultural, animal husbandry and industrial activities shall be prohibited and carefully monitored by all the competent agencies within their respective fields of jurisdiction;

4. The corps commanders shall carry out random bombardments using artillery, helicopters and aircraft, at all times of the day or night *in order to kill the largest number of persons present in those prohibited zones,* keeping us informed of the results; [emphasis added]

5. All persons captured in those villages shall be detained and interrogated by the security services and *those between the ages of 15 and 70 shall be executed after any useful information has been obtained from them,* of which we should be duly notified; [emphasis added]

---

[45] This is only one of numerous copies of directive SF/4008 which Middle East Watch has found in Iraqi government files, addressed to different agencies.

6. Those who surrender to the governmental or Party authorities shall be interrogated by the competent agencies for a maximum period of three days, which may be extended to ten days if necessary, provided that we are notified of such cases. If the interrogation requires a longer period of time, approval must be obtained from us by telephone or telegraph or through comrade Taher [Tawfiq] al-Ani;

7. *Everything seized by the advisers [mustashars] and troops of the National Defense Battalions shall be retained by them, with the exception of heavy, mounted and medium weapons.[46] They can keep the light weapons, notifying us only of the number of these weapons. The Corps commanders shall promptly bring this to the attention of all the advisers, company commanders and platoon leaders and shall provide us with detailed information concerning their activities in the National Defense Battalions.* [emphasis added]

For information and action within your respective fields of jurisdiction. Keep us informed.

[Signed]

Comrade
Ali Hassan al-Majid
Member of the Regional Command
Secretary General of the Northern Bureau

cc: Chairman of the Legislative Council;
         Chairman of the Executive Council;
         Party Intelligence;
         Chief of the Army General Staff;
         Governors (Chairmen of the Security Committees) of Nineveh,

---

[46] In other words, the Kurdish paramilitary *jahsh*, whose ranks had been greatly expanded in the period immediately following Ali Hassan al-Majid's appointment, according to a Middle East Watch interview with a former *mustashar*, Zakho, August 30, 1992. This clause of decree SF/4008, with its reference to booty, may offer some hint of the connection between the coming campaign and the concept of *Anfal* in the Koranic sense (see above, pp.31-32). Army documents reviewing the Anfal campaign make further reference to the approved role of the *jahsh* in seizing booty. See p. 289.

al-Ta'mim, Diyala, Salah al-Din, Suleimaniyeh, Erbil and Dohuk;
Branch Secretaries of the above-mentioned governorates;
General Directorate of Military Intelligence (*Istikhbarat*);
General Directorate of Security (*Amn*);
Director of Security of the Autonomous Region;
Security Services of the Northern Region;
Security Services of the Eastern Region;
Security Directors of the governorates of Nineveh, al-Ta'mim,
Diyala, Salah al-Din, Suleimaniyeh, Erbil and Dohuk.

Ali Hassan al-Majid evidently insisted on a high degree of personal control of even the smallest details of the campaign. For example, one order issued in the middle of the Anfal operation indicates that no town or village may be searched without his express personal approval.[47] Nonetheless, the list of institutions to whom his June 20 directive was copied gives some hint of the bureaucratic scope of the effort and the large number of civilian, party, military and security agencies involved in its execution.

* * *

DEFINING THE "NATIONAL RANKS": THE CENSUS OF OCTOBER 17, 1987

After June 20, the village destruction campaign temporarily abated. Although it had also targeted areas near the smaller roads that criss-cross Iraqi Kurdistan, its most striking effect was to remove a broad swathe of formerly government-controlled villages close to the highway that runs from Mosul to Erbil, Kirkuk and Tuz Khurmatu, before turning east through Kifri, Kalar, Peibaz and Darbandikhan. For the time being, the Iran-Iraq War deprived the regime of the military muscle that would have been required to press the campaign any further. But the political and bureaucratic logic of the spring 1987 clearances--as well as the incipient logic of Anfal--became apparent during the second half of the year. This was to effect a sharp division between the "national ranks" and the

---

[47] Northern Bureau Command letter no. 3321, July 6, 1988, cited in *Amn* Suleimaniyeh circular to all security directorates (number illegible), July 16, 1988.

generally more mountainous *peshmerga*-controlled regions to the east and north. These were the "prohibited areas" (*manateq al-mahdoureh*) and their inhabitants, regardless of age or sex, would be regarded without exception as "saboteurs."

They would, however, be given one last chance to change sides. As al-Majid's June 3 directive stated, it was still possible for Kurds to "return to the national ranks" --in other words to move to the cities, towns or *mujamma'at* and align themselves with the regime. To keep a close track, family by family, of how the two sides lined up, the Iraqi regime had an ideal instrument to hand, in the form of a national census. Iraq had carried out five censuses in the half-century since its independence. The results of the most recent, conducted in 1977, were classified as "secret." Designed to be held every decade, another was due in 1987. It was scheduled for October 17.

As the census date drew near, the authorities repeatedly insisted on improving security and intelligence measures to inhibit any contact or movement between the two sides, other than on the regime's terms. *Amn* Erbil ordered renewed vigilance on the complexes of Benaslawa, Daratou and Kawar Gosek, which all housed villagers relocated during the spring 1987 campaign.[48] Orders were issued to seize and destroy tractors, since these might help the "saboteurs" skirt the economic blockade of the prohibited areas. The tractor owners in question were to receive "the maximum exemplary punishment."[49]

On September 6, Ali Hassan al-Majid chaired a meeting of senior Ba'ath Party officials to discuss preparations for the census. Case by case, individual by individual, the make-up of the two sides was to be refined in the most legalistic fashion. "Subversives who repent" were to be allowed to return to the fold right up to the day of the census. No such returnees would be accepted after October 17, however, "even if they surrender their weapons." At the same time, al-Majid regarded it as unacceptable for the

---

[48] This letter also urged that "saboteurs should be dealt with strongly, like the Iranian enemy." *Amn* Erbil governorate to all branches, letter no. Sh.S1/13295 of October 15, 1987, classified "secret and personal to be opened by addressee only."

[49] Letter no. 542, classified "secret and confidential" and dated (month illegible) 30, 1988, from Suleimaniyeh governorate Committee to Fight Hostile Activity to all local Committees to Fight Hostile Activity.

families of unrepentant saboteurs to remain in government-controlled areas. These people were to be physically removed and forced to join their saboteur kin in the prohibited areas.

This general policy had been in effect for at least two years.[50] But al-Majid now demanded a full inventory of all such cases from the security committees of each of the northern governorates. This list was to reach his desk not later than September 15. As soon as it was complete, "the families in question should be expelled to the regions where their subversive relatives are, with the sole exception of males aged between 12 and 50 inclusive, who should be detained."[51]

The local security agencies appear to have cooperated with alacrity. Middle East Watch has examined dozens of individual expulsion orders by *Amn* Erbil, for example, during this pre-census period. One typical case in mid-September 1987 gives the full names, addresses, dates of birth and residence permit numbers of eighty women, children and old men aged from 51-89, taken from their homes and summarily expelled "to those

---

[50] It is mentioned, for example, in a letter from the Special Office of the Army Chief of Staff to Second Corps Command, no. RAJ/1/13/1/5033 of June 14, 1985; order no. 4087 of December 22, 1986 from the Security Committee of Erbil governorate; and communique no. 4151 of the RCC Northern Affairs Committee, dated June 15, 1987.

[51] The only exception was for "families which comprise martyrs [i.e. those killed in battle], missing persons, captives, soldiers or fighters in the National Defense Battalions [*jahsh*]. In those instances, only the mother is to be expelled, together with any subversive sons." The summary conclusions of the September 6 meeting are included in a cable, reference 4350, dated September 7, 1987, from the Northern Bureau to all regional security committees. These instructions evidently received very wide distribution. Middle East Watch has also found a second version of this document, in the form of a letter, number 2/237, classified "secret, urgent and immediate" and dated September 19, 1987, from the Shaqlawa district security committee to a number of local party and police agencies. Although in other respects identical, it gives the ages of those to be detained as "17 to 50." Whatever the final regulation on minimum age may have been--12, 15 or 17--it is apparent from survivor testimonies that the separation of those to be killed during Anfal depended less on birth certificates than on a quick visual inspection of the prisoners. See below p.212.

regions where the saboteurs are present."[52] A single male relative born in 1949 is mentioned as having been detained "to receive the proper sentence."

Most strikingly of all, the Northern Bureau Command ordered that:

> Mass seminars and administrative meetings shall be organized to discuss the importance of the general census, scheduled to take place on October 17, 1987. It shall be clearly emphasized that any persons who fail to participate in the census without a valid excuse shall lose their Iraqi citizenship. They shall also be regarded as army deserters and as such shall be subject to the terms of Revolutionary Command Council decree no. 677 of August 26, 1987.

The importance of this provision can scarcely be overstated, for RCC decree 677 stipulated that, "The death sentence shall be carried out by Party organizations, after due verification, on any deserters who are arrested, should the period of their flight or delinquency exceed *one year or should they have perpetrated the crime of desertion more than once*." [emphasis in original][53] Failure to register under the census, in other words, could in itself be tantamount to the death penalty.

The results of the 1987 census were never publicly divulged. Employees of the government census office in Suleimaniyeh told Middle East Watch that they estimated it to have been only 70% accurate--no doubt

---

[52] *Amn* Erbil to Erbil Police Directorate, letters nos. 9475 and 9478, September 16 and 17, 1987, classified "secret." The 44 families are broken down as follows: Agents of Iran (PUK)--22; Offspring of Treason (KDP)--7; Treacherous Communist Party--8; Socialist Party--3; unknown affiliation--4.

[53] RCC decree no.10 of January 3, 1988 modified some aspects of decree 677, but maintained this clause intact. Both were signed by Saddam Hussein as Chairman of the Revolutionary Command Council. Two additional comments are pertinent here. First, the census gave the regime a means of detecting deserters, a perennial problem for the Iraqi military. Second, and more important, it specified that executions of deserters would be carried out by agents of the Ba'ath Party itself--a hint, perhaps, of the identity of the executioners during the Anfal campaign.

because large expanses of Iraqi Kurdistan, as well of the rebellious southern marshes, could not be included. Most residents of the "prohibited areas" opted to stay where they were; some, especially in the more remote parts of the Badinan region, said they never even learned that the census was taking place, despite a vigorous campaign conducted over government radio and television.

The instructions were quite different from those of the five previous censuses. Those who were not included in the census would no longer be considered Iraqi nationals, the official broadcasts announced; they would cease to be eligible for government services and food rations. Only two options were offered by the census: one could either be an Arab or a Kurd--nothing else. These ethnic lines were drawn with great rigidity. A number of official documents from 1988 and 1989 transmit orders from Saddam Hussein and Ali Hassan al-Majid to the effect that any citizen may become an Arab by simple written application. By contrast, anyone wishing to be considered a Kurd will be subject to the destruction of their homes and deportation to the Autonomous Region.

People could be counted only if they made themselves accessible to the census-takers. For anyone living in a prohibited area, this meant abandoning one's home. Inclusion in the census involved registering oneself as the resident of a government-controlled town or *mujamma'a*. (The only hope of evading this regulation was to bribe an official--a time-honored means of survival in Iraq, which continued to apply even during Anfal.) Villages that had been destroyed in earlier army operations--the Arabization drive of 1975, the border clearances of the late 1970s, or the spring 1987 campaign--no longer existed as far as the government in Baghdad was concerned. Some inhabitants of the border zone had returned illegally to their homes to rebuild, but the census would not count them. The remainder were now in complexes.

As a partial indication of the scale of this exclusion, government statisticians provided Middle East Watch with figures for Suleimaniyeh, one of the four governorates in the Autonomous Region of Iraqi Kurdistan. The 1977 census had counted 1,877 villages in Suleimaniyeh; by the time of the 1987 census, this number was down to just 186. Almost 1,700 villages had thus disappeared from the official map. Of these, several hundred had been destroyed during the border clearances of the 1970s and at various stages of the war against Iran. Most of their inhabitants had been resettled in the nine complexes that were also listed in the 1987 census. The remaining villages were simply not counted, because they now lay in "prohibited areas" of *peshmerga* influence.

Once the population count was complete, the consequences of not registering soon became apparent. Shelling and aerial bombing intensified. When families went to the nearest town to seek their food rations, said one man from a village near Qara Dagh, they were told that they could now forget about them. "You are Iranians," officials said, "Go to the Iranians for your food rations!"[54] The same was true of villagers seeking marriage licenses or government permits for other civil transactions.

On October 18, the day after the census, Taher Tawfiq, secretary of the RCC's Northern Affairs Committee, issued a stern memorandum to all security committees in Kurdistan, reminding them that aerial inspection would ensure that Directive no.4008 of June 20 was being carried out "to the letter." Any committee that failed to comply would "bear full responsibility before the Comrade Bureau Chief"--that is to say, Ali Hassan al-Majid.[55] Several other documents from late 1987 insist, in a tone of distinct irritation, that paragraph 5 (mandating summary execution after interrogation) does not require the authorization of higher authority on a case-by-case basis. The Northern Bureau should no longer be troubled by these requests, since the standing orders are quite explicit.

The blockade of the north was now to be made even more systematic. On September 29, al-Majid agreed to a set of harsh new proposals from an ad-hoc committee chaired by Taher Tawfiq and including Khaled Muhammad Abbas, head of Eastern Sector *Istikhbarat*, Farhan Mutlaq Saleh, head of Northern Sector *Istikhbarat*, and Abd-al-Rahman Aziz Hussein, director of *Amn* for the Autonomous Region. The group complained that food, medicines, fuel and other supplies were still getting through to the "saboteurs." Accordingly, security would be stepped

---

[54] Middle East Watch interview, Naser complex, July 28, 1992. The existence of a subsidized food system was a key element of the national economy during the Iran-Iraq War and a significant source of political control for the regime.

[55] Northern Bureau Command, letter no.1216, dated October 18, 1987, classified "secret and confidential," to all Security Committees and Security Directorates in the Governorates of the Autonomous Zone and the Governorates of Diyala and Salah al-Din.

up at checkpoints; many grocery stores in the towns would be closed down; the secret police would monitor the stocks in all restaurants, bakeries and cafes; and a strict ban would be enforced on the sale of all agricultural produce from prohibited areas. Food rations would be cut back to the minimum necessary for human survival. The loyalty of all workers in the food distribution sector would be evaluated.[56]

Under this bitter regime, the inhabitants of the prohibited areas struggled to survive. During Ali Hassan al-Majid's first eight months in office, the groundwork for a "final solution" of Iraq's Kurdish problem had been laid. Its logic was apparent; its chain of command was set in place. But the events of 1987 were "just a preliminary step," a former *Istikhbarat* officer explained, "because the war was still going on. The Iraqi government was not so strong and many troops were tied up on the front. They postponed the anger and hate in their hearts"--but only until the beginning of 1988, when the major winter offensive that Baghdad had feared failed to materialize, and Iran's fortunes on the battlefield began rapidly to decline.

----

[56] A copy of the findings of Tawfiq's committee on the blockade was found attached to a letter from the head of the economic section of the Interior Ministry, Erbil, reference no.248, dated November 14, 1987.

First Anfal: February 23 - March 19, 1988

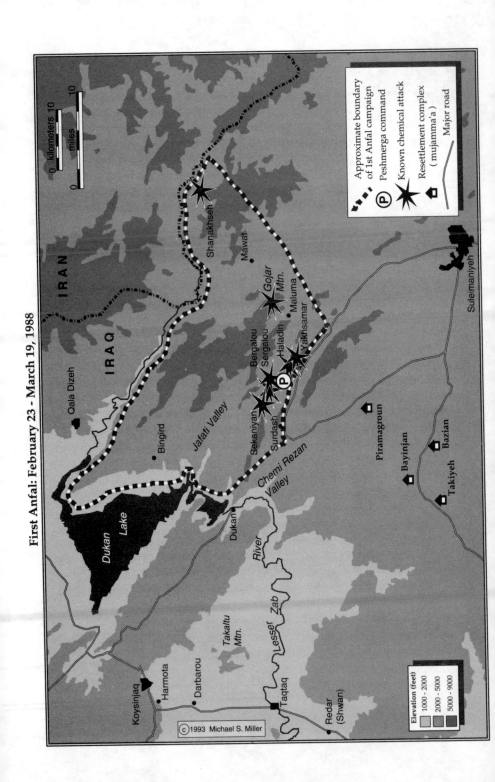

Legend:

- ▪▪▪ Approximate boundary of 1st Anfal campaign
- Ⓟ Peshmerga command
- ✸ Known chemical attack
- ⬛ Resettlement complex (mujamma'a)
- — Major road

Elevation (feet)
- 1000 - 2000
- 2000 - 5000
- 5000 - 9000

© 1993 Michael S. Miller

0 kilometers 10
0 miles 10

IRAN
IRAQ

Qala Dizeh
Bingird
Dukan Lake
Jafati Valley
Shanakhseh
Mawat
Gojar Mtn.
Bergalou
Sergalou
Haladin
Maluma
Yakhsamar
Sekaniyan
Surdash
Chemi Rezan Valley
Dukan
River
Takaltu Mtn.
Lesser Zab
Koysinjaq
Harmota
Darbarou
Taqtaq
Redar (Shwan)
Piramagroun
Bayinjan
Takiyeh
Bazian
Suleimaniyeh

3
First Anfal--The Siege of Sergalou and Bergalou, February 23--March 19, 1988

"I will, with engines never exercised,
Conquer, sack and utterly consume
Your cities and your golden palaces,
And with the flames that beat against the clouds
Incense the heavens and make the stars to melt,
As if they were the tears of Mahomet
For hot consumption of his country's pride.
-- Marlowe, Tamburlaine the Great, Part Two, (IV, i)

"It was like the Day of Judgment; you stand before God."
-- survivor of the poison gas attack on Halabja, March 16, 1988.

The nerve center of Jalal Talabani's Patriotic Union of Kurdistan lay deep in the mountains of Suleimaniyeh governorate in southeastern Iraqi Kurdistan. The organization's most important facilities were all housed here, in the long, narrow Jafati valley, so called because its inhabitants belonged to the important Jaf tribe. The PUK's top command, its politburo, had its headquarters in the small village of Yakhsamar. Nearby Bergalou ("Lower Valley"), a temporary settlement, was home to the PUK's radio station and its main field hospital. Talabani's deputy commander, Naywshirwan Mustafa Amin, had also taken up residence here, and in Talabani's absence abroad it was he who commanded the PUK during Anfal. Nearby Sergalou ("Upper Valley") was home to the PUK's second *malband*, or regional command, responsible for *peshmerga* operations in the governorate of Kirkuk. Other villages such as Maluma and Zewa were important additional links in the chain of command.

Sergalou was a village, almost a small town, of some 500 households (3,500 people), a half-hour by car on an all-weather gravel road from the nearby *nahya* of Surdash. Although the houses were of mud and stone, they boasted cement floors, and almost every home had its own water supply from springs. An hour away on foot, the village of Haladin, another sizeable place of some 350 households surrounded by vineyards, housed an additional contingent of PUK fighters. "[The valley] was as important to the *peshmerga* as Baghdad is to the government," was how one local trader put it.[1]

Hemmed in by steep mountains, this was a classic guerrilla stronghold protected by difficult terrain. But it had another strategic significance, too, for it lay just a few miles east of the vital Dukan Dam and hydroelectric power station at the head of the lake of the same name--an important source of electricity for the cities of Suleimaniyeh and Kirkuk.[2] Seizing the Dukan Dam was a crucial element of the PUK's plan to liberate large expanses of Kurdistan on an accelerated timetable. The goal was to take the cities of Ranya, Koysinjaq and Qala Dizeh (see map on p.92), thus encircling the lake and establishing a new front line along the Haibat Sultan mountain range, between Koysinjaq and the western shore. But that plan, which was ready to be executed in February 1988, was not to be realized.

Since 1985, and the breakdown of negotations between the PUK and the Iraqi government, the entire Jafati valley had been "redlined" as a "prohibited area." Attacks by aircraft and artillery occurred frequently, with shelling on an almost daily basis. But the PUK headquarters was well-defended, and all of the men and even some of the women in Sergalou, Yakhsamar and Haladin were organized into an armed self-defense force. Government checkpoints on the surrounding roads did a largely ineffective job of imposing the economic blockade.

The chemical weapons that had been used to such demoralizing effect against Iranian troops had also been brought into play repeatedly against the PUK redoubt during the previous summer. For an hour on the afternoon of June 8, 1987, chemical shells from a truck-mounted

---

[1] Middle East Watch interview with former Haladin resident Hakim Mahmoud Ahmad, Piramagroun complex, July 27, 1992.

[2] The PUK, together with the Iraqi Communist Party, the Socialist Party of Kurdistan and a number of Iranian parties, had formerly been based in Nawzeng, the "Valley of the Parties," some distance to the north. See Van Bruinessen, *Agha, Shaikh and State*, p.39. But they were driven out in 1983, when the Iranian army attacked and the Iraqis moved in to retake the area. The Jafati valley housed contingents of the Iranian KDP and Komala parties, in addition to the PUK.

multiple rocket-launcher, or *rajima*, rained down on Bergalou, Haladin and the nearby village of Sekaniyan ("Three Springs"). The *rajima* was a constant presence in the villagers' lives for many months after this, although the casualties appear to have been limited. One farmer told Middle East Watch that this was thanks in part to the high mountains, dense tree cover and natural shelters available, and in part to the notorious inaccuracy of the Iraqi gunners. The worst casualties were in Haladin, where one shell hit a house killing a man named Yasin Abd-al-Rahman and six members of his family. Otherwise, the main effects of the gas shelling were tearing and shortness of breath. Later chemical attacks produced additional symptoms, including blistering and burns. Those who died perished, in fits of shivering, within an hour of exposure to the chemicals; others acted as if deranged, and stumbled around laughing hysterically.[3]

The Iraqi Air Force also attacked the valley repeatedly. In the past, aerial harassment operations had been restricted to helicopters. But the Iranians had now supplied the PUK with anti-aircraft missiles that kept the Iraqi helicopters at bay, and fixed-wing aircraft were pressed into service. Sometimes the attacks were carried out by small Swiss-manufactured Pilatus planes, more commonly used as trainers or for crop-spraying. At other times, supersonic Soviet-made Sukhoi fighter-bombers took part, with as many as fifteen or twenty aircraft joining in the attacks. At first the raids used only conventional weapons, but on April 15, and again in July, the warplanes also dropped chemical bombs. Dispersed on the breeze, the main effect of the gas was temporary blindness, lasting two weeks or so. But it also killed a number of people, most of them civilians. By the summer of 1987, the *peshmerga* had supplies of gas masks, donated by the Iranians, and each division, or *teep*, had its own officer who was expert in defense against chemicals. But ordinary villagers had to defend themselves against the wind-borne gas as best they could, fleeing to higher ground, covering their faces with wet cloths as the Iranian-trained *peshmerga* doctors had instructed them, or

---

[3] Again, these symptoms suggest that a nerve agent such as Sarin was used here.

setting fires in the caves and underground shelters where they sought refuge.[4]

* * *

Throughout late January and February 1988, a flurry of intelligence reports from *Amn* Suleimaniyeh and the Iraqi Army's First Corps warned that new joint actions were being planned by the "agents of Iran" (*Umala Iran*) and the Teheran regime. According to *Amn*, "mercenaries" from the Iranian Revolutionary Guards, operating out of PUK base camps, were "carrying out surveillance missions in the direction of al-Ta'mim governorate"--in other words, westward, toward the Kirkuk oilfields. The PUK's first *malband*, based in Qara Dagh, was "facilitating the entry of Khomeini's guards from the Darbandikhan sector." On February 1, the Ba'ath Party branch in Qara Dagh informed *Amn* that "the Iranian enemy plans to help the saboteurs" in attacking a number of targets--including the sizeable Kurdish town of Halabja. On February 8, a report from a secret informant briefed *Amn* on the enemy's state of preparedness. It noted that Jalal Talabani himself was out of the country. "The number of saboteurs in Sergalou/Bergalou," it continued, "is between 600-800."[5]

---

[4] Confirmation of the Iraqi regime's intent to use chemical weapons, and of the fact that the *peshmerga* had obtained gas masks, is contained in a document in the captured Iraqi archives. Classified "urgent and secret," it is a telegram from Major Sa'di Mahmoud Hussein, Commander of Zakho District, dated 22/6 (year omitted, but from the context almost certainly 1987), reference no. AS/3/4181 and addressed to "Commander (A)". It reads:

> "[With reference to] letter of the command of the 38th Force Secret and Urgent 14665 on 20/6, we have learned the following: 4,000 gas masks arrived at the First Branch of the descendants of treason [i.e. the KDP] to guard themselves against poison gas and the saboteurs will wear them when we use chemical materials to attack their concentrations. Please check the accuracy of this information and take all necessary measures."

[5] These notes are drawn from a lengthy series of secret cables on conditions in the Sergalou and Qara Dagh areas that were sent to the Security Directorate of the Autonomous Region from *Amn* Suleimaniyeh. The cables are dated from January 25 to March 19, 1988.

Despite its long history of living under attack, the PUK seems to have been unprepared for the ferocity of the attack that broke on it later that month. Perhaps the *peshmerga* had overestimated the degree to which the Iraqi regime was now psychologically tied down by the war against Iran. But they quickly understood its thinking in laying siege to the Jafati valley. Success there would not only decapitate the PUK; it would also prove, to devastating psychological effect, that the regime could prevail over the *peshmerga* wherever it chose, in any terrain.

At about 1:30 or 2:00 a.m. on February 23, the people of Yakhsamar, Sergalou and Bergalou awoke in the dark and rain to the thunderous sound of shelling from *rajima*. Although there is no definitive evidence that the Iraqi army was yet using the word "Anfal" to describe its operations, these artillery shells may be considered to all intents and purposes the first shots fired in the Anfal campaign.[6]

It is evident that the regime attached a special significance to the new campaign right from the beginning. An Iraqi Defense Ministry order, for example, signed on February 23, passes on a Revolutionary Command Council decree that those who fall in the coming fight against the "saboteurs" and the attendant campaign of village "purification" are to be venerated as "Martyrs of the Glorious Battle of Saddam's *Qadissiyah*"--that is to say, the war against Iran.[7]

At daybreak on February 23, government ground forces attacked from all directions. "The army that laid siege to the headquarters was so big that it looked like a fence that was separating the area from the rest of Kurdistan," recalled one *peshmerga* who was in Sergalou that day.[8] The front line stretched for a full forty miles, from Bingird on the eastern side of the lake to Dukan, and thence to Suleimaniyeh and the towns of Mawat and Chwarta. The PUK held out for more than three

---

[6] Middle East Watch was given various dates for the opening of the Sergalou campaign, ranging from February 22 to 26, 1988; from the Defense Ministry order cited here, it seems apparent that the correct date is February 23. In field interviews, both *peshmerga* combatants and ordinary villagers could differ wildly in their recollection of dates, even for crucially important events.

[7] Defense Ministry Legal Department circular to Interior Ministry, no. Q2/236/6300, dated February 23, 1988.

[8] Middle East Watch interview, Goktapa, June 2, 1992.

weeks, even though the assault involved army, air force and the elite Republican Guards, who were apparently employed only during the initial stages of Anfal.[9] The armed forces' target was not just the PUK headquarters but all the villages in the valley, some 25-30 in all.[10] According to other PUK sources, between 200 and 250 people were killed in the course of the siege, most of them active *peshmerga*. As long as the *peshmerga* resisted, most of the villagers hid out in nearby caves. But in the early days of March, the villages began to fall one by one as tanks and armored vehicles smashed through the PUK's defensive lines. The inhabitants fled, most in the direction of Iran. After they had departed, crews of army engineers moved in with bulldozers and razed their villages to the ground.

Enveloping the Jafati valley on three sides, the army did leave one escape route open--to the east and the Iranian frontier, twelve miles or so as the crow flies from Sergalou across the mountains. According to official intelligence reports, by February 25 the PUK had opened at least two rough roads to the border with Iranian assistance.[11] At this stage, it appears that the government forces made no attempt to detain those who fled over the snow-covered mountains toward Iran. Mass disappearances had not yet become a matter of official policy.

Some survivors were offered an explicit choice by the army, backed up with a powerful warning: "You are free to remain or leave," one woman from Maluma village was told, "but we will not be responsible if you choose to stay. You may be killed or become the victim of

---

[9] The Republican Guard began life as a politically reliable paramilitary force, made up of three brigades from President Saddam Hussein's Tikrit district. Over time it expanded into a heavily mechanized élite corps, twenty-five divisions strong. It is easy to recognize Republican Guard troops in the field because of their camouflage uniforms and their distinctive red triangular shoulder-patches.

[10] This figure was given to us by Aras Talabani, a senior PUK official and nephew of party leader Jalal Talabani. Middle East Watch interview, Zakho, April 12, 1992.

[11] Secret cable, signed by "security colonel," *Amn* Suleimaniyeh to *Amn* Autonomous Region, no. 4610, February 25, 1988.

chemicals."[12] This was no idle threat, for chemical weapons were used repeatedly during the First Anfal.

The majority of the armed *peshmerga* managed to withdraw in relatively good order, with ideas of redeploying their forces further to the south, in the broad hilly plain known as Germian. But they found their way blocked by government troops and were forced instead to circle northward to the fastness of Qandil mountain, on the Iran-Iraq border near Haj Omran. Others fled to the grasslands on the shores of Lake Dukan, where they defended themselves until they ran out of ammunition. The bedraggled survivors eventually ended up in Iran. Others still set up a new, temporary base camp in the village of Shanakhseh, until that too was hit with chemical weapons on about March 22.

That morning, Iraqi warplanes flew over and dropped balloons. Six aircraft returned at about 2:00 p.m. and dropped the bombs. "The area was full of *peshmerga* and fleeing families," said a PUK fighter who was there. "There were thousands of people, many living in tents. I myself was injured, my face became black and my skin was painful. I had trouble breathing. But these were mild symptoms; others who were closer to the point of impact had severe blisters. Some men suffered from swollen testicles." A PUK local commander believed that as many as twenty-eight people were killed and some 300 injured, mostly *peshmerga* families. (Other sources believe the figure may be somewhat lower.) Some of the dead were civilians, who were already exhausted from their attempt to cross the mountains into Iran.[13]

* * *

Given the intensity of this new campaign, which they would soon come to know by the name of Anfal, the *peshmerga* had realized that there was little they could do to protect the civilians, and they told them as much, advising the villagers that they would have to take their chances alone. At this point, with the PUK leadership still relatively intact and with frequent warnings being broadcast over the clandestine *peshmerga*

---

[12] Middle East Watch interview with former resident of Maluma (*nahya* Mawat), Bayinjan complex, Suleimaniyeh, May 18, 1992.

[13] Middle East Watch interviews, Zakho, March 14 and April 6, 1993.

radio station, civilians seem to have been given fair notice of the dangers they faced. This, together with the army's decision to leave an escape route, no doubt led to countless lives being saved. But by the time Anfal spread to other areas, it was much harder to give civilians any warning. After the siege of the PUK headquarters, the *peshmerga* began to grasp the direction that the campaign would take. But there was little or nothing they could do about it.

Most of the villagers from the Jafati valley survived. While some fled to the city of Suleimaniyeh, the majority headed for Iran, through the heavily mined no-man's-land along the border, in the first large-scale refugee exodus since the crushing of the Barzani-led revolt thirteen years earlier. But it was March, and the harsh Kurdish winter was not over.

"We left behind all the properties accumulated over fifty years," added a middle-aged villager from Sergalou. "The people moved like a panicked herd of cattle through the mountains in the direction of Iran. It was raining. There were warplanes overhead....Six people from Sergalou froze to death along the way, and another thirty from other villages in the same valley."[14]

"The people were running, and lost their shoes," said a 57-year old woman from the village of Qara Chatan. "There was much snow. We were shivering from the cold."[15] People with children suffered especially in this way, since they could not move so quickly. The single most tragic incident involved a group of people who made it as far as Kanitou, a ruined village north of Sergalou that had been evacuated during the 1978 border clearances. *Peshmerga* from several parties were present in Kanitou, but they fell to bickering among themselves. In the chaos, a large band of fleeing villagers tried to cross the high snowpeaks into Iran. But they left too late in the day, and darkness overtook them when they were still several hours from safety. At least eighty died of cold and exposure; by one estimate, the number may have been as high as 160.[16]

---

[14] Middle East Watch interview, Piramagroun complex, July 30, 1992.

[15] Middle East Watch interview, Piramagroun complex, July 27, 1992.

[16] The lower figure was cited by former PUK officials; higher estimates were given by villagers interviewed by Middle East Watch.

Although the siege of the Jafati Valley was not accompanied by mass disappearances, some villagers from the First Anfal theater did vanish during late April, several weeks after Sergalou and Bergalou had fallen. One farmer from Haladin told Middle East Watch that after three days on the run, his family found refuge on the border, in tents supplied by sympathetic Iranian Kurds. "They stayed there for one month," he remembered. "Then the army came to the border and arrested all these people, including my entire family. This was on April 20. The army dropped troops from helicopters. There was a bad snow, and people were exhausted." The young man lost nine of his relatives that day. They included his mother, three sisters--two of them pregnant--and three nieces under the age of six. The witness escaped to Iran; only his father, a man in his late 50s, was ever seen alive again.[17]

Others who fled the siege of the PUK headquarters disappeared in a different manner. Three brothers from Sergalou recrossed the border into Iraq after two weeks in Iran, having heard false rumors of an amnesty for those who turned themselves in.[18] They surrendered to the *mustashar* at a complex called Sengasar, outside the town of Qala Dizeh. But the man turned them over to the government, and they were never seen again. Similarly, a group of fifteen army deserters who had been hiding in the mountains for several weeks gave themselves up to the *mustashar* in the village of Chermaga. The *mustashar* had given the family of one his word of honor that no one would be harmed. But these young men, too, disappeared into the custody of *Amn* in Suleimaniyeh. These trick amnesties and broken promises would be repeated over and over again in the subsequent stages of the Anfal campaign.

* * *

---

[17] Middle East Watch interview, Piramagroun complex, July 27, 1992.

[18] Amnesty decrees had long been a favored tactic of the Ba'ath regime. However, it was vital for citizens to know whether they were dealing with a genuine amnesty announced through official channels. The rumor of an amnesty could have devastating effects; fleeing civilians and *peshmerga* were often lured into government traps during the Anfal campaign by spurious offers of amnesty, local as well as general. Not until September 6, and the completion of the military campaign, was a genuine amnesty offered. See below, chapter 11.

THE MARCH 16 CHEMICAL ATTACK ON HALABJA

For years, the hostility between Iran and Iraq had appeared to the Kurdish parties as a geopolitical loophole that they could exploit to their advantage. After withstanding the siege of Sergalou-Bergalou for two weeks, the PUK took the desperate decision to open a second front with Iranian military support. As their target the *peshmerga* chose Halabja, a town on the plain just a few miles from the border, in a feint that was designed to draw some of the Iraqi troops away from the siege of Sergalou and Bergalou. But the plan turned out to be a tragic miscalculation, as the once beneficial alliance with Iran turned into a crippling liability. For the Halabja diversion only cemented the view of the Iraqi regime that the war against Iran and the war against the Kurds was one and the same thing.

At the end of February, Iraq had stepped up its missile attacks on Teheran as part of the "War of the Cities";[19] the escalation was designed to push the weakened Iranians to the negotiating table on terms favorable to Baghdad. A confident senior official even admitted to Patrick Tyler of the *Washington Post* that Iraq was trying to lure its adversary into a trap by overextending its forces. "For the first time in our history, we want the Iranians to attack," the official said.[20] At Halabja, the Iranians obliged.

Halabja was a bustling Kurdish town with a busy commercial section and a number of government offices. Villagers displaced from their homes by the war had swollen its population of 40,000 to 60,000 or more. The *peshmerga* had been strong here for almost thirty years, with several clandestine parties active--Socialists, Communists and others--in

---

[19] Jupa and Dingeman (*op. cit.*, pp. 5-6) believe that Iraq fired as many as 182 enhanced-range SCUD-B missiles in a 52-day assault, starting February 29, 1988. Developed with the help of East German and Brazilian engineers, these "souped-up" Scuds were capable of reaching the Iranian capital, 340 miles from the Iraqi border.

[20] According to this report, "The official explained that Iraq's confidence that it could repel a major offensive would demonstrate to Iraq's allies that Iran had no hope of breaching the country's defenses. Moreover, the world would be reminded, he said, that the war is a volatile flashpoint requiring a major diplomatic effort to bring it to an end." *Washington Post*, March 2, 1988.

addition to Jalal Talabani's PUK. One group with particular local strength was the pro-Iranian Islamic Movement Party (*Bizutnaway Islami Eraqi*). As a reprisal against local support for the *peshmerga*, Iraqi troops had already bulldozed two entire quarters of the town, Kani Ashqan and Mordana, in May 1987.[21]   Since about 1983, Iranian troops had been making secret reconnaissance visits to Halabja under cover of darkness. The town lay on the very edge of the war-zone, and dozens of small villages between Halabja and the Iranian border had been razed in the late 1970s, their inhabitants resettled in complexes on the edge of the city. But the greater strategic importance of Halabja was its location just seven miles east of Darbandikhan Lake, whose dam controls a significant part of the water supply to the Iraqi capital, Baghdad.

During the first two weeks of March, a stream of Iraqi intelligence reports noted the buildup of Revolutionary Guards and *peshmerga* to the west of Halabja and the shelling of the nearby town of Sayed Sadeq by Iranian forces.[22] On March 13, the Iranians officially announced that they had launched a new offensive named Zafar 7 in the Halabja area. According to Teheran radio, the offensive--conducted by a joint force of PUK *peshmerga* and *pasdaran*--was in retaliation for the Iraqi regime's recent chemical attacks on the Kurds.[23] A second attack, apparently coordinated, followed the next day. This one was called Bait al-Maqdis 4, and the Iranians claimed that it had taken their forces within twelve miles of Suleimaniyeh. On March 16, Teheran announced yet

---

[21] On the razing of the Kani Ashqan neighborhood, see the document cited at pp.78-79 above.

[22] Secret cable traffic from *Amn* Suleimaniyeh to Autonomous Region *Amn* headquarters, March 6-16, 1988.

[23] The two parties to the Halabja feint give differing accounts of the relative strength of the forces involved. While Iran played up its own participation, PUK sources interviewed by Middle East Watch claimed that the seizure of Halabja was a joint *peshmerga* operation, which the Iranians only joined in large numbers after the March 16 chemical attack. Neither version can be regarded as wholly reliable.

another offensive, codenamed Val-Fajr 10.[24]   Iran boasted that its
forces had now advanced to the eastern shore of Darbandikhan Lake,
controlling 800 square kilometers of Iraqi territory and 102 (presumably
destroyed) villages.   But the main thrust of Val-Fajr 10, Teheran
declared, was the "liberation" of the town of Halabja.

Halabja had been subjected to three days of heavy Iranian
shelling from the surrounding hills, beginning on March 13. One by one,
the small Iraqi military posts between Halabja and the border were
routed, and their occupants pulled back to the safety of the town. Some
stripped off their uniforms and took refuge in the mosques, while some
took up temporary defensive positions in local army bases. Others fled
altogether. Yet the Baghdad regime resisted the temptation to reinforce
Halabja with large numbers of ground troops, for it had an entirely
different strategy in mind.

Some Iranian *pasdaran* had reportedly begun to slip into town as
early as March 13. By the night of March 15 they were openly parading
through the streets, accompanied by Iraqi Kurds, greeting the
townspeople and chanting "God is Great! Khomeini is our leader!" They
billeted themselves on local Kurdish families and ordered them to
prepare dinner. Some rode around Halabja on motorcycles; others were
very young, barely teenagers, and carried only sticks and knives. Many
also carried gas masks. They asked bewildered people in the streets how
far it was to the holy cities of Karbala and Najaf.[25]   Militants of the
Iraqi Islamic Movement did a victory dance outside the headquarters of
Amn and the *Istikhbarat* building, which they took over for themselves.
But among the townspeople as a whole there was grave apprehension,
especially when public employees were ordered on March 15 to evacuate

---

[24] Among the many Iranian offensives of the war, the designation of Val-Fajr
carried special weight. Val-Fajr I, in February 1983, was Iran's first land assault
on Iraqi territory; Val-Fajr 8 and 9, in February 1986, resulted in the seizure of
the Fao Peninsula and the simultaneous occupation of mountain areas near
Suleimaniyeh, bringing Iranian forces close enough to shell that city. See
Cordesman and Wagner, *op. cit.*, pp.159, 219-224.

[25] Both cities contain important Shi'a shrines: Najaf is the burial place of the
Imam Ali, and Karbala of the Imam al-Husayn. The question asked by the
pasdaran says something about their naivete. Both cities are situated well to the
south of Baghdad--several hundred miles, that is to say, from Halabja.

their posts.[26] Swift Iraqi reprisals were widely expected; one *Amn* cable the next day spoke, with notable understatement, of the need for "a firm escalation of military might and cruelty."[27]

The Iraqi counterattack began in the mid-morning of March 16, with conventional airstrikes and artillery shelling from the town of Sayed Sadeq to the north. Most families in Halabja had built primitive air-raid shelters near their homes. Some crowded into these, others into the government shelters, following the standard air-raid drills they had been taught since the beginning of the Iran-Iraq War in 1980. The first wave of air strikes appears to have included the use of napalm or phosphorus. "It was different from the other bombs," according to one witness. "There was a huge sound, a huge flame and it had very destructive ability. If you touched one part of your body that had been burned, your hand burned also. It caused things to catch fire." The raids continued unabated for several hours. "It was not just one raid, so you could stop and breathe before another raid started. It was just continuous planes, coming and coming. Six planes would finish and another six would come."[28]

Those outside in the streets could see clearly that these were Iraqi, not Iranian aircraft, since they flew low enough for their markings to be legible. In the afternoon, at about 3:00, those who remained in the shelters became aware of an unusual smell. Like the villagers in the Balisan Valley the previous spring, they compared it most often to sweet apples, or to perfume, or cucumbers, although one man says that it smelled "very bad, like snake poison." No one needed to be told what the smell was.

The attack appeared to be concentrated in the northern sector of the city, well away from its military bases--although these, by now, had been abandoned. In the shelters, there was immediate panic and claustrophobia. Some tried to plug the cracks around the entrance with damp towels, or pressed wet cloths to their faces, or set fires. But in the end they had no alternative but to emerge into the streets. It was

---

[26] Middle East Watch interview with former municipal employee, Halabja, May 8, 1992.

[27] Secret *Amn* cable, unnumbered, to Autonomous Region *Amn* headquarters, March 16, 1988.

[28] Middle East Watch interview, Halabja, May 17, 1992.

growing dark and there were no streetlights; the power had been knocked out the day before by artillery fire. In the dim light, the people of Halabja could see nightmarish scenes. Dead bodies--human and animal--littered the streets, huddled in doorways, slumped over the steering wheels of their cars. Survivors stumbled around, laughing hysterically, before collapsing. Iranian soldiers flitted through the darkened streets, dressed in protective clothing, their faces concealed by gas masks. Those who fled could barely see, and felt a sensation "like needles in the eyes." Their urine was streaked with blood.[29]

Those who had the strength fled toward the Iranian border. A freezing rain had turned the ground to mud, and many of the refugees went barefoot. Those who had been directly exposed to the gas found that their symptoms worsened as the night wore on. Many children died along the way and were abandoned where they fell. At first light the next morning Iraqi warplanes appeared in the sky, apparently monitoring the flight of the survivors. Many kept away from the main roads and scattered into the mountains, despite the ever-present menace of landmines. According to one account, some six thousand people from Halabja congregated at the ruined villages of Lima and Pega. Another thousand or so gathered among the rubble of Daratfeh, the last village on the Iraqi side of the border.[30]

The Iranians were ready for the influx of refugees. Iranian helicopters arrived at Lima and Pega in the late afternoon and military doctors administered atropine injections to the survivors before they were ferried across the border. In Iran, all agree that they were well-cared for, although some had injuries that were untreatable, and they died on Iranian soil. The sickest were transferred to hospitals in the Iranian cities of Teheran and Kermanshah, and the smaller town of Paveh. The remainder spent two weeks in a converted schoolhouse in the town of Hersin, where they received medical attention. From there, they were taken to two refugee camps--one at Sanghour, on the Persian Gulf near

---

[29] The symptoms described by survivors are consistent with exposure to both mustard gas and a nerve agent such as Sarin.

[30] Resool lists these villages among those destroyed in the border clearances of 1978. Daratfeh appears as a village of thirty households in the *nahya* of Biyara; Lima and Pega, hamlets of eight and twelve houses respectively, are in the *nahya* of Sirwan.

Bandar Abbas, the other at Kamiaran in Kermanshah province, close to the Iraqi border. There they waited until Anfal was over, and they believed that it was safe to return home.

There would, however, be no homes to return to, for virtually every structure in Halabja was leveled with dynamite and bulldozers after Iraqi forces finally retook the city. So, too, were Zamaqi and Anab, two complexes that had been built on the outskirts of Halabja in the late 1970s to rehouse villagers from the destroyed border areas. So, too, was nearby Sayed Sadeq, a town of some 20,000. In both Halabja and Sayed Sadeq, the electrical substations were also dynamited.[31] Even after the razing of Halabja, many bodies remained in the streets to rot where they had fallen four months earlier.[32]

"The loss of Halabja is a regrettable thing," remarked Foreign Minister and Revolutionary Command Council member Tariq Aziz, adding, "Members of Jalal al-Talabani's group are in the area and these traitors collaborate with the Iranian enemy."[33] As the news of Halabja spread throughout Iraq, those who asked were told by Ba'athist officials that Iran had been responsible. A Kurdish student of English at Mosul University recalled his shock and disbelief at the news; he and his fellow Kurds were convinced that Iraqi government forces had carried out the attack, but dared not protest for fear of arrest.[34]

---

[31] This reportedly occurred in every one of the *nahyas* and *qadhas* that were demolished during the campaigns of 1987-1989. By way of comparison, see Middle East Watch's analysis of the targeting of Iraq's electrical system during the 1991 Gulf War (Operation Desert Storm), in *Needless Deaths in the Gulf War: Civilian Casualties during the Air Campaign and Violations of the Laws of War*, pp.171-193. In Halabja and Sayed Sadeq, of course, the evident intent was to make the towns uninhabitable. Both were subsequently declared part of a "prohibited area."

[32] The Iranian forces in Halabja had managed to bury an estimated 3,000 victims of the March 16 chemical attack in mass graves under a thin layer of dirt in the complex of Anab. Four years later, the corpses were still there, and they were beginning to pollute the local groundwater.

[33] Amman *Sawt al-Sha'b* in Arabic, March 25, 1988, in FBIS, March 25, 1988.

[34] Middle East Watch interview, Suleimaniyeh, May 20, 1992.

Not until July did the Iraqi regime move to recover Halabja, which was left under de facto Iranian control. In the days following the mass gassing, the Iranian government, well aware of the implications, ferried in journalists from Teheran, including a number of foreigners. Their photographs, mainly of women, children and elderly people huddled inertly in the streets, or lying on their backs with mouths agape, circulated widely, demonstrating eloquently that the great mass of the dead had been Kurdish civilian non-combatants. Yet the numbers have remained elusive, with most reports continuing to cite Kurdish or Iranian estimates of at least 4,000 and as many as 7,000.[35] The true figure was certainly in excess of 3,200, which was the total number of individual names collected in the course of systematic interviews with survivors.[36]

* * *

THE FALL OF THE PUK HEADQUARTERS

Halabja was a symbolic show of Iraqi force in a war that Iran could never win. But the mass gassing had also served a more important purpose by delivering a crushing psychological blow to the Kurdish *peshmerga* and their civilian sympathizers. Halabja was exemplary collective punishment of the most brutal kind, carried out in bald defiance of all international prohibitions on the use of chemical weapons. The PUK fighters had been exposed to poison gas several times during the preceding weeks; now the will of the civilian population was to be broken.

---

[35] See for example *Time*, "The Cries of the Kurds," September 19, 1988 and *The Washington Post*, "Rebel Kurds Say They Are Ready to Strike at Iraq," January 24, 1991, both of which cite the figure of 4,000; Kendal Nezan, "Saddam's Other Victims--the Kurds," *The Washington Post*, January 20, 1991 (5,000); Isabel O'Keeffe, "Flanders Fields Revisited," *New Statesman and Society*, March 1989 (5,500); "Massacre by Gas," in *The Kurds: A Minority Rights Group Profile*, 1990 (6,000); and *The Observer*, "Hitler-Style Genocide Threatens the Kurds," May 7, 1989 (7,000).

[36] This figure was collected by the Kurdish researcher Shorsh Resool.

The Halabja chemical attack was a harbinger of later Anfal policies. During each of the eight phases of the military campaign, these forbidden weapons would be used against Kurdish villages, dozens of them in all--enough to terrify their residents with a reminder of what had befallen Halabja. Yet Halabja, while remaining the single greatest atrocity of the war against the Kurds, was *not* part of Anfal. In that sense, it was the clearest possible illustration of the bureaucratic logic of the Anfal campaign. On March 15, the very eve of the Halabja attack, the Northern Bureau Command ordered that "the families of subversives who take refuge with our units should be detained in special guarded camps set up for that purpose under the supervision of intelligence officers from the First and Fifth Army Corps."[37] These camps were the first step in establishing the web-like bureaucracy of mass killing that operated during Anfal. But the fleeing survivors of Halabja were not detained and taken to the camps, because the Iraqi regime did not consider Halabja to be a part of Anfal. The reason was quite simple: Halabja was a city, and Anfal was intended to deal with the rural Kurdish population.[38]

* * *

After Halabja, the PUK headquarters did not resist for long. At 10:10 on the night of March 18, army units stormed into Sergalou causing heavy losses among its final defenders. Bergalou fell the following afternoon. Saddam Hussein had fulfilled his promise to cut off "the head of the snake." By the end of the day, the General Command of the Iraqi Armed Forces had prepared its official victory declaration,

---

[37] Letter no. 297 of the Northern Bureau Command, dated March 15, 1988. These instructions were conveyed to Suleimaniyeh *Amn* (Chamchamal, Sayed Sadeq and Darbandikhan) in an unnumbered letter from Eastern Region Military Intelligence (*Istikhbarat*), dated March 18 and classified "confidential and personal."

[38] By the same logic of Anfal--perverse yet utterly consistent--villagers from the Halabja region who returned to their homes in the "prohibited areas" after the chemical attack were later "Anfalized." Thus, twenty families who were found by Iraqi troops in the village of Tawella (*nahya* of Biyara) when the army retook this area in July 1988 were all reportedly arrested and disappeared. Middle East Watch interview with a former resident of Tawella, Suleimaniyeh, March 27, 1993.

and a jubilant announcer on Iraqi radio informed his listeners that
"thousands of the sons of our Kurdish people took to the streets of Erbil,
expressing their joy and chanting in support of President Saddam
Hussein."[39] The army communique contains the first official reference
that Middle East Watch has been able to find to the operation known as
Anfal. The successful conclusion of each subsequent phase of the
campaign would be announced in the Iraqi press with similar fanfare.

The March 19 communique reads:

> In the name of God, the merciful, the compassionate.
>
> Like all covetous invaders, the Zionist Khomeinyite
> forces relied on some of those who betrayed the
> homeland and people in the northern area of Iraq--those
> who our good Kurdish people expelled from their ranks.
> Those elements performed shameful services for
> foreigners. Among their shameful acts was facilitating
> the missions of the invading forces in entering in the
> Halabja border villages in the Suleimaniyeh Governorate.
>
> As an expression of the will of the great Iraqi people, the
> brave Armed Forces, and the good honorable nationalists
> from our Kurdish people; and in response to the treason
> of this stray clique; the brave Badr forces, the brave Al-
> Qa'qa forces, the brave Al-Mu'tasim forces, and the forces
> affiliated with them from our Armed Forces and the
> National Defense Battalions [jahsh], carried out the Anfal
> operation under the supervision of Staff Lt. Gen. Sultan
> Hashem, who is temporarily assigned to this mission in
> addition to his regular duties.[40] Our forces attacked

---

[39] Baghdad Voice of the Masses in Arabic, March 19, 1988, in FBIS, March
21, 1988, p.23.

[40] The various forces named correspond to divisions of the Iraqi Army. The
first of them is of course named for the Battle of Badr in A.D. 624, which is the
subject of the Koranic sura of al-Anfal. Lt. Gen. Hashem was later in command
of Iraqi forces during Operation Desert Storm, and negotiated the terms of the

the headquarters of the rebellion led by traitor Jalal Talabani, the agent to the Iranian regime, the enemy of the Arabs and Kurds, in the Sergalou, Bergalou and Zewa areas and in the rough mountainous areas in Suleimaniyeh. At 1300 today, after a brave and avenging battle with the traitors, the headquarters of the rebellion was occupied. The commander of the force guarding the rebellion headquarters, and a number of traitors and misguided elements, were captured with God's help and with the determination of the zealous men of Iraq--Arabs and Kurds. Many were killed and others escaped in shame.

This is unique bravery and faithfulness. This is a struggle admired by the entire world, the struggle of leader Saddam Hussein's people, Arabs and Kurds, who placed themselves in the service of the homeland and gave their love and faithfulness to their great leader, the symbol of their victory and title of their prosperity. Our people have rejected from their ranks all traitors who sold themselves cheaply to the covetous foreign enemy.

Praise be to God for His victory. Shame to the ignominious.

[signed] The Armed Forces General Command, 19 March 1988"[41]

———

Iraqi surrender on March 3, 1991, with allied commander Gen. Norman Schwarzkopf.

[41] Baghdad *Voice of the Masses* in Arabic, March 19, 1988, in FBIS, March 21, 1988, pp.22-23.

Second Anfal: March 22 - April 1, 1988

Elevation (feet)
1000 - 2000
2000 - 5000
5000 - 9000

Approximate boundary
of 2nd Anfal campaign
Main Anfal camp and
facility
Peshmerga command
Known chemical attack
Resettlement complex
(mujamma'a)
Major road

0 kilometers 10
0 miles 10

IRAN

IRAQ

Halabja

Sayed Sadeq

Darbandikhan Lake

Darbandikhan

Zarayen

Naser

Arbat

Suleimaniyeh

Glazerda Mtn.

Qaradagh

Chami Smor

Asteli Serru

Takiyeh
Koshk
Senan

Sayw

Dukan

Masoyi

Omer Qala

Zerda Mtn.

Chirchaqala

Balaglar

Tapa Garus

Qara Dagh

Mountains

Ja'faran

Serko

Sengaw

Bayinjan

Bazian

Takiyeh

© 1993 Michael S. Miller

4
SECOND ANFAL--QARA DAGH, MARCH 22-APRIL 1, 1988

"Bring your families; nothing will happen to them."
-- army officer to villagers fleeing from
southern Qara Dagh.

Although the siege of Sergalou-Bergalou consumed enormous resources, the Iraqi armed forces were not so rash as to neglect other targets. To block any attempt by the PUK to reinforce its beleaguered national headquarters, the regime maintained a steady rhythm of attacks against the other regional commands, such as the first *malband*, based on Qopi mountain in Qara Dagh and charged with all operations in the governorate of Suleimaniyeh. At each stage of Anfal, as the main assault changed its geographical focus, this pattern of secondary pressure was maintained.

Few parts of Iraqi Kurdistan are as lovely as Qara Dagh. Its chain of jagged, serrated peaks runs southeast for some seventy miles, as straight as a razor's edge. But the features of its beauty were also those that made Qara Dagh vulnerable. It took three weeks for elements of twenty-seven army divisions together with Kurdish *jahsh* to crush resistance in the Jafati Valley, which is hemmed in by steep mountains. But Qara Dagh was the opposite: a thin line of mountains flanked by almost indefensible lowlands. To the west lies the hilly plain of Germian, the "warm country." To the east, until 1988, dozens of small farming villages nestled in green valleys of astonishing fertility. Fields of winter wheat, barley, tobacco and rice flourished next to rich plots of okra, peas, green beans, tomatoes, melons and grapes. At the southernmost tip of the Qara Dagh chain lay the 6,000-foot sentinel of Zerda Mountain, a *peshmerga* stronghold. Beyond this, to the east, a narrow corridor carried the highway from Suleimaniyeh past the town of Darbandikhan and the lake of the same name, with its strategic dam. Even as the First Anfal raged to the north, Iraqi intelligence kept a watchful eye on the lake, ever fearful of a waterborne attack by Iranian forces on the dam and its power station.

113

The government had relinquished control of rural Qara Dagh since the early days of the Iran-Iraq War. In 1987, the *nahya* itself was emptied, and its population relocated to the nearby complexes of Naser and Zarayen. Troops and *jahsh* took over the deserted town, but they were quickly routed from their positions by the *peshmerga*. Retaliatory air-raids soon destroyed what was left of Qara Dagh, although PUK forces continued to control the rubble. Like the civilian population of the surrounding villages, they learned to live with constant artillery shelling from a half-dozen government firebases between Suleimaniyeh and Darbandikhan.

Since 1983 the twin hubs of *peshmerga* activity in Qara Dagh had been the villages of Takiyeh and Balagjar, which housed armed contingents of the Iraqi Communist Party as well as the PUK. A dirt path linked these two villages, which lay less than two miles apart. The district center of Qara Dagh--the *nahya*--was some three hours distant on foot; three miles off to the east was the large village of Sayw Senan, where the *peshmerga* had installed a field hospital that serviced much of the surrounding population.

During the early months of 1988, Iraqi intelligence cables were filled with references to Iranian *pasdaran* moving freely in and out of the Qara Dagh *peshmerga* camps. A force of Revolutionary Guards, 200-strong, was reported to be present in Balagjar on January 25; by March 6, their number had risen to 400.[1] Eighty members of "the imposter Khomeini's guard" were said to be in Sayw Senan on March 9, and they were heavily armed.

Sometime in February--the exact date is unclear--eight Iraqi aircraft carried out a chemical attack on Takiyeh and Balagjar. "Many bombs were dropped," said Omar, a Takiyeh man who witnessed the raid. "I don't know how many, maybe eight or nine. When they fell, there was a loud explosion, a little smoke, and it was like salt spread on the ground. People who touched it ended up with blisters on their skin. Animals that

---

[1] From a sequence of secret cables from *Amn* Suleimaniyeh to *Amn* Autonomous Region headquarters; no. 1754 of January 25, 1988; no. 5474 of March 6, 1988; and no. 5860 of March 9, 1988. The second of these cables also reported that sixty members of the "Treacherous Iraqi Communist Party" were present in Balagjar.

ate the affected grass died instantly." But there were no human fatalities; because of the daily attacks, all the Takiyeh villagers had fled to temporary shelters in the fields. "But in Balagjar, many of the *pasdaran* and PUK *peshmerga*, and many other people too, lost their sight for three days; the *pasdaran* moved out of Balagjar three or four days before the Qara Dagh Anfal began."[2]

The continual chemical attacks during the First Anfal, and now on Qara Dagh, seem to have had the effect that the Iraqi government intended. An *Amn* intelligence report dated March 16, the day of the Halabja massacre, noted that a dozen divisions (*teep*) of the PUK had dispersed from their bases throughout southern Iraqi Kurdistan during the previous few days in fear of further chemical attacks. Another cable the next day reported, "We have learned from our reliable secret sources that a few days ago the treacherous *Al-Hasek* group [the Kurdistan Socialist Party] took possession of an estimated 1500 protective gas masks. They received these from the Zionist-Iranian regime."[3]

These precautions, however, were of little help, for Anfal came to Qara Dagh on March 22 with one of the most lethal chemical attacks of the entire campaign, on the village of Sayw Senan. It was the day after *Nowroz*, the Kurdish New Year and the first day of spring, which the *peshmerga* had celebrated by lighting bonfires and discharging their guns

---

[2] This witness also claimed that the *pasdaran*'s weaponry included US-made HAWK anti-aircraft missiles--the type supplied to Teheran in the course of what came to be known as the Iran-Contra affair. Middle East Watch interview, Bayinjan complex, March 21, 1993. PUK officials deny, however, that any HAWKs were present inside Iraq and say that they had only SAM-7s. They also claim that the main function of the Iranian Revolutionary Guards was to conduct reconnaissance and intelligence missions.

[3] *Amn* Suleimaniyeh to *Amn* Autonomous Region headquarters, cables no. 6631 of March 16, 1988 and no. 6739 of March 17, 1988. Despite the dates, from other references in these documents to *pasdaran* activities in and around Halabja it is apparent that both reports were prepared by agents who were unaware of the March 16 chemical attack.

into the air.[4] Despite the news of the attacks on Sergalou-Bergalou and Halabja, and despite the recently reported presence of Iranian *pasdaran* in their village, the people of Sayw Senan seemed to have a curious and ill-founded sense of their own immunity. "People were saying, 'It will be the same as in the past. They will attack us and we will defeat them," recalled one villager.[5] Although Sayw Senan was home to a PUK division (*teep*), there were very few *peshmerga* in the village by this time; most had been summoned to the defense of Sergalou-Bergalou. But at the dinner hour on March 22, the villagers heard the whistling sound of shells fired from a *rajima* and smelled the odor of apples. One shell landed in the courtyard of a house, instantly killing thirteen of the fourteen people in the family of a man called Mahdi Hadi Zorab. Only one son, a *peshmerga*, survived by fleeing to the mountains. Six separate estimates given to Middle East Watch by local villagers and PUK officials place the total number of dead in the chemical attack on Sayw Senan at between seventy-eight and eighty-seven.

"When we received the news of the attack from people fleeing it, many men from our village went to Sayw Senan to help," said Omar, the farmer from Takiyeh. "We saw the bodies of those who had died inside the village. I helped bury sixty-seven with my own hands in Koshk village after we took them there on tractors. We laid them all in one big grave in the Haji Raqa graveyard, with their clothes on. Another fourteen bodies were buried in Asteli Serru village. They had died instantly. They were bleeding from the nose; it was as if their brains had exploded."

---

[4]   While a second witness gave the date of the Sayw Senan attack as March 18, the later date seems more credible, since the witness specifically referred to *Nowroz* falling on the previous day. All dates given by witnesses need to be treated with a certain amount of caution: although the Kurds use a 365-day solar calendar, the months do not correspond precisely to those of the Gregorian calendar. On the Kurdish calender and the traditional celebration of *Nowroz*, see Izady, *The Kurds*, pp. 241-243.

[5]   Middle East Watch interview, Naser complex, July 30, 1992.

The following day, March 23, the chemical *rajima* hit Dukan, another PUK base in a village of seventy houses.[6] On the night of the 24th it targeted Ja'faran, a farming village of 200 houses which had no PUK presence, but housed the small headquarters that controlled KDP operations in the governorate of Kirkuk. According to two villagers, this was not the first time that Ja'faran had been attacked with gas. In May 1987, MIG fighter planes had dropped chemicals on the outskirts of the village--one man counted fourteen bombs, which produced red, green and white smoke. Ja'faran was lucky, for neither of the chemical attacks killed anyone--even though hundreds of farm animals perished. The May 1987 bombing took place when most people were outside the village, and *peshmerga* paramedics from a nearby base provided emergency medical care.[7] The first attack scared people enough that they rarely returned to their homes, and even slept in temporary shelters in the fields. The March 1988 *rajima* attack found the village deserted.

* * *

THE EXODUS FROM QARA DAGH

By now the hillsides were alive with people fleeing Anfal, for the army's ground assault had begun on the afternoon of March 23. Troops from the army's 43rd Division, backed by *jahsh* and *Amn* Emergency Forces, converged from four directions on the area between Qara Dagh and Darbandikhan, driving the villagers from their homes like beaters flushing out game-birds.[8] The general sense of panic was enhanced by

---

[6] Not to be confused with the larger town of Dukan, to the north of Suleimaniyeh.

[7] Middle East Watch interviews, Ja'faran village, June 6, 1992.

[8] The army's day-to-day movements are detailed in a sequence of sixteen handwritten *Amn* cables, contained in a file entitled "The Purification of Qara Dagh Operation, [illegible] Darbandikhan." The documents, classified "secret and urgent," cover the period from March 23 to April 1, 1988, when *Amn* announced the capture of Takiyeh and Balagjar.

the news, carried by word of mouth and over the *peshmerga* field radios, of the devastating poison gas attack on Sayw Senan.

The mass exodus was mainly to the north, where people hoped to find sanctuary in Suleimaniyeh or in one of the complexes along the main highway. One group of villagers from Chami Smor smelled the nauseating odor of rotten apples, carried on the wind that was blowing from the direction of Ja'faran. Another family, from the village of Masoyi, took refuge in a cave a few minutes walk from their homes. But they made the mistake of leaving a lantern burning when they fell asleep. In the night they were awakened by the throb of helicopters, which had evidently been attracted by the light, and the sound of explosions. Suddenly the cave was filled with the suffocating smell of sweet melons. The family stumbled outside and fled, carrying two children who had been overcome by the fumes. By good fortune they survived, and hid out on the slopes of Zerda mountain. Three days later they watched as the army burned the village of Masoyi.[9]

What the regime intended to do with civilians caught up in the Second Anfal remains murky. By now, *Istikhbarat* had received orders from the Northern Bureau to set up special temporary camps to house those who were displaced. But the roundups during the last week of March were much less systematic than in the later phases of the Anfal operation. Between Qara Dagh and Suleimaniyeh, one physical obstacle loomed before the fleeing villagers--the 4,300-foot Glazerda Mountain. They found its slopes swarming with troops, *jahsh*, commandos in camouflage uniforms and members of the Emergency Forces (*Quwat Taware'*). Everywhere there were ragged people, tractor-drawn carts and farm animals. Helicopters hovered overhead. There was tank and artillery fire from every side: "It was like a boiling pot," said a man from Ja'faran who survived.

Yet the army's attitude was ambiguous. In the first few days of the Second Anfal, some villagers were told to make their own way to the city and the complexes (although *Amn* later carried out house-to-house searches of Naser, Zarayen and Suleimaniyeh to track these people down.) Others fled via back trails into the mountains as soon as they saw the soldiers, and eluded the dragnet that way. Word of the Qara Dagh exodus reached Suleimaniyeh, and the city relatives of some families made their way to Glazerda Mountain to fetch them.

---

[9] Middle East Watch interview, Bayinjan complex, March 21, 1993.

Despite the massive military presence, the survivors of the Sayw Senan attack heard rumors of a temporary amnesty, and remained on the mountainside unmolested for several days in the rain. But on the fifth day soldiers at the checkpoint on the Qara Dagh-Suleimaniyeh road began to arrest them. Some, especially the elderly and the infirm, were helped to escape by the *jahsh*, in an early hint of the contradictory role that the Kurdish militia would play throughout Anfal. But between twenty-five and thirty people from Sayw Senan were taken away at this point and never seen again.

The attitude of the troops seems to have changed with an incident that was witnessed by Omar, the farmer from Takiyeh village:

> When we arrived, the army had not yet started arresting people. The officers were just asking us if there were saboteurs in our area, and we told them that there were. But then something happened. A tractor cart laden with old wheat grain was blocking the road because it had a flat tire. The owner had abandoned it there. So a tank came and tried to move the cart out of the way. Instead, it overturned it completely and a lot of Kalashnikovs came tumbling out from underneath the grain, enough to arm a whole squad. Then the army put out a radio call to units in different areas to set up roadblocks, and they started to arrest people--men, women, children, even the people who had come from Suleimaniyeh.
>
> I was twenty meters away from the tank, behind the army lines. There were 500 of us. We fled into the mountains--it was the *jahsh* who told us to run if we were able to.... My brother Khaled was still behind the tractor cart when the incident occurred. We were close to one another, close enough to call out to each other. But he was arrested and taken to Suleimaniyeh.[10]

Khaled was never seen again; nor were three other young men from Takiyeh who were arrested with him. Omar escaped to the city and survived.

---

[10] Middle East Watch interview, Bayinjan complex, March 21, 1993.

Those who were arrested at the checkpoint were loaded into military IFA trucks and driven to the Emergency Forces base in the Chwar Bagh ("Four Orchards") quarter of Suleimaniyeh. There were thousands of prisoners there from the Qara Dagh region, and every day hundreds more arrived. The soldiers recorded their names and confiscated whatever valuables and identity documents they were carrying. One man from the village of Dolani Khwaru described being held at first on a nearby military base, supervised by *Istikhbarat* officers, before being transferred to the Emergency Forces headquarters.[11]

There the prisoners remained for as long as three or four weeks. Some groups of young men were blindfolded and separated from the rest, while others were taken out for a couple of days but later returned to their cells. The detainees were given almost nothing to eat, although it was possible to buy food from the guards. Although it was the army that had detained them, the villagers who passed through the *Taware'* base said that the daily interrogation sessions were conducted by *Amn* agents. "Are your sons *peshmerga*?," they were asked; "What *peshmerga* activity is there in your village?" The interrogators appeared to regard even children of grade-school age as potential "saboteurs." After an average of two or three weeks, buses and coasters arrived to take the detainees away. They drove off west, in the direction of Kirkuk.

Middle East Watch interviewed survivors from some ten Qara Dagh villages affected by the Second Anfal. In every case, they could name the young men of draft age who had disappeared after detention in the Suleimaniyeh Emergency Forces base. From Serko, nine never came back; four were lost from Takiyeh and another four from nearby Balagjar; two from Berday, three from Koshk, two from Dolani Khwaru, three from Deiwana, nine from Mitsa Chweir, five from Chami Smor. Repeated across the whole *nahya* of Qara Dagh, with its eighty villages, one may reasonably assume that several hundred young men disappeared during the Second Anfal.

But the story is more complex than this, as the experience of villages like Chami Smor suggests. The five young men of Chami Smor who vanished from Suleimaniyeh were army deserters who gave themselves up to the authorities as part of the general exodus. However, the village's location--at the very edge of the high Qara Dagh mountains-- tempted others into what proved to be a terrible mistake. While the

---

[11] Middle East Watch interview, Suleimaniyeh, April 1, 1993.

majority fled north, two families struck out across the forbidding peaks toward the Germian plain, hoping to be safe in the town of Kalar, which would not be touched by Anfal. There were seventeen people in the group altogether--men, women and children. None of them ever reached their destination. Nor did hundreds of others who fled south with the same idea. It must be presumed that they were all seized by the Iraqi authorities.[12]

* * *

FLIGHT TO SOUTHERN GERMIAN

There are very striking regional differences in the pattern of mass disappearances during the Anfal campaign. After the First Anfal, adult men and teenage boys who were captured by the army were disappeared--a pattern that was repeated in all areas. But in several places, notably southern Germian, huge numbers of women and children were also taken away and never seen again. The criteria for this selection seem to have included not only one's place of birth but the area in which one was captured. In many cases, but not all, the pattern of disappearances appears to have reflected the degree of resistance that the troops encountered. If the *peshmerga* fought back strongly, women and children captured in the vicinity were more likely to be disappeared along with their husbands and fathers. This may be what is implied in an *Amn* letter, dated August 2, 1988, which requests information on whether those who had been given into its custody had surrendered in an area where combat had taken place.[13]

Women and children who fled north from Qara Dagh toward Suleimaniyeh and the complexes were not harmed. Those who crossed into southern Germian vanished. Two men, three women and six children disappeared from the village of Aliawa. Forty-seven villagers

---

[12] Middle East Watch interview, Bayinjan complex, March 19, 1993.

[13] Confidential letter from *Amn* Autonomous Region to *Amn* Erbil governorate, August 2, 1988. The text reads, "Please take note of our telex no. 9887 of July 20, 1988 and inform us whether the persons who are the subject of the communication came from the fighting basin or not."

from Masoyi, including many children and nursing infants, were captured near Kalar and never seen again.[14]

The population of Omer Qala, a village of twenty houses at the southern tip of Zerda Mountain, had fled en masse on hearing of the gas attack on nearby Sayw Senan. Taking with them only a few essentials such as money and blankets, as well as their animal herds, they skirted the mountain and headed southwest in the direction of Germian. Although they were not *peshmerga*, all the men carried weapons, as is common practice among Iraqi Kurdish males; all but three of them were either army deserters or draft dodgers. The twenty families walked for several days, sleeping in caves or in the open air. They hoped to return to their homes when the government was driven out of their area, as had always happened in the past. But this time was different. Reaching the village of Bakr Bayef on the eastern edge of Germian, they learned that the whole Qara Dagh area had fallen to government forces. All of their villages had been razed to the ground; there were no homes to return to. Behind them, the army's chemical shells rained down on Zerda Mountain, and in the early morning of April 1 the army captured the crucial *peshmerga* villages of Takiyeh and Balagjar.[15]

Far from outrunning the army, the people of Omer Qala had run straight into the jaws of the enemy. Germian was the next target of Anfal, the villagers of Bakr Bayef told them, and its inhabitants had been given seventy-two hours to surrender. The twenty families gathered that night to decide on their next move. They concluded that there was no alternative but to surrender. After all, the more optimistic among them reasoned, walking toward government lines had offered protection in previous rounds of fighting between the army and the *peshmerga*. In the morning they headed in the direction of the government forces, as far as the village of Boysana. Less than a mile further on lay a place called

---

[14] Middle East Watch interviews, Bayinjan complex, March 21, 1993; Naser complex, March 26, 1993.

[15] A "secret and urgent" telegram from *Amn* Darbandikhan, no. 9507, 1740 hours, April 1, 1988, reports the seizure of "four bases of the saboteurs and agents of Iran, along with a base of the Guards of Khomeini the impostor and a base of the saboteurs of the Iraqi Communist Party." With these army victories, the military aspect of the Second Anfal was essentially complete.

Sheikh Tawil, which was to become perhaps the single most stubbornly defended target in the entire Anfal campaign.

In the course of the last week of March, the people of Sheikh Tawil, who belonged to the Tarkhani tribe, had offered refuge to hundreds of fellow Kurds fleeing from Qara Dagh. Although they were from different tribes, said one man, "We sheltered them; we became one."[16] In the wake of the panicked civilians came a fresh contingent of *peshmerga*, fleeing their rout on Zerda Mountain. The triangle between the mountain, Sheikh Tawil and Darbandikhan was by now a raging cauldron. There was constant shelling from all directions, some of it Iraqi and some from the Iranian side. No one could any longer tell the difference. Confusion reigned. From April 3 to 5, the army and the *peshmerga* fought their first, inconclusive battle for control of Sheikh Tawil. In the general chaos that preceded the fighting, most of the civilians of Sheikh Tawil evacuated their homes and made for the highway that runs southwest from Darbandikhan Lake to Kalar. Seventy-nine of them would be captured and disappeared. But this was not yet the Third Anfal, the Germian Anfal: the horror of that was still to come.

The Omer Qala families watched as four old men of Boysana went forward to meet the troops, carrying white flags. "Bring your families," they were told. "Nothing will happen to them." Trusting the officer's promise, a number of men, women and children turned themselves in. They were promptly arrested. Those who remained behind later learned that they had been taken to the army brigade headquarters in the town of Kalar. But that was the last that was ever heard of them.

The remaining Omer Qala villagers fled once more, walking until they reached the town of La'likhan on the main road. They found a huge crowd of people from many different villages milling around, and a large fleet of trucks which the army had brought to collect them. Again the villagers conferred. Despite their terror, they again agreed that surrender was their only hope. Akram, an eighteen-year old from Omer Qala, was still suspicious, however. Fearing punishment as a draft dodger, he hid himself in an empty barrel to observe the mass surrender.

---

[16] Middle East Watch interview with a former resident of Sheikh Tawil, Bawanur complex, March 28, 1993.

Five hundred gave themselves up; only twenty, including Akram, stayed behind. Akram survived; the five hundred disappeared.[17]

---

[17] Middle East Watch interview, Naser complex, July 28, 1992. Akram in fact later passed through a number of army lines and checkpoints along the way; but he never abandoned his goats, and this may have saved his life. Middle East Watch was told several stories of draft-age men being spared, especially in the southern Germian area, if they were tending their farm animals at the time of Anfal.

Third Anfal (North): April 7 - April 20, 1988

©1993 Michael S. Miller

Legend:
- Approximate boundary of 3rd Anfal campaign
- Main Anfal camp and facility
- Resettlement complex (mujamma'a)
- Major road
- Tribal area mentioned in report

JABARI

Elevation (feet)
- less than 1000
- 1000 - 2000
- 2000 - 5000
- 5000 - 9000

0 kilometers 10
0 miles 10

Piramagroun
Suleimaniyeh
Glazerda Mtn.
Bayinjan
Bazian
Takiyeh
Shoresh
Chamchamal
Qara Hanjir
Qara Ways
Qara Hassan
Hanara
Leilan
Mahmoud Parizad
Aliawa
Qader Karam
Ibrahim Ghulam
Qala Mikhaeil
Qeitawan
Golama
Bangol
Takiyeh Jabari
Qeitoul
Garawi
Gulbagh
Khidr Reihan
Sengaw
Sirqala
Banamurt
Drozna
Tapa Garus
Qara Dagh
Mountains
ZANGANA
JABARI
Kirkuk
Topzawa

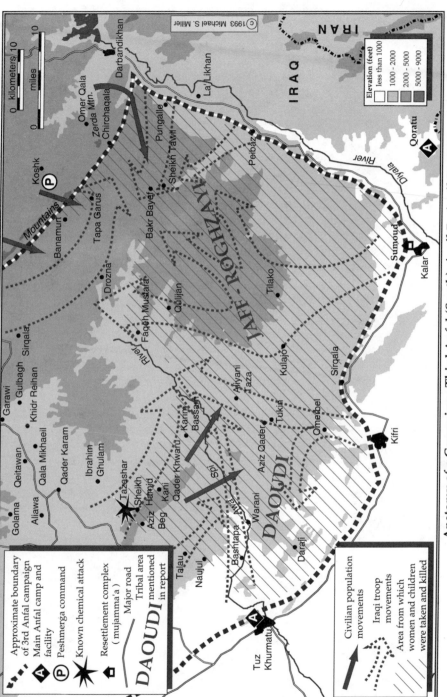

Anatomy of a Campaign. Third Anfal (South): April 7 - April 20, 1988

Elevation (feet)
- less than 1000
- 1000 - 2000
- 2000 - 5000
- 5000 - 9000

© 1993 Michael S. Miller

0 kilometers 10
0 miles 10

IRAN

IRAQ

JAFF - ROGHZAYI

DAOUDI

Mountains

Diyala River

Darbandikhan
Omer Qala
Zerda Mtn.
Chirchaqala
Koshk
Banamurt
Tapa Garus
Drozna
Pungalle
Sheikh Tawil
Lay Likhan
Peibaz
Bakr Bayef
Garawi
Gulbagh
Sirqala
Khidr Reihan
Faqeh Mustafa
River
Qulijan
Tilako
Qeitawan
Golama
Aliawa
Qala Mikhaeil
Qader Karam
Ibrahim
Ghulam
Tazashar
Sheikh
Aziz Hamjd
Beg Kani
Qader Khwaru
Karim
Bassam
Ahyani Taza
Kulajo
Sirqala
Tukin
Omerbel
Kifri
Aziz Qader
Warani
Spi
River
Talau
Naujul
Bashtapa Awa
Darari
Tuz Khurmatu
Kalar
Sumoud
Qoratu

DAOUDI

- Approximate boundary of 3rd Anfal campaign
- Main Anfal camp and facility
- Peshmerga command
- Known chemical attack
- Resettlement complex (mujamma'a)
- Major road
- Tribal area mentioned in report

- Civilian population movements
- Iraqi troop movements
- Area from which women and children were taken and killed

5
THIRD ANFAL--GERMIAN, APRIL 7-20, 1988

"This was the first time people were taken away to end them."
-- farmer of Golama village,
Qader Karam.

Germian--the warm country--is a large hilly plain at the southernmost tip of Sorani-speaking Iraqi Kurdistan, bordering on Iraq's Arab heartland. It is bounded to the west by the highway between the oil-rich city of Kirkuk and the town of Tuz Khurmatu; to the north by the Kirkuk-Chamchamal road; to the east by the Qara Dagh mountains; and to the south by a shallow triangle of towns--Kalar, Kifri and Peibaz.[1] Almost exactly in the geographical center of Germian lies the *nahya* of Qader Karam, once a busy market center of some 10,000 people.

By the end of the first week in April, the straggling remnants of the defeated *peshmerga* from the Sergalou-Bergalou area had worked their way southward to take refuge in the PUK's strongholds in Germian. Villagers fleeing from the second Anfal headed south and west as well. Some fighters from the second *malband* took up fresh defensive positions in Sheikh Tawil, which had been flooded with the refugees from Qara Dagh. Others headed for the village of Bashtapa on the Aqa Su river, which bisects the Germian plain.[2] (Local people call it the *Awa Spi*, or "white river," for the milky color of its flow.)

Compared to the Jafati valley and even to Qara Dagh, the flat terrain of Germian was much less favorable to guerrilla warfare. This was, however, the political heartland of the PUK revolt, and the sons of its farming villages made up the bulk of the organization's fighting forces.

---

[1] The town of Peibaz, on the main road from Kalar to Darbandikhan, is also known as Bawanur--"Father of Light"--in honor of a holy man who is buried there and whose shrine is said to emit light each Friday evening.

[2] Middle East Watch interview with former PUK commander in Germian, Suleimaniyeh, March 28, 1993.

The villages were also filled with deserters and draft dodgers, and the *peshmerga* enjoyed an extensive and well-organized network of local support. "They used to come at night and get food from the villagers and give political lectures for the villagers as to why they should fight the government and why they should not join the *jahsh*," said a woman from the village of Sheikh Hamid, which lay close to the important PUK stronghold at Tazashar.[3] "The *peshmerga* had ordered each family to buy one weapon," added a man from the nearby settlement of Kani Qader Khwaru. "It was like a law, and the people agreed with this because they saw it was necessary. The armed civilians would join the *peshmerga* in the defense of their villages. They were referred to as the 'backing force.' All the villages had this type of civil defense unit."[4]

Yet there was little the *peshmerga* could do to withstand the ferocious assault of the Iraqi Army. This was a more conventional war, though of a grossly one-sided kind. For more than a week, the area was enveloped in wave after wave of assaults by infantry, armored divisions, artillery, air force and *jahsh*. The people of Germian were persuaded to surrender by the near-impossibility of escape; never before had they seen such overwhelming concentrations of troops and militia. The army did not leave the area until all living things had been captured, and they pursued any fleeing villagers, by helicopter and on foot, into the mountains and into the towns and cities.[5]

The Iraqi Army mercilessly exploited the PUK's weaknesses in Germian. There were no strongly fortified bases here--no Bergalou, no

---

[3] Middle East Watch interview, Bayinjan complex, May 19, 1992. By this time, of course, there was absolutely no incentive for draft dodgers to turn themselves in, given the recent decrees establishing the death penalty for desertion. Public and even televised executions of deserters were commonplace. See above p.66.

[4] Middle East Watch interview, Suleimaniyeh, July 25, 1992.

[5] A "secret and urgent" field report from Eastern Region military intelligence to the Northern Bureau, for example, describes a dawn raid on April 26 on the abandoned village of Kilar. Three armored companies of the 444th Infantry Regiment encircled the village to search for "families that had infiltrated the village as a result of the Third Anfal Operation." All the fighting in this sector had ended at least a week earlier.

Yakhsamar, no heavy weaponry. The few *peshmerga* villages with a fixed troop detachment, or *teep*, were easily cut off from their supply lines; deprived of reinforcements, the isolated fighters could either flee or fight until they ran out of ammunition. *Peshmerga* arriving from the areas of the first and second Anfals were exhausted, and there was a general collapse of morale in the wake of the chemical attacks on the Jafati Valley, Qara Dagh and Halabja. The Iraqi regime seems to have found poison gas much less necessary during the Germian campaign, although it did come into play against at least one troublesome target.[6] Some beleaguered *peshmerga* strongholds held out for as much as five days, but in most places the resistance crumbled quickly.

* * *

It is possible to reconstruct the battle plan of the Iraqi Army in Germian in some detail, thanks to a sequence of some thirty-three "secret and urgent" military intelligence cables, which give an hour-by-hour update of conditions on the battlefield.[7] These documents depict a series of enormous pincer movements, with troop columns converging from at least eight different points on the perimeter of Germian, encircling *peshmerga* targets and channeling the fleeing civilian population toward designated collection points by blocking off all other avenues of escape. (see map) The cable traffic describes some 120 villages "stormed

---

[6] There are reliable reports of a chemical attack on the village of Tazashar (*nahya* Qader Karam). For details, see below pp.134-135. Middle East Watch has also received unconfirmed reports of a gas attack during Anfal on Khalo Baziani (Qara Hassan).

[7] These cables, generally headed "*Umala* Iran synopsis," are dated April 9-27, 1988. They were found bound together with a lace in a folder whose cover bears the handwritten title, "The File on the Third Anfal Operation (Qader Karam Sector), April 9, 1988. For all its detail, it is apparent that this is far from a comprehensive file on the Germian theater. Most of the documents originate with Kalar Military Intelligence or the Second Army Corps and describe operations in the southern part of Germian. A handful from Tuz Khurmatu and Chamchamal *Istikhbarat* report on actions further to the north. Some of these documents are reproduced in the February 19, 1993 report on Iraq by the Special Rapporteur of the U.N. Commission on Human Rights, *loc. cit.*, pp.102-117.

and demolished," or "burned and destroyed." Almost none of these is described as a military target; in only a handful of cases is there any report of resistance being encountered; in the rare cases where a village is searched, the soldiers tend to find nothing more incriminating than "pictures of saboteurs and the charlatan Khomeini."[8]

The intent of the operation could not be more clear: it was to wipe out all vestiges of human settlement. Several of the *Istikhbarat* field reports make this explicit. "All the villages that the convoy passed through were destroyed and burned, since most of the villages were not marked on the map," reports the Kalar column on April 13. The Pungalle column returns to base on April 20, "after completing the demolition of all the villages within its sector."[9] No matter how thorough, a single pass was not enough; in mid-August the troops returned to "burn and remove any remaining signs of life."[10] In one case after another, the names of the villages that have been eliminated correspond to the site of mass disappearances described to Middle East Watch by survivors.

* * *

THE PLAN OF CAMPAIGN: (1) TUZ KHURMATU

Early in the morning of April 7, the first troops and *jahsh* battalions moved out from their base in Tuz Khurmatu, at the southwestern corner of Germian. Over the next two days, other units left

---

[8] Second Corps cable no.10724 of April 14, 1988, describing the actions of the Kifri column. "After occupying the village of Aziz Qader, the force inside the village found nothing but furniture inside homes and documents and pictures of saboteurs and the charlatan Khomeini. It was burned."

[9] Kalar *Istikhbarat* cable no. 10687 to Eastern Region *Istikhbarat*, April 13, 1988; Second Corps cable no. 11386 to Northern Bureau Command, April 21, 1988.

[10] *Amn* Kalar, "secret and urgent" cable no. 19442, August 20, 1988. The order to "isolate prohibited areas from tilling and burn them" was given by Northern Bureau communique no. 3821 of July 3, 1988.

Kirkuk, Laylan, Chamchamal and Sengaw, all converging from different directions on the town of Qader Karam. The Tuz Khurmatu column quickly divided into three task forces. One headed southeast from the town of Naujul toward the Awa Spi river. A second, larger task force moved east along the sandy river valley. Preceded by airstrikes, it dealt quickly with the resistance from the second *malband* survivors at Bashtapa, and quickly reported having wiped out seventeen villages at the cost of just eleven dead--eight of them *jahsh*.[11]

Two of these villages were Upper and Lower Warani, a new fallback position for the *peshmerga* in Bashtapa. The Waranis had suffered grievously in the past, having been burned down on three separate occasions since 1963. The twin villages also provided a bitter illustration of the effects of Ali Hassan al-Majid's demand for aerial and artillery bombardment designed to "kill the largest number of persons present in those prohibited zones."[12]

In the months preceding Anfal, there were three fatal attacks by government helicopters. One killed an old man resting in his fields at harvest time; another, a fifteen-year old girl and her mother, fetching water from the river; another, two young shepherd boys, brothers aged eight and eleven.

But Anfal was different. The troops arrived at breakfast time, set fire to the houses, killed all the farm animals and rounded up many of the villagers. Others managed to flee into the hills, where they remained for several days. But they realized that they were encircled on three sides, and had no alternative but to head south toward the highway, where they surrendered to a *jahsh* unit commanded by a *mustashar* named Adnan Jabari. It was the first day of Ramadan, the Muslim month of fasting, one elderly man remembered--April 17. Trucks were waiting to take them away, and many of them were never seen again. The

---

[11] The task force was made up of the 65th Brigade of the Special Forces, supported by the 58th and 200th National Defense Battalions (*jahsh*). Tuz Khurmatu *Istikhbarat* cable no.10340 of April 10, 1988. The cable complains that another *jahsh* unit, the 25th, "has withdrawn from the task, having failed to carry out its mission." Such complaints of the shortcomings of the Kurdish militia occur frequently in these cables.

[12] Paragraph 4 of Northern Bureau Command directive SF/4008 of June 20, 1987, cited above at p.82.

surviving villagers later made a list of 102 people from Warani who had disappeared.[13] As with all the villages in the Daoudi tribal area, those who vanished included large numbers of women and children.

Meanwhile, the third Tuz Khurmatu task force launched a ferocious attack on the PUK base in Tazashar, some twelve miles due north of the Awa Spi river. Tazashar was a perfect example of the dilemma that the PUK faced in Germian. A small village of only about twenty households, it had assumed a certain strategic importance because of its location on an all-weather road close to the main Tuz Khurmatu-Qader Karam highway. A small contingent of 20-25 *peshmerga* dug in here to fight the army forces that were advancing south from the main road. The army brought in heavy weapons and tanks, and airplanes and helicopters lent aerial support. The outnumbered and outgunned *peshmerga* put up a spirited defense from 8 a.m. until the early afternoon of April 9. But in a valley surrounded by low hills, they were at a huge disadvantage; meeting resistance, it was a simple matter for the army to withdraw temporarily and send troops around behind Tazashar to encircle it. The soldiers seized control of the surrounding hilltops and destroyed three other villages that lay in their path--Upper and Lower Kani Qader, and Sheikh Hamid.

Several witnesses from neighboring villages say that the army resorted to chemical weapons in Tazashar. One man in Kani Qader Khwaru, four miles away, told Middle East Watch that he intercepted radio communications from the officer in command, saying that gas was the only way to dislodge the resistance.[14] This witness then saw

---

[13] Middle East Watch interviews with former residents of Warani, Benaslawa complex and Suleimaniyeh, April 19 and May 12, 1992.

[14] According to numerous witnesses interviewed by Middle East Watch, it was a common practice for *peshmerga* and ordinary villagers to tune in to frequencies used by the armed forces. One PUK commander in Germian was unsure whether chemicals were used in Tazashar, but eyewitness accounts, together with frequent references in other interviews, offer persuasive evidence that such an attack did occur. Middle East Watch interviews with former residents of Sheikh Hamid and Kani Qader Khwaru, Bayinjan complex and Suleimaniyeh, May 19 and July 25, 1992, and March 19, 1993. It is also possible that there was a second chemical attack on April 10. A sheep farmer in the nearby village of Talau reported that *peshmerga* survivors fled in that direction and were bombed by aircraft at about midnight. According to this man, the

British-supplied Hawker Hunter aircraft bombing Tazashar, sending up
billowing clouds of white smoke. An hour later the army entered the
village. All its defenders died.

Aisha, a pregnant 20-year old woman from Sheikh Hamid,
watched the attack from her family's hilltop wheat field. She did not
realize at first that chemicals were involved, since the Iraqi Air Force had
bombed the area so often in the past. But when she came down from the
hillside that evening, she saw the bodies of twenty-five *peshmerga*. "It was
then that I found out they had used chemical weapons, because I also saw
a lot of dead goats and cows and birds." On the night of April 10,
Istikhbarat in Tuz Khurmatu cabled to Eastern Region headquarters that
it had removed "the bodies of 15 subversives, who were buried in the
vicinity of the Tuz Military Sector Command; before burial they were
photographed, and the film will be sent in a further dispatch."[15]
Having dealt with Tazashar, the column proceeded south, eliminating
another half-dozen villages before finally wiping out the last *peshmerga*
resistance at Karim Bassam, and so reaching the north bank of the Awa
Spi river.

Like everyone else from Sheikh Hamid, Aisha fled. As she was
leaving the area, she encountered a *mustashar*, a man by the name of
Sheikh Ahmad Barzinji, who had come in search of his own relatives. She
asked him what had happened. "I don't know," the *mustashar* replied.
"You should just surrender to the army. This is the best thing you can
do. I cannot do anything; even my relatives have been killed."

Aisha took her children and made for the hills. She could not
find her husband. With the *mustashar*'s words in mind, she first struck out
north in the direction of Qader Karam to surrender; the army had in any
case closed off all other avenues of escape. But on the way, she changed
her mind and decided instead to hide out in a cave with a group of fellow
villagers. The mountainsides south of Qader Karam were covered with
clusters of refugees. They hid in the cave for three days. On the second,
Aisha gave birth to her baby. She was hungry and too weak to nurse, and
had no covering to protect her child against the cold night air. On the

---

chemicals killed ten people in Talau. Middle East Watch interview, Daratou
complex, April 18, 1992.

[15] Tuz Khurmatu *Istikhbarat* cable no. 10334, April 10, 1988.

third day, she ventured out in search of food, leaving her day-old baby in the cave.

As soon as she left the safety of her cave, however, Aisha was spotted by a *jahsh* patrol tracking down survivors. She was surprised at how kind they seemed; they promised they would take her to the *mustashar*, who would arrange for her to be amnestied. They found their commander on the outskirts of Qader Karam. It turned out to be Sheikh Ahmad Barzinji, the same man she had encountered three days earlier in the rubble of her village.

> "He took me and promised me that he would help me and he put
> me in a nearby school. I felt safe in the school, and he
> gave me some food. But after a few hours they brought a lot
> of people into the school. A lot of villagers were coming
> in to surrender; they were encouraged to do so by Sheikh
> Ahmad's *jahsh*. The army separated the men from the women,
> handcuffed all the men and put them in a separate room. When
> the army took charge, they pushed the *jahsh* aside. Sheikh
> Ahmad disappeared and I did not see him again. Then the
> soldiers took all the men and put them into military buses.
> Soon after that, they began to do the same thing to the women
> and children.[16]

Aisha's story remains one of the strangest of the Anfal campaign; in an apparently arbitrary act of clemency, an army officer eventually allowed her to leave the Qader Karam school and go to Suleimaniyeh. Aisha not only survived Anfal; she was even reunited in the end with the baby she had left behind in the cave. Most people from her area were less fortunate--if that is the word to use, since Aisha herself lost her husband, three brothers and twelve other members of her family. They were among a group of at least eighty men from Sheikh Hamid who surrendered to the *mustashar* and were never seen again. From nearby Karim Bassam, at least twenty-five people disappeared; from Aziz Beg, a village between Tazashar and Talau, the list ran to ninety-two, many of them women and children.

* * *

---

[16] Middle East Watch interview, Bayinjan complex, May 19, 1992.

THE PLAN OF CAMPAIGN:
(2) QADER KARAM AND NORTHERN GERMIAN

Meanwhile, other army units were pursuing a similar campaign of terror to the north of Qader Karam, under the direction of Special Forces Brigadier General (*'Amid*) Bareq Abdullah al-Haj Hunta, who appears to have been the overall commander of the Third Anfal operation in Germian.[17] Columns moving in from the west reported an uneventful advance--hardly surprising, since they were following the main Kirkuk-Chamchamal highway through an area that had largely been destroyed and depopulated during the spring 1987 campaign. They reached Qader Karam rapidly, by the late afternoon of April 10. The following morning, a column of *jahsh* under Sayed Jabari set out from the *nahya* to take care of the single, isolated village of Ibrahim Ghulam, in the rocky hills south of Qader Karam.[18] The population had already fled after hearing of the fighting nearby, but they straggled down from their hiding places after a few days to surrender. Middle East Watch was given a list of the names of fifty-one men from Ibrahim Ghulam who were never seen again.[19]

Ibrahim Ghulam was a village belonging to the Zangana tribe, and the Zangana and the neighboring Jabari were the victims of some of

---

[17] General Bareq, a "hero of al-Qadissiyah," (the Iran-Iraq War), was now in charge of a Special Forces detachment guarding the Kirkuk oilfields. Other witnesses also reported sighting him at Glazerda Mountain, during the Second Anfal. According to a former Iraqi police chief, Bareq was also the commander of military campaigns against Shi'a dissidents in the south in the mid-1980s. (Middle East Watch interview with Hamdi Abd-al-Majid Gilli, Suleimaniyeh, July 24, 1992.) Bareq was reportedly executed in 1991 on suspicion of being involved in a plot to overthrow President Saddam Hussein.

[18] Cable no. 10488 from Chamchamal *Istikhbarat* to Eastern Region *Istikhbarat* headquarters, April 11, 1988. There are unconfirmed reports of one chemical attack in this sector against the village of Khalo Baziani.

[19] Middle East Watch interview with a former inhabitant of Ibrahim Ghulam, Suleimaniyeh, June 28, 1992.

the worst ravages of the Third Anfal.[20] In April 1988, the Zangana
inhabited dozens of villages to the east of Qader Karam; the villages of
the Jabari dotted the low mountains to the north. Columns of troops
operating out of bases in Sengaw and Chamchamal wiped out all of them.

Some of the Jabari villages did manage to escape northward,
through a temporary breach that the *peshmerga* opened on the Kirkuk-
Chamchamal road. Others tried, but failed, to outrun the oncoming
army troops. At the time of the Third Anfal, the inhabitants of Taeberz,
a tiny Jabari hamlet on the paved road a half-hour west of Qader Karam,
were in the process of trying to rebuild the homes that the army had
burned down the previous summer. Hearing that waves of troops were
moving towards them in a huge pincer movement from Kirkuk and
Chamchamal, they fled at dawn, but were only two hours from the village
when the army and *jahsh* tracked them down. A convoy of army IFA
trucks was waiting for them on the paved road. It took them to Leilan,
a *nahya* a little to the south of Kirkuk.

Other Jabari hamlets were deserted by the time the troops
arrived.   Such was the case of Mahmoud Parizad, another small
settlement close to the main road and only a half-hour drive from both
Qader Karam and Kirkuk. In many ways Mahmoud Parizad was typical
of the whole Jabari area: twenty-five houses of mud or cement blocks,
each with its own bomb shelter; neither electricity nor running water; a
small mosque, as well as a schoolhouse that had been closed down and its
government teacher withdrawn when the area fell under *peshmerga*
control in the mid-1980s.

When Anfal reached Mahmoud Parizad on April 11, the army met
modest resistance from *peshmerga* in two neighboring villages, and the
people of Mahmoud Parizad fled to the mountains to escape the incoming
artillery fire. They were joined there by a steady stream of refugees from
other Jabari villages, perhaps 1,000 in all. Word had spread rapidly of
the previous day's chemical attack on Tazashar, and the women and
children decided to surrender to the army; their menfolk, most of whom
were active *peshmerga*, remained in hiding for another two days.

---

[20] The Zangana are one of the largest non-confederated tribes in Kurdistan,
with settlements on either side of the Iran-Iraq border. The Jabari were not
protected during Anfal by the pro-regime stance of their two *mustashars*, Sayed
and Adnan Jabari.   For general information on Kurdish tribes and tribal
confederacies, see Izady, *The Kurds*, pp.74-86.

At noon the women and children returned to their village, as a helicopter hovered overhead and shellfire sounded all around. The army had already taken Mahmoud Parizad, and with them was a small contingent of *jahsh*. The first houses were already in flames. The soldiers stripped the villagers of whatever possessions they had taken with them to the hills. Before torching the houses, the troops also looted whatever they could lay their hands on, even down to small domestic animals like rabbits and pigeons. Then they bundled the villagers into a line of waiting IFAs, and drove off north in the direction of Chamchamal, away from the flames that were now engulfing Mahmoud Parizad.

A few Jabari villagers did manage to escape the advancing troops, sometimes with the help of advance warning from their fellow Kurds in the *jahsh*. This happened, for example, in Hanara, which lay further north toward Chamchamal, and was linked by a rough mountain path to the local PUK headquarters at Takiyeh Jabari. There had been fighting in the vicinity for years, and a number of villagers had died in bombing raids. Whenever the injured were taken to hospital, said one who survived, the doctors told them that, "You deserve to be treated like this because you are traitors and work with the Iranians." The people of Hanara had grown accustomed to a routine of spending their days in the hills with their flocks, hiding when necessary in their air-raid shelters, and returning to their homes only at night to bake bread.

When Anfal came to Hanara--with helicopters and fighter planes in the morning, and ground troops in the evening--only a few *peshmerga* combatants were present. The other villagers took the risk of making contact with the *jahsh* units that they spotted nearby, and pleaded with them not to destroy Hanara. These *jahsh* did not take them into custody, but instead urged everyone to flee. That night, the villagers came down from the hills to find nothing but smoldering rubble. Everything had been bulldozed, including the mosque. Under cover of darkness, the villagers set out on foot and on tractors for the town of Leilan. "I turned off my tractor's lights," one man from Hanara remembered. "While I was driving to Leilan, it was all dark, but I could see my village burning. I cried; I knew it was the end of everything."[21]

In Leilan, the fleeing residents of Hanara met up with refugees from two other villages. Townspeople of Leilan, at great personal risk,

---

[21] Both quotations are from Middle East Watch interviews with a former inhabitant of Hanara, Suleimaniyeh, May 21 and June 28, 1992.

sheltered all of them until morning. From there, relatives succeeded in spiriting away many of the villagers, taking them to Kirkuk, where they hoped to find anonymity among the crowds. Some also managed to vanish into the crowds of displaced Kurds in the large new resettlement camp of Shoresh, outside the town of Chamchamal, which at this point was little more than an open field. Here, they survived. As a result, Hanara suffered proportionately less than many Jabari villages as a result of Anfal. According to survivors, twenty-seven people from a single family disappeared from Golama; nearby Bangol lost forty-one.[22] Hanara's disappeared numbered only seventeen--the *Imam* of the local mosque, and sixteen teenage boys who surrendered to an especially notorious *mustashar* named Tahsin Shaweis, whose empty promise of amnesty was repeated on a wide scale in the Qader Karam area. One survivor told us:

> [The *mustashar*] told the villagers that there was a general amnesty, and he gave his word of honor that the youths would be protected. He would help them reach a safe place if one could be found. Otherwise, they should surrender and they would be protected by the amnesty. A man brought the sixteen young men, all relatives of his, to the *jahsh* leader. None were *peshmerga*. After two or three months, the father went back to Tahsin to ask what had happened to the boys. Tahsin told him that Ali Hassan al-Majid had talked to all the *mustashars* and told them that no one should ask about the fate of those who had disappeared.[23]

* * *

---

[22] Middle East Watch interviews, Jedideh Zab complex, Erbil, May 2 and July 16, 1992.

[23] Middle East Watch interview, Suleimaniyeh, May 21, 1992. Many of the most hated *mustashars*, including Tahsin Shaweis himself, later changed sides and joined the *peshmerga* during the March 1991 uprising--creating a further twist in the complicated landscape of Kurdish politics.

The Zangana tribal villages to the east fared even worse. A large army task force, including scores of tanks, set out from the *nahya* of Sengaw and moved west, with the goal of subduing an important PUK base in the Gulbagh valley, less than ten miles east of Qader Karam. It took the army a whole day to crush the resistance in this area, although it was clear that the *peshmerga* were fighting against impossible odds. Three of them died in Qeitoul; another seven fell in Garawi. The PUK's 59th *teep*, together with survivors from the 55th *teep* in Qara Dagh, entrenched themselves in Upper and Lower Gulbagh on April 10 and held off the troops until nightfall. Two more *peshmerga* were "martyred" here, and by 8:00 p.m. the survivors realized that their position was hopeless and withdrew to the south.[24]

The people of Qeitawan, a village of one hundred mud houses on the Baserra river, were alerted to the arrival of Anfal by the sound of government aircraft bombing the nearby village of Garawi. Hoisting the small children on to their shoulders, with only the clothes they stood up in, they took flight. But the army dragnet caught up with them before nightfall. "We were rich," said an old woman who survived. "We had fruit, gardens, all was looted. They took our tractors, water pipes, even the lantern we used to light the rooms when it was dark."[25] Deciding that they had no alternative, her four sons, aged thirty-five to forty-one, made their way to Aliawa, an old destroyed village on the outskirts of Qader Karam, where they gave themselves up to a *mustashar* by the name of Sheikh Mu'tassem Ramadan, of the Barzinji tribe.[26] "But Mu'tassem handed them all over to the government" and she never saw them again.

The people of nearby Qeitoul, by contrast, had taken to the hills a full two weeks before Anfal reached them, as soon as they heard news

---

[24] Middle East Watch interview with a former PUK commander who took part in the Gulbagh Valley fighting, Kalar, March 30, 1993. The fall of Upper and Lower Gulbagh was reported in Chamchamal *Istikhbarat* cable no. 10488 of April 11, 1988.

[25] Middle East Watch interview, Suleimaniyeh, May 21, 1992.

[26] One of the most feared of the *mustashars*, Sheikh Mu'tassem was the brother of Sheikh Ja'far Barzinji, a Saddam Hussein loyalist who was governor of Suleimaniyeh and later became chairman of the official Executive Council of the Kurdistan Autonomous Region.

of the fall of the Sergalou-Bergalou PUK headquarters on March 19. There were no *peshmerga* in the vicinity at the time, and they felt unprotected. From their hiding places above the village, they saw the soldiers entering Qeitoul, preceded by *jahsh* units and with helicopters providing air support. After a brief debate they decided to make for the town of Chamchamal, several hours walk to the north. But they were captured in the mountains by troops under the command of Brig. Gen. Bareq. The army registered their names and sent them off in two groups of trucks. One headed east toward Suleimaniyeh; the other west, in the direction of Kirkuk. Many never returned.

Other villagers nearby were caught unawares in their homes by the army's lightning attack. This happened, for instance, in Qirtsa, a remote village of one hundred houses on a dirt road beyond Qeitoul. Qirtsa was a peaceful place--"We were living naturally, no *peshmerga*, no government," remembered one resident--and the attack, early in the morning, found the villagers still in bed. Only a handful managed to reach the safety of the mountains. Gen. Bareq himself was in personal command of the troops that came in that morning, rounding up all the village men on the spot and handcuffing their hands behind their backs.

The men were trucked away first. Then another army IFA departed, this one loaded up with the villagers' livestock. Finally the women, children and elderly were driven off, but only after the soldiers had looted their homes. As they waited for the IFAs and coasters that would take them away, the women watched the village set afire and then leveled with bulldozers. Sixty people disappeared from Qirtsa, including every male under the age of forty and many of the women. Another sixty vanished from neighboring Qeitoul. "I am not sorry for myself but for the young women," a female survivor of Qirtsa told Middle East Watch. "We do not know what happened to them. They were so beautiful. If they were guilty, of what? Why? What had they done wrong?"[27]

They had done nothing wrong, of course. They were simply Kurds living in the wrong place at the wrong time. But their fate may shed important light on one of the great enigmas of the Anfal campaign. Throughout Iraqi Kurdistan, adult males who were captured were disappeared en masse--as the standing orders of June 1987 demanded. In certain clearly defined areas, however, the women and children

---

[27] Middle East Watch interview, Suleimaniyeh, May 12, 1992.

vanished as well.[28]   In some cases, such as the Gulbagh Valley, these mass disappearances occurred in areas where the troops had encountered significant *peshmerga* resistance.

* * *

THE PLAN OF CAMPAIGN:
(3) SENGAW AND SOUTHERN GERMIAN

Some *peshmerga* had managed to escape to the north, hiding out in the hills above the Kirkuk-Chamchamal road. Others were driven in the opposite direction, however, as army units swept methodically southward from the *nahya* of Sengaw to the village of Drozna, near the source of the Awa Spi river. According to witnesses, close to twenty villages were overrun and destroyed in this one small area: the PUK bases at Darawar and Banamurt (from which large numbers of people reportedly disappeared); a nearby cluster of villages including Upper and Lower Hassan Kanosh, Tapa Arab, Kareza, Dobirya and three adjacent hamlets, each called Penj Angusht[29]; and a little further to the east, Hanzira, Segumatan, Kelabarza, Darzila, Kalaga and Darbarou.[30] The hundreds of villagers captured in this sector were taken to Chamchamal; the *nahya* of Sengaw would have been closer, but it had been destroyed during the campaigns of 1987. The surviving *peshmerga* were now driven hard up against the southern edge of the Qara Dagh mountains, where the Second Anfal had been fought to such devastating effect. This

---

[28] For a sense of these regional patterns, see Appendix D, p.365.

[29] A U.S. Defense Mapping Agency map of this sector, sheet no. 5060 III, shows the villages of Penj Angusht-i Haji Muhammad, Penj Angusht-i Haji Muhammad Agha and Penj Angusht-i Sheikh Mustafa. Such multiple naming is very common in rural Iraqi Kurdistan.

[30] Middle East Watch interviews with former residents of Hassan Kanosh and Drozna, Shoresh complex and Suleimaniyeh, May 9 and June 28, 1992. Resool lists all of these villages among a total of sixty-seven destroyed in the *nahya* of Sengaw during Anfal.

confined area, where the *peshmerga* now also had to contend with other troop units coming from the south, was one of the bloodiest cockpits of the Anfal campaign.

At the southernmost extreme of Germian, where it borders on the Arabized area of Diyala, the first column of troops had set out from the town of Kifri at 6:30 a.m. on April 9. Later that same morning, other columns departed from their bases at Kalar, Peibaz and Pungalle. Their basic strategy was the same as in northern Germian: to launch a huge enveloping movement from several directions at once; to carry out mass arrests of all the civilians they encountered; to destroy their villages; to funnel escaping villagers toward the main road or to prearranged collection points; and to channel the surviving *peshmerga* into confined areas from which there was no escape. The first step, however, was to annihilate known PUK strongholds.

The initial target of the Kifri column, under the command of a Brigadier General Sami of the First Corps, was the large village of Omerbel, home to the tribe of the same name.[31] There had been a PUK base on the outskirts of Omerbel ever since the founding of the organization in 1976, and a hundred fighters were on hand when the army attack began. This was a battle-hardened *peshmerga* force, one which had managed to repel a major army offensive the previous April. Although the assault force had included tanks and armored personnel carriers, it had been forced to retreat after taking heavy casualties, and its failure was emblematic of the regime's inability to achieve its goals during the spring 1987 campaign.

Brig. Gen. Sami's force reached Omerbel by mid-morning and immediately encountered fierce resistance from *peshmerga* using the heavy weapons that they had captured a year earlier. According to the PUK commander who directed the battle, the siege lasted for two whole days, and this is borne out by the terse battlefield reports from *Istikhbarat*.[32]

---

[31] The general's full name is not given. The Kifri column was made up of troops from the 417th and 444th Infantry regiments, supported by the 100th, 131st and 197th National Defense Battalions. Kalar *Istikhbarat* cables to Eastern Region *Istikhbarat*, nos. 10212 and 10238, April 9, 1988.

[32] Middle East Watch interview with PUK regional commander, Suleimaniyeh, August 1, 1992; supporting details provided by an interview with a former inhabitant of Omerbel, Banaslawa complex, July 7, 1992.

The army responded, however, as it had in Tazashar, by sending advance units on a flanking mission to destroy the villages that lay immediately beyond the target. "1015 hrs: village of Chwar Sheikh stormed and demolished," an April 10 cable reported. (The village of Chwar Sheikh lay three miles to the north.) Omerbel was now under siege from all sides, and by nightfall the *peshmerga*, realizing that further resistance was useless, had withdrawn. The civilian population had already fled, but they were quickly surrounded by troops in the mountains, arrested and trucked away.

The main column continued northward, mopping up a smaller PUK base at Tukin and then recording a monotonous sequence of another twenty villages "destroyed and burned" over the course of the next week, as far north as the Awa Spi river. One of these was Aliyani Taza ("New Aliyan"), a small village of twenty homes, where a retreating band of PUK fighters had taken up defensive positions.[33] "Muhammad," a 32-year old member of the *peshmerga* backing force, was at home when the troops arrived on the morning of April 13.

> The government was advancing from all directions, so it was impossible for us to stay. We headed for Mil Qasem village. We took our wives and children and put them in tractor carts, and we took the animals, and we put all our belongings on the carts. We thought that the army was going to put us in tents at the division base (*firqa*) on the other side of the [Diyala] river. That is what we heard as we were leaving. The *peshmerga* didn't stay; they dispersed and went to the mountains.[34]

It took Muhammad and his family three days to reach Mil Qasem, normally a journey of less than two hours. From there the soldiers led them to the main road, and ordered them to drive under armed guard to the fort at Qoratu, headquarters of the army's 21st Infantry Division.

---

[33] Aliyani Taza is reported as having been "burned and destroyed" at 08:30 a.m. on April 13, in a "secret and urgent" cable from Kalar *Istikhbarat* to Eastern Region headquarters, no.10687 of April 13, 1993.

[34] Middle East Watch interview, Aliyani Taza village, March 30, 1993. Identity concealed, at subject's request.

The fort would be the first stop in Muhammad's journey through the bureaucracy of Anfal.

Meanwhile, on April 11, a secondary task force under the command of Captain Abed Awad of the 417th Infantry Regiment had split off temporarily to take care of Daraji, an outlying village a few miles to the west of Omerbel. "The inhabitants who surrendered to the column were evacuated to a specially prepared camp close to the 21st Infantry Division," that evening's intelligence report noted--a rare official comment on the removal and mass detention of civilians, and an explicit reference to the fort at Qoratu.[35]

After pitching camp at Daraji that night, Capt. Awad's task force retraced its steps the next morning to rejoin the main column. On the way, it paused to burn Belaga al-Kubra and Belaga al-Sughra, which like Daraji were villages of the Daoudi tribe. Affection for the *peshmerga* ran deep here, according to Rashad, a farmer in his early 60s: "They were all our sons and daughters, all our brothers, all our people. We loved them." Rashad was at home when the bombing and shelling began at lunchtime. With the rest of the village, he and his wife Fekri fled to the hills, but the aircraft pursued them; Fekri was hit by gunfire and killed. Those who survived the air attack were soon hunted down by a contingent of *jahsh* headed by two *mustashars* from Kifri, Sheikh Karim and Sa'id Jaff, and trucked away--presumably also to the "specially prepared camp" at Qoratu, the first step in a journey that would end in their deaths. Among the villagers who disappeared from Belaga al-Kubra that day were Rashad's son Akbar, three nephews, two nieces and their six young children, all aged from one to seven.[36] Such a heavy proportion of women and children among the disappeared was characteristic of Anfal in the Daoudi tribal area.

* * *

The first targets of the army units that left Kalar on the morning of April 9, commanded by Major Munther Ibrahim Yasin, were the twin villages of Upper and Lower Tilako, where part of the shattered first

---

[35] Cable from Kalar *Istikhbarat* to Eastern Region *Istikhbarat* headquarters, no. 10468, April 11, 1988.

[36] Middle East Watch interview, Sumoud complex, May 20, 1992.

malband of the PUK had installed itself after the rout in Qara Dagh.[37] The troops' advance seems to have been relatively painless, and by the early morning of April 11 both Tilakos had been destroyed after a short firefight that left just four soldiers wounded. This area, inhabited by the Roghzayi branch of the Jaff tribe, was poorly mapped, and helicopters were needed to airlift troops into zones that were inaccessible by road. Major Yasin's forces passed through several villages whose existence was not even officially recorded. But they destroyed them all regardless.

Few, if any, Kurdish tribal groups were worse hit by Anfal than the Jaff-Roghzayi. The Roghzayi, one of a half-dozen subdivisions of the Jaff, used to inhabit more than one hundred villages in this area; all of them were wiped out during Anfal. The head of the Roghzayi, an elderly man named Mahmoud Tawfiq Muhammad (b.1927), lived in Barawa, a village tucked away in a narrow plain at the southeastern tip of Germian, close to the Qara Dagh mountains and ringed by important PUK bases. Although Barawa fell within the Third Anfal theater, its inhabitants had been terrified into flight by the chemical attacks that took place at the end of March during the Second Anfal.

Mahmoud was a prosperous man, and twenty-four members of his immediate family lived in a large, sprawling house surrounded by vineyards and the rich gardens where they grew apples, figs and pomegranates. Artillery fire and aerial bombing had become part of daily life, and it took chemical weapons to destroy their morale. After the attacks on Sayw Senan and other targets in Qara Dagh at the end of March, the people of Barawa held an urgent meeting. Even though the PUK was present in the village, Mahmoud remembered, "We decided to surrender to the government, the father of the people, since we were only poor farmers with no relations to any political party. Instead, they did what they did." His son added, "When we went to them, the government captured us, looted everything and Anfalized us. Nothing remained."[38]

The people of Barawa abandoned their homes and their property and headed for another Roghzayi settlement called Kulajo, a place of forty or fifty households that lay several days' walk away over the

---

[37] The officer is identified in Kalar *Istikhbarat* to Eastern Region *Istikhbarat* headquarters, cable no. 10212, April 9, 1988.

[38] Middle East Watch interview, Sumoud complex, May 20, 1992.

mountains, to the southwest. Although the Third Anfal had not yet
officially begun, the hills were already full of soldiers. At each
checkpoint, the villagers explained that they were making for the
government lines in order to surrender. The troops allowed them to pass
unhindered and eventually they reached Kulajo, where they spent two
nights safely. But on the third day they saw that the village where they
had sought refuge was surrounded.

According to army intelligence reports, the Kalar task force
arrived at Kulajo at 11:15 on the morning of April 13. Just before the
troops got there, they encountered a brief flurry of resistance on their
right flank, from a place called Tapa Sawz, "so this village was crushed
and destroyed, and four rifles were confiscated."[39] Taymour Abdullah
Ahmad, a boy of twelve at the time of Anfal, had lived in Kulajo since he
was three.[40] His father, a wheat farmer, owned a little land there, and
like all the men was a member of the village's "backing force." Taymour
was the eldest of four siblings. Since the family's move from nearby
Hawara Berza, three daughters had been born. Unlike their kinfolk
fleeing from other villages in the area, Taymour told Middle East Watch,
the people of Kulajo had stayed in their homes until the last moment.
But now, seeing the tanks and heavy artillery advancing toward them
from Tilako, an hour's walk away across the plain, each family ran up a
white flag from its roof and took flight. The men, including Taymour's
father, concealed their weapons in the village wells and other hiding
places. Taymour helped his parents to cram a few hastily collected
household possessions on to their rickety tractor-drawn cart. Assuming
that they would return to their homes before too long, they planned to
take temporary refuge in the large new complex of Sumoud, outside
Kalar, where some relatives had been relocated as a result of the village
clearance campaign of the previous spring. But the people of Kulajo, and
the fugitives from Barawa, found that the army had left only a single exit
route open for them, a "funnel" as it were, that directed them south

---

[39] Cable from Kalar *Istikhbarat* to Eastern Region *Istikhbarat* headquarters, no.
10687, April 13, 1988.

[40] The story of Taymour--for a long time the only known survivor of an
Anfal execution squad--has been widely reported. The account given here is
from a Middle East Watch interview, Sumoud complex, July 29, 1992.

toward the village of Melistura, close to the main Kifri-Kalar highway.[41] The journey to Melistura took two hours by tractor; they moved slowly because the vehicle was so heavily laden.

Having destroyed Kulajo, the troops pressed on to the north, followed by a line of bulldozers and empty IFA trucks. They soon reached Hawara Berza, Taymour's birthplace, and it, too, is recorded on the daily intelligence report as "burned and demolished."[42] The next tiny hamlet, Kona Kotr, was abandoned by the time the army arrived. All six of its families had already fled. But they ran into an army patrol in the mountains, and were also ordered to proceed to Melistura. An officer promised that no one would be harmed, and that they would all be rehoused in a new complex that would be built soon. As it turned out, however, thirty-four people were to disappear from Kona Kotr's six households--a pattern that was repeated across the Jaff-Roghzayi area. Mahmoud Tawfiq Muhammad of Barawa, the elderly tribal head, lost thirty-seven members of his extended family from Barawa village-- including his two wives and ten children, aged two to fifteen, as well as his son and daughter-in-law and their six small children. Another twenty-five relatives disappeared from neighboring Tapa Garus village, a *peshmerga* base--more than half of them children.[43]

On April 15, in heavy rain, the troops of the Kalar column reached the northernmost limit of their operations, storming and burning Qulijan, a village close to the Awa Spi river. One family fleeing Qulijan ran into a contingent of *jahsh* in the hills, headed by a local *mustashar* named Fatah Karim Beg. "Your time is over," he told them. "This is the

---

[41] Villagers from other parts of southern Germian were reportedly funneled toward the town of Maidan, on the far side of the highway.

[42] The army recorded the exact time of the burning of Hawara Berza as 17:27 hours on April 17. Cable from Kalar *Istikhbarat* to Eastern Region *Istikhbarat* headquarters, no. 11180, April 19, 1988.

[43] Middle East Watch interviews, Sumoud complex, May 20, 1992.

time of the government."[44] They, too, were left with no option but to
head south toward the main highway.

The displaced villagers spent two days in Melistura, unable to go
any further, sleeping in the open fields. The crowds swelled until it was
impossible to count them. "It was like the Day of Judgment," recalled one
man from Kona Kotr who reached Melistura safely with his family and
his farm animals. On the third day the soldiers instructed everyone to
move on. Army trucks were brought in from the military base at Kalar,
and those who had their own means of transport were ordered to follow.
This rough caravan crossed the Diyala river into a stony, arid area that
had been forcibly Arabized in 1975 and then laid waste in the border
clearances of the late 1970s and the first years of the Iran-Iraq War.
Their destination was the fort at Qoratu, headquarters of the Iraqi Army's
21st Infantry Division--the "specially prepared camp," in other words, that
had been set up under *Istikhbarat* control in accordance with the March 15
order of the Ba'ath Party's Northern Bureau Command.[45]

* * *

By about April 18 or 19, ten days into the Third Anfal, the Kifri
and Kalar columns had completed their missions. All resistance between
the Kalar-Kifri highway and the Awa Spi river had been crushed; not a
stone of any village remained standing. A little way to the east, the
Peibaz and Pungalle forces were able to report similar success. The
Peibaz task force, commanded by Lt. Col. Muhammad Nazem Hassan,
took a couple of days to subdue PUK forces in the villages of Sofi Rahim
and Ali Wasman, and there were complaints that an unnamed *mustashar*
in charge of the 75th National Defense Battalion had fled the field. But
once these problems had been surmounted, the rest of the expedition
proved uneventful, and after razing another fourteen villages the task
force returned to base.

More serious obstacles lay in the path of the troops operating out
of Pungalle, a village some eight miles south of the important

---

[44] Middle East Watch interview, Sumoud complex, May 20, 1992. Several
other witnesses name Fatah Beg as the commander of *jahsh* forces in this area;
according to one, he was from the Bagzada branch of the Jaff tribe.

[45] Northern Bureau Command letter no. 297 of March 15, 1988.

Darbandikhan dam. On its first day out, the task force ran into stiff resistance from a *peshmerga* unit defending the village of Sheikh Tawil, already the scene of a fierce battle a few days earlier. The army commander, Lt. Col. Salman Abd-al-Hassan of the 1st Commando Regiment of the 17th Division, was wounded in an early exchange of fire, and without him the chain of command fell apart. One of the supporting *jahsh* battalions, the 131st, retreated in disarray; part of the army force, including another officer, was cut off and pinned down by *peshmerga* fire. The remainder pulled back two miles and called in reinforcements from the 21st Division at Qoratu.

Even with the help of airstrikes, tanks, missile-firing helicopters and heavy artillery, it took the army five full days to subdue the fifty *peshmerga* in Sheikh Tawil. But on the night of April 13 the village's defenders received the order to withdraw.[46] At 14:30 hours the next day, the new commanding officer of the army task force, one Major Salem, reported to headquarters that Sheikh Tawil and the neighboring village of Bustana had both been "occupied and destroyed." Fifty-three families were duly reported to have "returned to the national ranks."[47]

With this, the troops were free to drive deeper into an area that had been partly abandoned two weeks earlier by the large group of villagers headed by Mahmoud Tawfiq Muhammad, tribal chief of the Jaff-Roghzayi. The PUK, along with smaller contingents of *peshmerga* from the Iraqi Communist Party and the Islamic Movement, had now been pinned back into their last redoubts in Germian--the string of bases along the western flank of the 5,900-foot Zerda mountain. This area had already been pounded from the east during the Second Anfal. Now it was under siege by troops advancing from the west, and by helicopter-borne Special Forces (*Quwat Khaseh*). It was impossible for the *peshmerga* to

---

[46] Middle East Watch interview with a *peshmerga* who fought at Sheikh Tawil, Kalar, March 31, 1993.

[47] This euphemistic terminology continued to crop up in official communications during the Anfal period, even though many of those captured were now to be killed rather than resettled. Cables from Second Corps *Istikhbarat* to Northern Bureau Command and other agencies, nos. 10780 and 10915, April 15, 1988. Bustana, it should be recalled, was the site of the surrender in late March of people fleeing from the village of Omer Qala as a result of the Second Anfal operation in Qara Dagh.

resist any longer. The last PUK defensive base at Zerda Likaw fell quickly; thousands of villagers flocked to the village of Faqeh Mustafa, where they were rounded up by troops and *jahsh* and trucked away; others made the arduous trek north along the spine of the Qara Dagh mountains, accompanied by the last of the *peshmerga* survivors. On the morning of April 20 the Pungalle task force returned to base, reporting that all its objectives had been accomplished.[48]

* * *

THE COLLECTION POINTS

"These people are heading toward death; they cannot take money or gold with them."
      -- *Iraqi Army officer during the looting of a village.*

Villages and small towns like Melistura, Faqeh Mustafa and Maidan in the south of Germian, and Aliawa and Leilan in the north, were the first collection centers through which the fleeing civilians were funneled. In some cases, their places of origin were noted down at this stage and their identity documents given some cursory examination. After their initial capture, the vast bureaucratic machinery of a number of specialized party, police and intelligence agencies would be brought to bear on the problem of the Kurdish "saboteurs." But at this early stage of the operation, almost all those in evidence on the government side were either regular Army troops or members of the *jahsh* militia. It would be inaccurate to describe the initial collection points as "improvised," since the Kurds were clearly directed toward them in a coherent fashion. Yet at the same time places like Aliawa and Melistura showed real signs of porousness--the only point at which the efficiency of the Anfal campaign seemed to break down. In part this was no doubt because even the Iraqi Army's considerable resources were stretched in dealing with such huge numbers of prisoners; but in part it also reflected

---

[48] Cable from Second Corps *Istikhbarat* to Northern Bureau Command and other agencies, no. 11386, April 21, 1992.

the deeply ambiguous role that would be played in the roundups by the *jahsh*. (For a description of the *jahsh*, see above pp.43-46.)

For the villagers swept up in the northern Germian campaign, there were at least four principal collection centers: Leilan, Aliawa, Qader Karam and Chamchamal. Many captives were processed through two or even three of these centers in succession.

Leilan, a small *nahya* to the southeast of Kirkuk, appears to have lacked any sophisticated infrastructure for handling the large numbers of Kurdish prisoners who passed through. People fleeing the Jabari tribal villages arrived in Leilan in a number of different ways. Some made their way there on their own initiative, perhaps hoping that a town--even one of this modest size--would offer more protection than the exposed countryside, as well as food and water. But they were given a hostile reception; as they approached Leilan on foot, said one woman from the village of Qara Hassan, soldiers fired into the air above their heads. Others, men, were taken to Leilan from Qader Karam, where they had gone to surrender, in the custody of the *jahsh*. They were blindfolded and handcuffed.

On arrival at Leilan, the army took down basic details on each newcomer. The women wept and begged for mercy, but they were repeatedly told that they had nothing to fear, that they would be granted land by the government in a new complex and allowed to lead a normal life. But the women grew fearful when they were forcibly separated from their husbands, sons and fathers, who were crammed into an animal pen in the open air behind barbed wire. There were "a huge number of people" there, said one witness; "more than 2,000 men, women and children," according to another. There were army and *jahsh* guards everywhere, although security was less vigilant for the women and children, and a number managed to slip away in the initial confusion before their names could be registered. At least one woman was allowed to leave by army officers after being interrogated. Those who remained slept in the open air for eight or nine days, in the rain and hailstorms of early April, before the men were driven away in army IFA trucks to an unknown destination.

While Qader Karam itself served as the main processing point for all the villages in its jurisdiction, Aliawa, a destroyed village a little to the west, was the primary collection center for many people. During the Third Anfal it was the headquarters of the notorious *mustashar* Sheikh Mu'tassem Ramadan Barzinji, brother of the governor of Suleimaniyeh.

Mu'tassem's name came up repeatedly in interviews with Anfal survivors, along with those of five other local *jahsh* commanders--Adnan and Sayed Jabari, Raf'at Gilli, Qasem Agha and Tahsin Shaweis--as one of the principal agents of the roundup and mass surrender of villagers from central Germian.

Many factors drove the fleeing villagers--naive expectations that this campaign was no different from its predecessors, slender hopes of escape, fear of being captured in a prohibited area, terror of the troops who were burning their villages en masse. But a further inducement was now added: the promise of amnesty for those who gave themselves up. Using loudspeakers attached to the mosques of Qader Karam, the authorities repeatedly broadcast the message that all villagers had three days to turn themselves in--from Sunday April 10 through Tuesday April 12. During that time, they would even be permitted to return to their hiding places in the hills and recover the possessions with which they had fled. All the males who gave themselves up would be obliged only to serve a tour of duty in the *jahsh*. News of the offer spread quickly among the refugees, as townspeople spread word to their relatives that they had nothing to fear. *Jahsh* units under Sheikh Mu'tassem and the other commanders also dispersed into the hills. "They said that the government would not harm the men who surrendered, and that they would be given *jahsh* papers. They told them to bring their families and surrender," reported one survivor.[49]

Mu'tassem's *jahsh* units detained a large group of male prisoners for two days in Aliawa, where army personnel registered their names. "There were thousands of men there," according to one who passed through this transit facility, "*peshmerga*, deserters, draft dodgers and ordinary civilians from *peshmerga*-controlled villages." Here, the *mustashars'* message was repeated: the men would be taken to *jahsh* headquarters in Chamchamal, an hour's drive to the north. There they would be issued with *jahsh* identity papers before being returned to Qader Karam. At that point they were to go and find their families and their livestock, prior to relocation in a government-controlled *mujamma'a*.

On the second or third day of the roundup, Aliawa received a personal visit from Brig. Gen. Bareq, commander of military operations

---

[49] Several survivors told similar stories about Sheikh Mu'tassem, including this witness from the village of Kani Qader Khwaru. Middle East Watch interview, Suleimaniyeh, July 25, 1992.

in the Third Anfal theater. In his presence, the prisoners were filmed. According to another witness, a similar scene unfolded, probably on the same day, at the police station in the center of Qader Karam, where several hundred prisoners were also being held.[50] This time a helicopter touched down on the adjoining landing pad, and three men stepped out--Brig. Gen. Bareq, First Army Corps Lt. Gen. Sultan Hashem, and Ali Hassan al-Majid himself. Again, there was a videotaping session, and this footage was later broadcast on national television as film of "captured Iranian saboteurs." The news clip was broadcast repeatedly over the following weeks, to the point where the National Security Council began to complain that its use was becoming counterproductive: people were beginning to see that these were ordinary villagers, not *peshmerga* fighters.[51]

Hundreds of other prisoners--as many as 2,000 according to one estimate--were briefly detained in the deserted complex of Qalkhanlou, just outside Qader Karam, which had been built originally to house relocated villagers from the spring 1987 campaign. Hundreds more were held in an elementary school in Qader Karam, where the sexes were separated. "I was put in a room with many other older women," one woman remembered. "I was the only young woman there. I was very scared so that I covered my face with my scarf. I did not want to see anybody. We were held there for two days. Through the window I could

---

[50] Middle East Watch interview with a former resident of Khidr Reihan, Shoresh complex, July 1, 1992.

[51] May 2, 1988 letter, reference no. L. Sh. D/397, classified "personal and secret," from the Secretary of the National Security Council (*Majlis al-Amn al-Qawmi*) to the Interior Ministry, Office of the Minister, with copies to the Northern Affairs Committee of the Revolutionary Command Council and to the General Security Directorate. The National Security Council is a high-level advisory group headed by President Saddam Hussein. The letter also warns that "underground cells of the PUK" may organize an anti-government demonstration in Kalar to protest the fact that "saboteurs who returned to the national ranks along with their families" are being detained. "Returning to the national ranks" continues to appear in army documents reporting the capture of civilians during Anfal operations. The National Security Council's May 2 warning clearly implied that Kurdish villagers had begun to suspect that the term had now become a euphemism concealing a more sinister intent.

see the soldiers blindfolding and beating the men."[52] After two days, a military bus came and took the older women to Chamchamal, where they were abandoned in the streets, far from their homes and with no means of sustenance. But this was an exceptional case, and the reasons for it remain obscure.[53] According to one of the very few young male survivors from the Qader Karam area, "The people who surrendered to the government all disappeared. Saved were those who managed to stay in the hills, or went into hiding with relatives in the towns, or were saved by relatives in the *jahsh*, or paid a bribe to the local *mustashar*."[54]

Qader Karam itself did not survive Anfal. Once the town had served its purpose as a holding center, soldiers and Ba'ath Party members came from house to house to register the names of the inhabitants. At the same time, *Amn* warned the population over loudspeakers that no one should shelter Anfal fugitives, as happened in a number of towns. The people of Qader Karam were given fifteen days to evacuate their homes and move to new housing in the Shoresh complex, outside Chamchamal, and in early May the town was bulldozed. However, in a telling illustration of the logic of Anfal, these people were not otherwise harmed. They were even paid compensation of 1,500 dinars ($4,500) each for the destruction of their homes. The population of Qader Karam, after all, had been recorded in the October 1987 census. Despite its location in the middle of the war zone, the town was still, in bureaucratic terms, within "the national ranks."[55]

Chamchamal was the last of the smaller-scale detention places for the captured villagers of northern Germian. A large town and *qadha*, it

---

[52] Middle East Watch interview with a former resident of Sheikh Hamid village, Bayinjan complex, May 18, 1992.

[53] Middle East Watch is aware of other groups being spared either because of a bribe being paid or as the result of some other private arrangement with a local official, but neither appears to have happened in this case.

[54] Middle East Watch interview, Erbil, September 12, 1992.

[55] The destruction of Qader Karam was described to Middle East Watch by a former resident; interview in Shoresh complex, June 29, 1992. In April 1988, according to this witness, Shoresh was merely an open field, and those relocated there built their own homes under the supervision of a government engineer.

is one of the few population centers that remains intact in this part of Iraqi Kurdistan. For those who were trucked to Chamchamal from some other preliminary assembly point such as Leilan or Qader Karam, the destination was either the headquarters of the local army brigade (*liwa'*) or the headquarters of the *jahsh*.

Some male detainees were brought here by bus, and soldiers came aboard to take additional statements from them. Again, the prisoners were reassured that an amnesty had been declared and they had nothing to fear. But the mood was ominous, and through the bus windows the detainees could see thousands of hungry, ragged men, women and children on the army base.

Other men were roughly transported to Chamchamal in open-backed army IFA trucks. "We suffered much at the hands of the guards," said one. "We were blindfolded and had our hands tied, and we were made to get on and off the trucks several times. The trucks had a door and one step, but because we could not see or use our hands, many fell. It was chaotic."[56] "At the brigade headquarters," another man added, "we were literally thrown out of the trucks, and they took our names and addresses."[57] After the stop at the army brigade headquarters, it became apparent that other government authorities were becoming involved for the first time. Winding through the streets of Chamchamal, the prisoners soon found themselves outside the offices of *Amn*, the feared secret police agency.

At this point, an almost unprecedented act of mercy and solidarity occurred. Anfal witnessed many quiet acts of individual courage, both by members of the *jahsh* and by Kurdish townspeople, and these saved many lives. But nothing quite compares to the response of the townspeople of Chamchamal as they saw their fellow Kurds being trucked through their streets. At enormous risk to their own lives--and in some cases at the cost of their lives--the townspeople staged a spontaneous unarmed revolt to liberate the detainees.[58]

---

[56] Middle East Watch interview, Erbil, September 12, 1992.

[57] Middle East Watch interview, Shoresh complex, July 1, 1992.

[58] A similar partial escape in fact occurred the following month in the town of Koysinjaq, during the Fourth Anfal, but on a much smaller scale.

The *jahsh* undoubtedly had a hand in the Chamchamal protest, and chance also played its part. The trucks that were being used to ferry the prisoners from the Chamchamal brigade headquarters were not military IFAs but commandeered civilian vehicles, with civilian drivers. Surreptitiously, the *jahsh* guards persuaded a number of these drivers to free their women prisoners. The drivers seized their opportunity to do so in the uproar that ensued when townspeople stoned the trucks and smashed their windows. "Even young children put stones in their dresses, threatening to break the windows," said Perjin, a 20-year old woman from Qirtsa village, who was able to break free.[59] The soldiers opened fire on the demonstrators, and even called in MIG fighter planes and helicopter gunships to rocket the crowd. "My dress was full of bullets from the Bareq soldiers," Perjin said. According to one account, five people died and twelve were injured.

The uprising seemed at first to have been a partial success. Several dozen people escaped, and the residents of Chamchamal offered them refuge--"for the sake of humanity." But this was not the end of the story. Those fugitives who were later hunted down by *Amn* agents were publicly executed, and in a macabre detail that recurs in many testimonies from Iraq, the surviving family members were even required to pay the cost of the bullets.[60]

On her second day in hiding in Chamchamal, Perjin watched a report about Anfal on the Iraqi TV news program. This was almost certainly the film shot while Ali Hassan al-Majid and his military commanders were visiting the police station at Qader Karam on April 10. It showed a group of "captured Iranian agents who belonged to [Jalal] Talabani." Despite his blindfold, Perjin thought she recognized her husband, Fareq, and a number of other men from her village. It was the last time she ever saw him alive.

---

[59] Middle East Watch interview, Suleimaniyeh, May 12, 1992. After the Chamchamal revolt, the authorities carried out house-to-house searches for those who had eluded the Anfal dragnet. It did not take a revolt to provoke this treatment: Similar searches were conducted in Kirkuk, Suleimaniyeh, Tuz Khurmatu and the large Sumoud complex, outside Kalar in southern Germian. All witnesses concur in identifying those who performed the searches as agents of *Amn*.

[60] Middle East Watch interview, Suleimaniyeh, April 1, 1993.

* * *

In the southern part of Germian, there were two principal counterparts to these holding centers. Kurds who were captured from the Daoudi tribal area, as well as other villagers who fled into this sector in the wake of the chemical attack on the PUK base at Tazashar, were taken first to an empty youth center in Tuz Khurmatu. Some had already been separated by sex at their point of capture; those who had been trucked in together were now placed in two separate buildings at the youth center and held there for periods that ranged from three days to about a week. The building that housed women and children contained about 4,000 people, according to one survivor who was able to recognize people from at least a dozen Daoudi villages.

As in Leilan, a few managed to escape with the help of the *jahsh*, who were placed on guard duty. A sympathetic *mustashar* even reportedly smashed one of the school's windows, allowing many women and children to escape at night. His action almost certainly saved their lives. The regular soldiers, most of whom were Arabs, behaved much more harshly, stripping the women of any money and valuables they were carrying and telling them that "they deserved all they got because they had supported the *peshmerga*." Those who disappeared forever from Tuz Khurmatu after the trucks came to collect them included hundreds of women and children. One elderly woman from a Daoudi village never again saw her brother, husband, father and cousin--or her two daughters-in-law and the elder one's six small children. Her younger daughter-in-law, "a very pretty girl called Leila, newly married," was dragged away by soldiers. She clung to her mother-in-law's dress, while the older women pleaded with the soldiers not to take her. But they shoved the old woman aside, and Leila was never seen again.[61]

For the rest of southern Germian, including the villages of the Jaff-Roghzayi, the main processing center was the 21st Infantry Division base at Qoratu, a large, ugly Soviet-designed fort typical of those erected throughout Iraqi Kurdistan during the 1980s. After the Kurdish uprising in Suleimaniyeh in September 1991, Qoratu was dynamited by Iraqi troops as they retreated to a new frontline further south. Two months later, the Iraqi writer Kanan Makiya visited the fort. On the side facing

---

[61] Middle East Watch interview with a family from the *nahya* of Naujul, Benaslawa complex, Erbil, April 19, 1992.

the Iranian border, he saw "forty, maybe fifty wagons of the sort Kurdish farmers hook up to the back of their tractors when carting feed or livestock." It was in just such a high-sided, wooden cart that Taymour, the 12-year old from the village of Kulajo, had arrived with his parents and three small sisters. Makiya went on, "Piles of faded dresses and *sharwal*, the traditional Kurdish trousers, were tumbling now from these wagons, or lay rotting amid the dirt and clumped yellow grass. Everywhere were plastic soles, all that remained of so many pairs of shoes."[62]

"There were at least ten thousand people in the fort," one villager recalled to Middle East Watch. "They were all tired, hungry and frightened. Nobody knew what was going on but I knew something horrible was in the making. No one could talk to each other. We were all silent and waiting to see what would happen."[63]

Some of the prisoners stayed in Qoratu for just a single night, during which they received neither food nor water; others said they were held there on a starvation diet for longer periods: "We stayed in tents at the division headquarters for three days. We received one piece of bread per person per day, and water. There were countless people there. The army registered all their names and asked them questions: the name of their tribe, whether they were with the *peshmerga* or the government. Everybody was afraid to say that they belonged to the *peshmerga*. They all said that they were farmers or shepherds."[64]

Taymour himself, recalled the scene at Qoratu clearly four years later. "All the people from the Kalar area villages were there," he said. "All the halls were filled. There were perhaps fifty halls, and each hall held from 100 to 150 people. We had very little food: soup, bread and water. Families were allowed to stay together. The guards all seemed to be army, all dressed in khaki. They didn't speak to the detainees. We were afraid that we were going to be killed, and everyone was talking to

---

[62] Makiya, "The Anfal: Uncovering an Iraqi Campaign to Exterminate the Kurds," *Harper's Magazine*, May 1992, p.55.

[63] Middle East Watch interview with a villager from Karim Bassam, Sumoud complex, May 20, 1992.

[64] Middle East Watch interview, Zammaki complex, July 24, 1992.

each other about this, because we knew this government campaign was different from the previous ones. The *jahsh* had lied to us."[65]

* * *

THE AMBIGUOUS ROLE OF THE JAHSH

The *mustashars* had indeed lied--or at least made promises that they were in no position to keep. A final word must be said here about the contradictory role of the *jahsh* forces during Anfal. As accomplices of the army, they undoubtedly helped send thousands of Kurds to their deaths. *Jahsh* units performed a wide range of appointed tasks. They protected army convoys and went into the villages ahead of the troops as advance scouting parties--or as cannon fodder. They combed the hillsides for those who had fled the army's advance and brought them down into custody, often flagrantly breaking their promises of safe conduct. They lied to the refugees, promising them the benefits of an amnesty that never existed--promising them, in effect, that this was to be just another in the government's unending series of resettlement campaigns, as a result of which they would enjoy the blessings of "modern life" in a government-controlled *mujamma'a*. On occasion, the *jahsh* also reportedly made false claims to army officers that villagers in their custody had been "captured in combat"--either to curry favor or, perhaps, in the hope of some monetary or material reward.

And material reward there was: It was the *jahsh* who benefited most directly from the application of Anfal in the literal, Koranic sense of the word--as the "spoils of the infidel." As the standing orders for the Anfal campaign had stipulated, "Every item captured by advisers (*mustashars*) of the National Defense Regiments or their fighters shall be given to them free with the exception of heavy, supportive and medium weapons."[66] "Give the men to us and you can have the property," was

---

[65] Middle East Watch interview, Sumoud complex, July 29, 1992.

[66] Northern Bureau Command directive no. SF/4008 of June 20, 1987. See above p.82.

how a Ba'ath Party "comrade" translated this to one *jahsh* leader.[67]
"The *peshmerga* are infidels and they shall be treated as such," a former
mustashar was told in a seminar run by army intelligence officers. "You
shall take any *peshmerga*'s property that you may seize while fighting
them. Their wives are lawfully yours (*hallal*), as are their sheep and
cattle."[68]   And indeed the *jahsh* looted the abandoned villages
mercilessly before they were burned and bulldozed to the ground. The
account given by one villager was typical of many:

> My husband and I were captured in a cave where we
> were hiding by *jahsh*, who did not say anything, tell us
> anything or give us any reason. They just asked for my
> husband's ID, took it and did not return it. The *jahsh*
> took everything from my house while I was standing
> there, everything, including all the furnishings. I did not
> have any money, but they took my jewelry and the
> animals and the tractor and loaded everything into a
> truck. They cleaned out all the houses in the village in
> the same way. Then I saw them burning the items that
> they found inside the house that were not useful to the
> soldiers and *jahsh*, like people's clothes. They used
> kerosene to set fire to the houses; I saw them.[69]

But while many *jahsh* assiduously performed the duties assigned
to them, it is also true that the Iraqi regime's old doubts about the
political reliability of the Kurdish militia were well-founded, and that
individual *jahsh* members were responsible for spiriting many people

---

[67] The remark was overheard by a villager during a conversation between
a military officer and a *mustashar* named Sa'id Agha in the village of Garawan
(*nahya* Rawanduz). Middle East Watch interview, Garawan, April 29, 1992.

[68] Middle East Watch interview with former *mustashar* Muhammad Ali Jaff,
Suleimaniyeh, May 11, 1992.

[69] Middle East Watch interview, Bayinjan complex, May 18, 1992. This
witness was from Galnaghaj, a village destroyed in early May during the Fourth
Anfal, but the essential details in her account were repeated in many other
testimonies from different stages of the Anfal campaign.

away to safety in the towns and complexes during the initial sweeps. It was only because of the *jahsh*, in fact, that this villager, having seen her home looted and burned, was able to survive at all. "Other *jahsh* guarded the Zils," she went on.[70] "They told the army at checkpoints that what was in the covered Zils was sheep. The *jahsh* saved most of the women and children from this village in that way."

It seems likely that some of the *jahsh*'s acts of clemency were inspired by bribery, a simple appeal to the same venal motives that also led to their looting sprees. One young man from the Zangana village of Qeitawan, in the *nahya* of Qader Karam, recalled how, at great personal risk, he persuaded the *jahsh* to help: "I was able to save many family members, women and children, taking them in groups to Kirkuk, Qader Karam and so forth. At the checkpoints I bribed the *jahsh* with yogurt and food and everything else I had."[71]

But other testimonies suggest that the most plausible reason for the *jahsh*'s occasional flashes of generosity was that they sincerely believed the lies that they told the villagers, having been told the same lies themselves. Middle East Watch did locate one former *mustashar* whose unit, or *fawj*, had been informed by the army that "they were going to arrest and kill or bring in men from the villages." But this was an isolated testimony, and it came from a village in the northern governorate of Dohuk, scene of the eighth and final stage of Anfal, during which the army's standing orders appear to have been modified in several important respects. A much more widespread sentiment, certainly representative of the Third Anfal in Germian, was that the *mustashars* and the men under their command remained ignorant of the regime's intentions until the roundups had reached an advanced stage.

"I was never told by the army where the captured villagers were being sent," said a *mustashar* from the Jaff-Roghzayi tribe, whose unit served in a number of villages in southern Germian, including Kulajo, the home of Taymour Abdullah Ahmad. "I always thought they were being

---

[70] Zils were an earlier Soviet model of the East German-manufactured IFA army truck, and the term is commonly used by Kurds to refer to either--even though by the time of Anfal IFAs were more widely used. We have generally referred to these vehicles as IFAs.

[71] Middle East Watch interview, Suleimaniyeh, May 21, 1992.

taken to the south.[72] I never thought that they might be slaughtered.
All the *jahsh* did was to assist the army in finding the best ways to get to
the villagers, and to capture the escaping villagers and deliver them to
the army." One day, he asked an officer what was to happen to the
captives. "We are taking them to modern villages," the man replied. But
this *mustashar* became suspicious later, when he had occasion to visit an
army camp (presumably Qoratu) and saw large crowds of detainees there.
Again he asked an officer what was going on. This man answered, "It is
none of your business." When the *mustashar*'s suspicions turned to
conviction, he says he was filled with remorse: "We spit on ourselves for
taking part in this operation; it was a crime."[73]

For some members of the *jahsh*, the moment of realization
appears to have come at the processing center in Tuz Khurmatu. Their
change of heart was quite visible to the prisoners. "When the *mustashars*
saw that the men and women were separated from each other," said one
former detainee, "they knew what was going to happen, and they were
upset. The *mustashars* tried to take the women away secretly."[74]

Another of the Warani villagers had been captured by *jahsh* who
took her to Tuz Khurmatu and handed her over to the army. Soon,
however, "the men were separated from the women and packed into
trucks that took them to Tikrit. When we asked what was happening, the
officers said that Tikrit would be more comfortable for them." At this the
jahsh became suspicious. "Some of them came to rescue the same people
they had previously captured and handed over to the army. One *jahsh*
freed ten women in this way. Then they took us to their homes and hid
us."[75]

But the real question about the role of the *jahsh* is what power
they actually enjoyed. In the operational hierarchy of Anfal, the Kurdish

---

[72] As had happened, initially, in other words, during the well-known
deportations of the Barzanis and others in the 1970s.

[73] Middle East Watch interview with Muhammad Ali Jaff, Suleimaniyeh, May
11, 1992.

[74] Middle East Watch interview with a former resident of the Daoudi village
of Warani, Suleimaniyeh, May 12, 1992.

[75] Middle East Watch interview, Suleimaniyeh, May 12, 1992.

militia was at the bottom of the pyramid, lower than the most ordinary foot soldier of the regular army. Until the appointment of Ali Hassan al-Majid, membership in the *jahsh* had conferred some measure of protection. *Amn* documents on village destructions carried out during 1986 explicitly spare those whose menfolk were *jahsh*.[76] Now, however, the rules had changed, and a number of pro-regime villages were burned and bulldozed along with those of the other Kurds.

The promises that the *jahsh* made to the captured villagers, even if sincerely meant, were empty. A prosperous farmer from the Jaff-Roghzayi village of Qulijan in southern Germian, fleeing his burning village, sought out the forces of Fatah Karim Beg, the most powerful *mustashar* in the district, for help. He was told to have no fear. "He issued me with a paper saying that I was with him, the *mustashar*, and that I had seven families with me. He told me that if I carried this letter the army would leave me alone."[77] Comforted by this encounter, the farmer made his way down to the main road to Sarqala, where a group of soldiers ordered him to halt. With confidence, he handed them the *mustashar's* letter of safe conduct. "Who is this Fatah Beg?" a soldier asked. And using an expression that is grossly insulting in Arabic, he sneered, "He is my shoe." The letter was worthless, and the farmer was taken with all the other detainees to the 21st Division fort at Qoratu.

* * *

Several former *mustashars* have given Middle East Watch accounts of a number of meetings in Erbil and Kirkuk with Ali Hassan al-Majid and the commanders of the Army's First and Fifth Corps. At one of these meetings, in August 1988, al-Majid told the *mustashars* that the Anfal campaign was now to be taken into Badinan, the mountainous northern stronghold of Mas'oud Barzani's KDP. But on the personal orders of Saddam Hussein, the Badinan Kurds were to be given one final chance to "return to the national ranks." Clemency would be shown to any

---

[76] A handwritten December 1986 letter from the Northern Affairs Committee of the Revolutionary Command Council reports on the destruction of three villages, but approves a First Army Corps recommendation to spare others because their inhabitants are members of the *jahsh*.

[77] Middle East Watch interview, Sumoud complex, May 20, 1992.

saboteurs who surrendered from that area--presumably until military operations began in the north.[78]

Al-Majid asked for questions, and several men rose to speak. Among them was Sheikh Mu'tassem Ramadan Barzinji, the powerful and widely feared *mustashar* from Qader Karam who had handed over thousands of civilians to the army. According to another *mustashar* who was present that day in Erbil's Hall of the Cultural Masses, Sheikh Mu'tassem appeared skeptical. Would the promise be honored, he asked, given what had happened in the earlier stages of Anfal?[79] But the qualms of even such an influential Kurdish collaborator, a man who had done all that the regime had demanded of him, were contemptuously flicked aside. Al-Majid told Mu'tassem that he was "a black spot on a white mirror"; if he did not sit down, al-Majid would have him taken away and executed, "even if Allah intercedes." Before the Secretary General of the Ba'ath Party's Northern Bureau, even God Himself had limited powers.

———

[78] A memorandum from *Amn* Suleimaniyeh, dated July 11, 1988, appears to confirm this new policy. This document reads in part:

"Comrade Ali Hassan al-Majid, Member of the Regional Command and Secretary General of the Northern Bureau, has announced the following:

1. The saboteur who turns himself in and hands over his weapon and who is returning from areas that have not been included in Anfal operations up until now, will be granted amnesty for all crimes, including those of delinquency and flight [from military service].

2. *The saboteur returning without a weapon from those areas not included in Anfal operations will be pardoned* for the crimes of affiliation with a saboteur group and of delinquency and flight. [emphasis in original]

3. There is nothing barring the enlistment of the aforementioned in the National Defense Battalions [the *jahsh*]."

[79] Middle East Watch interview with former *mustashar*, Suleimaniyeh, June 30, 1992.

Fourth Anfal: May 3 - May 8, 1988

Legend:
- Approximate boundary of 4th Anfal campaign
- Main Anfal camp and facility — △ A
- Peshmerga command — Ⓟ
- Known chemical attack — ✶
- Resettlement complex (mujamma'a) — ▣
- Major road

Elevation (feet):
- less than 1000
- 1000 - 2000
- 2000 - 5000
- 5000 - 9000

SHEIKH BZEINI — Tribal area mentioned in report

Area from which women and children were taken and killed

© 1993 Michael S. Miller

6

FOURTH ANFAL--THE VALLEY OF THE LESSER ZAB, MAY 3-8, 1988

"Some were blind; some could not reach our village. The spirit left them on the way; they were all black."
-- Na'ima Hassan Qader of Galnaghaj, describing the exodus of villagers from the chemical attack on the neighboring village of Goktapa, May 3, 1988.

After the initial blitzkrieg in Germian--there is no other word for what took place there--the remaining *peshmerga* forces headed north. While the army prepared to confront them there, the intelligence apparatus spared no effort to track down those who had slipped to safety in the towns or *mujamma'at*. On May 4, the General Security Directorate (*Amn*) issued orders for anyone who had surrendered in combat areas of the first three Anfal operations to be rounded up and handed over by the army into its custody for case-by-case evaluation.[1]

In the northern part of Germian, many villagers escaped this dragnet and survived by melting into the anonymous crowds of Kirkuk and the smaller Kurdish towns. But those in the south were less fortunate. Hemmed in on all sides by troops, mountains, well-guarded main roads and an Arabized desert area, they had little chance to elude their captors. Only a few lucky ones made it as far as Tuz Khurmatu or the new complex of Sumoud ("Steadfastness" in Arabic), outside the town of Kalar. Those who were caught accounted for the heaviest single concentration of disappearances during the Anfal campaign. While males

---

[1] "The following has been deemed appropriate," reads a communique from *Amn* Suleimaniyeh to the agency's local office in Chamchamal: "All persons who surrender in the theater where fighting took place during the First, Second and Third Anfal Operations, shall be sent to the Security Directorates with an explanation regarding the political stance of each one of them, in order to take the necessary measures [word illegible]." Communique no. 2827, May 4, 1988.

169

aged from 15-50 routinely vanished en masse from all parts of Germian, only in the south did the disappeared include significant numbers of women and children. Most were from the Daoudi and Jaff-Roghzayi tribes. Yet their tribal affiliation was unlikely to be the cause; there seems no reason why the Iraqi regime should have harbored any special hatred for these two groups. Furthermore, people from other tribes who fled or strayed south of the Awa Spi river were subject to the same treatment. Nor can the explanation lie with brutal or over-zealous local army commanders, since the detainees were transferred within a matter of days--still alive--to centralized processing camps. It was there that the intelligence services singled them out, referring to the highest authorities where necessary for a ruling on what to do in the cases of individual detainees.[2]

No single theory can adequately explain the mass disappearances of women and children from southern Germian, although they may in part reflect a mentality of reprisals for the stiff resistance that the army faced in such PUK-controlled villages as Tazashar, Omerbel and Sheikh Tawil. It was the inhabitants of these places, and scores of others like them, who suffered so grievously; in some cases, entire village populations appear to have been wiped out, with the exception of some of the elderly. In the absence of a comprehensive statistical survey, it is hazardous to estimate the total numbers who perished during Anfal. But by the most conservative estimate, it is safe to say that at least 10,000 Kurds disappeared from this one small area alone.[3] In only one other area was a similar pattern repeated; this was in a cluster of villages along the Lesser Zab river during the Fourth Anfal, in the first week of May 1988.

---

[2] This, in addition to the emphasis on the place of capture, is the particular significance of the *Amn* correspondence cited above at p.121. The governorate office of *Amn* in Erbil has evidently found it necessary to appeal to the agency's headquarters for a ruling on what to do with particular individuals in its custody.

[3] Resool, *op. cit.*, calculates that some 200 villages were destroyed in this sector during Anfal, with a total population in excess of 35,000. On the basis of numerous Middle East Watch interviews with survivors, a disappearance rate of 30 percent seems conservative. Middle East Watch hopes to prepare a comprehensive statistical survey that will allow for a more precise estimate of the numbers who died or disappeared as a result of Anfal.

Beyond the town of Chamchamal, the land falls away sharply. Immediately to the north is the broad valley of the Nahr al-Zab-al-Saghir, the Lesser Zab river, which forms the borderline between the governorates of Erbil and Al-Ta'mim (Kirkuk). (The Kurds call the river Awi Dukan--the Waters of Dukan--because it flows from the dam on the lake of that name.) It was this area which offered temporary sanctuary to PUK forces fleeing from the Third Anfal.

By about April 13, the *peshmerga* in Germian realized that further resistance was futile. The military leadership met secretly that day in Tilako--two days after the village had been burned by the army--and decided to organize an orderly retreat. They pulled back first to the village of Masoyi Bergach (Sengaw *nahya*), and then, on April 15, split up into three columns, with each taking responsibility for the safety of large contingents of women and children. Two groups headed for the Redar (Shwan) area, northwest of Chamchamal.[4] The other, led by the surviving nucleus of the first *malband*, made for the town of Askar, a few miles south of the Lesser Zab.[5]

In 1988, the river valley was studded with little Kurdish towns: *nahyas* like Aghjalar, Taqtaq and Redar, as well as other population centers of local importance such as Askar and Goktapa. Further north the Koysinjaq plain spread out, with its untapped oil reserves; to the northwest lay the city of Erbil, and the handful of villages on the Erbil plain that had escaped the army's spring 1987 assault. These were now targeted as part of the Fourth Anfal. To the north and east, the operation extended as far as the western shore of Dukan Lake and the last outcroppings of the Qara Dagh mountain chain.

As the Fourth Anfal began, the morale of the Iraqi troops could hardly have been higher. On April 17-18, in a devastating counterattack that cost 10,000 enemy lives, Iraq had retaken the Fao peninsula at the

---

[4] Redar is the town in the center of the *nahya* and tribal area of Shwan, and the two names are often used interchangeably.

[5] This account of the PUK withdrawal is based on Middle East Watch interviews with two former *peshmerga* commanders in Suleimaniyeh and Kalar, March 28 and 30, 1993.

head of the Persian Gulf, reversing the most humiliating loss of the eight-year war and paving the way for Iran's final defeat.[5]

* * *

THE CHEMICAL ATTACKS ON GOKTAPA AND ASKAR

Goktapa means "green hill" in Turkish--a language whose influence is often apparent still in this former part of the Ottoman Empire's Mosul *vilayet*. Although the whole village had originally been built on the slopes of the hill, some families had resettled on the flat farmland on the south bank of the Lesser Zab after Goktapa was burned in 1963, during the first Ba'ath regime, after the first of many fierce battles between government forces and the *peshmerga*. In truth Goktapa was more a small town than a village, with at least 300--some say as many as 500--households, as well as a school, a clinic and two Sunni mosques. The surrounding fields produced rich harvests of cotton, wheat, tobacco, sunflowers, potatoes, eggplant, sweet pepper, beans, okra, grapes, apricots, figs and watermelon. Goktapa even had electricity, although the women still carried water from the river on donkeys.

Goktapa had endured the repression familiar to most villages in the prohibited areas. From a checkpoint outside the *nahya* of Aghjalar, half an hour away by car on a paved road, the army tried with mixed success to impose a blockade on all foodstuffs reaching the villages on the south side of the Lesser Zab. In 1982 or 1983, after a pitched battle between government forces and *peshmerga*, Goktapa was savagely attacked by helicopters, aircraft, tanks and ground troops. Among those killed was a 45-year old woman named Miriam Hussein, shot from a helicopter. There had been *peshmerga* in Goktapa since the far-off days of Mullah Mustafa Barzani, and after 1984 the village housed an important PUK command post. As a result it was bombed frequently. "We spent most of our lives in shelters," said one woman. When asked to describe the attitude of the civilian population towards the *peshmerga*, Fawzia, a woman of sixty, smiled. "The *peshmerga* were loved by the people," she said. "No one hates his own people." The *peshmerga* protected them from the army

---

[5] See Jupa and Dingeman, *op. cit.*, pp.6-7.

and *jahsh*, she added: "Naturally; if there were no *peshmerga*, they would kill us with knives, cut out our tongues."[6]

May 3, 1988 was a lovely spring day. The river valley was carpeted in green and dotted with roses and other flowers. Although it was still Ramadan, and the people were fasting, the women of Goktapa were baking bread, and the children were splashing in the Waters of Dukan. Throughout April, Goktapa had seen a lot of *peshmerga* coming and going, stopping briefly in the village to eat, bringing news of the rout in Germian and Qara Dagh, spending the night and then moving on. But there had been no fighting in Goktapa itself, and ten days had now passed since the last Kurdish fighters had been sighted.

An hour or so before dusk, the late afternoon stillness was broken by the sound of jet engines. Abd-al-Qader Abdullah Askari, a man in his late 60s, was a little distance from his home when he heard the aircraft. Everyone in this part of Iraqi Kurdistan knew of Abd-al-Qader and his famous family. His late father, Abdullah, had been the head of the Qala Saywka tribe, which owned thirty-six villages in the hills around Aghjalar. By the time he died, the old man's property had dwindled to seven villages, which he divided among his sons. Abd-al-Qader was given Goktapa, although "I always worked with my hands; I never liked to exploit anyone."[7] His brother Ali received the nearby village of Askar-- hence the name "Askari." In time Ali became a senior PUK commander and a close confidant of Jalal Talabani.

Askar, an hour and a half on foot from Goktapa, seems to have been the aircraft's first target on May 3, no doubt because the PUK's first *malband*, in retreat from Germian, had tried to set up its new base here. A formation of MIGs swooped low over the village, which was now full of *peshmerga*. There were eight dull explosions, followed by a column of white smoke that smelled pleasantly of mint. Borne on a southeasterly wind, it drifted as far as Haydar Beg, a couple of miles away. When it cleared, nine villagers of Askar lay dead. Members of the PUK rushed

---

[6] Middle East Watch interview, Bayinjan complex, May 18, 1992.

[7] The 1958 land reform did away with these old patterns of ownership. Abd-al-Qader Abdullah Askari continued to be acknowledged, however, as the effective leader of the village of Goktapa.

around administering atropine injections to those who had been exposed to the gas.[8]

Askar was not visible from Goktapa, and Abd-al-Qader was not especially alarmed when he looked up and saw the aircraft approaching. "I did not pay attention because we suffered from many bombardments. I thought it would be the same as in the past. We did not go into the shelters in front of our houses. No one paid any attention to the planes; we were accustomed to them. But when the bombing started, the sound was different from previous times. It was not as loud as in the past. I saw smoke rising, first white, then turning to gray. I ran away." But the wind from the southeast carried the smoke toward him. "I ran 50 meters then fell down. The smoke smelled like a match stick when you burn it. I passed out."

The bombs fell at exactly 5:45 p.m., according to Abd-al-Qader's daughter-in-law Nasrin, the 40-year old wife of his son Latif, a former schoolteacher. Nasrin remembered the time with precision because her family had a rare luxury: a clock mounted on the wall. She recalled counting four aircraft, although some other villagers say there were six-- and some added that a second flight of six dropped their bombs later. The smoke, said Nasrin, was red and then turned to blue. It smelled of garlic.

There was general panic and confusion; villagers were screaming, running in all directions and collapsing from the fumes. Nasrin remembered the general advice that the *peshmerga* had given: in the event of a chemical attack, head for the river and cover your faces with wet cloths. She grabbed a bunch of towels and ran to the riverbank with seven of her eight children. Her eldest daughter, who ran off in another direction, was later arrested and disappeared. The advice about wet towels may well have saved the lives of Nasrin and her family, since the wind blew the gas straight across the Lesser Zab river where she had fled, and one bomb even fell in the water. Dead fish floated to the surface.[9]

Today, a simple monument on top of the "green hill" memorializes those who died in the chemical attack on Goktapa. Survivors say that they buried as many as 300, although a list compiled

---

[8] Middle East Watch interviews with former residents of Askar and Haydar Beg, Askar village, August 2, 1992.

[9] Middle East Watch interview, Suleimaniyeh, August 1, 1992.

later by the PUK gives the names of 154.[10] Some died in the fields as
they tended their crops. Other bodies were found in the river. With the
help of a borrowed bulldozer, some of the villagers dug a deep trench in
front of the mosque that had been destroyed by the army in an earlier
raid, and buried many of the bodies that same night. Menawwar Yasin,
a woman in her early 60s, helped with the burial. "Some of their faces
were black," she said, "covered with smoke. Others were ordinary but
stiff. I saw one mother, nursing her infant, stiffened in that position."
Other corpses were covered over by the army with a rough layer of dirt
when the ground troops destroyed Goktapa several days later. There was
no time to do it any other way, an officer explained to a visiting member
of the Askari family--it was hot and the bodies were beginning to smell;
if they were left uncovered they might cause health problems for his
men.[11]   Whatever the exact number of those who died, it was the
heaviest toll from any confirmed chemical attack other than Halabja, six
weeks earlier.

* * *

In the wake of the Goktapa attack, villagers remembered, the
waters of the Lesser Zab rose quickly. It was a trick they had seen the
regime use in earlier campaigns, opening the sluices at the Dukan Dam
to block any attempt at flight across the river. The survivors from
Goktapa, Askar and Haydar Beg scattered in all directions. Some fled
south in the direction of Chamchamal, hoping to find sanctuary in the
complexes of Takiyeh and Bayinjan, on the main road to Suleimaniyeh.
Others headed west by back ways and goat tracks, travelling parallel to
the river into the area inhabited by the Sheikh Bzeini tribe. More than
fifty families from Askar were arrested on the morning of May 4 by

---

[10] Middle East Watch was given the names of thirty-eight people in two
families who died in the attack. More than half of these were children.
Interviews with Abd-al-Qader Abdullah Askari and other former residents,
Daratou complex and Goktapa village, April 20 and May 24, 1992.

[11] Middle East Watch interview, Suleimaniyeh, July 4, 1992. As a result of
his official contacts, this relative--who, as a city resident, was unaffected by Anfal--
was granted permission to return to Goktapa after the attack to search for
members of his family.

troops approaching along the main highway and were taken east in trucks to the complex of Suseh.

After passing out from the effects of the chemicals, Abd-al-Qader knew nothing more until he awoke the next morning in a strange room. A voice told him that he had reached the village of Mamlesi, some five miles west of Goktapa. He had been brought here unconscious by his son, the former teacher Latif. There was a smell of burning, and looking out they saw that most of the houses in Mamlesi were on fire. Abd-al-Qader and Latif crept into an air-raid shelter and waited there for three days and two nights until they were forced out by a sudden burst of gunfire at the entrance. Outside were four armored personal carriers, a contingent of troops under the command of an army major, and an IFA truck; the old man and his son surrendered and were driven away.

Meanwhile, Abd-al-Qader's daughter-in-law Nasrin and her seven crying children had found refuge in a cave. With her were thirty refugees from Goktapa, and another twenty from Mamlesi. At first light on May 4, 5:00 a.m., they went outside and saw helicopters hovering over the valley below. Some of the men had fieldglasses, and they watched in silence as the troops entered Goktapa later that morning. This account is borne out by army documents from the Fourth Anfal campaign, which note that troops had reached Askar at 5:30 a.m. on May 4 and were advancing north toward Goktapa.[12] Seeing the troops approach, Nasrin and her children fled into the hills, where they survived for ten days by extraordinary good fortune before finally reaching safety in the complex of Takiyeh. Another daughter-in-law, Fahima, was less lucky; she was captured by troops in the village of Jelamort and disappeared. (Yet another member of this ravaged family, a three-month old child named Avan, was involved in an incident that is reminiscent of the baby-snatching practiced by the Argentine military during the "dirty war" of the 1970s. Avan survived the chemical attack, although her mother, brothers and sisters all died. But a member of the *jahsh* abducted the infant from her crib and took her to his childless wife in Koysinjaq. The child was eventually retrieved by an uncle.)

* * *

---

[12] Handwritten daily report no. 8184 of May 4, 1988 from (signature illegible), Commander of First Army Corps, to Army Operations Headquarters.

THE ANFAL DRAGNET: EAST OF TAQTAQ

As in Germian, it appears that the army pursued a strategy of envelopment, attacking the Fourth Anfal area with at least a dozen separate task forces from several directions at once. Fragmentary handwritten field reports of the Fourth Anfal from the commander of the First Army Corps, Lt. Gen. Sultan Hashem, show that troop columns hit the Lesser Zab valley at first light on May 4, twelve hours after the chemical bombing of Askar and Goktapa. Some, operating out of Koysinjaq, attacked the villages along the north bank of the river; others converged on the south bank from Suseh and Chamchamal; two convoys moved out of Taqtaq, one headed north toward Koysinjaq, and the other crossing the river and cutting through the area inhabited by the Sheikh Bzeini tribe.

Most of the task forces reported only token resistance, but in a couple of places the *peshmerga* fought back hard, and even pinned the troops down under sustained artillery and rocket fire. On the morning of May 4, Lt. Gen. Hashem reported "fierce opposition" on Takaltu Mountain, a few miles to the northeast of Taqtaq. But by the end of the day, the mountain had been "cleansed after killing nine of them, whose bodies were left on the site." In the rugged Chemi Rezan valley, to the east of Goktapa, the task force operating out of Suseh ran into difficulties in one village after another: "0740 task force reached Surqawshan village, confronted saboteurs numbering 20-25....0900 task force was able to burn Awdalan and Kalabash after removing resistance....0945 Talan village burned after destroying resistance consisting of four groups of ten saboteurs." Lt. Gen. Hashem even found it necessary to call in reinforcements, more than 700 helicopter-borne *Amn* troops from Suleimaniyeh.[13]

By the late afternoon of May 4, however, the Chemi Rezan valley was quiet.[14] The next day was punctuated only by brief firefights in Goktapa and across the river in Gomashin. By May 6, the entire area was under army control. Over the next two days, military units moved

---

[13] Handwritten daily field report from First Corps Commander to Army Operations Headquarters, no.19/8179, 0500 hours, May 5, 1988.

[14] Handwritten daily report no. 8276 from First Corps Commander to Army Operations Headquarters, May 6, 1988.

north along the shore of Dukan Lake, burning everything in their path. By May 8, the Fourth Anfal was over.

Along both sides of the Lesser Zab river, the consequences for the civilian population were devastating. Those to the north, with few escape routes, were the worst hit, and some 1,680 people are listed as having disappeared from the six large villages of Kleisa, Bogird, Kanibi, Qizlou, Kani Hanjir and Gomashin. Many people from the south bank villages, such as Nasrin and her children, reached the safety of complexes; even so, the losses were catastrophic. As many as 500 are estimated to have disappeared from Goktapa alone, and hundreds more from villages such as Galnaghaj, Gird Khaber, Jelamort, Qasrok and Qamisha.[15]   One daily field report from the Army's First Corps for May 6 gives some notion of how many of these people were women and children. In addition to thirty-seven saboteurs, this notes the surrender close to Taqtaq that day of sixty men, 129 women and 396 children.[16]

Those who lived north of the river had no way of learning about the chemical attack on Goktapa, since the army had disabled the cable ferry that the villagers used to pull their rafts across the river. But the panicked flight of the survivors, many of them blind or dying, alerted people in the villages on the south bank to the fact that Anfal had now reached them. Some fled as soon as they heard the news from Goktapa; others stayed where they were. At midnight on the day of the gas attack, survivors arrived, "smelling of apples," at the village of Darbarou, an hour and a half to the west on foot. Despite this, the people of Darbarou did not seem to feel that they were at immediate risk, and stayed in their own beds that night. But at 10:00 the next morning, they found themselves surrounded by *jahsh* and regular army troops arriving from

---

[15] These are merely the villagers from which Middle East Watch was able to interview survivors. According to Resool, *op. cit.*, some seventy-five villages in the *nahya* of Aghjalar were destroyed during the Fourth Anfal, along with twenty-four in the *nahya* of Koysinjaq center, fifty-two in the *nahya* of Taqtaq, and sixty-one in the *nahya* of Redar. Army documents speak of 138 villages "burned, destroyed or purified" during the Fourth Anfal. As in the case of the Third Anfal, these lists include most of the villages whose survivors reported mass civilian disappearances to Middle East Watch.

[16] Handwritten daily report no.8280 of May 6, 1988 from First Corps commander to Army Operations.

Taqtaq. Aircraft flew overhead, bombing, and helicopters hovered over the village, with their loudspeakers announcing "Come out; there is a pardon for you." The villagers were rounded up and trucked away in IFAs as their homes went up in flames.[17]

Goktapa survivors also turned up toward midnight at Gird Khaber, a village of the Sheikh Bzeini tribe. People here had already sensed that trouble was brewing, and some of the men had taken the precaution of sending their wives and children away to the safety of the towns, taking refuge themselves in caves in the surrounding hills. As in Germian, there were false promises of an amnesty for those who surrendered, issued in this case by Qasem Agha, a one-eyed *mustashar* from Koysinjaq, whom people called "Qasma Kour" (Qasem the Blind). With the aid of this trick, Qasem Agha's forces captured 200 men fleeing from the Gird Khaber area.

But others in Gird Khaber were still at home when the Goktapa survivors arrived. They met early the next morning, in the pre-dawn darkness, to decide what to do. Some of the young men decided to take their chances in the mountains with the *peshmerga*, and it seems that some survived in this way. But most felt there was no alternative but to surrender. Accordingly, they made their way that morning to the village of Qamisha, where they knew the army was located, fearing that otherwise they too would be attacked with chemicals. It took them two hours to reach Qamisha, travelling packed into nine tractor-drawn trailers.

Army tacticians appear to have assigned Qamisha a role similar to that of Germian villages like Melistura and Aliawa--an initial assembly point toward which fleeing villagers could be funneled. The refugees from Gird Khaber found Qamisha occupied by a *jahsh* unit commanded by a *mustashar* named Borhan Shwani. Regular army troops were also in attendance, as well as a camouflage-clad contingent of commandos (*Maghawir*). "The army was firing into the air over people's heads, scaring them," one elderly resident of Gird Khaber said. "They were merciless with the old people."[18] A man from Gird Khaber recognized

---

[17] Middle East Watch interview, Koysinjaq, April 22, 1992. This witness supplied the names of eleven disappeared men from the village of Darbarou.

[18] Middle East Watch interview, Taqtaq, April 24, 1992.

faces from a half-dozen villages. An army officer with the two stars of a
first lieutenant was carrying out body searches and confiscating "money,
gold earrings, everything." Identity documents were taken away and
never returned.

A somewhat different procedure appears to have been followed
during the army attack on Jelamort, another Sheikh Bzeini tribal village
a few miles to the south of Gird Khaber. The troops did not reach
Jelamort until May 6, but the inhabitants had already heard of the
Goktapa bombing from fleeing *peshmerga*. They took to the mountains,
where they joined hundreds, perhaps thousands, of other refugees, hiding
in caves or under trees. But they were quickly surrounded by the army.
The troops opened fire, killing two men, and everyone else came out
quickly with their hands held high. Men and women were separated on
the spot and those from Jelamort were marched back to their village.
Again, as in Qamisha, the troops stripped everyone of their money,
valuables and documents, while other soldiers and *jahsh* completed the
business of looting their homes. Some of the houses were already
burning, and the bulldozers were at work on the cement structures.
Three empty army trucks waited nearby. The sight of the looting was
apparently too much for one member of the *jahsh*, who protested loudly.
But he was confronted by an angry military officer, who told him, "These
people are heading toward death, they cannot take money or gold with
them. The law of the state says they are going to die." The commander
of the *jahsh* unit came over at this point and disarmed his rebellious
underling, telling him, "It is the law of our state; you cannot do
anything."[19]

In Jelamort, then, the sexes were separated at the point of
capture rather than later at one of the regime's processing centers. This
was also the procedure in Galnaghaj (although married women from this
village were eventually trucked away with their husbands), and in
Qaranaw, just outside the town of Taqtaq, where all the women were
spared for reasons that remain obscure. "The army officers took all the
men," an elderly woman from Qaranaw told Middle East Watch. "Then
they held us in the village for two days. We could not eat or do anything.
We just sat in one big line. When we were waiting in the village, the

---

[19] Middle East Watch interview, Erbil, April 23, 1992.

jahsh and the soldiers burned all the houses."[20]   After two days, the women of Qaranaw were driven to Chamchamal in army buses and dumped in the street. "I asked one of the soldiers why they were leaving us like this in the city where we didn't know anybody. They replied, 'You are lucky that you have ended up here; your men have gone to hell.'"

To the north of the Lesser Zab, it was much the same story, as one village after another was captured and demolished by the task forces operating out of Koysinjaq. The villages of Gomashin and Kleisa, for example, lay on the north bank of the river, almost directly across from Goktapa. Anfal reached Kleisa on May 4, the day after the chemical attack. Like Gomashin, it housed a PUK headquarters and the village had a large *peshmerga* presence. ("Our souls were on their heads," was how one woman put it.) Most of the villagers had moved out of Kleisa two years before Anfal, to build new homes along the Lesser Zab, which narrows to a gorge at this point. They called the place Qolti Karez, "the pit of the underground stream." It was here that Anfal surprised them, and after a brief attempt to hide out in caves in the mountains, they were arrested en masse and disappeared.

In October 1986, Gomashin and neighboring Qizlou had provoked the wrath of the regime when a group of Iranian *pasdaran* passed through the two villages, making an unusual sortie so far from the border. Aircraft had rocketed Gomashin a short time afterwards, and villagers assumed that the raid was in reprisal. One projectile hit a woman named Aisha as she carried water from the spring, killing her instantly. Another pierced the wall of a house, wounding a woman named Hajer and her 18-month old child. Since there were no cars to take them to a hospital to have their wounds treated, both died within hours.

Peshmerga fleeing the rout in the south had converged upon Gomashin in the days before the Fourth Anfal. One teenager from Gomashin, a boy of thirteen at the time, estimated that 200-300 *peshmerga* were in the vicinity at the beginning of May. The day after the chemical attack on Goktapa, they decided to try to make their way to Iran, appropriating the village's tractors for transport. The people of Gomashin pleaded with them not to deprive the villagers of their only means of escape, but the *peshmerga* brushed aside their objections. At dawn, however, the empty tractors came back with their drivers, and the

---

[20]   Middle East Watch interview, Bayinjan complex, May 18, 1992.

villagers now used the vehicles to flee in the direction of Koysinjaq.[21]
The following day Iraqi aircraft and groundforces attacked Gomashin.
Many of the villagers were captured in flight and disappeared. One
witness said that 115 people from Gomashin were "Anfalized"; another
put the number at 130.[22]   On May 6, the First Corps reported that
Gomashin had been razed to the ground, together with Gird Khaber and
a string of other villages.[23]

---

[21] Like Chamchamal in the Third Anfal, Koysinjaq was the target of massive
house-to-house searches to locate survivors of the Fourth Anfal. Many people
disappeared as a result of these *Amn* sweeps.

[22] Middle East Watch interviews, Erbil, July 7 and 8, 1992.

[23] Handwritten daily report no. 8276 from First Corps Commander to Army
Operations Headquarters, May 6, 1988. This phase of Anfal also seems to have
sucked in some people who were not its direct targets. One curious case concerns
a driver and two porters--one of them a 25-year veteran of the Iraqi police named
Khasraw Khidr Sa'id--in the town of Koysinjaq. Sometime in early May, the
three men were approached in the bazaar by an *Amn* agent and three members
of the *jahsh* of Qasem Agha. They ordered the men to accompany them, saying
only that they had some belongings that needed to be moved. Khasraw Khidr
Sa'id's family later heard that the three men had been taken to the village of
Kanibi, just across the river from Goktapa.

Three days later the former policeman's family received a message via a guard
at the Topzawa camp, to say that the man had been arrested. (Topzawa's crucial
role in Anfal is described in detail below, at pp.209-217.) Beyond this, the family
dared not approach the authorities, for fear that they too might be disappeared.
This was the last word they received from any of the three men, who then
vanished into thin air.

Then, in January 1992, they learned that Khasraw Khidr Sa'id's name had
appeared on a document pasted to the wall of a local mosque. The paper turned
out to be a transmittal order from the Erbil office of *Amn* to the morgue at the
city's Republic Hospital. The letter was numbered 10160, classified "confidential"
and dated June 29,1988--six weeks after the porter's disappearance, in other
words. It ordered the hospital to bury and provide death certificates for four
"saboteurs," including Khasraw Khidr Sa'id; the list also included the name of
Hassan Muhammad Hassan Mawloud, the Koysinjaq driver abducted with him.
The name of the second captured porter appeared on a similar document posted
on another part of the mosque wall. Four days later, the family of Khasraw
Khidr Sa'id obtained his death certificate from the Erbil Hospital. It listed the

THE SHWAN AREA

While the region east of Taqtaq was being devastated in this way, other army units turned their attention to the *nahya* of Shwan (Redar), a short way to the west. Once again they were assisted by *jahsh* contingents under the command of the short, stoutly built *mustashar* Qasem Agha of Koysinjaq. The small town of Shwan itself had been destroyed in September 1987; several of the seventy villages in its jurisdiction had already been razed during the clearances that spring, their inhabitants being relocated to the newly built complexes of Daratou and Benaslawa on the southern outskirts of the city of Erbil.

As one moves west, the landscape becomes flatter and less dramatic. Here, the Lesser Zab valley begins to broaden out into the plain between Erbil and Kirkuk, although it is still broken up by craggy hills and horizontal rock outcroppings. On the face of it, the terrain here was far from ideal for guerrilla warfare. Yet from the evidence of a dozen interviews that Middle East Watch conducted with Shwan villagers, it is apparent that small *peshmerga* units (both PUK and a few KDP) hung on here for several weeks, fighting occasional skirmishes before retreating. A considerable number of civilians also managed to escape to safety through the army lines.

Many of the Shwan villages, being in relatively low-lying land closer to the highway and the cities, had never been "liberated territory" in the same sense as the more mountainous interior. More than one survivor spoke of government forces and *peshmerga* "taking turns" at controlling these villages. During periods of greater *peshmerga* influence, there was brutal, if intermittent, government harassment in all the forms familiar in the rest of Iraqi Kurdistan--punitive *jahsh* incursions, burning and looting, shelling from artillery, rocketing and occasional bombing from the air. After the spring 1987 campaign of village destruction, many army deserters had rebuilt crude homes in sheltered areas, and most of the remaining villages harbored large numbers of draft dodgers. In the Shwan village of Dellu, for example, a village of eighty mud and stone houses, fully half the men considered themselves active *peshmerga*,

---

cause of death as execution. This case strongly suggests that *Amn* may have forced civilian bystanders to play an auxiliary role in the removal of the property and effects of villagers during the Fourth Anfal, and then killed them to preserve the secrecy of the operation.

and the population was swelled by some fifty or sixty fugitives from military service.

Dellu had been destroyed and rebuilt twice before--once in 1963 and then again in 1976. The Fourth Anfal reached the village on the morning of May 5, with rocket attacks from helicopters and fixed-wing aircraft softening up the area for advancing ground troops from the 77th Special Forces. Some died in their homes. According to one witness, three or four elderly women and four or five children died in the initial attack, either burned to death or killed by artillery fire.[24] Twenty-eight villagers were arrested in the army roundup and disappeared; they included three women and one small child. The remainder fled to the hills, and many managed to hide out, eluding *Amn's* house-to-house searches, in Kirkuk, Chamchamal or in the Benaslawa complex, which had been built to house people from this area a year earlier, some six miles outside Erbil.

Many people were also lucky enough to escape from Khala Kutia, a 15-minute walk from Dellu, and from Zigila, where remarkably the army managed to capture only six elderly people, including the *mullah*, from a village of thirty households. All the rest had been forewarned and fled. From a hideout on a nearby mountain side fifty villagers from Darmanaw, in the Sheikh Bzeini area, watched as the army and *jahsh* looted and burned their village; they survived for twelve days in caves, eating nothing but wild grasses. Hunger eventually drove them down to the town of Taqtaq, where "we threw ourselves on the mercy of the people, kissing their hands." With the help of the townspeople and a local *mustashar*, hundreds of fugitive villagers from the Sheikh Bzeini area hid out for several days in a poultry farm, huddled together in the chicken sheds. Remarkably, the army never found them.[25]

Even some draft-age males escaped the Anfal sweep in the Shwan area. This happened, for example, in the village of Palkana, after it was attacked by regular troops and commando units, backed up with artillery fire, aerial bombardment and tear gas. The villagers took flight on the morning that Anfal reached them, crossing the Lesser Zab river on wooden rafts to outrun the approaching troops. Even without food supplies, this group managed to remain in the mountains for two months,

---

[24] Middle East Watch interview, Benaslawa complex, July 7, 1992.

[25] Middle East Watch interview, Daratou complex, April 20, 1992.

after which a number of young draft dodgers and army deserters slipped into the Benaslawa complex, which appears to have been sloppily monitored by the security forces.

More remarkable still in some ways was the escape of a group of sixty young draft dodgers from the village of Ilenjagh, a little to the east of Palkana and a few miles to the south of Taqtaq. Although Ilenjagh lay in the Shiwasur valley, a *peshmerga* stronghold, the village was vulnerable, since it was situated close to an army base and the paved road. In 1987 it was destroyed after a fierce battle, but the villagers defiantly returned to rebuild their homes in a secluded location a little further away from the army base. Almost the entire population survived Anfal. First, the women and children were sneaked into hiding in Taqtaq. Then the sixty young men fled with their weapons and dug into hiding places in the hills. Only two were captured. Moving from one place to another, the rest held out until the public amnesty of September 6, 1988, which marked the official end of the Anfal campaign.[26]

* * *

ZBEIDA'S STORY

The drama of the Shwan villagers' flight from Anfal with the help of the *peshmerga* is well captured in the testimony of Zbeida, a young woman who was nineteen at the time. Zbeida was a native of Serbir village, a sizeable place on the plain, toward the main Erbil-Kirkuk highway. Although Serbir was not a *peshmerga* village, it had been destroyed in the spring 1987 campaign that leveled scores of government-controlled villages on the Erbil plain. At first the villagers had been given two months to evacuate; officially, they were told that their homes were being razed to "protect them from harassment" by the *peshmerga*. A week later, their period of notice was shortened to just twenty-four hours, and they were ordered to move into the Benaslawa and Daratou

---

[26] It should be noted, however, that the amnesty did not put an end to their troubles. The sixty deserters were sent back to their army units, where at least some were beaten and mistreated before finally being released. Middle East Watch interview with Ilenjagh villager, Taqtaq, April 24, 1992.

complexes, which at this time were merely open fields with neither shelter nor infrastructure.

Zbeida and her parents moved into the city of Erbil--not into one of the complexes as the soldiers had ordered. Her two brothers, however, who were both active *peshmerga*, made for the PUK stronghold in the Sheikh Bzeini area. After being harassed by *Amn* in Erbil for three months on account of their sons' affiliation, the parents and Zbeida eventually moved to the "prohibited area" as well, in September 1987. Their new village was under constant government attack, and during one air-raid in February 1988, the family smelled a powerful aroma of apples from their shelter. When they emerged two hours later, they found that a number of *peshmerga* had suffered chemical burns although none had died.[27]

Anfal reached them on the morning of May 4, a year to the day after the destruction of Serbir. A helicopter had been seen circling overhead the previous day, so the attack was not entirely unexpected. At 4:00 a.m., the shelling began and the villagers immediately sought refuge in caves in the mountains. From this vantage point they could see the army entering a number of villages along the north bank of the Lesser Zab, rounding up the population and burning their houses. They witnessed the destruction of the villages of Qashqa and Khurkhur on the far shore. What they did not realize was that the soldiers were not only in the valley below but also in the mountains above their hideout.

Zbeida's family decided to flee in the opposite direction, to the east. They were fortunate, for the army soon descended on the caves and captured and disappeared their occupants. Zbeida's family, which was now accompanied by Rahman, one of the two *peshmerga* brothers, returned to their homes and paused there for a few minutes. But they could see the army approaching with tanks and armored personnel carriers, and they ran again. Looking back, they could see the soldiers tossing barrels of kerosene over their houses and setting them aflame. They ran on, with the troops in hot pursuit. Shells fell around them, but after crossing a series of small streams, they seemed to have thrown off

---

[27] A chemical weapons attack on this area was not mentioned by any other sources, and is not included in any of the PUK and KDP listings of such attacks. Nevertheless, the details of this account are persuasive, and the witness was extremely credible in all other respects. Middle East Watch interview, Daratou complex, July 15, 1992.

their pursuers, and they stopped to rest in the village of Turki, another *peshmerga* stronghold.

Turki itself soon came under shellfire, and the refugees ran toward the Lesser Zab, hoping to cross to the other side. They tried to wade, but gave up when the water reached their necks. Behind them, the *peshmerga* were putting up a determined defense with rocket-propelled grenades and mortars. Eventually, Zbeida's brother Rahman managed to fashion three crude rafts from planks and inner tubes, and Zbeida, her parents and sister managed to get across. Rahman, who remained on the bank, yelled at them to make for the safety of the *peshmerga*-controlled Qala Saywka area.[28]

On the north bank of the river, they found themselves in another abandoned village; this was Shaytan. In one of the empty houses, they found bread and dry clothes. Behind them, they could still hear Rahman shouting, "Go! Go! Run to Qala Saywka and follow the *peshmerga*!" They walked all that night of May 4-5 along a narrow path, resting for a few hours at dawn, until they reached the mountains, and a safe-looking cave. Setting out from their shelter in mid-morning, they could see the army continuing to burn villages in the flood plain below. In the late afternoon, by an extraordinary coincidence, they chanced upon Omer, the second *peshmerga* brother. He wept to hear that Rahman had been left behind and insisted on going back to join him, to try and help civilians cross the river and get away from the advancing army. But first he led his parents and sisters north, away from the river, to another village, Nerajin, where they managed to pay for places in a grossly overcrowded tractor-drawn cart. Finally, at about 4:00 a.m. on May 6, the exhausted family reached the relative safety of the Benaslawa complex.

Omer came to Benaslawa just once, in the middle of May. He stayed for two weeks, then left again in search of his brother. In August, the family received news that the two brothers had found each other and fought together in a battle with the army near Turki village in June. In this part of Iraqi Kurdistan, in other words, some *peshmerga* units held out for at least a month after the initial assault of the Fourth Anfal. But the *peshmerga* who brought news of the reunion of Omer and Rahman also brought news of their capture. Through binoculars, their comrades had

---

[28] In the *nahya* of Aghjalar. Rahman was evidently unaware that other army units were simultaneously laying waste to this area in the wake of the chemical attack on Goktapa.

seen them being arrested by the *jahsh* and driven away in army IFAs. Their parents, and their sister, never saw the two again.

* * *

THE FOURTH ANFAL COLLECTION POINTS

The villagers who were driven from their homes by the Fourth Anfal were subsequently taken to at least three temporary holding centers in the Lesser Zab valley. Harmota, an army camp outside the town of Koysinjaq, held a number of detainees from Gomashin and other villages for three days after their capture. Takiyeh, a complex that had been built in 1987 on the main road leading east from Chamchamal, was the initial destination for the trucks that carried away the survivors from the chemical attack on Goktapa and its environs. One Goktapa woman learned that her daughter, son-in-law and five children had been seen in an army truck at Takiyeh; another held her brother-in-law and his family of twelve. "The elder girl was seen crying to people to save them. She caught sight of a relative and yelled at him to try to save them, but he could do nothing."[29] Many refugees also made their way to Takiyeh in the wake of the Fourth Anfal, hoping to find refuge there, even though the residents of the *mujamma'at* had been warned that anyone offering shelter to an Anfal escapee would have their home demolished.[30]

But it was the town of Taqtaq itself, an important regional center of some ten thousand people on the north side of the Lesser Zab, which acted as the principal collection point for villagers rounded up during the Fourth Anfal. As in Qader Karam to the south, the numbers of detainees were such that more than a single holding center was pressed into service. Some prisoners described being taken to the *ameriya*--the town's military garrison, housed in one of the innumerable forts that dotted Iraqi Kurdistan, built to a standard design during the 1970s. An elderly man from the village of Darbarou told of being brought here in a convoy of IFAs, some carrying his fellow-villagers and the remainder loaded

---

[29] Middle East Watch interview with former resident of Goktapa, Bayinjan complex, May 18, 1992.

[30] Middle East Watch interview, Suleimaniyeh, August 1, 1992.

down with their chickens, sheep, goats and cows.[31] Along the way a pregnant woman in his truck gave birth. At the garrison he recognized people from more than a dozen villages in the valley, from both sides of the river, packed into a number of inner rooms, with men and women held separately. The villagers spent a single night there before being trucked off to a new, unknown destination.

The second location was variously referred to by survivors as "a corral"; "a fenced-in area used for animals"; "a livestock pen near the bridge"; and "some sheds used for cows and horses." Once again, there were hundreds of people here from a number of villages along the Lesser Zab Valley. Some witnesses said that families remained together here; others disagreed, saying that young and old were segregated. Guards stood watch, but at this point there was no interrogation. These were extremely primitive facilities, and they were used only for a few hours. The soldiers also had less than total control of the crowds, and, as in Germian, members of the *jahsh* aided in a number of escapes. As one convoy of trucks pulled into the detention area, a young woman jumped off, clutching her baby, and managed to run away even though the military guards opened up on her fleeing form with machineguns. In the confusion of arrival, two siblings from the village of Qasrok--an 11-year old boy named Osman and his elder sister--were approached by a *jahsh* guard, a stranger, who whispered to them, "Take a chance, there are no soldiers here, run away. If anyone asks you where you are from, tell them Taqtaq." Being a resident of a town or a complex would of course offer immunity, given Anfal's rigid bureaucratic logic. The pair ducked into a *jahsh* car that was bringing food to the corral and managed to slip out through the army lines. It was the last time that Osman saw his parents, two brothers and remaining three sisters--the youngest of them just three years old.

After their brief sojourn in the cattle-pen, the family was hustled once more into the waiting trucks, which lumbered across the bridge over the Lesser Zab and headed south, like so many of their predecessors, in the direction of the oil city of Kirkuk, home of the Ba'ath Party's Northern Organization Bureau. Army documents from the Fourth Anfal provide revealing evidence, from the government side, of what happened to the detainees. Buried in the scrawl of his handwritten field reports, Lt. Gen. Hashem notes briefly that two groups of captured civilians from the

---

[31] Middle East Watch interview, Koysinjaq, April 26, 1992.

Shwan area--fourteen men, twelve women and twenty children in all--
have been "sent on to the *Amn* administration of al-Ta'mim [Kirkuk]
governorate"--the clearest possible proof of the destination of those
heavily laden convoys of IFA trucks.[32]

---

[32] Lt. Gen. Hashem notes that on May 5 "forty-one persons... from various
villages came to our mobile base at Shwan"; on May 6, four men and one woman
"were detained in the prohibited village of Turki." Both groups were "sent on to
the *Amn* administration of Ta'mim governorate." Handwritten reports (numbers
illegible) from First Corps Commander to Army Operations Headquarters,
0600 hours May 6 and 0700 hours May 8, 1988.

Fifth, Sixth and Seventh Anfals: May 15 - August 26, 1988

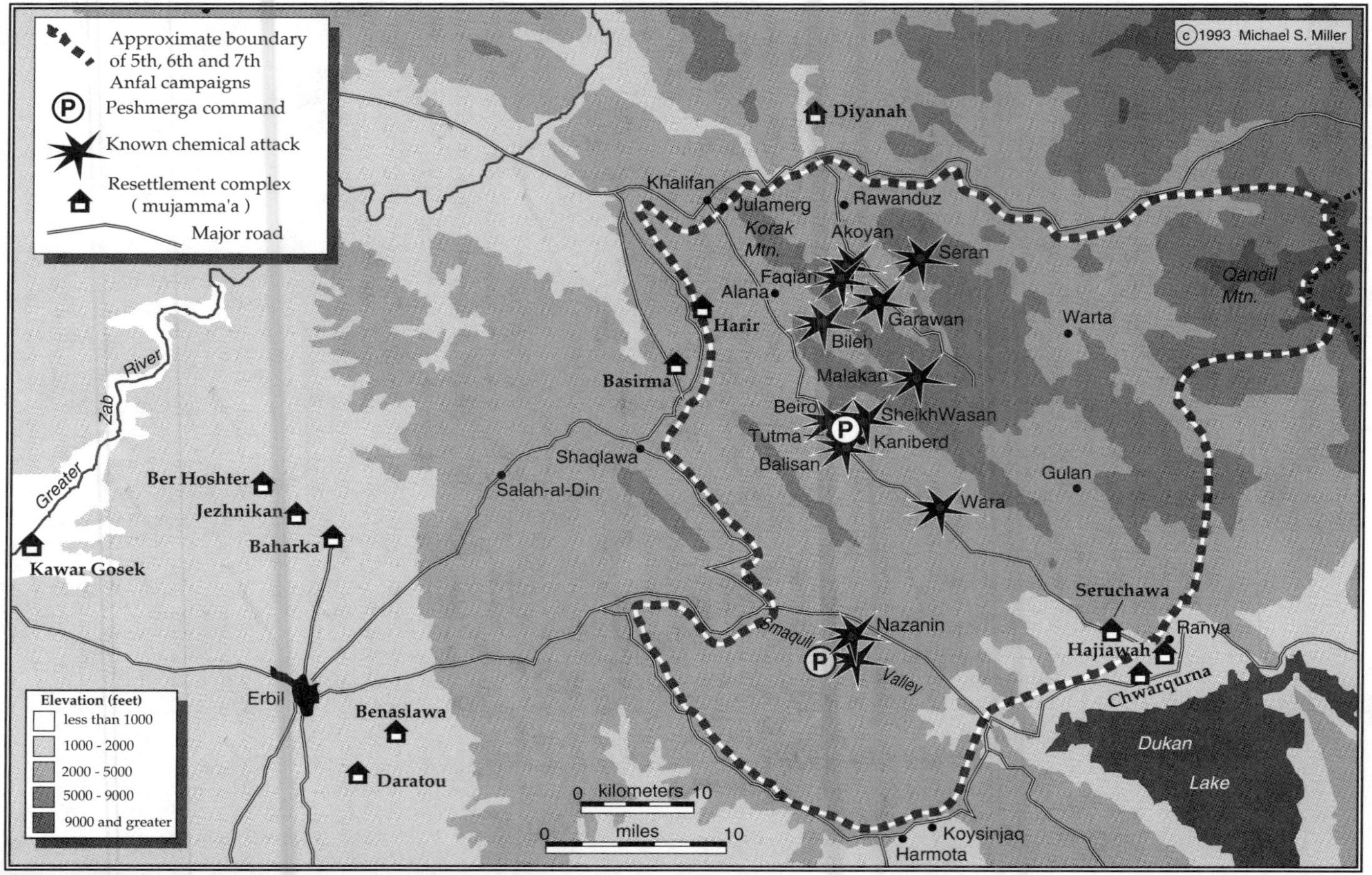

7

FIFTH, SIXTH AND SEVENTH ANFALS: THE MOUNTAIN VALLEYS OF SHAQLAWA AND RAWANDUZ, MAY 15-AUGUST 26, 1988

The forces of the "agent of Iran" Jalal Talabani had now been driven from their principal headquarters in the Jafati Valley, from their mountain strongholds in Qara Dagh, from the broad plains of Germian and the valleys and flatlands that stretch west to Erbil. Here and there, in caves and isolated outposts, pockets of resistance lingered. Several dozen *peshmerga* even remained behind in the desolation of Germian throughout Anfal and beyond. But most of the remnants of the PUK were now making their way to the remote fastnesses to the north of Dukan Lake for their final stand, to the steep mountains and narrow valleys that lie south of the town of Rawanduz and west of the Iranian border.

To the west of the lake, battered units of *peshmerga* had learned of--and in some cases witnessed--the rout of the villages around Goktapa in the first week of May. Along the lakeshore, in the final engagements of the Fourth Anfal, the survivors of the battles at Takaltu Mountain and the Chemi Rezan Valley tried vainly to resist the army's onslaught. They hid out as best they could for three or four days, some of them hunkered down in the grasslands by the water's edge, and resisted until their ammunition ran out. At night, according to one *peshmerga*, when the government helicopters could no longer spot them, they pulled back, leaving the last civilians behind. At last, by the second week of May, they had reached Korak mountain and their familiar sanctuaries in the Balisan Valley.

It was to Balisan and the neighboring thinly populated valleys that Anfal came in the middle of May 1988. This was the climax of the regime's drive to destroy the PUK once and for all as a fighting force, to punish those civilians who continued to sustain it and to expel the last

Iranian troops from the northern front of the Iran-Iraq War.[1] The mass relocation--and mass killing--of civilians would not be a pressing issue for the army in this phase of Anfal. The borderlands of Erbil governorate were now empty, their Kurdish population having been removed in two great sweeps, the first in 1977-1978 and the second in 1983-1984. And the valleys to the south and southeast of Rawanduz had been largely evacuated by civilians after the chemical attacks of April 1987.

From a strictly military point of view, the Anfal campaign continued to follow the logic of the great sweep that had begun three months earlier with the siege of Sergalou-Bergalou. The movement of the troops somewhat resembled the motion of a car's windshield wiper, first clockwise and then counter-clockwise, driving the diminishing forces of the *peshmerga* before it at every stage and "purifying" the countryside of the last of the Kurdish villages to remain intact under PUK control. Yet the Fifth Anfal, unlike the earlier stages of the operation, gave the Iraqi Army a great deal of trouble. A second and a third assault on these recalcitrant valleys would be required, and the Iraqi Army would designate these new campaigns Anfal VI and Anfal VII.

* * *

The Balisan Valley was the headquarters of the PUK's third *malband*, controlling operations in Erbil governorate from the villages of Beiro and Tutma. Other parties were also present in this rugged and beautiful area, where bears and other wild animals still roamed the steep mountainsides. The Socialist Party of Kurdistan had been present here since its foundation in 1979, and there were also armed units from the Iraqi Communist Party and from Mas'oud Barzani's KDP, whose main strongholds lay further to the northwest, near the Iraqi-Turkish border.

The leadership of the third *malband* knew full well that Anfal was on its way north. As the Fourth Anfal ended, the *peshmerga* began to

---

[1] Losing ground rapidly after the loss of Fao, Iran attempted one final offensive in the south on June 13, 1988, but it was contained by Iraqi forces. Simultaneously, the Iraqi Army's First Corps--which handled the Fifth, Sixth and Seventh Anfal operations in the area south of Rawanduz--recaptured a number of strategic mountain peaks that the Iranians had been holding in the north. See Jupa and Dingeman, *op. cit.*, p.8; on the overall military situation in June 1988, see also Cordesman and Wagner, *op. cit.*, pp.384-390.

gather food and ammunition, carrying supplies through the high mountain passes on muleback to hide them away in inaccessible caves, stockpiling enough to withstand a prolonged siege.[2] Hundreds of fighters congregated around the twin villages of Upper and Lower Garawan, seven or eight miles to the southeast of Rawanduz, while others took up positions in nearby Malakan, Akoyan and Warta.[3]

At least this time the *peshmerga* did not have to worry about how to protect the civilian population. Almost all the residents of these valleys had fled from their homes after the murderous poison gas attacks of the previous spring. There were only a few exceptions, such as Lower Bileh and Wara, where for very different reasons the villagers felt secure. Lower Bileh, tucked into folds of the mountains far from the road, had been a *peshmerga* base since even before the start of the Iran-Iraq War. Despite the chemical attack on the upper village on May 27, 1987,[4] the people of Lower Bileh felt that they were protected by the remoteness of the place, and had chosen to stay where they were. But now, Bileh was newly vulnerable, since it was a transit point for *peshmerga* defending the frontline on nearby Chilchil and Jajouk mountains.

Wara was a different matter. There were no *peshmerga* in the vicinity, and the village was planted squarely on the paved road from Khalifan to the rundown town of Ranya, close to Dukan Lake. Its location made it useless as a base for the *peshmerga*, and past experience had taught the residents of Wara that their closeness to the government lines conferred a measure of safety. Although some had moved a few miles to Hartal, higher on the mountainside, most stayed put.

---

[2] Middle East Watch interview with a PUK *peshmerga*, Galala complex, March 23, 1993.

[3] The two Garawans, like much of this area, had been a thorn in the regime's side for a long time. One *Amn* report, dated April 22, 1987 (less than a week, that is, after the chemical attacks on Sheikh Wasan and Balisan a few miles away) speaks of an attempt--presumably unsuccessful--by a joint force of army, police, *Amn* and Ba'ath Party Special Forces to raze the villages of Upper and Lower Garawan. *Amn* Shaqlawa to *Amn* Erbil, letter no. 5614, classified "secret and confidential" and dated April 22, 1987.

[4] See page 51.

At dusk on May 15, the people of Wara were preparing for the 'Id al-Fitr, the festival which breaks the fast of Ramadan. Some of the former residents of the village, now living in Hartal, saw two airplanes fly low overhead, but they paid little attention to them, never thinking that Wara might be their objective. The nearest *peshmerga* units immediately realized what was happening, however, when they saw the *jahsh* lighting fires on the darkening mountain peaks--a sure sign that chemicals were being used. The people in Hartal were stunned when the first survivors came running to them, two hours later, to report that Wara had been hit with gas. "As soon as we arrived," said one man from Hartal, "we saw four or five people in the orchard on the hillside. They were obviously dying. Then we walked on a little further and found three people dead in the graveyard. When we reached the center of the village, we saw that the place was a mess. Food was still on the stoves. There were animals lying all around, dead or dying, and we could hear their screams."

A young woman named Amina was outside her house when the aircraft made their bombing run over Wara. "The sound I heard was like when a car races at very high speed and then you step on the brake. Then there were four explosions, and smoke covered the village." Amina's two-year old daughter, Najiba, was one of thirty-seven villagers who lost their lives that night.[5] The survivors buried thirty-three bodies in a mass grave outside the village. Three were interred in the nearby village of Khateh, where they had been taken by tractor cart to the PUK field hospital, and one in the complex of Seruchawa, which already held the graves of fifty of the victims of the previous year's gassing of Sheikh Wasan.

* * *

Morning brought an unnatural calm, which lasted for more than a week. Then, in the early afternoon of May 23, waves of aircraft dropped chemicals in Balisan, Hiran and other neighboring valleys. The attacks became so frequent at this point that the *peshmerga* lost count of them. An old woman from Upper Garawan, hiding in a cave, saw two warplanes swoop down over nearby Malakan and release bombs that produced a blue smoke which "covered the place and made everything

---

[5] Middle East Watch interview, Wara, March 24, 1993.

dark." The gas, which smelled pleasant at first, quickly made the cave's occupants dizzy. Several of them fell to the ground, vomiting and teary-eyed, their skin turning black. A mother and her son in the cave died.[6]

While the entire valley suffered the effects of gas attacks against the *peshmerga* on Chilchil mountain, witnesses said that the largely abandoned villages of Sheikh Wasan and Balisan were hit directly for the second time. Soviet-built Sukhoi fighter-bomber aircraft carried out a 20-minute raid on Sheikh Wasan with both cluster bombs and chemical weapons. Although some of the *peshmerga* had German-made gas masks, there were not enough for their families, and everyone fled, combatants and non-combatants alike. In Bileh, the chemicals killed at least three children, including two siblings, Suran and Haydar Saleh Majid, aged two and three.[7] Two people also reportedly died in the village of Nazanin; gas and cluster bombs fell over Seran village; chemical shells from a *rajima* rained on the mountain of Rashki Baneshan, and the heavy vapor drifted down into Akoyan village. Late in the night of May 23, or early the next morning, the ground troops made their simultaneous advance from three directions.

Most of the remaining civilians had fled to the hills as soon as this latest round of attacks began. "There was a nasty smell in the places that had been bombed," recalled one woman who fled, and the corpses of horses and sheep overcome by gas still littered the fields. Like many others, the people of the village of Akoyan scattered in three directions. Some set out on foot or on horseback for the Iranian frontier, thirty-five miles away. Others sought sanctuary in the complex of Hajiawa, which had been built in 1987 at the northern edge of Dukan Lake, a three- or four-day walk distant. Others tried to hide out in the mountains.

After an arduous journey across rough, steep terrain, hundreds of refugees, including many of those from Akoyan and Garawan, converged on the uninhabited village of Gulan, almost half way to Ranya. They spent up to a month there, sleeping in the open air and surviving on the charity of the local people. They found themselves in the fiefdom of a powerful local leader called Swara Agha, of the Ako tribe. "He was the government in Gulan," said one fleeing villager who arrived there.

---

[6] Middle East Watch interview, Garawan, April 29, 1992.

[7] Middle East Watch interview, Ramhawej village, July 18, 1992.

"He had his own soldiers and *jahsh*; he owned everything except Saddam's airplanes."[8]

But tribal loyalties are relatively loose in this part of Iraqi Kurdistan, and even though they were not his people, Swara Agha made a deal with the newcomers that seems to have been unique in the story of Anfal. Those who wished could stay in his village, he told them; he would not let the military touch them. "He told the government we were all *jahsh*," according to a man from Garawan. And indeed those who made it as far as Gulan seem to have been spared. Some chose to remain there, while others--especially those who had family members in the *peshmerga* and were not in the mood to take any chances--opted for the sanctuary of Iranian refugee camps. The chieftain, Swara Agha, guaranteed them safe passage as far as the border--a trek that took all day and all night, with frequent detours to avoid Iraqi troop patrols.

Others who reached Gulan decided to surrender to the army and be relocated to the Hajiawa complex, outside the town of Ranya. It appears that they were allowed to do so freely, although conditions in the *mujamma'a* were abysmal. For the remainder of the summer it was hot and insanitary and there was no regular water supply; the camp was monitored by a police post, and its agents warned the inmates not to go too far: only to shop in Ranya or the larger complex of Seruchawa. After September, the searing heat gave way to bitter cold, and Zara, a woman from Garawan, lost two of her seven children that winter--Shilan, aged three, and Isma'il, aged two.[9]

The experience of the third group of fugitives from Akoyan, those who tried to survive in the mountains, is summed up in the experience of Amina, a woman in her early thirties. Amina had left home one day at 7:00 a.m., before the soldiers could reach her village.

---

[8] Swara Agha was reportedly a former PUK member who had surrendered and made his own separate peace with Baghdad, promising that areas under his control would stay neutral. Middle East Watch interviews with villagers from Akoyan and Garawan, April 28 and 29, 1992.

[9] Middle East Watch interview, Garawan, April 29, 1992. It remains a mystery why those who surrendered in Gulan were spared, while people from the same villages who surrendered to the army at Julamerg were sent to the Anfal camps. The difference may be explained by the clemency of a local army commander.

By noon she had found a hiding place, where she met up with other refugees from Bileh and Garawan. They were some fifty households in all in the group, and they hid out for several days until word came that the troops were closing in on them. After wandering around in the mountains for hours, they reached another hiding place overlooking the village of Faqian. Here, too, they remained for four days, until the artillery fire came too close for comfort. They walked on again, losing all track of time, heading northwest over the high peaks, venturing out only after nightfall, until they reached the government-controlled village of Julamerg, exhausted and out of food.[10]

These were the unlucky ones, even though the first signs were encouraging; *jahsh* manning the checkpoints at Julamerg declined to arrest them, telling them that "this is not the appropriate time to come to the butcher's hand."[11] Despite this, they were quickly rounded up by army troops. Their names were recorded, their photographs taken, and they were taken to the nearby military post at Spielk, outside the town of Khalifan, where they were housed for several days under canvas, eight or nine families to each tent, in an area enclosed by barbed wire. The women and children who had surrendered after the attack on Lower Bileh were also here; their menfolk, who fled to the mountains briefly before turning themselves in, were brought to Spielk later.

According to survivors, Lower Bileh was the only village in the area to suffer large-scale civilian disappearances during Anfal. The events in Lower Bileh are also referred to in official Iraqi documents. One handwritten *Amn* field report notes that "on the night of June 2-3, thirty families from the village of Lower Bileh were received by the military command of FQ 45. They were counted and surveyed by us. We will presently send you lists of their names, addresses and birth

---

[10] Julamerg lies a little to the south of the town of Khalifan, at the head of the Alana Valley. It was near here, on the banks of the Alana river, that the survivors of the April 1987 Sheikh Wasan and Balisan chemical bombing had been dumped by *Amn*.

[11] Julamerg itself survived intact until September 3, when it was destroyed, according to a September 3, 1988 telegram from *Amn* Shaqlawa to *Amn* Erbil, no. 4799, alluding to the "purification" of the Alana Valley by the army's 37th Division.

dates."[12]   Here is further official confirmation of what survivors reported with numbing frequency--that a specific civilian group was in government custody at the moment it vanished. The *Amn* note indicates again that there was nothing indiscriminate about these disappearances; no one was to be "Anfalized" until his or her personal data had been recorded and analysed on a case-by-case basis.

Some of those affected by the Fifth Anfal disappeared from Spielk. Others were glimpsed through a window in a prison in Rawanduz. Others still vanished into the custody of *Amn* in Erbil. But as in the previous four phases of Anfal, the same detail recurs in one account after another: from these interim places of detention, the prisoners were bundled into army IFA trucks, which always departed south in the direction of Kirkuk.

* * *

THE PUK'S LAST STAND

The battles raged on and off for more than three months. During the periods of fighting, says a *peshmerga* who saw action in the Balisan region, "the heaven was never empty" of government aircraft.[13] Although government forces quickly occupied some twenty villages in these valleys, the *peshmerga* felt that the difficult landscape had frustrated the regime's goal of cutting off their main escape routes to Iran. The villagers who remained in the mountains also saw that their homes were being left intact for the time being. With the terrain limiting the

---

[12] According to survivors, this list ran to 267 villagers from Bileh. "Secret and confidential" telegram no. 1130 of June 3, 1988, from *Amn* Sadiq to *Amn* Erbil. "FQ 45" appears to refer to the Army's 45th Division (*firqa*), based in Khalifan. This report is one of a sequence of forty-two *Amn* telegrams giving daily field updates on the period from June 3 to September 18, 1988. These papers make it possible to reconstruct in some detail the course of the Fifth, Sixth and Seventh Anfals--as well as providing a glimpse of the evident frustration of the First Army Corps as it attempted to "purify" these recalcitrant areas of "saboteurs."

[13] Middle East Watch interview, Ramhawej village, July 18, 1992.

movement of ground forces, the campaign of village demolition would wait until special helicopter-borne engineering units were flown in towards the end of the year.

Upper and Lower Garawan seem to have been a particularly tough nut for the army to crack. The twin villages are the subject of a number of contradictory field reports exchanged by local and regional branches of *Amn* during June 1988. Telegram no. 1132 from *Amn* Sadiq to *Amn* Shaqlawa, dated June 3, refers to the "purification and burning of Lower Garawan." However, telegram no. 1136 from Sadiq to Erbil, dated June 6, refers to a continuing "siege of Upper and Lower Garawan," indicating that *peshmerga* forces there were still putting up resistance; telegram no. 1137, dated the next day, announces the "fall of Upper and Lower Garawan." A further telegram, no. 1179, dated June 14 and again from *Amn* Sadiq, informs regional headquarters in Erbil that a number of villages have now been burned, including Garawan.[14]

After hiding out in the mountains for weeks, several people from Garawan crept back into their village in search of food. Some homes had been destroyed by shelling, but most were still standing at this point and official records suggest that the destruction was carried out sporadically over the next several months.[15] But leveled they were: When

---

[14] Burning may not be the same thing as demolition. It is worth noting that Resool lists the date of destruction of the two Garawans, as well as the neighboring villages of Akoyan and Faqian, as August 28, 1988. He also lists many villages in these sectors as not being destroyed until December 1988. This is the case, for example, with eleven villages in the *nahya* of Salah al Din and eight in the *nahya* of Harir (both *qadha* of Shaqlawa). See also below, p.325.

[15] This appears to have been a frequent practice. For example, an extensive file of *Amn* and army documents dated August 18-22, 1988 indicates that many of the villages that had been occupied during the Third and Fourth Anfals--including the sites of important clashes such as Sheikh Tawil and the Chemi Rezan Valley--were not destroyed until several months later. This campaign also destroyed any crops, vehicles and stores that remained, with the goal, as one document put it, of "removing any signs of life" in the Anfal areas. *Amn* Kalar, "secret and urgent" cable no. 19442 of August 20, 1988.

Similarly, even while the Fourth and Fifth Anfals were underway, other military units were burning scores of villages in the Qala Dizeh area, to the east of Dukan Lake, where there were no hostilities at this time. This parallel campaign of village destruction was described to Middle East Watch in an

inhabitants were at last able to return to Garawan in 1991, after the post-war uprising, they found that "everything had been destroyed, exploded by dynamite; even the pipes were taken that brought the water from the spring." All signs of life had vanished, even the beehives. The poplar trees used for roofing material had been cut down. Even this was not enough, it seems. "They also destroyed a martyrs' cemetery [for *peshmerga* who had fallen] that had been built in the area of Zenia," said a fighter from Garawan, who was hiding nearby and had relatives interred there. The man watched from the mountainside through binoculars as a group of *jahsh* and soldiers dynamited and desecrated the graves.[16]

* * *

From the regime's point of view, the Fifth Anfal had been a messy and inconclusive operation--the only phase of the operation so far that had lacked a clear beginning and end. The government's intention had been to wipe out the PUK and then move on to the Badinan area, running up to the Turkish border, which was controlled by the KDP. But this goal had to be postponed for several months, because the resistance of the third *malband*'s forces was more tenacious than the Iraqi Army had anticipated.

The atmosphere of frustration and repeated delays can be gleaned from the telegrams that flew back and forth between local *Amn* offices. June 4: "Met strong resistance while advancing on Korak mountain"; June 8: "Special Anfal Operations: Attack by Saboteurs"; June 27, and again July 8: "Purification of Gelli Resh, Badawara, Gilga"; August 15: "Request complete picture of purification of the region within 24 hours."[17]

The sense that the Fifth Anfal was not a great success also emerges clearly from an unusually detailed military document entitled

---

interview with a survivor from the village of Binowshan, May 23, 1992. These villages, however, were not considered to be part of the Anfal operation.

[16] Middle East Watch interview, Garawan, April 29, 1992.

[17] From, respectively, "secret and urgent" *Amn* telegrams nos. 1333 (Sadiq to Erbil); 3215 (Shaqlawa to Erbil); 1293 (Sadiq to Shaqlawa) and 3550 (Shaqlawa to Erbil); and 12233 (Erbil to Shaqlawa).

"Analysis: Final Anfal Operation," (*Khatimat al-Anfal*). This is a report to the Army General Command from Brigadier General Yunis Muhammad al-Zareb, Commander of the Fifth Army Corps. It is classified "Strictly confidential and personal." In essence, the report is a glowing review of the brief, triumphant campaign against the KDP-held areas of the north, between August 28 and September 3, 1988. But in reviewing the background to the Final Anfal, it speaks of innumerable delays in "purifying" the Rawanduz-Shaqlawa sector. It also provides a revealing picture of the chain of command that ordered the successive stages of the Anfal operation.

"After the completion of Operation Anfal V on June 7, 1988, preparations and plans were embarked upon for Operation Anfal VI," Gen. Zareb writes. "A cleansing operation was planned to crush the saboteurs in the Alana and Balisan valleys (Anfal VI). This plan was sent to the Army Chief of Staff on May 30, 1988 in my strictly confidential and personal communication no. 1049." But this first plan did not materialize, for, "The Army Chief of Staff, in his confidential and urgent communication no. 1475 of June 7, 1988, ordered the postponement of the operation until a more suitable time. The Chief of Staff, in his strictly confidential and personal communication no. 519 of June 7, 1988, ordered a plan to be devised to crush the saboteurs in the Balisan and Smaquli regions."

The main reason for the decision to suspend the campaign temporarily seems to have been the obstinate resistance of the PUK around Korak mountain, a 7,000-foot peak at the head of the Alana Valley. But the temporary ceasefire, which held until well into July, may also have been connected to the June visit to Washington, D.C. by PUK leader Jalal Talabani. Although the *peshmerga* were excited by this trip, which was seen as a diplomatic breakthrough, it can scarcely be considered a success. Senior U.S. officials declined to meet with Talabani, and the mid-level State Department personnel who did see him commented only that, "Because of his Iranian alliance, his group has enjoyed a certain degree of military success at the expense of the Kurdish population as a whole."[18] This remark essentially reflected the line of the Iraqi government toward the PUK. Since Talabani is known to have informed U.S. officials about the Anfal operation and the recent chemical attacks against the Kurds, his visit also raises the question of how much

---

[18] *The New York Times*, June 22, 1988.

Washington may have known about the Kurdish genocide as it was happening.[19]

"The plan for the destruction of the saboteurs' headquarters in the Smaquli area," General Zareb continues, "was provided in our communication no, 1572, dated August 15, 1988 [sic]."[20]

"In a confidential and personal communication no. 2544/K of June 23, 1988, sent to us by the Army Chief of Staff in communication no. 641 of June 24, the Presidency of the Republic (Secretary) gave its agreement to launch the operation and destroy the headquarters of the saboteurs in the Balisan basin and the Smaquli region."

President Saddam Hussein himself, then, evidently saw fit to involve himself in operational decisions about Anfal, at least when the campaign was running into difficulties. Gen. Zareb went on:

"In a confidential and personal communication no. 14671 of July 16, 1988 from the office of the Presidency of the Republic, relayed to us by the Army Chief of Staff in confidential and personal communication no. 861 of July 20, we were informed that the Anfal operations should be

---

[19] Middle East Watch conversation with PUK officials, Washington, D.C., May 2, 1993. Documents obtained through the Freedom of Information Act by Middle East Watch and the National Security Archive throw scanty light on this contentious issue.

One Defense Department cable, dated April 19, 1988, notes that "an estimated 1.5 million Kurdish nationals have been resettled in camps"; that "approximately 700-1000 villages and small residential areas were targeted for resettlement"; that "an unknown but reportedly large number of Kurds have been placed in 'cowcentration' (sic) camps located near the Jordanian and Saudi Arabian borders"; and that "movement by the local population throughout the north has been severely restricted." The long section that follows is heavily deleted.

A second Defense Department cable, dated June 15, 1988, makes reference to Talabani's visit to the United States and reports on a new Iraqi offensive against Iranian forces in Kurdistan. It also makes a clear allusion to the Fifth Anfal: "The offensive, if confirmed, follows sweeps against Kurdish and Iranian positions in both V and I Corps that have continued for about two weeks. Iran and the Kurds have accused Iraq of using chemical weapons in the operations."

[20] In view of the chronology laid out below, this date is evidently incorrect.

completed with a high momentum after the religious feast [of the 'Id al-Adha], if God so desires."[21]

But God did not appear to be smiling on the enterprise, and several days after the 'Id al-Adha the offensive remained stalled. "In a meeting held at the headquarters of the First Army Corps in Kirkuk on the morning of July 29, 1988, attended by the Assistant Chief of Staff for Operations and the Director of Military Movements, and pursuant to confidential communication no. 943 of July 29, Anfal operations VI and VII were postponed until operational requirements were completed."

* * *

While the Iraqi regime grappled with the delays to the Sixth and Seventh Anfals, events elsewhere were giving the *peshmerga* fresh cause for alarm. On July 17, then Iranian President Ali Khamenei notified UN Secretary General Javier Perez de Cuellar that his country was willing to accept UN Security Council Resolution 598.[22] As far as the PUK was concerned, Iran's decision to end the fighting was a breach of the terms of their October 1986 Teheran agreement, which had stipulated that neither party would make a unilateral deal with Baghdad. But they were powerless to do anything about it--as powerless as Mullah Mustafa Barzani had been when the Shah cut off his supply lines to the KDP in 1975.

On July 26, the day after the 'Id al-Adha, the commanders of the third *malband* held an emergency meeting and decided that a partial withdrawal was its only option. Anyone who was unable to fight should now take their families to safety in Iran; the able-bodied *peshmerga* would stay behind to harass the troops and protect the retreat. Even as the evacuation began, the Iraqi Air Force launched another fierce chemical attack. Again, it struck all the main valleys: Balisan, Malakan, Warta, Hiran, Smaquli. Thirteen people died in a number of different locations,

---

[21] The 'Id al-Adha, in the Muslim calendar, occurs 50 days following the eighth day of Ramadan. In 1988, when Ramadan began on April 17, this would have fallen on July 25.

[22] Security Council Resolution 598, adopted on July 20, 1987, called for an immediate ceasefire to be monitored by UN observers. The full text is contained in Hiro, *The Longest War*, pp.309-310.

said one *peshmerga* who fought in this theater; fifteen, according to another account. The clouds of gas drove the *peshmerga* to seek safety on the upper mountain slopes; but early the next morning a second attack with cluster bombs drove them down again. Many of those who remained now scattered in confusion, and the last of the civilians were mopped up quickly.

A contingent of *jahsh* arrived in the Smaquli valley one August morning to find the population fleeing from artillery fire. Via loudspeaker, the *mustashar* urged them to surrender, and after five days a considerable number of people had turned themselves in. They were divided into three groups by age and sex and their names were registered. The men were told that they would be pardoned, but only if they surrendered with their weapons. Since many of them were unarmed civilians, this was difficult, and they were reduced to digging up caches of *peshmerga* arms in order to hand over whatever guns they could lay their hands on. Some were even allowed to buy guns from the *jahsh* in order that they might qualify for a pardon. The men were then ordered to sign a confession that they were indeed *peshmerga*. Once this grim charade was over, the *mustashar* recalled, "all these people disappeared via Topzawa"-- the Popular Army camp outside Kirkuk that served as the main processing center for the victims of Anfal.[23]

* * *

During the weeks that followed, hardly a day went past without further chemical attacks, even after the Iranians had accepted Saddam Hussein's terms for the ceasefire on August 8. Although the *peshmerga* were now in full flight, the Iraqi Army never did manage to cut off the two main avenues of escape to Iran. Sympathetic *jahsh* commanders like Swar Agha helped the last families to reach the border, and on August 26 or 27 the remaining *peshmerga* contingents in the Balisan Valley dynamited their headquarters and fled. By the 28th, ground and airborne forces had occupied the entire area. The PUK was finished as a fighting force, and the whole territory where it had once held sway was under the control of the Iraqi government.

---

[23] Middle East Watch interview with former *mustashar*, Suleimaniyeh, June 30, 1992.

With this, the regime turned its attention further north, to the region of Badinan, the principal stronghold of the KDP. This time, the campaign would not be given a number; it would simply be designated the Final Anfal. As Brig. Gen. Zareb's report indicates, the plans had been in the works for several weeks, concurrently with preparations for the Seventh Anfal. Zareb writes: "In a highly confidential and personal communication no. 941 of July 28, 1988, sent to us by the General Commander of the Armed Forces, instructions were given to deal the saboteurs a crushing blow in the Badinan sector."

"A meeting was held on August 7 at the headquarters of the First Army Corps in Kirkuk," the general continues, "chaired by Comrade Ali Hassan al-Majid, member of the Regional Command and Secretary General of the Northern Bureau. This meeting was also attended by the Deputy Chief of Staff and the Directors of Military Movements and the Air Force." There is a laconic hint of what must have been al-Majid's fierce mood: "Instructions were given to put an end to all acts of saboteurs in the northern region."

After some additional meetings to fine-tune the details, the army's responsibilities were assigned. "It was decided that the First Army Corps should operate in the Balisan-Smaquli sector, and that the Fifth Corps should operate in the two areas of Sheikhan and Zakho in the Badinan strip. This was in accordance with a highly confidential and personal communication no. 1076 of August 16, 1988 from the Army Chief of Staff."

It remained only to fix dates. There were two. The preparatory, or softening-up, stage of the final Anfal would commence on August 25, and as in almost every preceding phase of Anfal, this meant attacks from the air with chemical weapons. On August 28, the ground troops would go in, "with the first rays of the dawn."[24]

---

[24] All these extracts are taken from the 60-page report from the Fifth Army Corps Commander to the Command of the Staff of the Army, "Analysis: Final Anfal Operation, for the Period August 28 to September 3, 1988," dated December 25, 1988 and coded H2/2422.

8
THE CAMPS

"Away with them I say and show them death."
    -- *Marlowe, Tamburlaine the Great, Part One (V, i)*

"For the young, the final stage was Topzawa."
    -- *Rahman, an elderly man from Darbarou village,*
    Taqtaq.

THE POPULAR ARMY CAMP AT TOPZAWA

TOPZAWA is one of the commonest place names in northern Iraq; the map of Kurdistan is dotted with Topzawas. Most of them were tiny anonymous hamlets, of the sort that perished by the hundreds during Anfal. Like many place names, it is incongruous. Goktapa, site of the May 3 chemical attack, meant "green hill." Buchenwald, the Nazi concentration camp, was a "beech forest." *Top*, in Kurdish, means "artillery"; *zawa* is betrothed. Combined, the two words evoke sniggers among schoolchildren, for they refer, somewhat brutally, to the act that is performed by the male on his wedding night.

But just as no Kurd will ever again think of "Anfal" as a *sura* of the Koran, so no one will ever again hear the secondary meaning of "Topzawa" as a smutty joke. For the Topzawa they will remember is a sprawling army base on a highway leading southwest out of the oil-rich city of Kirkuk. Covering about two square miles, Topzawa is bounded by two underground oil pipelines, a railroad repair yard and a military airfield. For the villagers who were trucked away from their burning villages by the army during Anfal, all roads seemed to lead to Kirkuk, and to Topzawa. At Topzawa, any notion that Anfal was simply a counterinsurgency campaign evaporates.

No official documents have so far come to light from the Kirkuk headquarters of the various agencies that were involved in Anfal. But a letter from *Amn* Suleimaniyeh to the unnamed director of security of the Autonomous Region, dated October 29, 1988, alludes to the Topzawa operation and gives some small hint of its scale. Almost two months have now passed since the completion of Anfal, and the regional security director in Kirkuk has evidently telephoned to ask for a progress report from the Suleimaniyeh governorate. The reply is classified "Secret and personal, to be opened by addressee only."

It begins, "In the name of Allah, the Beneficent, the Merciful: Distinguished Director of the Autonomous Region, with reference to our telephone conversation, the statistics requested are as follows..." There is a brief recitation of actions taken: nine criminal subversives executed, along with eighteen members of their families, as ordered by Ali Hassan al-Majid's office; another nineteen people executed for being found in prohibited areas, in violation of directive no. 4008 of June 20, 1987; another forty-seven subversives sentenced to death by the Revolutionary Court; and finally this: "2,532 individuals and 1,869 families totalling 9,030 persons, who were among those arrested during the heroic 'Anfal' operations, were sent to the Popular Army[1] camp in the governorate of al-Ta'mim (Kirkuk)."[2] In other words, to Topzawa.

* * *

From the collection points at Qader Karam and Qoratu and Leilan they came, from Chamchamal and Aliawa and Taqtaq, crammed into the swaying IFA trucks like farm beasts. "From Taqtaq we were taken the next day [about May 7] in a military truck with a cow," remembered Abd-al-Qader Abdullah Askari, the dignified old village leader of Goktapa, with a rueful laugh. "This was insulting. You know what cows do, they shit. At the turn-off on the road from Redar to Erbil,

---

[1] The Popular Army (*Jaysh al-Sha'abi*) was founded in 1970 as a party-controlled militia which would provide Ba'ath cadre with basic military training and act as a counterweight to the regular armed forces. Despite its nominal strength of 250,000 the Popular Army was largely ineffective as a combat force in the Iran-Iraq war; its most important role was to guard buildings in the cities during the absence of the regular army.

[2] *Amn* Suleimaniyeh to *Amn* Autonomous Region Headquarters, letter no. 25163 of October 29, 1988. Unfortunately, no time period is indicated, making it impossible to extrapolate from these numbers to estimate the total of those who passed through Topzawa during the Anfal campaign.

they dropped off the cow. I said to the cow, 'We're both going to be slaughtered, pardon me if I have done something wrong to you in the past'"--this being a traditional Muslim way of bidding final farewell.[3]

The truck lumbered on to Kirkuk, where it stopped for an hour or so outside the Ba'ath Party building. (Many witnesses recalled making a brief halt either here or at the Kirkuk headquarters of *Amn*.) Abd-al-Qader counted fourteen young men being hustled on to the truck by soldiers. Before long the vehicle drew up outside the gates of Topzawa. The minority of villagers who were literate could read the name on a sign at the entrance.

"It was very late at night when we arrived at Topzawa," said Yawar, a 70-year old man who believed he was Anfal's only survivor from his home village of Karim Bassam (*nahya* Qader Karam).

> We were all hungry and exhausted. We were almost dead. We had not eaten for several days. We had even lost our sense of time. We did not know what they wanted to do with us. When we reached the base they announced over the loudspeakers that we should not get out of the trucks until they told us to do so. There were eight or nine trucks that arrived together. Their backs were covered; we could not see anything inside. We stayed in the truck for about one hour before the soldiers opened up the back and said, "The men, just the men will get off first." I was so hungry and exhausted that I could not move, so I was the last to get off. The young ones got off first; as soon as they did, they were handcuffed.[4]

With only minor variations, this was the standard pattern for sorting the new arrivals. Men and women were segregated on the spot, as soon as the trucks had rolled to a halt in the base's large central courtyard or parade ground. The process was brutal, and it did not spare the elderly. One 70-year old man from the *nahya* of Shwan was dragged

---

[3] Middle East Watch interview with Abd-al-Qader Abdullah Askari, Goktapa, May 24, 1992.

[4] Middle East Watch interview, Sumoud complex, May 20, 1992.

out of line for no apparent reason, beaten by an officer wearing the three stars of a captain on his shoulder and robbed of 3,000 dinars ($9,000 at the official 1988 exchange rate). Abd-al-Qader of Goktapa recalled that a colonel (*aqid*) was in charge of processing the new arrivals, assisted by a captain (*naqib*).[5]

A little later, the men were further divided by age--small children kept with their mothers, the elderly and infirm shunted off to separate quarters, and men and teenage boys considered to be of an age to use a weapon herded together. Roughly speaking, this meant males of between fifteen and fifty, but there was no rigorous check of identity documents-- and strict chronological age seems to have been less of a criterion than size and appearance. A strapping twelve-year old could fail to make the cut; an undersized sixteen-year old could be told to remain with his female relatives. A prematurely gray or grizzled-looking peasant could be spared, even though he might be in his forties.

"We joined thousands of other Kurds who had been brought there before our group," said one such man, Jalal, a 45-year old farmer from southern Germian who was transported to Topzawa in mid-April from the 21st Division fort at Qoratu.

> We just did not know what would happen. We could not speak; fear would not let us speak, everyone was mute. The only sound that we heard was when the military officers called out names. "Accused Ali Rahman, son of so and so... Accused Mustafa Taher, son of so and so..." They were announcing the names of the youths over the loudspeakers. They did not call the old men."[6]

It was time now to process the younger males. They were split up into smaller groups--lines of eight, one said; seated in a smaller courtyard, said another. No one told the prisoners why they had been

---

[5] These officers may have been from *Istikhbarat*, given the demonstrated role of military intelligence in overseeing the initial transit camps. See above p.109. But they may equally well have been from *Amn*, which uses the same ranks as the military. Middle East Watch interviews with Abd-al-Qader Abdullah Askari and with a survivor from the village of Zijila (*nahya* Shwan), Taqtaq, April 24, 1992.

[6] Middle East Watch interview, Sumoud complex, May 20, 1992.

brought here, or what was to happen to them. After separation into groups, they were body-searched by soldiers or *Istikhbarat* agents. Some had their IDs removed at this point, but not all--perhaps, as one survivor suggested, because the guards were simply overwhelmed by the magnitude of their task. Combs, razor blades, mirrors, knives, belts, worry beads: everything was taken from the prisoners but the clothes they stood up in. "I saw a pile of watches, belts and money taken from the villagers and heaped up on the floor," one woman remembered. "You could weep."[7]

Some of the detainees were interrogated immediately, others hauled out later from their cells at night. In any event, for most of the newcomers the interrogation was quite perfunctory--no more, really, than the taking of a brief statement and a few simple questions: name, mother's name, number of siblings, marital status, year of marriage, number of children.[8] "How long have you been a *peshmerga*?" the men were asked. "What actions did you take part in?" Many feared to give truthful answers. "I have never been a *peshmerga*," one young man answered typically. The interrogator, who was wearing the uniform of the army Special Forces (*Quwat al-Khaseh*), wrote down "*peshmerga*" anyway.[9]

Once duly registered, the prisoners were hustled into a number of large rooms, or halls, each filled with residents of a single area. One witness counted twenty-eight of these halls, and estimates of the numbers

---

[7] Middle East Watch interview, Benaslawa complex, April 21, 1992.

[8] These sessions appear to have followed a standard "information form" used by the Iraqi security agencies. Middle East Watch has found many examples of this form among official files. The only unusual feature of the questioning described at Topzawa is the asking of the mother's name; under standard procedures only the father's name was requested.

[9] Middle East Watch interview, Erbil, September 12, 1992. One survivor did recall a more extensive interrogation, in which he was asked not only whether he was a *peshmerga*, but to which party he belonged, whether he knew any *peshmerga*, whether he had relatives who were *peshmerga*, whether he had any relatives living abroad, whether he had any relatives who had been executed, and whether he was an army deserter. Middle East Watch interview, Shoresh complex, July 1, 1992. Both of these men were among the handful of execution survivors located by Middle East Watch. For their full stories, see below, chapter 9.

of prisoners held in each varied from one to two hundred. Using these figures as a rough yardstick, the total population of the Topzawa base at any given time may have been some 4,000-5,000. But the inmates shifted constantly, with most remaining there for as little as a single night or as much as four days before being taken on to their next destination.

While the conditions at Topzawa were appalling for everyone, the most grossly overcrowded quarters seem to have been those in which the male detainees were held. "We could not leave our hall," said one boy from near Qader Karam, who was held with others who were considered younger than military-service age but too old to stay with their mothers. "It was made of cement, heavily built and very strong with bars on the windows and doors but no glass. The hall measured about six meters by thirty, and was very crowded. There was no room to lie down."[10] Other men described being forced to squat on their haunches all night, and beaten if they attempted to stand up. Many of their companions fainted from exhaustion.

Sanitation was non-existent. The prisoners used cans in the room for their bowel movements, and urinated out of the door or simply on the floor where they stood. If they were fortunate, they might be taken to the toilet twice a day at gunpoint, in groups of five or ten, by guards who sometimes beat them on the way with a strip of coaxial cable. Most were suffering from diarrhea by this time, especially if they ate the prison food. "It was something that it is better not to describe," said one of the few young men who survived Topzawa. "If you were not hungry you would not eat it. It was a type of soup with left-over bones and a lot of oil floating in it. Everybody got sick." For many inmates of Topzawa, there was not even this--merely two small pieces of stale pita bread (samoun) each day, and a little water. Some received no food at all. Again, women and children fared a little less harshly, and some of them told of occasionally being given meager rations of rice, tea, cheese or even, in one case, a little meat.

But the women and children suffered grievously in their own ways. After a short time in which they remained together, baton-wielding guards dragged the older women away violently from their daughters and grandchildren and bundled them away to yet another unknown destination. In at least two reported cases, soldiers and guards burst into

---

[10] Middle East Watch interview with a survivor from the Jabari village of Mahmoud Parizad, Shoresh complex, May 9, 1992.

the women's quarters during their first night at Topzawa and removed their small children, even infants at the breast. All night long the women could hear the cries and screams of their children in another room. In one instance, the children were returned to their mothers the next morning, without a word of explanation, after a six or seven-hour separation. In the other, the families were not reunited until the next stage of their ordeal, when they were herded once more into army IFAs and transferred from Topzawa to a prison for women and children at Dibs, on the road that leads northwest from Kirkuk to Erbil and Mosul. Taymour Abdullah Ahmad, the twelve-year old boy who had been captured by the army on April 13 in the village of Kulajo, said he was held at Topzawa with his mother and three sisters for a month--an exceptionally long stay.[11] During that time, he witnessed the deaths of four children, aged five to nine, apparently from starvation. Soldiers removed their bodies, and Taymour learned later that they were thrown into a pit outside.[12]

But above all the women and children of Topzawa endured the torment of seeing their husbands, brothers and fathers suffer and, in the end, disappear. Through the barred windows of their halls, they could see their menfolk in another part of the prison. Every two or three days, said Taymour, the inmates of his cell were let out for air and allowed to mingle in the central courtyard. The children would take advantage of the moment to slip across to the men's quarters and throw bread in at the windows.

For the men, beatings were routine. Even old Abd-al-Qader Abdullah Askari of Goktapa was beaten, a man in his late 60s still weak and disoriented from the chemical bombing of his village several days earlier. On the night of his arrival, a guard ordered him to stand. He replied that he could not, because of the gas. The guard rushed at him

---

[11] Taymour has been interviewed many times by journalists and human rights delegations visiting Iraqi Kurdistan. See, for example, Middle East Watch and Physicians for Human Rights, *Unquiet Graves: The Search for the Disappeared in Iraqi Kurdistan*, February 1992; Taymour is also the subject of a chapter in Kanan Makiya's book, *Cruelty and Silence*, pp.151-199.

[12] Middle East Watch interview with Taymour Abdullah Ahmad, Sumoud complex, July 29, 1992.

in a fury and beat him, screaming that it was forbidden for anyone to speak of poison gas attacks.[13]

A young army deserter from the Qader Karam area, known to his friends as Ozer, was held captive for four days in Topzawa. During that time one of his cellmates was a bearded man from the village of Khalo Baziani, in the *nahya* of Qara Hassan. The man told Ozer he had been tortured. They had to talk discreetly because of the ever-present guards, but Ozer was able to learn that the man had been beaten with a cable, hung from a ceiling fan and scorched with a piece of hot steel. Guards had stamped on his back with their boots while he lay face-down on the floor. The man was in great pain. He said he had been singled out for harsh treatment because of his beard--which was presumably taken as a sign of Islamic fundamentalism and pro-Iranian sympathies.[14] An officer had told him that he would be executed if the beard was not gone by the following day. That evening, Ozer cut off the beard of this man and five others with a small pair of nail scissors that one of the prisoners had managed to keep hidden.

On the fourth day of Ozer's confinement, at 1:30 in the morning, an army captain came in and ordered the prisoners to stand. He told them that he would read a list of names; anyone who failed to answer when they were called would be executed on the spot in front of the others. One after the other the prisoners were summoned to the officer's table. Ozer saw that each man had been assigned a serial number; his own was 375. As their names were called, the prisoners were led out of the room in groups of eight. After four days on a starvation diet, they were weakened and disoriented. Ozer found himself in a second, empty hall. After the stuffy heat of his previous overcrowded quarters, he was chilled by the cold of the mid-April night. The floor was stained with diesel oil, and there were three patches of fresh blood. A bloodstained

---

[13] After Topzawa, Abd-al-Qader never again saw his two sons, Omed and Latif, or his daughter-in-law, Fahima. Middle East Watch interview, May 24, 1992.

[14] A letter from *Amn* Shaqlawa, ref. Research/11408, and dated December 31, 1987, refers to a Northern Bureau directive of December 13, 1987, to the effect that, "It is completely prohibited for bearded people to have access to the center of the governorates and other towns for any reason whatsoever, unless permitted by the proper authorities."

Kurdish headscarf lay in a corner, along with a coat and a pair of baggy Kurdish pants. At about 4:00 a.m. the prisoners heard the sound of engines outside. They tried to peer out of the keyhole, but it was impossible to make out anything in the darkness. For another four hours they waited, numb with cold, hunger and fear.

These early morning movements of male prisoners were observed by women and older people in other sections of Topzawa. "We saw them taking off the men's shirts and beating them," said one elderly man. "They were handcuffed to each other in pairs, and they took away their shoes. This was going on from 8:00 a.m. until noon."[15] Sometimes the men were blindfolded as well; according to some accounts they were stripped to their shorts. And at last they were packed into sinister-looking vehicles, painted white or green and windowless; these were variously described as resembling buses, ambulances or closed trucks.

This was the last that was seen of the men who had been held at Topzawa. As the windowless vehicles left in one direction, buses drove off in another, filled with the other detainees. For many of the women and children--but by no means all of them, as we shall see--the next destination was the prison of Dibs. For the elderly, the road led south, through the river valleys of central Iraq, before turning southwest, into the desert. "The Kurds are traitors, and we know where to send you," a military officer told one old man from Naujul. "We will send you to a hell that is built especially for the Kurds."[16] Its name was Nugra Salman.

* * *

THE POPULAR ARMY CAMP AT TIKRIT

Many tens of thousands of Kurdish villagers swept up in the third and fourth stages of Anfal passed through the Popular Army base of Topzawa in this way. So did smaller numbers of Kurds from the second, fifth, sixth and seventh Anfals. A note should also be added here about the Popular Army barracks in the town of Tikrit, which lies southwest of

---

[15] Middle East Watch interview, Sumoud complex, May 20, 1992.

[16] Middle East Watch interview, Benaslawa complex, April 19, 1992.

Kirkuk on the banks of the Tigris river, close to the birthplace of President Saddam Hussein. Tikrit appears to have performed a broadly similar function to Topzawa, but on a smaller scale and for a much shorter period. Indeed, all the witnesses who had spent time in Tikrit belonged to a single large batch of prisoners from the Daoudi tribal area along the Awa Spi river in southern Germian. All of them were captured in the initial stages of the Third Anfal by army units operating out of Tuz Khurmatu, and all of them were brought to Tikrit after first being detained at the Tuz Khurmatu Youth Hall (see above, pp.159).

It seems reasonable to surmise, then, that Tikrit was pressed into service as a temporary overflow center for a few days in mid-April, when the Third Anfal was in full swing in Germian and Topzawa was filled to capacity. As at Topzawa, the guards were identified as regular army troops, with *Amn* and *Istikhbarat* agents also in attendance. But one man also said that he recognized members of the Popular Army (*Jaysh al-Sha'abi*).

Conditions at Tikrit were extremely brutal. According to the account of Muhammad, a man from the village of Talau who was aged 63 at the time of Anfal:

> On the first morning, they separated the men into small groups and beat them. Four soldiers would beat one captive; the other prisoners could see this. About fifteen or twenty men were in each group that was taken a little way off to be kicked and beaten with sticks and [coaxial] cables. They were taken away in the early morning and returned in the afternoon. The soldiers did not gather the men by name, but just pointed, "you, and you" and so on. They were *Amn* from Tikrit and Kirkuk; butchers, we know them.[17] When one group of beaten men returned, they took another and beat them. That night, I was in a group of ten or twelve men that was taken out and blindfolded, with our hands tied behind us. They took us in three or four cars to somewhere in Tikrit. We drove around all night, barely stopping. They asked me

---

[17] Most members of *Amn* are drawn from Ramadi, Tikrit and Samarra, a triangle of Sunni-dominated towns west of Baghdad, the heartland of Saddam Hussein's political support.

no questions. The captured men could not talk to each other. Everyone was thinking of his own destiny. Of the ten or twelve they took out that night, only five returned. The next night, when I was back in the hall, *Amn* came and asked for men to volunteer for the war against Iran. Eighty men volunteered. But it was a lie; they disappeared. A committee was set up by *Amn* to process the prisoners, who were ordered to squat while the *Amn* agents took all their money and put it in a big sack. They also took all our documents. The *Amn* agents were shouting at us to scare us. "Bring weapons to kill them," said one. "They are poor, don't shoot them," said another. And another: "I wish we had killed all of them. "Later that night the *Amn* came back and took all the young men away. Only the elderly remained. The young men were taken away in Nissan buses, ten or more of them, each with a capacity of forty-five people. Their documents had already been taken; they left with nothing but the clothes on their backs.

Among the young men who disappeared that night were Muhammad's son Salah, his brother's son, and several other relatives. "I never heard from them again," he concluded. "There were no messages, nothing. No one ever saw them again. Only Saddam Hussein knows."[18]

* * *

THE PRISONERS FROM BILEH AND HALABJA

The treatment of those captured in other phases of the Anfal campaign appears to have been slightly different. During April and early May 1988, Topzawa was processing Anfal victims on what can only be described as an industrial scale. But by the end of May, when Anfal reached the areas north of Dukan Lake, the rules had changed somewhat.

Middle East Watch interviewed some three dozen former inmates

---

[18] Middle East Watch interview, Daratou complex, April 18, 1992.

of Topzawa. Of these, five were from the areas affected by the Fifth, Sixth and Seventh Anfals. Four were from Upper and Lower Bileh; the other was a young woman named Amina, from the nearby village of Akoyan.[19] These witnesses reported being held apart from the other prisoners. Almost the entire group was from Bileh, although they also recognized a handful of people from nearby Kandour--the village whose residents had shown such kindness to the victims of the May 1987 chemical attack on the Malakan Valley. All of them had been brought here after a few days in the army fort at Spielk, near Khalifan. One man told of an additional night in an underground cell at the *Amn* headquarters in Kirkuk; several others reported an overnight stay in Erbil.

The Bileh group was apparently held at Topzawa for eight to ten days, considerably longer than most of the detainees from earlier periods. Their conditions also seem to have been marginally less harsh, and the women were able to take water and cigarettes to their husbands, who were detained in a separate large cell. After a week or so the women and children were transferred, like their predecessors, to another army base at Dibs. Most of the elderly were driven south to the prison at Nugra Salman, although one old man was taken directly from Topzawa to Arbat, a town to the south of the city of Suleimaniyeh. This was in mid-June. From Arbat, he made his own way to Basirma, a government-controlled complex that had been set up after the chemical attacks on the Balisan Valley in April 1987.

An even more notable exception to the earlier pattern of detentions was the case of Faraj, a 39-year old teacher from Halabja. His testimony shows again how survivors from that town were treated differently from those who were swept up in Anfal. It also demonstrates that Topzawa remained in operation until the very end of the campaign. Faraj had fled to Iran with his wife and two of his six children immediately after the March 16 chemical attack. After two and a half months in Iranian hospitals and refugee camps, the family crossed back into Iraq, but they were soon picked up by soldiers at a checkpoint in Ranya. After a period of interrogation by *Amn* agents in Suleimaniyeh,

---

[19] Middle East Watch interviews, Ramhawej village, July 18, 1992, Rawanduz, May 5, 1992, Khalifan and Basirma complex, March 24, 1993.

Faraj and his family were transferred to Topzawa in a bus that contained twenty-five people from Halabja and the Kalar area.[20]

The conditions that Faraj observed in Topzawa were broadly similar to what earlier witnesses had described. The sexes were still being segregated on arrival; 150 people or so were crowded into a single large cell; and they existed on starvation rations. But there was now a Kurdish army doctor in attendance, a man named Najib, who hailed from Khanaqin. Faraj became aware that all of his fellow-prisoners were from Halabja, and that many of them had not fled to Iran as he did, but had been captured inside Iraqi Kurdistan after the bombing of the city.

At night, he heard the sound of weeping from other parts of the building, and asked a guard what was going on. "Those are the Anfal prisoners," the guard replied, "and they are leaving the prison." Halabja, in other words, was not part of the Anfal operation. "Where are the Anfal prisoners being taken?" Faraj asked another guard the next morning. "That is none of your concern," the man answered. "If you ask that question again, you will be sent off with them too, to be lost forever."

From eavesdropping on their conversations, Faraj, who could speak Arabic, learned that the Topzawa guards had all been posted here from Baghdad. One of them even gave the prisoner his telephone number, and suggested that he call if he was ever in the capital to see if "we may have a job for you." Later, the same guard aroused the teacher's suspicions further when he gave him a letter which he said was from a Kurdish girl in another section of the prison, telling her relatives in the men's cells about her failing health and her fears of death. Faraj refused to get involved. Some time later his suspicions about the guard were confirmed when the man told him point-blank that *Amn* was interested in having him spy on his fellow Kurds.

Amn's clumsy attempts to recruit Faraj may partially explain the leniency that was shown to him, although it is clear from his testimony that Halabja survivors were treated more indulgently than the Anfal prisoners. For the first two weeks, Faraj was even allowed brief visits to

---

[20] The *nahya* of Kalar in southern Germian was included in the third stage of Anfal. Thousands of villagers from the Kalar area were brought to Topzawa in early and mid-April, but this is the only case reported to Middle East Watch of their being taken there any later. The witness offered no explanation of what had happened to them during the three months since the Third Anfal. Middle East Watch interview, Halabja, May 8, 1992.

his wife, although those privileges were withdrawn when another prisoner was caught trying to escape through a hole in the ceiling. To discourage any further thoughts of flight, guards beat the man to death in front of his fellow inmates. The Halabja teacher remained in Topzawa for fifty-two days altogether--a much longer period of confinement than any other surviving witness has described. He was eventually released shortly after the end of the Iran-Iraq War and resettled in the Bayinjan complex, between Suleimaniyeh and Chamchamal.[21]

* * *

THE WOMEN'S PRISON AT DIBS

Karim, a 20-year old technology student from Dibs, had been aware for some time of unusual troop movements on the outskirts of town, close to the junction with the Kirkuk-Mosul highway.[22] Residents of Dibs had seen civilian buses and coasters approaching from the direction of Kirkuk, and converging on the Dibs army base--a so-called "Fighting School" where Iraqi commando forces (*Maghawir*) were trained. They had also seen sealed green police buses leaving the base, accompanied by armed men in olive fatigues. Local shopkeepers grew accustomed to visits from groups of six or seven female prisoners, accompanied by guards, and soon learned that they came from the Dibs base.

These women, and their children, were being transported from Topzawa to Dibs in large numbers from mid-April onwards, part of the three-way segregation process that took their elderly relatives off to the prison of Nugra Salman and their menfolk off, stripped to their shorts, handcuffed and blindfolded, to an unknown destination. One of the Dibs

---

[21] The supposition must be that Faraj was released under the general amnesty of September 6, 1988. By this reckoning, he would have been brought from Suleimaniyeh to Topzawa on or about July 16. The Bayinjan complex was used to resettle the survivors of several phases of Anfal. Two other testimonies suggest that its other main purpose was to rehouse returning refugees from the Halabja attack. Middle East Watch interviews, Halabja, May 8 and May 15, 1992.

[22] Middle East Watch interview, Benaslawa complex, July 6, 1992.

guards told a newcomer that the camp--two buildings within a single compound--held 7,000 Kurdish prisoners. On arrival, some of the women found themselves reunited with the children who had been plucked from their arms by the guards at Topzawa. They would remain at Dibs for between four and five months, until the Iraqi regime declared its final victory over the *peshmerga* and announced a general amnesty for the Kurds.

The women were tormented by not knowing what had become of their husbands, brothers and fathers. Yet after the abysmal conditions at Topzawa, Dibs offered significant relief. There was room to stretch out and sleep on the filthy concrete floor, and there were no restrictions on the use of the bathrooms. Water was readily available from a faucet. The food was bad, but it was at least more regular--lentil soup and hard pita bread (*samoun*) or rice, twice or three times a day. After a few weeks, there was even a little added variety in the diet. By the time that Amina, the young woman from Akoyan, arrived in June, the rations at Dibs included two eggs a week, yogurt and tea, and toward the end even a little watermelon. The guards sold soap, tea and sugar to those women who still had money, and the authorities provided one blanket for every seven prisoners. The women were allowed to do their washing in the prison courtyard, sit under trees in the shade or even sleep outdoors if the heat inside was oppressive. At least some were allowed out into the town under guard to shop. One woman who was pregnant when she arrived at Dibs was taken (albeit under military guard) to a hospital in the town, where her delivery was attended by a Kurdish woman doctor. Another said that doctors visited the base twice a week, dispensing shots and tablets, although other witnesses disputed this.

Yet for all these comparative advantages, Dibs was also a regime of unremitting horror. Ironically, the inmates found that the base was run by a fellow Kurd, a man from the Erbil area named Haji Ahmad Fatah who had made the pilgrimage to Mecca. Children who were old enough to do manual labor were forced by the guards to sweep out the halls and clean the bathrooms. "We were guarded by *Amn*, *Istikhbarat* and Ba'ath Party people," recalled a 14-year old boy who spent five months at the Dibs base. "They were always coming and beating the prisoners without any reason. They tied up my hands and beat me several times. Three *Amn* agents beat me with a stick on my back and legs. Twice they kept me tied up without food for a whole day for no reason, inside the hall where I slept, from morning until night. I could not ask why. It was impossible for anyone to intervene in Ba'ath rules."[23]

This child at least survived; many, perhaps hundreds, did not. There were few fatalities at first, but the rate increased as spring gave way to the heat of summer. Amina, the woman from Akoyan, had given birth to a baby daughter in Dibs, but within two months the child sickened and died. Four or five children died from Bileh alone. Nabat, a 28-year old mother from Qader Karam, lost two of her infant children within a month of each other. Her three-year old daughter Sharo died first; a month later, it was the turn of her two-year old son Diar. "They died of fear," Nabat said. "They were scared, got sick and died. They had diarrhea and were vomiting."[24] Sherzad, a boy of fourteen, counted seven infant deaths at Dibs in a single night. Muhammad, a boy of nine, estimated that there were fifty deaths in his family's large cell during the five months of their captivity; most were small children, but some older women also died. Habiba, who was eight at the time of Anfal, recalled being forced to sleep among dead bodies before guards came to remove them.[25]

The emaciated bodies of Nabat's two children, Sharo and Diar, were taken away by two guards from the Popular Army, who washed the bodies and interred them in the town's Gumbat Cemetery as Nabat watched. Other infant corpses were simply dumped at the town's Old Mosque, according to Karim, the 20-year old student who had watched the Dibs commando base fill up with prisoners earlier that spring. Townspeople would come to the mosque to wash the bodies, and young men from the locality--including Karim himself--would dig the burial plots in an old, abandoned children's cemetery just over a mile away. Karim helped bury four infants, and between them his friends buried at least fifty, all of them less than a year old. The people of Dibs marked

---

[23] Middle East Watch interview, Shoresh complex, May 9, 1992.

[24] Middle East Watch interview, Chamchamal, September 19, 1992.

[25] Middle East Watch interviews, Rawanduz, April 28, 1992; Shoresh complex, May 9, 1992; and Zammaki complex, July 24, 1992.

off a special plot for the new arrivals, and each of the tiny graves was marked.[26]

At regular intervals, sealed buses would drive up to the Dibs base and carry off large numbers of prisoners. On at least two occasions, these groups were made up of people from the Kalar area of southern Germian--some five hundred women and children in all, according to one estimate--and they were transported to the prison at Nugra Salman, for reasons that remain obscure.[27]   (See below p.304.) But thousands of others--perhaps half the total population of Dibs--were driven off to other, unknown destinations and vanished into the darkness of Anfal. Sherin, for example, a 23-year old woman from the village of Qeitoul Rasha (*nahya* of Qader Karam), lost two of her young nieces in this way: Perjin Ja'far Hassan, aged 12, and her younger sister Nabat. Given that the survivors of Anfal were eventually resettled in complexes that corresponded to their places of origin, and that five years have now passed without a word of news, the strong presumption must be that these two girls, and the thousands who vanished from Dibs with them, were murdered by the Iraqi authorities.[28]

---

[26] The town of Dibs lies in an area of Iraqi Kurdistan that is still controlled by the Baghdad regime. Neither the Gumbat Cemetery nor the old children's cemetery was therefore accessible to Middle East Watch for an independent forensic examination.

[27] Middle East Watch interview with a woman from Omerbel village, Kifri, March 30, 1993.

[28] Middle East Watch interview, Shoresh complex, June 29, 1992. The witness's nieces were from the Gulbagh Valley, from which, it may be recalled, a significant number of women were reported to have disappeared.

A PRISON CAMP FOR THE ELDERLY

"If you know about hell, this is hell. We have seen it."
--Muhammad Hussein Muhammad (b.1912), a
survivor of Nugra Salman.

While the trucks and buses drove north to Dibs, others headed
south from Topzawa and Tikrit, through Iraq's Arab heartland and then
further south still, into the vast deserts that stretch toward the Saudi
border, until at last they reached the abandoned fortress prison of Nugra
Salman--the "Pit of Salman." The prisoners came in four main batches,
and the total population of Nugra Salman during Anfal appears to have
been somewhere between 6,000 and 8,000.[29] The first to arrive were
thousands of captured villagers from Qara Dagh and Germian (Second
and Third Anfals), aged from about fifty to ninety, who came in huge
caravans of sealed buses in mid-April, 1988. Next, in early May, a
somewhat smaller number of elderly people arrived from the valley of
the Lesser Zab (Fourth Anfal). Third, over the course of the summer,
several busloads of women and children from southern Germian were
transferred from the prison at Dibs, to be housed in separate quarters at
Nugra Salman. Finally, in late August, just a few days before the military
declared a formal end to its Anfal campaign, several hundred returning
refugees from the gas attack on Halabja were brought to Nugra Salman,
having surrendered to the Iraqi Army as they crossed the border from
Iran. According to some reports, the Halabja contingent was of all ages,
and may even have included some young men.[30]

---

[29] These figures are based on interviews with twenty-one former inmates of
Nugra Salman, as well as a former Iraqi military officer with first-hand experience
of the prison. The interviews included seventeen men, ranging in age from
forty-five to eighty-three, and four women, aged from fifty to sixty. Asked to
estimate the total prison population, a dozen witnesses gave figures ranging from
5,000 to 11,000. Two gave much higher figures, which we have discounted.
With the exception of deaths and new arrivals, the population of Nugra Salman
remained stable until the general amnesty of September 6, 1988.

[30] One witness also told of a number of Arab prisoners being held in the
basement of Nugra Salman, wearing distinctive white *disdashas*; this could not be
corroborated in other interviews.

One of the Halabja survivors was a 33-year old woman named Urfiya. One of her five children had died on the road to Iran after the bombing. With the other four, Urfiya crossed the border and spent five months in the Iranian camps. On August 23, she recalled, the Iranians bussed some 2,000 Halabja families back to the border. The Iraqi Army was waiting for them, and took them in military trucks to Suleimaniyeh, where the Emergency Forces held them on a bread-and-water diet for five days. The place where they were confined, said Urfiya, was "full of people from Qara Dagh." At the end of this time, the young men were separated from their families and driven off in vehicles that resembled ambulances, painted white or green with a single tiny window in the rear. They have never been seen again. The women and children and the elderly were crammed into civilian buses and driven via Kirkuk, Tikrit, Baghdad and Samawa to Nugra Salman, arriving there on August 29.[31]

* * *

The journey from the outskirts of Kirkuk to Nugra Salman took between twelve and fifteen hours, with fifty or sixty prisoners crammed into windowless buses designed to hold half that number. At the head and tail of each convoy, *Amn* and *Istikhbarat* agents rode in cars with walkie-talkie radios. Some convoys moved off early in the morning and arrived at Nugra Salman late the same evening. Others left in darkness and drove all night. By guessing at the time and direction, or by peering out of the rear door if it was left open a crack for air, the prisoners could tell when they passed through a city--first Tikrit, several hours later Baghdad, and then finally Samawa. They could hear sirens wailing and glimpse curious Arab crowds lining the streets to watch the sealed vehicles go past with their human cargo. There were no stops; the detainees were

---

[31] Middle East Watch interview, Zarayen complex, July 28, 1992. Anfal, of course, cannot explain the disappearances of these young men from Suleimaniyeh, since Halabja was not included in the operation. Their disappearance may be taken, rather, as part of the routine practice of terror by the Iraqi security forces. Later press reports suggest that some younger people from Halabja may also have been disappeared from Nugra Salman. "Halabja Wounds Still Open Years After Gas Attack," (*Reuter's*, March 7, 1993), cites the case of one woman from Halabja who has not seen her four children, aged 10-24, since they were interned there.

given no food or water, and the presence of guards with Kalashnikovs silenced any complaint.

At Samawa, the elderly prisoners sometimes became aware that the convoys were dividing into two; while their vehicles continued to head south, others peeled off in a different direction. These were the buses that carried the younger Kurdish prisoners from Topzawa, and they were never seen again. After Samawa, there was nothing but barren desert, dotted with the rubble of destroyed settlements--"like our villages, flattened by bulldozers," said one woman.[32] Three hours to the southwest of Samawa, the table-land dropped away sharply, and there in the depression below, visible only at the last moment, lay the town of Al-Salman. And a mile and a quarter away in the desert, surrounded by a barbed-wire perimeter fence and guarded by watch towers at each corner, was the prison of Nugra Salman itself.

The buses entered through one of the two large gates and came to a rest in a huge central courtyard, "three times as long as the soccer field at Suleimaniyeh."[33] The first arrivals from Topzawa in mid-April found Nugra Salman dark and empty. It was an old building, dating back to the days of the Iraqi monarchy and perhaps even earlier.[34] It had been abandoned for years, used by Arab nomads to shelter their herds. The bare walls were scrawled with the diaries of political prisoners. On the door of one cell, a guard had daubed "Khomeini eats shit." Over the main gate, someone else had written "Welcome to Hell." Over the rear entrance, another sign read: "It is rare for anyone to survive three months in this place."

Whatever interrogation the Iraqi authorities deemed necessary for these elderly and infirm victims of Anfal had already been carried out at Topzawa. Here, at Nugra Salman, there was only a quick registration of name, occupation and place of residence, accompanied by jeers and threats from the guards. "You are here to die," said one, "on the orders of Saddam Hussein and Ali Hassan al-Majid." With this, the new arrivals

---

[32] Middle East Watch interview, Erbil, April 23, 1992.

[33] Middle East Watch interview, Ja'faran, Qara Dagh, May 11, 1992.

[34] The Iraqi monarchy was overthrown in a military coup on July 14, 1958. Its main architect was Brigadier Abd-al-Karim Qasem, who subsequently became Prime Minister.

were shoved into the cells, or halls, that filled both stories of the prison. These bare rooms varied greatly in size: some of them held only fifty or sixty prisoners, others several hundreds.[35] The doors were locked from 10:00 p.m. to 7:00 a.m. At other times, the inmates could circulate freely.

The arrival of the first detainees coincided more or less with the beginning of Ramadan on April 17, and during the holy month the food was better than it had been at Topzawa.[36] There was rice, vegetable soup, potatoes and tomatoes, even meat and fruit on occasion. Water came from a well, through a standpipe in the yard, though it was hot, salty and bitter--"like snake poison," said one man. Many inmates believed that the first health crisis at Nugra Salman was connected to drinking this water. The first deaths occurred early in May, soon after the arrival of the second wave of prisoners, those from the valley of the Lesser Zab.

* * *

One of those who arrived in this batch was Abd-al-Qader Abdullah Askari, the 68-year old village head from Goktapa, who had lost sixteen members of his family in the chemical weapons attack on May 3. During his four months in Nugra Salman, Abd-al-Qader--one of the few literate prisoners and an Arabic speaker to boot--emerged as a natural

---

[35] There are persistent, if somewhat contradictory, reports of a basement level at Nugra Salman, from which the sound of weeping and screams could be heard. A former Iraqi infantry officer who visited the prison before Anfal said that this basement was entered through a heavy barred trapdoor with a double lock. The space beneath was approximately two meters high--just enough for a prisoner to stand up. The officer also described a punishment cell at Nugra Salman, built "like a bird cage, with only enough room to sit down." Middle East Watch interview, Erbil, April 26, 1992.

[36] Ramadan, the ninth month of the Muslim calendar, is a time of fasting from sunrise to sunset. After sunset, meals tend to be more lavish than at other times, and the rations given to the inmates of Nugra Salman--assuming they were intended to be eaten in the evening--may be taken as a sign of relative lenience by the authorities toward the elderly. (By the same token, of course, if these foods were offered during daylight hours, they could be construed as a mockery, or a temptation of the Kurds' Muslim faith. The context, however, seems to make this explanation unlikely.)

leader of the inmates, and his testimony is worth quoting at length here. After the first night at Topzawa,

> At 8:30 a.m. a military man came in and announced, "Prepare yourselves." We had nothing, we were ready, we had nothing to pack. They told us to leave the room. We noticed 150 or 200 vehicles waiting in two groups, like ambulances, but green.[37] These could only take ten people, but they put twenty-seven in ours. There were two doors: a small narrow one which only the guard could enter, and a second door through which they pushed us. It was very hot, but they closed the door and locked it. In our car there were only elderly people.

> After an hour or an hour and a half, we called for water. I told them in Arabic, "We are thirsty; give us water." -- "Water is forbidden for you, it is not allowed." After a while, one friend wanted to get out and relieve himself. I informed the soldier. "It is not allowed for you," he said. After ten minutes the man could not hold himself any longer and we smelled a bad smell in the car. Five fainted from the smell and the heat. We wished for death. Nothing was allowed to us. All the men took their clothes off because of the heat, wearing only their shorts. The car went on moving and we did not know where it was going.

> One and a half hours before nightfall we arrived at a fort and got out. It was deserted. They took us into a long yard, with soldiers and police all around. More cars were arriving and emptying out men and women. The number reached 400. They brought water in buckets without any glasses. We were like cows, putting our heads down to get the water at once, three at a time

---

[37] Although Abd-al-Qader's estimate of numbers here may be high, his figures in general appeared to be unusually reliable, especially where the numbers of deaths at Nugra Salman were concerned. See p.232.

drinking from the bucket. The water was hot, the temperature to wash with, and it was salty.

[After registration] a guard asked for newcomers and told them to go with him. It was fifteen minutes before dark. We went to the second floor and they put sixty-four of us into one room, about eight meters by six. I objected: "We are not animals to be crowded all in one room. How can we sleep and eat." The man in charge answered, "Shut up. This is what we prepared for you." After three minutes he left and another came to the door with a sack on his shoulder. It was a prisoner. He said, "Brothers, we know you were not given anything because you are newcomers. We brought our shares for you tonight. Take this bread, since they will not give you any food until the morning."

In the morning a prisoner from another hall came and recruited four of us to go with him to get the bread rations for the cell. After twenty minutes the four men came back with three sacks of bread. Each prisoner got three *samoun* for the entire day, breakfast, lunch and dinner.[38] The bread was not made from wheat but from *zorat* [a coarse grain normally used as animal feed].

* * *

DEATHS AT NUGRA SALMAN

The Ramadan rations were now a thing of the past, and on the new starvation diet of bread and contaminated water, the conditions at Nugra Salman deteriorated sharply. The prisoners were fatigued and infested by lice. By late May there was a steady stream of deaths, some days three, some six or seven, and sometimes as many as a dozen. Abd-

---

[38] Other witnesses said that the ration was only two *samoun* a day--one at 10:00 a.m. and the other at 10:00 p.m. It may be that this varied from time to time.

al-Qader tried his best to keep count of the deaths. By early September, when he was finally released, he had tallied 517--victims of the inhuman conditions at Nugra Salman and the depraved indifference of the Iraqi authorities. Later, after his release, he heard that another forty-five had died over two successive nights in September.

Abd-al-Qader's figures, which suggest an average of four or five deaths a day during the period of his imprisonment from starvation, disease and physical abuse, are extremely credible. Certainly they bear out the more impressionistic estimates given by many other witnesses. The additional forty-five deaths may have been connected with an epidemic that some survivors say broke out after the arrival of the returned refugees from Halabja at the end of August 1988. This outbreak prompted the arrival of a dozen white-coated doctors from Samawa, who advised the prisoners to stop drinking the water.

The authorities at Nugra Salman appear to have responded to the steady stream of fatalities in two ways. The first was to arrange for a daily delivery of water by tanker truck from Samawa; the second was for the guards to initiate a petty extortion racket, selling food at grossly inflated prices to those prisoners who had managed to make it through Topzawa with some cash still in their pockets.

The tanker usually came from Samawa twice a day, although sometimes it missed a day altogether. When the water arrived, there was pandemonium as the prisoners rushed the truck. They were allowed only a few minutes to fill their pitchers, struggling for access to the plastic hosepipe as the guards taunted them, allowing the precious fluid to splash on to the ground and lashing out at people randomly with sticks and strips of coaxial cable. Sensing easy money, the truck driver took to selling the prisoners buckets of water for four dinars ($12) each. Later, he also offered to bring canned milk and meat, lentils, tomato paste and soap.

The driver's example was quickly taken up by the guards, who were from *Amn*, according to some witnesses, or from *Istikhbarat*, according to others. A cup of rice was one dinar. Cigarettes were three dinars ($9) a pack. Tomato juice in cans past their expiry date cost twelve ($36). According to Abd-al-Qader:

> We told the prisoners in charge of the food to speak to
> the guards to find a way to get rid of the bad food and
> get sugar and tea, even if we had to buy them, because

the deaths were very bad. They managed to get sugar, tea and oil with our money. The food came secretly at night. They sold us tomato paste for four dinars, in cans which were priced for sale by the government at six dirhams.[39] We paid eighty dinars for a sack of sugar and seventy dinars for a sack of rice--official price, eleven dinars.

The first thing we got was the tomato paste. We managed to borrow a pot from a cell whose prisoners had been there longer than us, and we cooked food in it. We put our bread into the tomato paste soup and absorbed all the liquid. This was really like a feast to us.

But the effects of this black market were short-lived, other than for the lucky few who had managed to keep money back after Topzawa. The prisoners grew weaker, scarcely able to take advantage of the brief afternoon exercise period, when they were allowed to mingle in the central courtyard. The deaths continued, and among the dead were some of the children who had been newly transferred to Nugra Salman from Dibs.

The dead were not permitted the dignity of a decent burial. Indeed, they were often not even moved from the spot where they died, but left there for as long as three days to rot in the summer heat. This was evidently a matter of deliberate policy. "After a few weeks," one woman recalled, "my husband died in my arms. He had gotten extremely weak and thin and he had been badly beaten by the prison guards. My husband's body lay in the prison hall for one day. The guards did not let me bury him and I had to beg them; the guard said the body had to remain in the prison until it rotted."[40]

Eventually *Amn* agents would register the names of the dead, strip them of any remaining money and valuables and order the corpses to be stuffed into sacks and loaded onto handcarts of the sort normally used for

---

[39] The dinar is made up of 1,000 fils; 50 fils are one dirham, and 20 dirhams one dinar.

[40] Middle East Watch interview with a woman from Qala village (*nahya* Naujul), Benaslawa complex, April 20, 1992.

garbage disposal. The theft of money in particular infuriated Abd-al-Qader:

> One man died with 400 dinars [$1,200] on him. An *Amn* man came, took the money, kissed it, and said this was for the government. I insulted the prisoners about this, telling them, "You are not animals! Anything that the dead relatives leave is yours. Do not leave it for others. Use it, you need it." -- "What else could we do?" they answered. "We are afraid." -- "Inside this building, nothing can be sent to you from the outside," I told them. "You cannot live without that money. You may be afraid of God, but God will not punish you, I assure you. I will answer for you on the Day of Judgment." They followed my advice. From then on, they left only one dinar or a half dinar in the pockets of the dead for the guards. The guards came two or three times, but when they found such small amounts they abandoned the search.

The prisoners tried as best they could to wash the bodies and prepare them for burial according to Islamic doctrine. At first, if there was money, the tanker driver from Samawa might be persuaded to bring a shroud. But when the money ran out, the only shroud available was the dead person's Kurdish headscarf (*jamadani*) or one of the scarce prison blankets. Groups of prisoners--at least two, sometimes four or six men, weakened and fatigued by hunger--would be assembled to carry the corpse away, while prison guards kicked and punched them to hurry the process along, shouting epithets all the while. "You are saboteurs, and you deserve to die like dogs," one guard shouted.

A ten-minute trudge through the stony desert brought them to the gravesite, which lay a few hundred yards to the east of the prison. It comprised a series of long trenches, no more than a meter deep, dug by bulldozers. There were no markers, although the mourners tried when they could to mark the spot with stones. The bodies were laid roughly inside and dirt tossed over them. The guards allowed no time for prayers for the dead. When thirty or forty corpses filled a trench, the bulldozer would smooth it over to remove all traces and proceed to dig another.[41]

When the burial party returned the next day, broken limbs and bloody rags would be strewn around, for during the night the freshly turned gravesite attracted packs of wild desert dogs. The guards were terrified by these animals, believing that they became rabid after eating human flesh, and shot at any they could see. But few of the remains of those who died at Nugra Salman were allowed to rest in peace. "Go bury the bodies for the dogs," the guards would taunt the survivors.

* * *

The man who presided over this cruel regime was named Hajjaj, an *Amn* lieutenant by most accounts.[42]   Hajjaj was a feared and detested figure, described by one witness as a "bald, husky young man" from *Amn* headquarters in Baghdad, who drove a red Volkswagen Passat manufactured in Brazil. His deputy was a man called Shamkhi. An uncle of Lt. Hajjaj, one Khalaf, was one of the guards.

Hajjaj and his associates were notorious for beating prisoners on the slightest pretext, or on none at all. One man in his sixties was beaten for requesting a light bulb. "Go to [PUK leader Jalal] Talabani for bulbs," a guard told him mockingly.[43]   Another inmate, weakened by hunger, fell asleep one day when Hajjaj was in his cell. "He slapped me right away," the man recalled, "and said, 'You shall never sleep in my

---

[41] The only exception to this harsh behavior was if the guard was a Shi'a Muslim; witnesses described the Shi'a (including even Shi'a military officers commanding troops during Anfal operations) as having shown the Kurds numerous small kindnesses.

[42] One witness queried this, and thought Lt. Hajjaj was an army officer. The same witness identified the "head of the prison" as a man named Sa'id Hama, but was unable to specify to which agency he belonged. There was a general and understandable confusion among witnesses when it came to identifying particular government agencies by their uniforms or other visible signs. At Nugra Salman, as at Topzawa and the earlier processing centers, witnesses variously identified their oppressors as being from *Amn*, *Istikhbarat*, the regular army and police.

[43] Middle East Watch interview, Erbil, April 23, 1992.

presence.' Then he made me go and sit in the place where the garbage was kept."[44] Age and gender offered no protection. "Is this child a *peshmerga?*," the same man asked a guard one day. "Is this woman?" -- "Yes, they are," the guard answered. "They are all *peshmerga* and they are criminals." On another occasion, Abd-al-Qader Abdullah Askari saw Hajjaj kicking a group of young women who had recently arrived from Dibs and hitting them with a length of plastic tubing.[45]

Hajjaj also punished prisoners by forcing them to crawl on their bellies. If the result was not to his liking, a guard would stamp on the small of the prisoner's back to force him lower. But the punishment most favored by Hajjaj, according to many accounts, was to expose prisoners to the blazing midday sun. Men, women and children alike were subjected to this treatment, even if they were too weak to walk and had to be dragged to the spot. The prisoners would be forced to squat with their heads lowered, normally for two hours. Any movement would be punished with a beating. A variant on this routine was to tie the prisoner to a metal post in the sun. There were nine of these posts sunk in concrete in the central courtyard at Nugra Salman, each taller than a person and thicker than an electricity pole.[46] Some prisoners were reportedly suspended upside down from the posts, tied at the feet by their Kurdish cummerbund, and with their unbound hands barely clearing the ground.

---

[44] Middle East Watch interview, Sumoud complex, May 20, 1992.

[45] One even more lurid account spoke of a large group of single women being kept apart from the other prisoners and regularly raped by *Amn* agents. One of these women reportedly killed herself with a knife as a result. The rape of female detainees in Iraq has been well substantiated elsewhere, and is even known to have been recorded on videotape. Middle East Watch did not succeed, however, in speaking to any witnesses or victims of rape at Nugra Salman. The Kurds, it should be noted, are reluctant to talk to outsiders about matters involving sexual abuse.

[46] The description strongly suggests that one original purpose of these posts would have been for the use of firing squads. Prisoners can be seen tied to similar posts in captured videotapes of the execution of Kurdish prisoners.

The inmates of Nugra Salman had to endure Lt. Hajjaj's brutal custody until September 6, when the general amnesty allowed them to go free--but not to go home.

———

9
THE FIRING SQUADS

"Hell and Elysium swarm with ghosts of men
That I have sent from sundry foughten fields
To spread my fame through hell and up to heaven."
     --*Marlowe,* **Tamburlaine the Great, Part One** *(V, i)*

"It was God's wish."
     -- *Mustafa, who escaped a mass execution*
     during Anfal.

MUHAMMAD'S STORY

At least six people--the youngest a boy of twelve, the eldest a man of thirty-eight with nine children of his own--have survived to tell the truth about what happened to the tens of thousands of Iraqi Kurds who were driven away in the convoys of sealed vehicles from the Popular Army camp at Topzawa. All six were from the Germian area, scene of the Third Anfal.

Muhammad, the 32-year old member of the *peshmerga* backing force from the village of Aliyani Taza in southern Germian, had arrived with his family at the army fort at Qoratu on about April 16. (see above p.145) They spent three days there before being moved to Topzawa, where Muhammad was separated from his two wives and seven children. None of his family ever returned alive, with the exception of his parents, who survived Nugra Salman.[1]

Muhammad spent two days in Topzawa. He was not questioned. He was given nothing to eat. On the third day the guards came to his "hall," which held about 500 prisoners. They handcuffed the men in pairs and took them to a line of vehicles painted in camouflage colors. Each vehicle held twenty-eight prisoners; Muhammad counted the seats. It was

---

[1] Muhammad's story is based on a Middle East Watch interview with him on the site of Aliyani Taza village, March 30, 1993.

the middle of the afternoon when the convoy moved off. They drove for perhaps six hours, but Muhammad quickly lost all sense of direction and had no idea where they were going. All he could tell was that most of the journey was on the paved highway; the final hour was on a bumpy dirt road.

When the convoy eventually stopped, the driver kept the motor running. Over the throb of the engine, Muhammad could hear the sound of gunfire outside. The prisoners were hustled out into the darkness and searched for any identity cards and money that might have been missed earlier. Muhammad lost his last 700 dinars. When the search was completed, the guards removed the handcuffs that bound Muhammad to his neighbor, a man from the village of Babakr, close to Aliyani Taza. In place of the handcuffs, the guards brought a length of string, which they used to tie the twenty-eight prisoners in a single line by their left hands. The men were ordered to stand facing the edge of a freshly dug trench, just long enough to accommodate the twenty-eight bodies as they fell.

The knot binding Muhammad's left hand had been carelessly tied, and he managed to tug it free of his wrist and bolt a moment before the soldiers opened fire. Beyond the trench was an open field, and the springtime grass had grown tall enough to conceal Muhammad from the truck headlights that were now trained in his direction. To his astonishment, the guards did not give chase. Behind him, the clatter of gunfire continued.

Muhammad ran and walked for four days without food, drinking rainwater from puddles along the way. Trying to chart his route by the sun, he set out in what he thought was the direction of Germian, across an endless flat plain planted with wheat and barley. From the clothes of the shepherds he spotted at intervals, he could tell that he was in an Arab area. After four days, so exhausted that he could not walk another step, he stumbled into an Arab village. The people gathered around to stare. "Look," they said, "it is a Kurd who has fallen out of an airplane."

The remainder of Muhammad's odyssey is too long to recount in detail here. Imprisoned and beaten by the Arab villagers, handed over to the police, interrogated, taken to Mosul, jailed again, transferred to the Kirkuk police and then to Suleimaniyeh, to Kalar and back once more to Suleimaniyeh, amnestied and finally inducted into the army. Miraculously, the police believed his story--which he never varied--that he was a member of the *jahsh* of Fatah Beg, the *mustashar* from Kalar. The ordinary Iraqi police, who were almost certainly not privy to the truth about the Anfal mass executions, never realized that they were dealing with an *Anfalaki*. *Amn*, which would certainly have pressed the matter further, was never brought in to elucidate Muhammad's case. The man was truly blessed with a talent for survival.

* * *

OZER, OMAR AND IBRAHIM

Remarkably, four of the other five survivors of the Anfal firing squads travelled together to their execution site as part of a single convoy. Three of them were even in the same vehicle--although one of the three did not know the others, and has not met them since. It is possible, then, to reconstruct their composite story in considerable detail.

Ozer, the young man who had spent his last night at Topzawa shivering with cold as he listened to revving bus engines and contemplated the pools of diesel oil and fresh blood on a cement floor, was perhaps the most articulate of these witnesses. Ozer was twenty-five at the time of Anfal, an unmarried construction worker who had seen action in the war against Iran and deserted several times from the Iraqi Army. He had been born not ten miles from Topzawa, in the village of Tarjil, on the main road between Kirkuk and the *nahya* of Leilan. But he had moved around a lot before settling in nearby Jafan, a tiny hamlet of just seventeen houses. There he stayed until April 1987, when the army attacked and burned the village. This time Ozer moved to Khidr Reihan, a peaceful village two and a half hours on foot from the *nahya* of Qader Karam that was home to several other deserters and draft dodgers.

Like so many others, Ozer took to the hills when the Third Anfal approached his home on about April 10. Hearing the rumor of a temporary amnesty in Qader Karam, he was one of the thousands who surrendered to the *jahsh* forces commanded by Qasem Agha, the one-eyed *mustashar* from Koysinjaq. Over the next few days, Ozer passed through the Qader Karam police station and the army brigade headquarters in Chamchamal. The truck that took him from there to the local office of *Amn* was part of the convoy that was caught up in the attempted revolt of the townspeople of Chamchamal. But Ozer was not one of those they succeeded in rescuing, and finally, on April 14, he arrived at Topzawa.

At this stage, Ozer met up with an acquaintance whom we shall call Omar, a 22-year old draft dodger who had also fled from Jafan the previous year and resettled in Khidr Reihan. Omar had fled to the hills when Anfal began, and surrendered to Qasem Agha's men two days after Ozer. From Chamchamal, they were trucked together to Topzawa, where most of their cellmates were strangers. But two of these men were destined to share with Ozer and Omar what was intended to be their final journey.

Both of them were draft dodgers from *peshmerga*-controlled villages in the *nahya* of Qader Karam. The elder of the two was "Mustafa," a 38-year old resident of Top Khana; the other, "Ibrahim," was a 23-year old father of four from Kani Qader Khwaru. Neither man was an active fighter, but Ibrahim had carried an Iranian-made Kalashnikov rifle as a member of the civilian "backing force," and was a friend or blood relative of most of the *peshmerga* who had died in the army's bloody assault on the PUK base at Tazashar, at the opening of the Third Anfal campaign. Like Ozer and Omar, both Mustafa and Ibrahim had been fooled by the phony offer of a three-day amnesty in Qader Karam. Mustafa had turned himself in to the *jahsh* led by Sheikh Mu'tassem; Ibrahim had surrendered to the forces of the *mustashar* Raf'at Gilli. Both men had passed through the first-stage collection facility at Aliawa.

The testimonies of these four men contain some minor discrepancies over dates. But at some point between April 15 and April 17 (the first day of the holy month of Ramadan), at about 8:00 in the morning, they were hustled, together with hundreds of others, into the prison yard at Topzawa. A caravan of sealed vehicles waited under military guard, with their engines running. They were of two kinds. Some (eighteen, by one count) were windowless police buses, painted green or white, and Ozer, Ibrahim and Omar were shoved into one of these. Ozer had time to notice that it had a Mosul registration; its license plate read "Nineveh Police," and the number was 5036 or 5037. Mustafa traveled in a second type of vehicle, which resembled a large ambulance or covered truck. The smaller police buses held thirty-four or thirty-five people each, in forward-facing rows two abreast, divided by a central aisle. Mustafa's truck held between fifty and sixty prisoners, squashed together on four benches that ran lengthwise along the vehicle.

To the last, it appears that the prisoners were grouped together according to their places of origin. Ozer recognized faces from a number of places in the Leilan-Qader Karam area--Khidr Beg, Qashqa and

Qarachiwar--as well as two others from his own home village of Khidr Reihan. Everyone in the bus was young, aged from 20-40, Ibrahim recalled. But Ozer thought that some of the men were much older, "with white beards."

The inside of the buses was hellish. The vehicle in which Ozer, Ibrahim and Mustafa rode was thick with old urine and human feces. Its previous occupants had scrawled brief messages in Kurdish on the seat-backs: "To the Saudi border"..."To the Kuwaiti border"..."To Ar'ar."[2] In these smaller buses, the prisoners were separated from the driver's compartment by a padlocked sliding door. The driver himself entered by a separate door on the right of the bus. A military guard rode alongside him, armed with a Kalashnikov with a folding stock and wearing the distinctive uniform of the army's Special Forces (Quwat al-Khaseh)--camouflage fatigues of yellow drab with irregular green splotches and a red beret with the golden insignia of a bird of prey with outstretched wings.

Set into the sliding door that separated the two compartments was a small wire-mesh opening, perhaps six inches square, through which the prisoners closest to the front could see the road ahead and the driver's rear-view mirror. Ozer estimated that his was the thirty-fifth vehicle in the convoy.[3] To the front and rear of each bus, he could glimpse pick-up trucks of the sort used by Amn, with mounted machine-guns.

Seated toward the front of the bus was a man named Anwar Tayyar. A dark, stoutly built man, Tayyar was a former peshmerga; he had also worked as a driver, and knew the roads intimately. For this reason, his fellow prisoners asked him to figure out where they were heading. Sneaking glances through the wire grille, Tayyar at first reported that they were following the road to Mosul. There was a gasp of fear,

---

[2] Ar'ar, an Iraqi-Saudi border post and a way-station for pilgrims traveling to Mecca, was mentioned in several interviews as a site for internments and mass executions during Anfal. A guard at Nugra Salman, for instance, told one elderly detainee that Kurdish prisoners from Anfal were being held there.

[3] Again there are some minor discrepancies in the witnesses' estimates of the size of the convoy. But the various figures given to Middle East Watch would suggest that it contained between 1,000 and 1,500 prisoners.

because, as Ibrahim recalled, "most of the government's killers are in Mosul."[4] The passengers were convinced they were going to die.

Soon, however, the bus swung off the Mosul road and turned to the southwest. "We have been saved," said Anwar Tayyar with a sigh of relief. Perhaps, the men speculated, they were merely being transferred to another prison. But the buses drove on, stopping occasionally for a few minutes. At intervals, the men begged the *Quwat al-Khaseh* guard for water. "Just a minute," the man would answer, but the water never arrived. In the airless heat and stench of Mustafa's bus, the prisoners were reduced to drinking their own urine from their shoes.

As the afternoon wore on, Anwar Tayyar began to lose his bearings. "Samawa!" he exclaimed at one point, but then someone else recognized Falluja, a sizeable town on the Euphrates. Just outside Falluja, Ozer noticed that the convoy was splitting into two parts. The majority of the vehicles continued in a different direction; five, including Ozer's bus and the larger green truck carrying Mustafa, drove due west, into the rapidly approaching sunset. Before long, they passed the larger city of Ramadi to their left. After leaving Ramadi behind them, they continued for at least another fifteen minutes, perhaps as much as a half-hour, on the paved highway, turning right once at a junction to cross a heavily guarded bridge over a river--presumably the Euphrates once more.

At the far end of the bridge, the five vehicles halted. It was now about 6:30 p.m., and ten hours had passed since their departure from Topzawa. Through the wire-mesh screen, the prisoners could see that they had stopped outside a police station, under a clump of date palms. They could hear a conversation between one of their army guards and an officer at the police station. Although the man was addressed as "sir," his uniform bore no insignia of rank. It was clear that the guard was transferring the prisoners into this officer's custody. He handed over a list of their names, and told the officer that the vehicles were to remain with the police "until the mission is completed," at which time they should be returned.

The drivers and Special Forces guards climbed down from the vehicles at this point. Their replacements were dressed all in green with black berets--a uniform that is characteristic of both *Amn* and the Ba'ath Party, as well as the regular Iraqi police. The officer and several other

---

[4] The reference is apparently to the high proportion of Republican Guards from Mosul.

men jumped into two Toyota Landcruisers. There were also two bulldozers.

With the bulldozers in the lead, the new nine-vehicle caravan drove west along a bumpy paved road that ran parallel to the Euphrates. In the fading light, the silhouettes of date palms fringed the road to the right. One of the prisoners in Ozer's bus was weak and faint, and a prisoner who spoke a little Arabic begged the new driver for water. This was not allowed, the driver answered. "Let the man die," he said. "You are all men of Jalal Talabani."

After half an hour, the convoy turned right on to a dirt road. Ahead the prisoners saw only desert and darkness. Some began to pray, muttering the Shehadeh--"There is no God but Allah, and Muhammad is his Prophet..." Remembered images of his family flashed through Ibrahim's mind. By now all the men were weeping, asking what they had done to deserve such a fate, kissing each other's beards and exchanging words of forgiveness, as is the Muslim custom among those who know they are about to die.

* * *

It was almost dark, and the meaning of time had begun to dissolve. Ozer thought that the sealed buses traveled along this rutted desert track for about ten minutes; Omar estimated that the journey took from 15-30 minutes; Ibrahim said that it felt more like an hour. Suddenly, the bus lurched to a stop, bogged down in the deep sand. The vehicle behind, the last one in the convoy, swerved to the right to avoid it and got stuck as well. Through the wire-mesh screen in the sliding door, Ozer could see that the three remaining buses, as well as the two Landcruisers and one of the two bulldozers, had driven on ahead. In the half-light he could just make out the tops of the vehicles bobbing as they crested a rise and dipped into a shallow depression in the desert a quarter of a mile or so ahead. The driver turned off the engine.

Since the final turn on to the dirt road, there had no longer been any room for denial or wishful thinking. The men knew exactly what lay in store for them, and they began to plan feverishly, speaking in Kurdish in the knowledge that neither the guard nor the driver could understand them. When the guards arrived to kill them, they would put up a struggle. "Even if only one of the thirty-five survived, it was worth the try," said Ibrahim.

In the sudden quiet, the prisoners could hear the steady chatter of gunfire from automatic weapons, and the churning, whining sound of bulldozer engines. After perhaps twenty minutes, the guns fell silent. Out of the darkness, a bulldozer lumbered toward them and took up position behind the bus. Gears screaming, it tried several times to push the vehicle out of the sand, but the front wheels only dug in deeper. Next it tried to lift the bus out by its rear end, and Ozer thought the driver meant to tip them headlong into a trench, bus and all. At last, the bulldozer managed to drag the stalled vehicle out frontwards. The driver climbed down from his cab, exhausted by the effort, and took out his hip flask. The prisoners begged for water, banging on the windowless steel walls. The driver drank deeply and jeeringly held up his flask as the rest of the liquid trickled away into the sand.

It was now 7:30 p.m., and quite dark. The men were just able to tell the time by squinting at a watch that a prisoner from the village of Khidr Beg had somehow managed to hang on to at Topzawa. Twice more, there were volleys of gunfire and the sound of screams. After about half an hour, the two Landcruisers returned, with the officer who had joined the convoy at the bridge over the Euphrates. The driver of Ozer's bus climbed down from his seat, walked around to the back of the vehicle and turned off the overhead light in the rear compartment. Having done this, he went back to his cab and turned his headlights on full-beam. As Ozer and his companions whimpered in panic, the three dozen occupants of the second stalled bus were dragged into the pool of light, and a uniformed firing squad opened up on them with Kalashnikovs and pistols. When the firing stopped, the men were dragged into a freshly dug pit. Ozer noticed that some of the bodies were still moving. Only one busload of prisoners now remained.

The men's plan was this: When the first guard entered the bus to take the prisoners away, the strongest of them would overpower him, grab his weapon and try to wedge the door open. Most of the men were too weak to assist, but Ozer, Omar and a handful of others watched the sliding partition door. Ibrahim waited fearfully at the back, ready to bolt if he could. Through the grille, Ozer could see that two guards with pistols had taken up position on either side of the door; another, who carried a Kalashnikov stood by the driver's seat; while a fourth man, also armed with a Kalashnikov, guarded the outer door, with one foot planted on the step and the other on the ground.

After a few moments, one of the uniformed guards, a burly man with a thick neck, removed the padlock and slid back the connecting door to the driver's compartment. As soon as he did so, a prisoner named Salam lunged forward to strike him. But a second guard in the driver's cab opened fire with his pistol, killing Salam instantly, and slammed the door shut again. Ozer heard the first guard, apparently an officer, declare that he would execute the prisoners one by one.

Seizing command of the situation, Ozer issued his instructions. When the guards took the first prisoner out, Omar would throw his weight against the rail of the sliding door to prevent it from being closed. The other men would hurl themselves into the breach. And that is essentially what happened. The burly guard returned, pulled one prisoner into the open doorway and tied a white cloth around his eyes as a blindfold. As he turned to drag the man away, half a dozen prisoners rushed forward. Several of them laid hold of the shoulder strap of the guard's Kalashnikov, while he kept a firm grip of the stock and the barrel. Ozer yelled at another prisoner to punch the officer in the face. Although the man, like everyone, was weakened by several days without food, he succeeded in landing a blow on the officer's eye. Ozer wrenched the rifle free, but the officer managed to break loose, unclip the magazine and hurl it out of the bus behind him, rendering the weapon useless.

Pouring through the open door, the prisoners cut off the escape of the guard who had been standing by the driver's seat. Gunfire erupted, and two men fell dead on top of Ozer. Another prisoner tried to leap from the bus and was also cut down. As Ozer struggled to free himself, he saw the second of the four guards--the one who had killed Salam--stagger toward him, bleeding profusely from the shoulder. The man was screaming, "Abu Saleh, come and help me!" It appeared that he had been shot by his own side. Ozer reached for the man's pistol but could not find it; instead, he wrestled him to the ground by his injured arm, and the guard lay still, apparently unconscious. Meanwhile the soldiers or police outside continued to rake the bus with gunfire, and the men in the passenger compartment cowered under the bus seats. Bodies piled up inside the bus, and Ibrahim took a painful flesh wound in the right buttock. He was also dimly aware that he could no longer see through his right eye. In the confusion, Omar managed to wriggle under the vehicle as bullets ricocheted from it on all sides. Ozer felt his leg grazed by a flying piece of shrapnel. As he lay there, he heard a strange sound between the bursts of firing. At first he could not place it; then he realized that it was the sound of blood dripping from the bus. Almost all of his fellow prisoners were dead.

* * *

MUSTAFA'S STORY

The remaining three vehicles that had accompanied the convoy from Kirkuk had come to a halt a few hundred yards ahead, in the shallow depression that Ozer had glimpsed through the driver's window. Here, the executions had proceeded in a more orderly and efficient fashion. It was *maghreb*--sunset--when guards flung open the rear door of the truck in which Mustafa, the 38-year old father of nine from the village of Top Khana, had travelled from Topzawa. The men were dragged out in pairs. In his fear, Mustafa left his shoes behind; he had taken them off in the bus because of the heat. He, too, was aware of the constant rat-a-tat of gunfire, which seemed not to come from a single site but from many directions at once. But he could see nothing, only darkness and desert.

The guards carried out a hasty body search, stripping Mustafa of his military ID papers but somehow failing to find the 200 dinars that he had managed to keep hidden in his clothing at Topzawa. He felt his hands being roughly bound behind him with his Kurdish cummerbund. His eyes were blindfolded with his headscarf, as were his companion's. The two men were ordered to walk. Mustafa, knowing that he was to die, began to recite under his breath the *Ayat al-Kursi* from the Koran. "God: there is no god but He, the Living, the Everlasting..."[5]   He moved forward for about twenty yards, then felt himself stumbling down a slight incline. From a distance, the voice of a guard ordered the two men to lie

---

[5] The *Ayat al-Kursi*, "the Throne," is verse 255 of the second *Sura* of the Koran. It reads in full, "God: there is no god but He, the Living, the Everlasting. Slumber seizes him not, neither sleep; to Him belongs all that is in the heavens and the earth. Who is there that shall intercede with Him save by His leave? He knows what lies before them and what is after them, and they comprehend not anything of His knowledge save such as He will. His Throne comprises the heavens and the earth; the preserving of them oppresses Him not. He is the All-high, the All-glorious." Arberry (trans.), *The Koran Interpreted*, p.65.

down on their backs. As he obeyed the command, Mustafa felt himself sandwiched between his companion and another, inert body. His ears picked up the sound of a bulldozer's engine revving.

The next thing Mustafa heard was automatic weapons firing. To his side he felt a jolt and heard a groan. The clatter of gunfire ceased, and Mustafa heard the guards walk away. He realized that the bullets had missed him. Praying that he was unobserved, he tried to wriggle sideways, feeling more dead bodies as he moved, and struggling to loosen the cummerbund that bound his hands. Minutes later, he heard the guards return with another two prisoners, who lay down in the trench and were riddled with gunfire; then another pair, and another round of firing, this time a little further away. Mustafa was still unharmed. "It was God's wish," he thought.

This time, when the guards departed, Mustafa managed to work his blindfold loose. He saw that he was lying in a long, shallow trench, perhaps twenty feet wide and eighteen inches deep. The end of the trench, where the bulldozer had exited, was close by: this was the shallow incline into which he and his fellow prisoner had stumbled. In the other direction, the trench stretched away as far as Mustafa could see. It was filled with hundreds of corpses.

This macabre scene was illuminated by the headlights of the bulldozer, which now stood at the shallow entrance to the mass grave, its engine running. The driver appeared to be waiting for orders to cover the bodies with dirt when the trench was full, as it now almost was. Over the lip of the trench, Mustafa could still make out the dark shape of the vehicle that had brought him here. For fifteen minutes he lay where he was, listening to staccato gunfire and screams. After a while he realized that the sound was not in fact coming from all sides. The area behind him was silent, and Mustafa began cautiously to clamber over the bloody piles of dead bodies, away from the noise of the firing squads. Peering out, he saw that his was the last of many trenches. Behind him there was only desert. Mustafa ran.

He ran until morning, stopping only occasionally to catch his breath. Wild dogs chased him, smelling blood, and he kept them at bay by throwing stones at them. He saw lights in the darkness, but was afraid to go toward them. When the sun rose, he stumbled on to a dirt road. In the distance, he could see a city. But before he could reach it, he realized that the nearest building was a military base; two soldiers caught sight of him and waved him away on to another dirt road, but did not come close enough to see the bloodstains on his clothes. The road that the soldiers had indicated brought Mustafa to a river. When he had washed the bloodstains from his clothes, he set off once more in the direction of the city. Before long, he ran into a shepherd, and asked the old man where he was. "Ramadi," the shepherd answered.

The old man explained that he was an Iranian Kurd who had been resettled in a nearby *mujamma'a*.[6] He was curious about why Mustafa was barefoot. Thinking quickly, Mustafa replied that he was a government public works employee, and had been in a car crash. Since he had left all his papers in the wreck, he was anxious to avoid military checkpoints. The old man gave Mustafa an address in the complex and told him how he could sneak in without being observed by the guards.

Reaching the house, Mustafa smelled the aroma of fresh bread. He found a woman baking. What was this place, he asked. She told him it was a complex that had been built for Iranian Kurds, although she herself was an Iraqi Kurd from Khanaqin.[7] Her husband was at market, she explained, but would return before long. When the man arrived, Mustafa repeated his car-crash story and asked for advice on how he could get back to Baghdad. A bus would soon be leaving the complex for Ramadi, the man said. He gave Mustafa instructions on how to evade the checkpoints, and pressed on him some food and a pair of slippers. When Mustafa got to the entrance to the complex, the bus was just pulling away, but he flagged it down and the driver stopped. As Mustafa boarded the bus, he recognized one of the other passengers. It was someone he knew from the Jafan area. It was Ozer.

* * *

---

[6] The old shepherd was presumably one of the thousands of Iranian Kurds relocated from their border villages after the Iraqi Army's occupation of portions of Iran's Kermanshah province in 1980. The location described by Mustafa is strongly suggestive of a camp called Al-Tash, outside Ramadi, which once held as many as 30,000 people. According to the International Committee of the Red Cross, which had access to this camp, some 12-15,000 prisoners remained there in mid-1992. Middle East Watch interview, Geneva, July 14, 1992.

[7] And therefore probably a victim of the Arabization campaign of the mid-1970s. Khanaqin lies in the extreme southeastern part of Iraqi Kurdistan, in the Arabized section of Diyala governorate.

After the massacre in the bus, Ozer had managed to slip away into the darkness. He ran for a while, confused and angry, before tripping headlong into a trench. He fell on top of a body. It was bleeding from the nose, but the man was still breathing. This trench was very different from the one in which Mustafa had been laid for execution. It was ten or twelve feet deep, Ozer remembered, and only about six feet wide. He estimated that it contained 400 bodies. Scrambling out again, he fled into the desert. Fearful of being recognized as a Kurd, he stripped off his clothes and rolled them into a bundle, which he carried on his shoulder. Like Mustafa, he had left his shoes behind.

He walked or ran for hours. "I passed only trenches filled with bodies; I could tell what they were by the smell," he recalled. "I also saw many mounds made by bulldozers. The whole area was full of trenches with corpses."

At one point he crossed a paved road and came to water, perhaps a lake. On the other side he could see the tall shapes of date palms. He knelt down to drink, but stopped short when he saw the headlights of a vehicle approaching. Afraid that it was one of the Landcruisers from the execution squad, he plunged into the water and started to wade toward the far shore. But when he was waist-deep, he noticed with relief that the car had turned in another direction. Now, Ozer also saw the lights of distant buildings, and he headed toward them. It was perhaps 4:00 a.m.

It turned out to be the same complex that Mustafa had reached. Ozer later learned that it housed thousands of people from the Qaser Shirin border area, who had been kept here as virtual hostages since the early days of the Iran-Iraq War. The complex was encircled with barbed wire, and its residents were barred from leaving, other than on eight-hour passes that allowed them to shop at the market in Ramadi.

Ozer peered through the doorway at the first building he passed. He saw two people asleep in an inner courtyard, and knocked. A man's voice called out in Kurdish, "Who's there?"

"A poor man in need of bread and water," Ozer answered.

Neighbors, aroused by the noise, came out from the building next door to see what was happening. But when they saw Ozer, they promptly slammed their door shut again. In answer to his repeated knocking, it was opened once more, and Ozer saw an old man and his two sons brandishing sticks at him. When he blurted out his story to the men, they agreed to give him some food--bean soup and bread. But they were too afraid to shelter a ragged Kurdish fugitive in their home. In the early dawn, Ozer went begging from door to door, until a man named Ahmad agreed to take him to the terminal where he could catch a minibus to Ramadi. On the bus, he met Mustafa. The two men traveled together as far as the Baghdad bus terminal, where Mustafa thought he recognized an *Istikhbarat* officer he had seen in Topzawa, and fled on his own into the crowds. Ozer eventually reached the Kurdish quarter of Kirkuk. That night, watching television, Ozer saw himself in a news flash that showed the Iraqi Army watching over captured "Iranian agents"--the film shot at the Qader Karam police station on April 10.[8]

* * *

TAYMOUR'S STORY

Through a series of chance occurrences in the desert, five men--Muhammad, Ozer, Mustafa, Omar and Ibrahim--survived the culmination of the Iraqi regime's Anfal campaign. From the testimony of these five survivors, it is apparent that one of the principal purposes of Anfal was to exterminate all adult males of military service age captured in rural Iraqi Kurdistan. Firing squads murdered these Kurds by the tens of

---

[8] Ibrahim and Omar, the remaining two survivors of the massacre in the bus, also made it back to Kurdistan. But for both men the ordeal was not yet over. Ibrahim, who like Ozer and Mustafa passed through the complex of Iranian Kurds on his way to Ramadi, was recaptured as a deserter in Baghdad, and passed through a series of military jails before taking refuge with a contingent of *jahsh* in Suleimaniyeh. Omar spent a further period in hiding in Kurdistan before eventually surrendering to the army in September, after the general amnesty. He was forced into another period in the military and sent to serve in Kuwait (as was Ozer) after the August 1990 Iraqi invasion. He deserted for the last time three days before the beginning of the air war in January 1991.

Anwar Tayyar, who had been on the same bus as Ozer, Ibrahim and Omar, also escaped from the execution site and was seen in late May or early June by *peshmerga* hiding out in the Qader Karam area. He had sustained four flesh wounds during the shooting in the bus, and had been left for dead. After the encounter near Qader Karam, Anwar Tayyar disappeared for good. The last *peshmerga* to see him alive speculate that he either starved to death or was captured by the army and killed. Middle East Watch interview with former PUK commander, Kalar, March 30, 1993.

thousands with no semblance of due process, by virtue of nothing more than their age, their ethnicity and their presence in "prohibited areas" supposedly influenced by the parties of the Kurdish *peshmerga*. As Ali Hassan al-Majid had insisted on many occasions, paragraph five of Northern Bureau Command directive SF/4008 was being carried out to the letter.[9]

The bodies of many of the victims of Anfal lie in mass graves outside the Iraqi town of Ramadi, ploughed under by bulldozers in a desert area that, for the moment, remains inaccessible to outside observers. But it is apparent that this was not the only mass execution site used during Anfal. On this score the testimonies of Ozer, Mustafa, Omar and Ibrahim leave a number of enigmas still unanswered. Their accounts indicate that thousands lie buried outside Ramadi; yet they also say that only five buses from an original convoy of more than thirty took the road to Ramadi that night. The remainder broke off outside Falluja and drove off in another direction, and the inference must be that these prisoners were taken to be executed elsewhere.

Middle East Watch has received detailed reports, based on hearsay, of at least three other mass execution sites that were used during the Anfal campaign. One of these was in the vicinity of the archeological site of Al-Hadhar (Hatra), some sixty miles south of the city of Mosul. (There is ample material here for the connoisseur of historical irony, since Saddam Hussein had spent lavish resources on excavating Al-Hadhar as part of his search for the ancient origins of the Iraqi Arab nation--only to dig it up again as a burial place for his non-Arab enemies.)[10]

---

[9]   This, it should be recalled, stated that, "All persons captured in those [prohibited] villages shall be detained and interrogated by the security services and those between the ages of 15 and 70 shall be executed after any useful information has been obtained from them." See above p.64.

[10]   Saddam Hussein's fascination with Al-Hadhar is detailed in Baram's *Culture, History and Ideology*, pp.53-54. Al-Hadhar may also be the site referred to by a former Zakho *mustashar* interviewed by Neil Conan of National Public Radio in the U.S.; this man spoke of 12,000 Kurdish men being executed at an unknown site in August 1988 after being imprisoned in Mosul. Conan's interview is cited in Makiya, *Cruelty and Silence*, p.144. There are also persistent but unconfirmed reports of mass Anfal graves near Ar'ar on the Iraqi-Saudi

Another reported execution site was near Hamrin Mountain, to the south of Tuz Khurmatu. One account, citing an eyewitness, speaks of forty busloads of Kurds, in the custody of Republican Guards, being machinegunned by a dirt road leading to the Otheim river. A third report speaks of mass executions at another part of Hamrin Mountain, between Tikrit and Kirkuk--this one involving an estimated 2,000 women and children.

The lists of those who disappeared during Anfal, which are routinely pressed on all visitors to Iraqi Kurdistan, are by no means restricted to the names of young and middle-aged men. Indeed, from the fragmentary lists given to Middle East Watch, it is apparent that more than half of those who disappeared from southern Germian and the Lesser Zab Valley were women and children. Some of those who disappeared were no doubt infant refugees who perished on the freezing roads to Iran or Turkey. Many other small children were allowed to die of starvation and disease in the prison at Dibs. Hundreds of children (whose fates are known, and thus do not figure in these lists of the disappeared) were among the victims of the chemical gas attacks on Halabja, Goktapa and other sites. But many children also went before the firing squads.

One of these children of Anfal was Taymour Abdullah Ahmad, the 12-year old from Kulajo in the *nahya* of Tilako in southern Germian, just six or seven miles from Muhammad's home village of Aliyani Taza. Taymour was the first--and until recent Middle East Watch interviews the only--known survivor of a mass execution during Anfal. He remains the only eyewitness to the mass killing of women and children. His story has been well documented elsewhere, but it bears repeating here in its proper context.[11]

Taymour had lived in Kulajo from the age of three. His father, Abdullah, was a wheat farmer, and the family--Taymour, his parents, and his three younger sisters--lived in a humble four-room mud house. The

---

border, and in Diwaniyah and Naseriyah governorates in southern Iraq.

[11] See for example, Middle East Watch/Physicians for Human Rights, *Unquiet Graves: The Search for the Disappeared in Iraqi Kurdistan*, February 1992, pp. 23-25; and Makiya, *Cruelty and Silence*, chapter 5. Taymur has also been featured extensively in television reports, including "Saddam's Killing Fields," CBS "60 Minutes," February 23, 1992.

siblings were closely bunched in age. In 1988, Taymour was twelve. His eldest sister, Jelas, was a year younger; Laulau was ten, and Sunur nine. Kulajo was swept up in the massive three-day army sweep through southern Germian in the second week of April, and fleeing before the advancing troops, Taymour and his family were funneled through the first collection-point at Melistura. They hoped to make their way to the complex of Sumoud, where some relatives had been relocated in 1986 and 1987, but this was impossible. From Melistura they were taken by tractor-hauled cart to the fort at Qoratu, and thence, after ten days, to the Popular Army camp at Topzawa.

By now Taymour knew that this campaign was different from any of the past, and even in Qoratu he began to fear that he and his family were to be executed. At Topzawa, his father was taken away, and Taymour never saw him again. Through the window of his hall, he watched as male prisoners were handcuffed together, stripped to their undershorts and hustled away. The rest of Taymour's family remained at Topzawa for a month, and were fed on bread and water and a little cheese. During this time Taymour saw several younger children weaken and die.

One day in late May, at about six in the morning, the guards led Taymour, his mother and sisters out into the courtyard and checked their names off on a list. A convoy of vehicles awaited, apparently the same kind in which Mustafa had been driven to Ramadi about a month earlier. They were painted green or white, and Taymour thought that the absence of windows made them look like oversized ambulances. He counted fifty or sixty women and children, seated along the four benches that stretched the length of each bus. To enter the passenger section, the prisoners had to pass through two small guards' compartments, connected by an interior door. Other guards rode in front with the driver. The only ventilation came from a small wire-mesh opening at the rear. Taymour could not see outside.

They drove until sunset along a paved highway, halting only once. Taymour craned to look out through the wire-mesh screen, but all he saw of their stopping place was a large water tank painted in camouflage colors. The heat was oppressive, the doors remained locked, and there was nothing to drink. As the bus drove on, three children collapsed and died, all of them younger than Taymour. But still they did not stop. No one spoke: "They were too afraid," Taymour remembered, "too exhausted, too hungry and thirsty, too desperate."

It was nightfall when the caravan stopped and the guards took the prisoners outside. In the darkness, Taymour could see nothing but endless desert. But he could see now that there were about thirty vehicles in the convoy. Dozens of soldiers milled around; they appeared to have been accompanying the buses in Toyota Landcruisers.[12] They gave the prisoners a little water to drink from their canteens and then blindfolded each one with a strip of white cloth. Since there were hundreds of people, the process took a long time--about an hour, Taymour thought. When it was over, the prisoners reboarded the buses, and Taymour promptly removed his blindfold. The jolting of the bus told him that they had left the highway and were driving along a dirt road into the desert.

After half an hour the bus stopped again and the guards threw open the rear doors. Taymour saw that each vehicle was neatly positioned next to its own burial pit, some fifteen feet square and less than a yard deep. A fresh mound of dirt rose up behind each pit. The guards shoved the prisoners roughly over the edge, and in the panic and confusion Taymour was separated from his mother and sisters. Almost at once an officer and a soldier opened fire with their Kalashnikovs. Taymour was hit in the left shoulder. Despite the pain, he began to stagger toward the soldier who had shot him. He remembered noticing that the man had tears in his eyes. But as Taymour tried to grab hold of him and climb out of the pit, the officer barked out an order in Arabic, and the soldier fired again. This second bullet caught Taymour on the right side of his back, just above the waist. This time he lay still.

Apparently satisfied, the soldiers walked away. Taymour could no longer see the men, but he could hear their voices in the darkness some distance away. He also became aware of a movement next to him. He could see that it was a young girl, and she appeared to be unhurt. "Let's run," Taymour whispered to her.

"I can't," the girl answered. "I'm too afraid of the soldiers."

Without stopping to argue, Taymour clambered on to the hard-packed mound of dirt behind the grave. He later heard a rumor that a young Kurdish girl had been found alive in the desert at this time, and surmised that it was the companion he had left behind. As for his mother

---

[12] Although Taymour referred to the executioners as "soldiers," he had no specific recollection of their uniforms, and it is much more likely that the men belonged to another agency, such as the Ba'ath Party or *Amn*.

and three daughters, they did not survive the execution squads that night.[13]

Like the girl, Taymour was at first too scared to run, since the Landcruisers were still driving around the execution site, their headlights sweeping in circles through the darkness. Taymour scooped out a shallow hole in the top of the mound and lay down flat. Each time the headlights moved away, Taymour dragged himself to the next trench. His had been the last one filled with bodies; in the direction he was now heading, the pits were still empty. As he reached each one, he stopped and flattened himself against the earth mound, hoping that he was invisible from below.

The next thing he knew, it was much later. He had passed out on top of the fifth or sixth mound. The blood was still flowing freely from his wounds. But the whole area was quiet now. The sealed buses and landcruisers had gone, and although Taymour never saw or heard any bulldozers, the pits that contained the bodies of that night's execution victims had been filled with dirt and smoothed flat. No fresh bodies were visible, and Taymour passed another twenty empty trenches as he fled into the darkness. He remembered thinking just one thing as he dragged his injured body away from the killing grounds: "If I get out of this alive, I will give five dinars to the poor."

There was no moon. Once he saw car headlights in the distance behind him. He came to the intersection of two dirt roads and struck out blindly along one of them. After a couple of hours, he discerned the shadowy outline of a Bedouin encampment. Dogs barked, and the noise woke the owner of the nearest tent, who emerged with a flashlight. Seeing a boy in Kurdish dress, covered in blood, he yanked Taymour inside. They could not communicate--the Bedouin spoke no Kurdish, and Taymour knew not a word of Arabic. And the man could do nothing to treat Taymour's wounds--although these proved not to be life-

---

[13]   Taymour, in fact, lost a total of twenty-eight relatives in Anfal. In addition to his father, mother and three sisters, they included his uncle, Omar Ahmad Qader; his aunt, Ayna Ahmad Qader, her husband, Hama Sa'id Mohi-al-Din Abd-al-Karim and their three young children; his aunt, Mahsa Muhammad Mahmoud and her nine children; an unmarried aunt, Hamdia Muhammad Mahmoud; his uncle, Osman Muhammad Mahmoud, his wife, Amina Ali Aziz, and four of their fourteen children. Middle East Watch interview with Taymour Abdullah Ahmad, Sumoud Complex, July 29, 1992.

threatening. But he kept him safe in the tent for three days and then drove him in his truck to the nearest town. This was Samawa, the city south of Baghdad that had been the final stop for the convoys of sick and elderly people who were taken to Nugra Salman. Taymour stayed there, sheltered by a friendly Arab family, for more than two years. Eventually the family managed to smuggle a message through intermediaries to a surviving uncle of Taymour's in Kalar, letting him know that the boy was alive and well. In October 1990, Taymour and his uncle were reunited. The following year, after the failed Kurdish uprising, Taymour's story began to filter out, giving the outside world its first real glimpse of the horror that was Anfal.

———

Final Anfal: August 25 - September 6, 1988

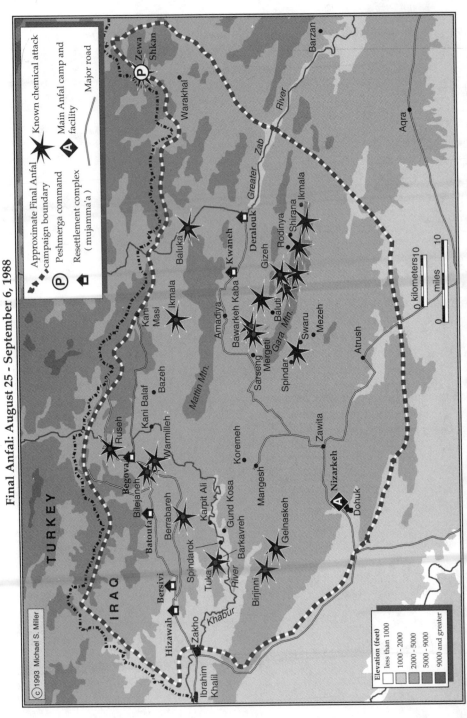

© 1993 Michael S. Miller

Elevation (feet)
- less than 1000
- 1000 - 2000
- 2000 - 5000
- 5000 - 9000
- 9000 and greater

- ✦ Approximate Final Anfal campaign boundary
- Ⓟ Peshmerga command
- ◆ Resettlement complex (mujamma'a)
- ✴ Known chemical attack
- Ⓐ Main Anfal camp and facility
- Major road

10
FINAL ANFAL: BADINAN, AUGUST 25-SEPTEMBER 6, 1988

"There was medicine from the airplane."
*-- victim of the August 25 chemical attack on the
village of Gizeh, Amadiya.*

With only the last remnants of the PUK continuing to resist, Baghdad's plans for wiping out Mas'oud Barzani's Kurdistan Democratic Party (KDP) now began to advance rapidly. On August 7, 1988, as we have seen, Ali Hassan al-Majid personally stepped in to urge the Iraqi Army to hasten the completion of the Anfal operation. The following day, the Army High Command issued its "communique of communiques," to announce that a ceasefire had come into effect on Iraq's terms, putting an end to the eight-year Iran-Iraq War that had cost as many as a million lives.[1]

The ceasefire gave the Iraqi Army the critical boost it required to bring Anfal to a close. The First Corps, which had handled the earlier phases of Anfal from its base in Kirkuk, would now mop up the lingering resistance in the Shaqlawa-Rawanduz valleys. The Fifth Army Corps, based in Erbil, would take charge of operations in Dohuk governorate, along the Iraqi-Turkish border. Other divisions, reportedly including elements of the Third, Sixth and Seventh Armies, were now redeployed to Iraqi Kurdistan from the southern war front around Fao and Basra.

In his review of the Final Anfal campaign, Fifth Corps commander Brig. Gen. Yunis Zareb wrote, "The morale was so high and was clear on the faces of the fighters from the beginning, and especially after the collapse of the Iranian enemy in the victorious campaigns starting from the eternal battle of Fao through the battle of Muhammad

---

[1] Cordesman and Wagner, *op. cit.* p.3, calculate that there were between 450,000 and 730,000 Iranian and between 150,000 and 340,000 Iraqi deaths. These figures are based on unclassified CIA estimates.

the Prophet of God.[2] The formations which took part in [Anfal] had
also taken part in those battles."[3]

This massive concentration of firepower was necessary, the
general felt, because of the difficult logistical problems that his troops had
to face in classic guerrilla warfare country:

> The land is generally hilly with a hard terrain in its
> northern and eastern parts which lie parallel to the
> border line of Iraq and Turkey. There are many
> gardens, forests and natural trees. The surface of the
> earth consists of rocky lands and a sedimentary surface
> in the highlands. And the lowlands are a combination of
> hard land with a mixed soil of sand and mud which
> gradually descends westward and southward in the
> direction of the Sleivani and Aqra plains. This area has
> many rivers and valleys which run from the north and
> east toward the south and west, forming streams. The
> movement of the forces and machinery is greatly
> hindered by the series of mountains, high knolls, valleys
> and other obstacles.[4]

It was a military planner's inelegant description of Badinan, the
traditional mountainous heartland of Mullah Mustafa Barzani and his
sons, the "offspring of treason."

Although the terrain complicated the logistical needs of a regular
army, the campaign against the KDP was in other respects more
straightforward than the drive to destroy the PUK. The KDP *peshmerga*
were largely concentrated in a single geographical area, Badinan, where

---

[2] The Battle of Muhammad the Prophet of God was the Iraqi drive to
remove Iranian troops from the mountainous northern front in mid-June 1988.

[3] *Analysis: Operation End of Anfal*, p.39.

[4] ibid.

its operations were run from a headquarters at Zewa Shkan, an abandoned village hard up against the Turkish border.[5]

* * *

Although the Ba'ath Party had devoted five months to "purifying" the areas that were under the control of the PUK, it had never abandoned its particular hatred for the KDP. Once allied with the Shah, the KDP had rekindled a close relationship with the clerical regime in Teheran, and on several occasions acted as scouts for the Iranian army on the northern front. The strength of this alliance was curious in a sense, for religious fervor had never been a part of the KDP's identity. Instead, the party was deeply imbued with the traditional values of the steep, narrow valleys of Badinan, a 4,000 square-mile chunk of the Zagros Mountains bounded to the east by the Greater Zab river and to the north by Turkey. There are no major cities in this inhospitable terrain. Badinan has none of the cosmopolitan sophistication of a Suleimaniyeh, none of the thriving industry of an Erbil or a Kirkuk. Tribal structures and loyalties remained powerful, and the KDP had long made common cause with conservative local *aghas* and *sheikhs* who were still touched by a certain nostalgia for the days of the Ottoman Empire, when tribal fiefdoms in Kurdistan were granted a large measure of autonomy.[6]

While the KDP inspired a devoted partisan following, historically centered on the Barzan Valley, it had also made powerful enemies among other tribal leaders. These schisms in turn meant that the final stage of

----

[5] While the PUK had regional commands (*malband*), the KDP had four branches, or *lak*, which handled both political and military affairs. Zewa Shkan housed the first *lak*; the second *lak*, based in the Smaquli Valley, handled operations in Erbil governorate; the third, in the Qara Dagh village of Ja'faran, ran KDP affairs in al-Ta'mim (Kirkuk) governorate; and the fourth, in the Chwarta area, was responsible for Suleimaniyeh. The KDP also had special units known as the Barzan Forces in Hayat (*nahya* Mergasur). Middle East Watch interview with Hoshyar Zebari, Washington, D.C., June 7, 1993.

[6] Among Kurdish tribes, *aghas* are the secular and *sheikhs* the religious leaders. The definitive work on the subject is Martin Van Bruinessen, *Agha, Shaikh and State, op. cit.*.

Anfal had some characteristics that set it apart from the rest of the operation. Some of the tribal groups who had made a separate peace with Baghdad managed to avoid the worst of Anfal. A considerable number of villages survived in Badinan and on its fringes, at least for a time--especially those of the Surchi, the Zebari, the Bradost and the Dolamari. And Kurdish villagers who might otherwise have died were spared if the local *mustashar* could convince Baghdad that they were not contaminated by *peshmerga* sympathies.

It was never easy for outsiders to guess the numbers of active *peshmerga* in the KDP. According to one 1985 estimate, the party had some 6,000 fighters, compared to 5,000 for the PUK.[7] A later estimate put the strength of each group at 10,000 in 1988.[8] In fact these figures, cited by sympathetic writers, may have been inflated. Military and civilian intelligence reports told the Fifth Corps Commander, Brig. Gen. Zareb, that the total strength of the "saboteurs" in Badinan was no more than 2,600.[9]

Against this puny force, and against the civilian population of Badinan, Ali Hassan al-Majid's Northern Bureau sent as many as 200,000 troops. According to several former Iraqi military sources interviewed by Middle East Watch, between fourteen and sixteen regular army divisions of 12,000 men each took part in the Final Anfal campaign, in addition to a Chemical Weapons Battalion, units of the Iraqi Air Force and the National Defense Battalions, or *jahsh*. The regime's strategy, wrote Gen.

---

[7] Van Bruinessen, "The Kurds Between Iran and Iraq," p.27.

[8] A. Sherzad, "The Kurdish Movement in Iraq, 1975-1988," in Kreyenbroek and Sperl, eds., *The Kurds: A Contemporary Overview*, p.138.

[9] The Army estimated that the KDP itself had between 1,800 and 2,000 fighters in Badinan, divided into a half-dozen local committees. In addition to the KDP, there was a unit of 250-300 PUK *peshmerga* in the valley of Zewa Shkan, close to the Turkish border and northeast of the summer resort of Amadiya; 200-220 combatants of the Iraqi Communist Party; and seventy "saboteurs" of the Kurdistan Popular Democratic Party of Sami Abd-al-Rahman, a KDP breakaway group. The KDP continues to dispute the accuracy of the army figures. According to senior KDP officials, the organization's combat strength on the eve of Anfal was 8,000, with an additional 36,000 villagers formally registered as members of the civilian "backing force." Middle East Watch interview with Hoshyar Zebari, Washington, D.C., June 7, 1993.

Zareb, was "based on the guidelines issued by the Northern Bureau and those of the Chief of Staff in the August 7 Kirkuk conference." The underlying doctrine was the simple one that worked so well in the earlier phases of Anfal--the application of overwhelming force, "to operate by moving from the outside toward the inside in order to encircle the saboteurs, with "different forces act[ing] simultaneously to guarantee the encirclement."[10]

Larger geopolitical considerations also seem to have played a part in this thinking. "The area of operations was adjacent to the international Iraqi-Turkish border," Gen. Zareb observed, "and this caused some perplexity....Accordingly, all forces were ordered to tackle the matter in the best possible way and ensure the secrecy of the operation by not transgressing the frontier."[11]

The general's final headache was a logistical one. "The magnitude of the engineering work needed for the destruction and removal of the remnants of the saboteurs and their premises in the areas covered by the operation...was so great that it put an extra burden on the shoulders of the command of the unit."[12] The removal of the remnants of the "saboteurs" and their premises: in other words, the destruction of some 300-400 Kurdish villages of Badinan.

* * *

BADINAN ON THE EVE OF THE FINAL ANFAL

In the days that preceded the Final Anfal, there were ample signs of what was to come. The massive buildup of ground troops was visible along the main highways of Dohuk governorate, and the area was softened up by intense shelling and aerial bombing, sometimes with cluster bombs. In the village of Spindar, for example, on the southern slopes of Gara Mountain, aircraft dropped cluster bombs on August 24,

---

[10] "Analysis: Operation End of Anfal," p.2.

[11] ibid, p.32.

[12] ibid, p.33.

killing two small boys, cousins aged four and five, as they tended their family's goats in the fields.[13]

Even as these preliminary attacks began, some families began to flee, especially if their villages lay within walking distance of the Turkish border. But others stayed where they were, waiting for the violence to pass. After all, they reasoned, villages like Spindar had been attacked many times since the mid-1960s. Although Spindar itself had been burned down more than once, the government had never prevented the inhabitants from returning to rebuild.

The regime's control of Dohuk governorate had dwindled to a handful of towns and complexes along the main roads. From these strongholds, army troops had maintained brutally thorough checkpoints since the mid-1980s. "No food was allowed through," one villager recalled, "not even small cans of infant formula, and produce was not permitted to be taken to market."[14] Another villager added, "For three or four years before Anfal only women were able to pass through the checkpoints. People resorted to smuggling--flour, rice, salt, oil, kerosene, soap, detergent and sesame paste--but everything cost much more this way. At the checkpoint [in the town of Sarseng] the soldiers confiscated anything they found and set fire to it. Sometimes women were able to hide things underneath their dresses."[15] But several witnesses told stories of boys and men being arrested, and disappearing, if they were found concealing food, which was presumed to be destined for the *peshmerga.*

In Badinan, as in the Sorani-speaking areas to the south, the Kurds had long grown accustomed to the harsh routines of wartime. Aircraft bombed, strafed and rocketed them whenever the armed forces received intelligence reports of *peshmerga* movements. When the planes approached, villagers fled to caves, makeshift shelters or "shades." Occasionally, helicopters would drop infantry troops into a village for house-to-house searches for draft-dodgers and deserters. Artillery

---

[13] Middle East Watch interview, Dohuk, June 10, 1992.

[14] Middle East Watch interview, Gund Kosa village, September 5, 1992; see also the 1987 government recommendations on tightening the economic blockade, above p.90.

[15] Middle East Watch interview. Kwaneh complex, August 29, 1992.

emplacements in the nearest large town or military base rained down poorly directed shellfire, which would sometimes kill some luckless farmer working his fields. As if these Iraqi attacks were not enough, the inhabitants of some border areas also had to contend with raids from Turkish aircraft on search-and-destroy missions against contingents of guerrillas from Turkey's Kurdistan Workers' Party (PKK), which maintained bases inside northern Iraq.[16]

In the spring of 1987, in accordance with the first decrees issued by the newly appointed Ali Hassan al-Majid, virtually the whole of Dohuk governorate--an area a little smaller than the state of Connecticut--was "redlined." As in the Sorani-speaking areas, there was a fresh flurry of village-burning that April and May, with some forty-nine villages being destroyed in various parts of Badinan.[17] The "redlining" was announced over the official radio, said a man from a village near the town of Mangesh. Those who came over to the government side would be considered "our people," the broadcast declared. Those who did not would be regarded as Iranians. To drive home this message, the government blocked off the dirt roads leading to prohibited villages with mounds of earth.[18] When the October census came, it had only a very limited effect in rural Badinan; many villages, Middle East Watch was told, did not even know of its existence.

Despite the grim news about Anfal that had filtered through to Badinan via KDP radio broadcasts from Iran, villagers do not appear to have believed that the government campaign of 1988 would be any different from its predecessors. Inexplicably, this absence of any unusual alarm afflicted not merely the civilian population but the KDP itself, whose central committee was meeting inside Iran as the Final Anfal approached, and seemed not to be anticipating anything out of the

---

[16] Since the 1930s, Turkey and Iraq had frequently cooperated in suppressing Kurdish dissent. In 1982 the two governments signed an agreement authorizing Turkey to send its armed forces into Iraq in pursuit of rebel Turkish Kurds or in joint operations with the Iraqi Army against Iraqi Kurdish *peshmerga*. See *The Economist*, June 18, 1983.

[17] According to surveys by the Kurdistan Development and Reconstruction Society (KURDS), a local relief agency.

[18] Middle East Watch interview, Dohuk, September 4, 1992.

ordinary. Although local *peshmerga* alerted villagers to the possibility that chemical weapons might be used, the KDP leadership does not appear to have broadcast any emergency alert. "After Halabja, we thought the international community would stop Saddam Hussein," one regional commander said--an astonishingly sanguine attitude, in view of the dozens of chemical attacks that had followed that spring and summer.[19]

Even in its own highly classified internal documents, the Iraqi military was evasive--almost to the point of silence--on the matter of chemical weapons during the Final Anfal.[20] Gen. Zareb's report noted only that a battalion specialized in their use had played "a unique role" in the campaign, "just like all the other groups." The unit was kept in a state of readiness and supervised the use of flamethrowers by infantry troops. Otherwise, Zareb wrote, "It did not have another role during the battle because the battle was within the national geographical boundaries"--a curious scruple on the general's part, given how widely chemical artillery had been used on Iraqi soil in the earlier stages of the Anfal campaign.

Gen. Zareb's assertion may appear contradictory, given that the use of chemical weapons in the Badinan campaign was given wide publicity by the international press. But the explanation is quite simple: chemical bombing operations during the Final Anfal were the exclusive responsibility of the Iraqi Air Force, and the army's chemical artillery

---

[19] Middle East Watch interview, Zakho, September 1, 1992.

[20] Even in internal communications, the Iraqi government evidently treated the matter of its chemical weapons with the utmost secrecy. Letter no. Sh 5/19299 from the *Amn* director of the governorate of Erbil to all branches, dated December 17, 1988 and classified "secret and personal for addressee only," reads: "Pursuant to the memorandum from the Honorable Office of the Presidency, no. 4/4/11/44154 of December 4, 1988, a decision has been taken to give all letters (memoranda) which contain information about the production of chemical weapons the highest degree of secrecy. Take all necessary measures, keep this memorandum to yourself, and sign for its receipt."

pieces that reportedly were deployed in a half dozen locations remained silent.[21]

Through the testimonies of traumatized Kurdish refugees in Turkey, the world learned quickly of the use of mustard gas and nerve agents in Badinan.[22]   Listing forty-nine villages that had been "exposed" to gas, Galbraith and Van Hollen concluded that Iraq had "used chemical weapons on a broad scale against its Kurdish population beginning August 25, 1988," and that the attacks had "been accompanied by large loss of civilian life."[23]

* * *

"APPLES AND SOMETHING SWEET": THE CHEMICAL ATTACKS OF AUGUST 25

The first gas fell on the KDP headquarters at Zewa Shkan, close to the Turkish border, late in the evening of August 24. Ten *peshmerga* reportedly died. The next morning, August 25, between about 6:30 and

---

[21] One *mustashar* did allege that chemical artillery was used against the village of Warmilleh, but this could not be confirmed in interviews with residents. Middle East Watch interview, Zakho, September 1, 1992. On the events in Warmilleh, see below pp.272-273.

[22] There have also been persistent rumors about Iraq's use of biological weapons, including reports of mysterious and localized outbreaks of disease in *peshmerga*-controlled areas. At least one document proves that the Iraqi Army did possess stockpiles of such weapons. In a "highly confidential and personal" letter no. H1277, dated August 8, 1986, Erbil district commander Gen. Abd-al-Wahab Izzat instructs all units in his area to carry out a half-yearly stocktaking of all biological and chemical agents in their possession.

[23] Galbraith and Van Hollen, *op. cit.*, pp.1, 42. Their list appears to include a number of villages that were affected by windborne gas from other locations. A persistent difficulty in documenting Iraqi chemical attacks is in distinguishing primary sites from other places suffering the secondary effects, and the list on pp. 323-327 includes only proven primary targets. This is not only a problem of methodology; it is also the most vivid illustration of the indiscriminate character of these weapons.

8:30 a.m., Iraqi warplanes launched a number of separate and almost simultaneous attacks, perhaps a dozen in all. Many of them were probably carried out by the same flight of aircraft, since they were concentrated within a strip measuring approximately sixty miles wide and twenty deep. Some of the aircraft targeted a single village or *peshmerga* base, but in at least two cases the planes hit a whole string of villages in rapid succession. (see map) The intent seems to have been less to kill than to spread mass terror. Perhaps twenty civilians died on the spot, and about the same number of *peshmerga*. But hundreds more, especially children, succumbed in the weeks that followed.

The precise cause of their deaths remains unknowable; it may have been the lethal after-effects of a combination of mustard gas and Sarin nerve gas; or the consequences of exposure, cold and hunger in the mountains where they fled; or the malnutrition and disease they endured in the camps after they were captured; or a combination of all three. In a sense, the question is academic; whatever the precise cause may have been, it was the Iraqi government that was responsible for their deaths.

In one interview after another, those who lived through the chemical attacks of the Final Anfal told very similar stories.

• The village of Birjinni, in the *nahya* of Zawita, had the misfortune to lie almost midway between two of the KDP's most important bases--one, the party's regional headquarters, located due north in the village of Tuka, just across the Khabour river, and the other a little way to the east, in the village of Gelnaskeh. All three places were hit by chemical weapons at breakfast time on August 25. The people of Birjinni had been watching the sky since dawn. For several days they had been aware of unusual numbers of aircraft overhead, and they were fearful of a conventional bombing attack. As eight airplanes came into view, many of the villagers fled in fear to the shelters they had built nearby. Three of the planes made a low pass over the village, from east to west, and dropped four bombs each. Surviving villagers told of clouds of smoke billowing upward, "white, black and then yellow, rising about fifty or sixty yards into the air in a column. Then the column began to break up and drift. It drifted down into the valley and then passed through the village. Then we smelled the gas."

It was a pleasant smell at first; "it smelled of apples and something sweet." Others said it reminded them of "pesticides in our fields." Soon, however, "it became bitter. It affected our eyes and our mouths and our skin. All of a sudden it was hard to breathe."[24] The villagers later found that four people from a single Birjinni family had died, including a 58-year old man and his five-year old grandson. The aircraft continued to circle overhead for perhaps a half hour, apparently observing the results of the raid. Others came later that day, dropping conventional weapons that set the tinder-dry late summer fields ablaze. From the mountain saddle on which Birjinni was built, the villagers could see that the surrounding area was filled with refugees, all fleeing northward in the direction of the Turkish border.[25]

• A few miles to the north of Birjinni, close to the Khabour river, the planes hit Tilakru, a large village that was home to many army deserters. A woman named Halima was preparing breakfast for her children when the bombs fell. She heard muffled explosions and looked out to see clouds of white smoke turning yellow. Her husband, a *peshmerga* on active duty, had told her how to recognize the signs. Having served in the Iran-Iraq War, he knew very well what a chemical attack looked like.

Halima's children had been asleep on the roof, so she pulled them down as quickly as she could, one by one, and bundled them into the family's air-raid shelter, a hole in the ground covered with wood, leaves and dirt. Looking round in horror, she realized that her one-year old baby, Zozan, was missing. Halima found her crawling around in the courtyard. But by the time she reached her, the child's face had turned yellow and she was gasping for breath and trying to vomit. Halima rushed her into the shelter and flung wet blankets over the walls. But

---

[24] Soil samples from Birjinni were collected on June 10, 1992 by a forensic team assembled by Physicians for Human Rights (PHR) and Middle East Watch. They were subsequently analyzed at the Chemical and Biological Defence Establishment of Great Britain's Ministry of Defence at Porton Down, and found to contain trace evidence of the nerve gas GB, also known as Sarin, as well as of mustard gas. See the PHR-Human Rights Watch statement, "Scientific First: Soil Samples Taken from Bomb Craters in Northern Iraq Reveal Nerve Gas--Even Four Years Later," April 29, 1993.

[25] A full account of the chemical attack on Birjinni is contained in Middle East Watch/Physicians for Human Rights, *The Anfal Campaign in Iraqi Kurdistan: The Destruction of Koreme*, pp. 31-44.

her infant daughter could not be saved, and she died several days later in a prison camp, as did several other children from Tilakru.[26]

• From a vantage point in the village of Spindarok, on the far bank of the Khabour, a farmer named Suleiman watched through binoculars as two aircraft attacked the KDP base at Tuka and the hamlet of Barkavreh, a few hundred yards away. With his radio tuned to an air force frequency, Suleiman even overheard snatches of the two pilots' cockpit conversation:

"They are firing at us."

"Drop the bombs on the high places."

"Don't fire while you are behind me. Hold your fire until you are next to me."

Suleiman concluded that the pilots were responding to ground fire. A friend, Obeid, said that in this area at least, there had been specific warnings of reprisals: "The government had told people that if a single bullet were to be fired from a village, a chemical bomb would be dropped. People came from government-controlled areas bringing this information." In the course of some 350 Middle East Watch field interviews, this was virtually the only example cited of the government issuing any prior warning of its intentions.

Suleiman counted thirteen bombs in all. Although most of them fell outside the village, he learned later that two bombs had landed close to the *peshmerga* headquarters, on the western outskirts of Tuka. According to three separate accounts, fourteen *peshmerga* died there, and one civilian. Since the wind was blowing from the east, all the farm animals on the western side of the village died, although no one inside the perimeter of the village was harmed.[27]

• The village of Warmilleh lay a little nearer to Turkey, between the Khabour and the western edge of Mattin Mountain, a *peshmerga* stronghold. The nearest guerrilla camp was in Bazeh, a three and a half hour walk across the mountains to the east. The people of Warmilleh, like those of Birjinni, had been expecting an attack on the morning of

---

[26] Middle East Watch interview, Gri Gowr complex, August 27, 1992.

[27] Middle East Watch interviews, Hizawah complex and Zakho, September 1, 1992.

August 25. Again, it came at about 8:00 a.m. This time, they counted six aircraft, but only two of them took part in the attack, dropping six bombs each. "We were lucky," a villager remembered, "for the wind was in the opposite direction to where the people were sheltering under the trees, half a kilometer away."[28] Five people were affected by the drifting gas. They vomited; their skin turned black and peeled off. But a *peshmerga* doctor arrived later that afternoon, administered injections, and the five injured villagers joined their families' northward flight to the Turkish border.

Directly across the river, the planes also hit the village of Bilejaneh. The chemicals drifted on the wind to a hamlet called Bani. "I got sick and had to vomit," said a man who lived there. "We left Bani that afternoon and went to Bilejaneh and Girka. After that we had to cross the main road [from Begova to Kani Masi]. The army was not there yet. The first troops arrived at 2:00 a.m. on August 26 and cut off the escape route to Turkey. Those who crossed the main road before this were lucky. We got there at about 1:00 a.m., just before the soldiers."[29]

• North of the main road, one direct route to Turkey led through the villages of Ruseh and Nazdureh. "When the military came and began camping out on the road to Nazdureh, people expected an attack and fled," according to a KDP *peshmerga* from Ruseh, who had sent his family on ahead to Turkey.

> The army attacked the next morning. The Iraqis were trying to seal the border area. People who were close to the border managed to cross, but those who failed were arrested and disappeared. I was near the border when the chemical attack happened. I saw yellow smoke. I was on top of the mountain, but people in the valley below were affected. My brother, who was two or three hundred meters away from me on the mountain side, was also affected by the chemicals. He began frothing at the mouth and choking and his skin became dark. Then

---

[28] Middle East Watch interview, Warmilleh village, August 31, 1992.

[29] Middle East Watch interview, Batufa, April 9, 1993.

he died. His name was Salim, and he was 45-years old. We buried him there on the spot.[30]

• The most concentrated attacks, however, came along Gara Mountain, the great ridge that begins near the town of Sarseng and stretches east for twenty miles or more. Here, the air force targeted at least fifteen and perhaps as many as thirty separate villages.[31] On the southern slopes, the neighboring villages of Avok, Swareh, Sidara and Spindar (*nahya* of Sarseng) were all hit at about 8:00 a.m. on the same morning, August 25. There was a *peshmerga* base in the mountains nearby, and the people of Swareh had moved to the ravines and caves of Avok a year or so earlier in response to the government's continuous bombing and shelling.

A young women named Khadija was in one of these caves with her nine children when the bombs fell. Her elder sister, Aisha, had just gone outside to wash the dirty plates from breakfast. Khadija heard a series of powerful explosions, as if the bombs had fallen right overhead, and the mouth of the cave was quickly obscured by white smoke. The smoke smelled like "the same medicine that is sprayed on apples," and everyone inside the cave grew dizzy and found it hard to breathe. Their eyes burned and teared. Two teenage boys who had been hiding among the bushes outside tried to sprint to safety. But the planes cut them down with machinegun fire, and both youngsters died.

After about an hour, when the smoke had cleared, the family ventured out fearfully to look for Aisha. They found her lying on the ground outside the cave. She was sighing and moving her lips as if she wanted to speak, but no words came. She had vomited, and her skin was black. A few yards away the grass was blackened and burned, and dead farm animals lay all around. Aisha lived only another two or three hours. When the family washed her body that night for burial in the village

---

[30] Middle East Watch interview, Batufa, April 9, 1993.

[31] A number of Middle East Watch interviews produced strikingly similar lists of the villages attacked with chemicals along Gara Mountain: to the northern side, Dehukeh, Bawarkeh Kavri, Mergeti, Havintka, Birozana, Drisheh, Mijeh, Kavna Mijeh, Spindar Khalfo and Geyrgash; on the mountain itself, Garagu, Goreh, Zewa Shkan, Baluti, Gizeh, Zarkeh, Razikeh, Sarkeh, Rodinya, Shirana and Ikmala; and on the southern side, Spindar, Swareh, Avok and others.

cemetery, her dry and blackened skin came off in their hands.[32] Another young woman, Amina, also died in the attack. Others died later as they tried to hide out in the mountains, but many families managed to escape by walking through the narrow Ashawa Valley, close to the extravagant mountaintop palace which President Saddam Hussein had recently built himself.

• To the north side of Gara Mountain, the villages of Bawarkeh Kavri and Mergeti ("Meadow of the Mulberry Tree") lay next to each other in a small valley, separated only by a 10-minute walk. The army had burned Bawarkeh Kavri four times before Anfal, but the village had always been rebuilt. The valley had been "redlined" by the government in 1987, and both villages housed *peshmerga* bases.

Again, the bombing began at about 8:00 a.m. on August 25. Five or six bombs fell in Bawarkeh Kavri and nine or ten in Mergeti, witnesses said, but they struck some distance away from the KDP base. There was white smoke, and all the chickens and birds died, as did the goats. But none of the villagers lost their lives in the attack, even though those who were downwind of the gas suffered the usual symptoms-- vomiting, tearing and dizziness. They ascribed their good fortune to the *peshmerga*, who had warned them a few days before that an attack might be imminent and showed them how to protect themselves by closing all the doors and windows and shrouding their heads in wet towels and blankets. That same evening, the villagers saw the ground forces approaching and fled to the mountains.

• It was a similar story in Sarkeh and Gizeh, neighboring villages deep in the folds of Gara Mountain, about ten miles south of the town of Amadiya. There were no guerrilla bases here, although fighters did pass through at frequent intervals. As the villagers sat down to breakfast, Mushir, a *peshmerga* in his early twenties, saw six aircraft discharge their bombs over Sarkeh before flying on to attack Shirana, the next village to the east. Mushir ran west toward Gizeh, the village of his birth. But it was deserted; the warplanes had already paid their visit.

"There was medicine from the airplane," said Khadija Sa'id, an old, partially sighted woman from Gizeh. "We noticed smoke, felt dizzy

---

[32] Middle East Watch interview, Dohuk, June 10, 1992.

and fell down. My sister went blind. The smoke smelled like old alcohol, but the smell did not stay."

"I felt dizzy, about to faint," added her sister, Fahma. "Tears were coming from my eyes, and I fell down. I tried to wash my face. I vomited. Those who vomited survived. Others died at the beginning. Now I am like this; I can see only a little bit." The villagers of Gizeh fled to caves in the mountains, as they had in the past. On the evening of the same day, they watched ground troops enter the village and burn it to the ground.[33]

* * *

In psychological terms, these attacks were every bit as devastating as the regime presumably intended them to be. The raids terrified *peshmerga* and civilians across Badinan. With no village farther than twenty miles from the chemicals, word of them spread rapidly. The suddenness and intensity of the attack on so many fronts at once threw the KDP into disarray, and many *peshmerga* simply abandoned their posts to try and rescue their families and reach the border. Said one fighter,

> I could not find any of my fellow *peshmerga*. They had all gone to help their relatives, and the chemical weapons had created a lot of fear among the people. We did not know how to fight them. We knew how to fight tanks, how to chase a military caravan until we ambushed it, and how to escape aerial bombardments. But we did not know how to fight chemicals.[34]

Immediately after the bombs had fallen, word reached the villages that resistance was useless. According to a young man who was a *peshmerga* in Spindar, the next village to the west of Swareh,

> Even before the army entered our village we received a message from Mas'oud Barzani not to resist. The [KDP]

---

[33] Middle East Watch interviews, Jezhnikan complex, May 3, 1992 and Sarseng, April 11, 1993.

[34] Middle East Watch interview, Dohuk, June 6, 1992.

leadership command told us, "Everything has ended; the revolution is over; we cannot fight chemical weapons with our bare hands; we just cannot fight chemical weapons." The KDP's First Branch told us, "You have a choice: if you want to surrender, do so in order to save the civilians, because the party does not have the ability to care for so many civilian casualties." We could not take so many elderly people and children to the border.[35]

Such scattered fighting as did take place after the first wave of chemical attacks cannot properly be called resistance. The best that the KDP could manage was a string of isolated rearguard actions, in which splintered groups of *peshmerga* tried to slow the army's advance. But their efforts were useless, for the places where the *peshmerga* tried to make a stand, such as the narrow defile known as Darava Shinyeh (or "Shinyeh Passage"), were also acutely vulnerable to renewed attacks from the air. According to one KDP veteran, these battles were "all very short ones, like pinpricks," and military helicopters continued to harass the fleeing *peshmerga* throughout the next day, August 26.[36]

Perhaps the most cowardly of all the chemical attacks was the bombing of the bridge at Baluka, one of the main crossing points on the fast-flowing Greater Zab river. The village of Baluka itself had been emptied during the border clearances of 1976, although a few families had straggled back, accompanied by the *peshmerga*. Now, with the sanctuary of Turkey barely four miles away across the mountains, villagers had begun to converge on the Baluka bridge from all directions, in flight from the army. At about 1:00 p.m. on August 25, the warplanes appeared over Baluka. They released two bombs on the village and several more over the river. The bridge was quickly covered in a greenish cloud and the corpses of farm animals piled up on the bridge, making it impassable.

By nightfall on August 26, the combat was effectively over. "The zealousness of the [army] fighters was boosted by the collapse of the

---

[35] Middle East Watch interview, Dohuk, June 2, 1992.

[36] Middle East Watch interview, Amadiya, August 29, 1992. According to this fighter, the helicopter attacks included the renewed use of chemical weapons.

saboteurs and their complete inability to resist," Gen. Zareb noted with satisfaction in his written report on the Final Anfal.[37]

In many cases, the ground troops and *jahsh* -- or *chatta* ("bandits"), as they are known in the Kurmanji-speaking areas--moved into the abandoned villages on the same day as the chemical attacks. In others, they waited a day or two. But the occupation of Badinan was effectively complete by dawn on August 28, exactly on Gen. Zareb's original schedule. Tens of thousands of refugees headed for Turkey; others were captured in their homes, or surrendered after a brief, vain attempt at flight; others hid in the mountains until the September 6 amnesty.

* * *

In coordination with the first wave of attacks, the Iraqi Army occupied the highway that runs east from the small border city of Zakho until it meets the Greater Zab river at Baluka. The idea was evidently to seal off the Turkish border and stem the flood of refugees. In this, however, the army was strikingly unsuccessful. Although many died along the way, some were caught, and others were chased and strafed by fighter aircraft, between 65,000 and 80,000 Kurds did manage to make the crossing. In the impromptu camps that a reluctant Turkish government found itself obliged to open along the border, the refugees told their stories and displayed their injuries to the few members of the foreign press who managed to gain access. Those who lived in villages south of the highway found it more difficult to escape, and a lower proportion of them reached safe havens in Turkey.[38]

---

[37] "Analysis: Operation End of Anfal," p.39.

[38] It is clear that a very serious incident occurred either in the Bazeh gorge, through which thousands of civilians fled in an attempt to cross the main Zakho-Baluka road, or in nearby Bazeh village, a *peshmerga* headquarters. During their September 1988 interviews with refugees in Turkey, Galbraith and Van Hollen spoke with two people who reported witnessing a massacre of some 1,300 people, including women in children, in Bazeh village. According to these accounts, the victims were machinegunned and then buried in mass graves dug by bulldozers.

The British film-maker Gwynne Roberts interviewed two teenage refugees in Turkey, who claimed to have witnessed a chemical attack on the Bazeh gorge in which "more than 3,000" people died. According to one of these witnesses,

Many of those who could not break through the blockade line along the Zakho-Baluka road still managed to evade capture by hiding out in the mountains. They watched impotently as the bulldozers crawled back and forth through the valleys below, crushing everything in their path. Along the great east-west spine of Gara Mountain, south of Amadiya, the scattered *peshmerga* fighters took charge of a sprawling caravan of thousands of refugees. On foot and on horseback, they travelled east for three days, but found it impossible to get across the Greater Zab, because all the bridges were now controlled by the army. Retracing their steps to the west again, the refugees heard on the radios that the *peshmerga* carried that thousands of their fellow Kurds had found sanctuary in Turkey. As news of the recent chemical attacks spread, the *peshmerga* tried to keep up the morale of the civilians by telling them that foreign pressure on the Iraqi regime would soon force Saddam Hussein to declare a halt to the fighting.

Although they had no bread or other supplies, there was meat aplenty in the form of abandoned farm animals. But the most pressing problem was the lack of drinking water: all the rivers and springs lay in the valleys below, and these were in the hands of the army and *jahsh*, who were shooting at anything that moved. The fugitives went for three days without water, and according to at least one account many young children died on Gara Mountain as a result of diarrhea and dehydration.[39] But a surprising number did survive the ordeal, and on their twelfth day in hiding, just after the radio had broadcast noon prayers, news came that the Revolutionary Command Council had decreed a general amnesty.

Many thousands of others were less fortunate. The villagers of Gizeh, for example, which had been attacked with chemical weapons on August 25, held out in the mountains for ten days--not quite long enough to benefit from the amnesty. Starving and exhausted, they were

---

"thousands of soldiers with gas masks and gloves" entered the gorge the next day, dragging the bodies into piles and setting fire to them. However, Middle East Watch interviews in Bazeh and surrounding villages turned up no recollection of such an event four years later. Neither were there any reports of significant deaths or disappearances of women and children that might have occurred during an attack such as those described. Exactly what took place at Bazeh remains an enigma.

[39] Middle East Watch interview, Dohuk, September 7, 1992.

eventually hunted down by soldiers who made them walk for four hours to Amadiya. There they were hustled into trucks that drove off to the west, in the direction of Dohuk. Gizeh was one of the worst hit villages in the whole of Badinan: according to Mushir, the young *peshmerga* from Sarkeh, ninety-three of its men were captured by the army and were never heard from again. Only Mushir and two others survived.

Some were captured in their homes on the first day of the assault. Part of the population of Mergeti, on the north side of Gara Mountain, did flee immediately after the August 25 chemical attack, but almost a hundred other people, including many of the older residents, were seized as soldiers and Kurdish *chatta* forces reached the village that evening. The troops warned them that if there was any resistance from *peshmerga* in the vicinity, they would all be executed on the spot.

In Warakhal, some way to the east in the *nahya* of Nerwa Reikan, a local *mustashar* told the village elders that their people should turn themselves in to the army; since they were not *peshmerga*, they had nothing to fear. The villagers obeyed, and were rounded up and packed into trucks. Their first destination was the complex of Deralouk, built where the main east-west highway crosses the Greater Zab. They remained there for three hours, crowded into animal pens, before being separated by age and sex. The women counted as eighty-three men from Warakhal were loaded into IFAs and driven off. They asked the *jahsh* what was to become of them, but were ordered to shut up. But there is evidence that the militiamen knew the answer only too well, for some of the women heard them muttering among themselves that it would be "a great loss for these people to disappear."[40]

From this point on, the story of the Final Anfal closely parallels what had happened during earlier stages of the campaign. The captured villagers were detained, for a few hours or a few days, in temporary holding centers on or near the main east-west highway. Sometimes there was a rudimentary interrogation. Several of these processing points were complexes like Deralouk, built to house displaced Kurds during earlier periods of the Iran-Iraq War. Captives from the area around Gara Mountain were kept briefly in the complexes of Sori Jeri and Kwaneh, and in a school in Sarseng. In the town of Amadiya itself, the police station, the army base and the headquarters of the Teachers Union were

---

[40] Middle East Watch interviews, Jezhnikan complex, May 3 and July 13, 1992.

all used. The temporary facilities were badly stretched, and transportation of so many prisoners also proved to be a problem, with many of the army IFAs breaking down. One civilian truck driver told Middle East Watch that his vehicle was commandeered, along with two civilian buses, to transport fifty or sixty prisoners--men, women and children--from the army brigade headquarters in Amadiya to Sarseng, and thence to Dohuk.[41]

Closer to Zakho, the complexes of Bersivi and Hizawa served the same purpose. Many people also told of being taken to the army fort in Mangesh, or to a primary or intermediate school in that town, sometimes lured there by false promises of amnesty. They remained in Mangesh for up to three days. Some were given meager rations of Kurdish flat bread and sun-heated water; others received nothing at all, although sympathetic townspeople reportedly threw food in at the windows.[42] After three days, the IFAs were set to move again, this time to the south, toward Dohuk.

* * *

ON-THE-SPOT MASS EXECUTIONS

In the Sorani-speaking areas of Iraqi Kurdistan, faced with orders to exterminate their prisoners on an industrial scale, the executioners were sometimes sloppy about their work. From the Third Anfal alone, the Germian campaign, at least six survivors have surfaced to tell their stories. This is not the case in Badinan, where after more than a year of intensive research Middle East Watch has been unable to find a single male who emerged alive from the camps and the firing squads.

Between April and September 1992, and again in April 1993, MEW staff travelled extensively in Badinan, conducting dozens of interviews with survivors of the Final Anfal--*Khatimat al-Anfal*. In each

---

[41] Middle East Watch interview, Amadiya, August 29, 1992. Gen. Zareb, in his "Analysis: Operation End of Anfal," acknowledged the problem of frequent vehicle breakdowns.

[42] There is a brief account of conditions at the fort in Mangesh in *The Destruction of Koreme*, p.58.

former village group, surviving witnesses were asked to construct a list of those who had died or disappeared. In many cases, they were able to do so, giving complete names where possible and identifying anyone who had been an active *peshmerga*, a draft dodger or an army deserter. The lists provided by villagers from Badinan invariably included only adult and teenage males--with the signal exception of Assyrian and Chaldean Christians, as well as Yezidi Kurds, whose fate is detailed below.

The numbers reported to MEW from thirty-six villages give some hint of the probable death toll from the Badinan campaign. Some places went unscathed, with everyone making it across the border into Turkey; some lost a single man; many a dozen or twenty; a few suffered brutally, losing almost their entire adult male population--seventy-four from the village of Ikmala in the *nahya* of Al-Doski, for example, either eighty-three or eighty-seven (according to two separate accounts) from the village of Warakhal in the *nahya* of Nerwa Reikhan, and ninety-three from Gizeh. In all, these thirty-six villages lost 632 of their menfolk to Anfal, including a few boys as young as twelve or thirteen.[43]

All of these men and boys were last seen alive in Iraqi Army custody, either crammed into IFA trucks, handcuffed by the roadside at their place of capture, or (predominantly) in the fort at Dohuk, which functioned, so to speak, as the Topzawa of the North.[44] None of them has been seen alive since their disappearance almost five years ago, and the only possible conclusion is that they were killed en masse by firing squads, just as their predecessors had been in the earlier stages of Anfal.

Hundreds of women and young children perished, too, as a result of the Final Anfal campaign. But the causes of their death were different--gassing, starvation, exposure and wilful neglect, rather than bullets fired

---

[43] According to a dossier compiled by the Kurdistan Reconstruction and Development Society, some 310 villages were destroyed in the Dohuk governorate during the Final Anfal. The internal Iraqi Army figure for the total number of males taken into custody during the Final Anfal, including "saboteurs" who surrendered or were captured, is 3,063. See below p.289. The pattern of male disappearances from villages surveyed by Middle East Watch suggests that the total numbers may be rather higher.

[44] It should be noted, however, that at least some of the Dohuk prisoners were subsequently transferred to Topzawa, which remained in operation to the very end of the Anfal campaign.

from an AK-47. In the first seven Anfal operations, the mass disappearance of women and children frequently mirrored the pattern of *peshmerga* resistance. In the Final Anfal, there was no resistance to speak of. The KDP was simply routed, and this may help explain why the women and children of Badinan were spared. As for their menfolk, the standing orders could not have been clearer:

"We received orders to kill all *peshmerga*, even those who surrendered," Middle East Watch was told by a former lieutenant colonel in the Iraqi Army. "Even civilian farmers were regarded as *peshmerga* if they were working within a prohibited area. All men in the prohibited areas, aged from 15-60 [sic], were to be considered saboteurs and killed. The prohibited areas were shown in red on the army maps, and they covered everything except the paved highways." These orders, the officer explained, were conveyed in writing to the divisional level (*tahriri*) and then passed on orally to the lower-ranking officers. The reference is clearly to Northern Bureau directives 3650 and 4008 of June 1987, which contained the standing orders for the two-year period including Anfal. The lieutenant-colonel went on to explain that women and children in his own local area of operations, were to be rounded up, trucked to the army's divisional headquarters at Begova where he was stationed and then later resettled in a government complex.[45]

"Ali Hassan al-Majid's orders were clear," agreed another former officer who had served in the *Istikhbarat*. "They were to kill all men aged from 15-60. He did not want to see them again, they must be killed off." However, "people were killed according to the mood of the officer in charge. Some were good-hearted and let people go, while others killed them."

The "good-hearted" behavior of some officers is borne out by the testimony of witnesses. A Yezidi Kurd from the village of Mezeh (*nahya* of Sarseng) was among the thousands who hid out in the mountains after fleeing before the army's attack at the end of August. "Some forty to fifty women could no longer bear the hardship," he recalled, "and surrendered to an army unit in Shkafkeh village. The commander, who was friendly, gave them food and water, but told them he was under orders to kill everyone. So he sent them back into the mountains, saying that he was incapable of killing women and children, and told them to wait for an

---

[45] Middle East Watch interview, Zakho, June 24, 1992.

amnesty."[46]   *Chatta* units in this area also crossed *peshmerga* lines to warn everyone to stay where they were, since there was a general order to kill anyone who surrendered.

At least one large group of villagers was spared as the result of a private deal with the army. This startling case involved a group of 160 families from the village of Spindarok, who tried to flee toward Turkey on the first day of the Final Anfal. They had only made it as far as the main road when they encountered an important tribal leader, the father of one of the *mustashars*. They assured the man that there were no *peshmerga* in their ranks, and he in turn approached military intelligence on their behalf. The following afternoon they surrendered to the army, which trucked them to the Zakho headquarters of *Istikhbarat*. There they handed over their weapons and gave statements. After this they were allowed to go free, moving in with relatives in Zakho. (Their own village of Spindarok was burned and bulldozed.)[47]

* * *

Some of the captured men and boys of Badinan were lined up and murdered at their point of capture, executed by firing squads on the authority of a local army officer. The most notorious case is that of Koreme, a village of some 150 households just two and a half miles north of the town of Mangesh.[48]   Koreme was known locally as a pro-government village, and many of its men served as agents of *Amn*. By

---

[46] The commander himself is extremely unlikely to have been under orders to kill all those he apprehended, regardless of age or gender, since there are no documented instances of this occurring. If this report of his comments is accurate, he may have had in mind what would happen later to those he handed over into the custody of *Amn* and *Istikhbarat*. Middle East Watch interview, Khaneq complex, August 27, 1992.

[47] In a curious footnote to this story, the families were detained after the September 6 amnesty by *Amn*, which sent them on via the fort at Dohuk to the complex of Baharka—entirely in line with the bureaucratic logic of Anfal. Middle East Watch interview, Hizawa complex, September 1, 1992.

[48] The story of this village is told in considerable detail in *The Destruction of Koreme*, especially pp.12-29, 45-52.

the time of Anfal, however, Koreme was already a village-in-hiding; since the previous year its population of 1,000 or so had taken refuge beneath damp rock overhangs in the ravines nearby. In the aftermath of the August 25 chemical attacks, Koreme--like innumerable other villages-- held a fierce debate about what to do. By the 27th, several hundred people had decided to risk fleeing to Turkey. But later that same day other terrified villagers they encountered in the mountains warned them that they had left it too late; all routes to the border were now blocked by soldiers.

The Koreme refugees turned back, accompanied by a number of people from the village of Chalkey who had joined them in the ravines. They walked all night, in constant fear of attack. By the afternoon of August 28, they had reached the outskirts of Koreme once more. The soldiers and the *jahsh*, however, had got there first. As soon as they saw the troops, the men raised their hands high in the air to signal surrender.

The officers in charge, two young lieutenants in their twenties, had the villagers separated on the spot by age and sex. This done, they appeared unsure of what they should do next, but after a pause one of the lieutenants ordered a group of thirty-three men and teenage boys to stand apart from the others.[49] Their ages ranged from thirteen to forty-three. As the other villagers were led away behind a hill, out of sight, the men were made to squat on their heels. The soldiers continued to tell them that no harm would come to them, and even offered them cigarettes and water. While they waited, one of the officers called his superiors in nearby Mangesh on his walkie-talkie. He reported that he had captured a group of "armed subversives" and asked for instructions. As soon as he put the radio down, the lieutenant shouted the order to his men to open fire. Twenty-seven of the thirty-three prisoners were killed- -eighteen from Koreme and nine from Chalkey. Remarkably, however, six survived--even though the soldiers later went down the line to administer the coup de grace.[50] The bodies were left to lie where they

---

[49] There was some debate among the villagers as to whether all the members of this group had been carrying weapons when they surrendered. See *The Destruction of Koreme*, pp.45-47.

[50] The sloppiness of the Koreme execution was remarkable in itself. Even more surprising was the fact that one of the six who survived, a 34-year old man, was wounded by the gunfire, but removed to the hospital in Mangesh the next

had fallen and to rot in the hot summer sun for more than a week before soldiers returned to bury them in two shallow pits.

To this day there is considerable speculation as to why Koreme should have been singled out in this way. Of all the theories that have been floated, the most plausible may be that their former role in *Amn* holds the key to the mystery. As a loyalist village, Koreme would have been expected to abide by the "redlining" of 1987 and register its inhabitants under the October census. Instead the village went into hiding. The regime would therefore have regarded its former *Amn* agents as especially traitorous, and captured official documents make it clear that this kind of desertion was punishable by summary execution.[51]

Koreme was not the only case of a mass execution in the field. Something similar took place on a smaller scale in Mergeti, the village on the northern slopes of Gara Mountain that had been attacked by chemical weapons on August 25. Most of the men were *peshmerga*, and they escaped to the mountain. But as we have seen, as many as one hundred villagers were captured in their homes by soldiers that same night. They were held for an hour or so by the spring that was Mergeti's only source of water. As they waited there, the soldiers set fire to their homes.

An *Istikhbarat* officer then reportedly called his superiors by walkie-talkie and told them that a number of "saboteurs" had been arrested. A member of the *jahsh*, who was standing nearby and spoke some Arabic, quietly told the villagers what the man had been ordered to do: "Separate the men and women and kill all the men older than fifteen." Twelve men were made to stand aside, and at nightfall the women were taken away on foot to the nearby town of Sarseng. In the confusion and darkness, an apparently tender-hearted infantry officer managed to conceal four of the men in the larger group of women in an

---

day by a *jahsh* unit. He was treated there and eventually transferred to the fort at Dohuk--which he also, inexplicably, survived. See *The Destruction of Koreme*, pp.51-52.

[51] According to Ba'ath Party membership forms found in the Iraqi government archives, merely concealing prior membership in another political party constituted grounds for the death penalty.

attempt to save them.[52] The other eight were taken by their captors to the nearby village of Bawarkeh Ka'ba, away from the mountains.

The soldiers' commanding officer was furious. "Why did you bring them here?" he shouted. "I ordered you to kill them. Why did you not implement my orders?" The man repeated his command: the men were to be taken back to their place of capture and shot. At a spot about 300 yards outside Mergeti, the prisoners were bound together hand and feet, blindfolded and handcuffed, and shot with Kalashnikovs.[53]

* * *

Thanks to Brigadier General Zareb's meticulous account of troop movements during the Final Anfal, it is possible to say with some precision who was responsible for the Mergeti and Koreme murders.[54] Although Mergeti is not mentioned by name in Gen. Zareb's report, the village clearly fell within the area of operations of the Iraqi Army's 41st Infantry Division. The 41st controlled a detachment of commandos from the Sixth Army Corps, as well as three infantry brigades, numbers 103, 114 and 706. The commander of one of these three brigades--it is not specified which--was in charge of the division's first joint task force that was deployed against Gara Mountain from its base in Sarseng and would

---

[52] These four were later disappeared from the fort at Dohuk, according to a Middle East Watch interview, Dohuk, June 9, 1992.

[53] This account is based on the testimony to relatives of one of the eight men, who was wounded in the shooting, escaped temporarily to a nearby *jahsh* post in the complex of Qadish, but was later handed over by his fearful family to *Amn* in Sarseng. From there he disappeared. The seven men who died were Muhammad Saleh Abd-al-Qader (b.1938), Serdar Sa'id Muhammad (b.1957), Mustafa Abd-al-Qader Mustafa (b.1926 or 1928), Suleiman Sha'aban Checho (b.1956), Adel Muhammad Khaled (b.1961), Ramadan Ahmad Hamou (b.1968) and Hamid Ahmad Hamou (birthdate unknown). The temporary survivor was Banjin Mustafa Abd-al-Qader (b.1966). The full names of the twenty-seven men executed in Koreme are given in *The Destruction of Koreme*, p.50.

[54] "Analysis: Operation End of Anfal," pp.17-19.

have moved eastward through Mergeti in the first hours of the campaign.[55]

Within the plan of attack devised by the Fifth Army Corps, Koreme was part of the Khabour Basin area of operations. (see map) Stretching from Zakho and Batufa in the north to Mangesh in the south, this theater was in the hands of the 29th Infantry Division. Three infantry brigades were also assigned to the operation--numbers 84, 238 and 435--together with a tank battalion, an assortment of mechanized forces, field engineers, artillery units and waterborne troops, and sixteen National Defense Battalions, or *jahsh*.

The campaign was further subdivided into eight joint task forces, two of which--the sixth and seventh--were based in Mangesh.[56] While the seventh task force was instructed to drive eastward and take the villages of Majalmukht and Alkushki, the sixth was to move north, as far as the twin villages of upper and lower Baroshki, on the south bank of the Khabour river. A secondary detachment was to peel off to the northeast, and to take Koreme. It was this unit that carried out the executions, and from the testimonies of witnesses, the assumption must be that the order came from the sixth task force commander of the 29th Infantry Division, based in Mangesh.

Gen. Zareb was well pleased by the performance of his officers. By August 29, he was able to report that the 29th and 41st Infantry Divisions had "occupied all [their] target places" and "completed all the duties assigned to [them]."[57] Over the course of the next week, other units and task forces continued mopping-up operations and drove the last of the *peshmerga* into Turkey and Iran. By September 6, the last strategic border hilltop had been occupied, and from a military point of view the Final Anfal was complete. Gen. Zareb applauded the "military and civilian security authorities" for laying the groundwork for the successful campaign, and paid tribute to the comrades of the Ba'ath Party for "raising the degree of enthusiasm and zealousness of the fighters."[58]

---

[55] ibid, p.16.

[56] ibid, pp.17-19.

[57] ibid, p.27.

[58] ibid, pp.38-39.

The general detected the same sterling fighting qualities in the *jahsh*. "The combatants of the National Defense Battalions zealously and enthusiastically fought to achieve the target of destroying the saboteurs in their positions," he wrote. "In all the convoys, they used to march ahead of the troops because they knew the area and also because of their good physical fitness, especially for mountain-climbing. They...played an active role in the destruction of villages and the collection of plunder."[59] There was a meticulous inventory of the "plunder": cattle and goats; rugs, mattresses and blankets; watches, cash and pieces of gold; picture albums, eating utensils, packets of powdered milk, toothpaste...[60]

His forces had met "almost no resistance," the general reported, and this was reflected in the army's casualty figures. Only thirty-one men died in the Final Anfal, and eighteen of those were *jahsh*, who had dutifully played the role of cannon fodder assigned to them by the army and the Ba'ath Party. As for the "saboteurs" taken into army custody during the Badinan campaign, they were listed as follows:

Saboteurs Surrendered	803
Saboteurs Captured	771
Men	1,489
Women	3,368
Children	6,964
Total	13,395

Others, of course, had died in the field. But these were not tallied accurately, with the exception of forty-eight *peshmerga* reported killed in clashes with the 29th Division. Instead, Gen. Zareb contented himself with a terse notation: "Too many bloodstains were seen in all the places cleaned by our forces."

* * *

---

[59] ibid p.39.

[60] ibid pp.57-60.

THE FORT AT DOHUK AND THE WOMEN'S PRISON AT SALAMIYEH

The Dohuk Fort squats by the roadside at Nizarkeh, on the eastern outskirts of the capital of the governorate. It is a huge concrete structure, built of Soviet design in the 1970s and protected by a battery of four anti-aircraft guns on the roof. Of the 13,395 "saboteurs" captured in Badinan, most were taken to the fort, trucked there in army IFAs from their place of capture. Some male prisoners from the southern part of Badinan were reportedly also taken to the city of Mosul, but no one has apparently returned alive to tell the story of what happened there.

Most of the inmates were held on the second floor of the fort, which was so crowded that the prisoners spilled over into the corridors. They stayed in Dohuk between two and five days, although some old people were kept there longer, for periods of as much as a couple of weeks. Some women spent the whole of the first night in the courtyard of the fort, confined to the same trucks that had brought them. As in Topzawa, the newcomers were segregated on arrival: men and boys of military service age to one side and women, children and the elderly to the other. Soldiers took brief statements from the men and confiscated their IDs, but no one else was questioned. With their customary fondness for keeping documentary records, security agents made videotapes of these brief interrogation sessions.

As their wives and sisters stood by, powerless to help, the men were beaten with wooden batons and lengths of plastic tubing, kicked, punched and slapped. Army guards amused themselves by putting lighted matches to the prisoners' beards and mustaches. Children screamed and tried to run to their fathers, but were driven back with kicks and blows. Iram, a young woman from Gizeh, on Gara Mountain, watched as soldiers beat her brother-in-law bloody. She begged them, "by God and by the Prophet," to let her cross the courtyard to wash his wounds. The soldiers refused. "You have no God and no Prophet," they sneered.[61]

When the registration process was completed, the prisoners were dispersed to filthy communal cells that were strewn with human waste. "It was like living in a toilet," one elderly woman recalled in disgust. There were thousands in the fort, men packed into the ground level cells and women, children and the elderly on the floor above. Hundreds more

---

[61] Middle East Watch interview, Jezhnikan complex, May 3, 1992.

arrived each day. They were from all the major tribes of the Badinan area--Doski, Sindi, Reikan, Barwari, Sleivani and others. Several hundred of the prisoners were from Yezidi and Assyrian Christian villages, and these people were segregated from the Muslim detainees by a partition wall.

In many respects the conditions at Nizarkeh were even more squalid than at Topzawa. Most strikingly, there was no attempt to feed the inmates. Although there were faucets in the courtyard, guards barred the prisoners from using them. Small amounts of insanitary, sun-warmed water were available from barrels in the yard, but there was no effort to distribute this systematically. There was not even bread. "You Kurds have been sent here to die," was the comment that many prisoners reported hearing from their guards.

Small gestures of sympathy from local townspeople helped to ward off starvation--something that happened at a number of other detention facilities for Kurds during Anfal. Once, a Kurdish guard dumped two sacks of bread in the courtyard, and the fitter children scrambled for these. But other children, and some of the older adults, did succumb to hunger and disease. As many as twenty died in one two-day period in early September, according to one account.[62] Over time, the longer-term elderly inmates were able to buy food from their jailers, in the same way as their fellow Kurds in Nugra Salman. When only the elderly remained, security also became more lax, and some relatives even managed to slip inside the fort for brief visits. At night the prisoners would slip out to the barbed wire perimeter fence to collect large plastic sacks of food that the people of Dohuk left there.[63]

For the younger inmates, the guards' brutality continued as a matter of daily routine. New arrivals saw recent bloodstains on the floors and walls. Any woman attempting to visit her husband on the lower level

---

[62] Middle East Watch interview, Telkabber complex, August 28, 1992.

[63] Apart from a handful who reportedly died of disease and starvation, the elderly prisoners survived Nizarkeh. So, by a curious quirk, did at least two younger men who were confined with the elderly because of their injuries. One was the wounded survivor of the execution squad at Koreme; the other was a man suffering from the effects of the poison gas attack on Warmilleh, the only adult male to survive from that village. Middle East Watch interviews, Koreme and Warmilleh villages, May 30 and August 31, 1988.

of the fort was beaten back. Men were savagely beaten with pruning hooks of the sort that Kurds customarily use in their fields. One overweight young man was pummeled senseless, stuffed into the trunk of a Volkswagen Passat and driven out of the fort. He was not seen again. Others were pounded on the head and upper body with concrete blocks, sometimes when they were tied to posts in the courtyard. "I saw it myself when officers killed one young man with such a block," said an old man from the Amadiya area. "I cried and prayed to God to save us all."[64]

On another occasion, a prisoner saw soldiers and *Istikhbarat* officers taking turns to beat a group of twelve young men in *peshmerga* dress. The army men were yelling and cursing them: "Are you not ashamed of being saboteurs, donkeys, sons of dogs!" Later, the witness saw the bloodied bodies of the twelve young men being dragged away by soldiers. He was told by a guard that they were *peshmerga* who had surrendered or been captured by helicopter on Mattin Mountain.[65]

Another young man who was a carpenter in Dohuk learned that a friend's father was among the detainees in the fort, and rushed there immediately with sacks of bread and grapes. At the gate of the fort he asked an *Amn* agent for permission to enter. "How could you go in?" the man asked. "You'll get beaten. Let me show you what happened to some of the people in there." The *Amn* man took the carpenter to a patch of lower ground outside the fort and pointed to a number of bloodstains, as well as what appeared to be the remains of human brains. The guard explained that these belonged to people from the villages of Spindar and Swareh, on the slopes of Gara Mountain. Eighteen of them had been killed here, summarily executed.[66]

After a few days in this hellish atmosphere, the first groups of women and children were told to assemble in the huge central courtyard, where vehicles were waiting to take them away to a new destination. Sometimes these were closed buses with two small windows in the rear,

---

[64] Middle East Watch interview, Jezhnikan complex, May 3, 1992.

[65] The witness identified two of the *peshmerga* as Muhammad Taher Musa, age twenty-five, from Zewa Shkan village (Sarseng), and Lazgin Omar, age between twenty and twenty-two, from Ikmala village (Mangesh). Middle East Watch interview, Bateli, Dohuk, June 12, 1992.

[66] Middle East Watch interview, Dohuk, September 4, 1992.

sometimes minibuses or coasters, sometimes ordinary army IFAs. Armed guards--identified as *Amn* and *Istikhbarat*--waited to accompany the convoys. The final images that the women took with them from Nizarkeh were of the continued sufferings of their menfolk. As one group waited to depart, they saw cursing soldiers beating a number of men in the courtyard with cement blocks and sticks. The men were blindfolded and handcuffed. As the buses pulled away, one woman cried, "Let our children die too, now that their fathers are dead."[67] And in the days that followed, the older inmates of the Dohuk Fort saw more buses come--some of them khaki-colored, others blue--to take away the younger men.[68] With hardly an exception, they have never been seen again.

* * *

The vehicles carrying the women and children headed south toward Mosul, before turning on to the Baghdad road. In one truck, a pregnant woman from the Amadiya area began to go into labor. The other women yelled at the driver to stop, but he refused, and a belligerent soldier aimed a kick at the pregnant woman. But as the crowded truck continued to bump along the highway, she gave birth to her baby. The child survived, and they called it Hawar, or "scream."

About five hours after leaving Dohuk, the convoys pulled up outside a prison, or military base, in the small town of Salamiyeh, on the east bank of the Tigris a few miles south of Mosul. On arrival, there was a brief registration process and *Istikhbarat*, which had overseen the Dohuk Fort, handed the women and children over into the custody of new guards, whom witnesses identified as belonging to the Iraqi police and Popular Army. The prisoners found themselves in a huge single-story building, divided into perhaps two dozen large, overcrowded halls, each some fifty yards in length. Every hall held people from a particular region, but all the inmates were from Badinan; not a word of Sorani was

---

[67] Middle East Watch interview, Kwaneh complex, August 29, 1992.

[68] One witness described the blue vehicles as being "as long as buses, but not looking like buses," with a single small window high up on one side, near the driver's compartment. This witness saw between seven and ten of these buses leaving the fort each day for several days. Middle East Watch interview, Dohuk, September 4, 1992.

heard. Here the women were to stay for anything between ten days and two weeks.

The prison regime at Salamiyeh was a distinct improvement on the Nizarkeh fort, and none of the women reported being specifically harassed or abused. Recollections of Salamiyeh varied from case to case. Perhaps memory is dimmed by time and trauma; on the other hand, it may well be that prison conditions changed over time. Some women recalled a diet of nothing but "hard, rough bread" and water from tanks in the yard; other said that they received three meals a day, including bread, rice, soup and jam, and that water was readily available from faucets. There were even iceblocks to counter the summer heat, and a small prison shop that sold a few basic staples. Although there was no soap, the women could wash their clothes each day in the courtyard.

Even so, conditions at Salamiyeh were grim. The prisoners were detained here with no semblance of legal process; no charges were ever brought against them, and they were never given any reason for their confinement. Women and children slept on the bare concrete floor without blankets and used filthy, overflowing toilets. The inmates of different halls were forbidden to communicate with each other. There was no medical attention, and at least two deaths were reported during the two weeks that the Salamiyeh prison was in service. One of the dead was a child from Gizeh village, who was crushed beneath a water tank. Soldiers removed the body, and refused to tell the child's mother where they were taking it.

Above all the women suffered the constant mental torment of not knowing what had become of their husbands and brothers. At least two witnesses said that some of the Badinan men *were* taken for a time to Salamiyeh, although they were held in separate quarters. One woman from the *nahya* of Guli learned from the guards that her husband and three brothers were alive in the prison. Another, who was held in Hall No.7 with other prisoners from the Sarseng area, found one day that the steel door of her cell had been locked. It remained that way for six days. On the sixth morning, it was left open for two hours. From her vantage point close to the door, the woman had a partial view of the courtyard outside. "I saw men, blindfolded with their hands cuffed behind them," she told Middle East Watch. "They were wearing Kurdish cummerbunds and headscarves (*jamadani*)." It was the first time she had been aware of male prisoners at Salamiyeh. "I saw those men being put into military vehicles, closed vehicles with only a small hole in the back." As each pair of vehicles was loaded up, they drove away. Another two took their place, then another two, and another. She saw many men moved out of Salamiyeh in this way. She surmised that this had been going on during the six days that the door of Hall No.7 had remained locked: "It had to be for a purpose; otherwise the doors were always left open."[69]

Shortly after the removal of these blindfolded male prisoners, there was a sudden burst of gunfire. But it turned out to be nothing more ominous than joyful guards letting off their weapons into the air. President Saddam Hussein had declared a general amnesty, they told the women. Now their husbands would be safe. There was to be music, a big party. They even expected the Kurdish women to dance with them.

---

[69] Middle East Watch interview, Bateli, Dohuk, June 12, 1992.

11
THE AMNESTY AND ITS EXCLUSIONS

"We were useless. They said it was unjust to waste bread on us."
-- Rahman Hamid Nader of Darbarou village,
Taqtaq, on his release from Nugra Salman prison.

Decree no. 736 of the Revolutionary Command Council was read out on the radio early on the afternoon of September 6, just after the mid-day prayers. It declared "a general and comprehensive amnesty for all Iraqi Kurds...both inside and outside of Iraq"--with the sole exception of "the traitor Al-Talabani...because of his wilful and repeated violations of law and order, even after he was granted opportunities to reform his ways." Ali Hassan al-Majid was infuriated by the amnesty, he later told aides, but went along with it as a loyal party man.[1]

The optimists among the *peshmerga* believed that the amnesty came as the result of outside pressure, that the regime of Saddam Hussein had been compelled to back down by the international reaction to revelations that chemical weapons had been used during the Final Anfal. But such outrage as there was over the Badinan attacks was not a significant contributing factor to the amnesty. The most scathing comments, and those likely to have had the greatest influence on Iraq, came from U.S. Secretary of State George Shultz. But these comments were not made until September 8, a full two days after the amnesty had

---

[1] Iraqi News Agency, as reported in *Al-Thawra*, September 7, 1988. Other, broader amnesties were also decreed in the immediate post-Anfal period. On November 30, 1988, Revolutionary Command Council decree no. 860 announced "a comprehensive and general amnesty" for all "persons who have engaged in dissident political activities and subsequently gone into hiding." On February 28, 1989, RCC decree no. 130 declared a general amnesty for all Iraqis who have fled the country, although again "with the exception of the traitor Jalal al-Talabani and agents of the Iranian regime." Al-Majid's comments on the amnesty are from an audiotaped meeting held on April 15, 1989.

been declared.[2]   It is clear from the Fifth Corps report on the Final Anfal that the decision to declare a general amnesty was made because Baghdad was convinced by September 6 that the *peshmerga* forces had been crushed.   In the words of the press release that accompanied the amnesty, "These [traitorous] Kurds had relinquished control of their cities and villages to Khomeini's troops, but God foiled their evil plans."[3]

The next day, September 7, the Presidential Cabinet issued an additional order granting Ali Hassan al-Majid and the Northern Bureau of the Ba'ath Party special powers to facilitate the return of refugees from Turkey, where their stories had been causing Iraq considerable embarrassment and annoyance--despite the best efforts of the Turkish government to minimize the tragedy.[4]

The refugees would only be allowed to return at two approved entry points, where special reception camps would be set up. One was the Ibrahim Khalil international bridge outside Zakho. The other site was "to be determined by the First Army Corps with all due swiftness." After processing by a newly constituted Returnee Reception Committee (*Lajnet Istiqbal al-'A'idin*), which would operate under Ba'ath Party control, the refugees would be assigned to complexes. There, they would have the responsibility of building their own homes; the plot allocated to them would become their property free of charge after five years--"on condition

---

[2] At its noon briefing on September 8, after Shultz had met with Iraqi Minister of State Saadoun Hammadi, the State Department described Iraq's use of chemical weapons against the Kurds as "unjustifiable and abhorrent" and "unacceptable to the civilized world." See Middle East Watch, *Human Rights in Iraq* (New Haven: Yale University Press, 1990), pp. 108-110.

[3] *Al-Thawra*, September 7, 1988.

[4] Two versions of the document spelling out al-Majid's powers over refugee resettlement have come to light. One, apparently the original order, is an unclassified letter to various departments from the Presidential Office of the Iraqi Republic, no. Q/1509 of September 7, 1988. The other, dated September 12, is "secret and confidential" letter no. Sh 3/13631, from *Amn* Erbil to all Security Directorates in the governorate.

that the family receives a favorable assessment by the Party and Security authorities of its conduct from the point of view of loyalty."[5]

Once the assignment to a *mujamma'a* had been made, the Kurds who returned under the amnesty would not be allowed to move. They were obliged, in fact, to sign or affix their thumbprint to a sworn statement which read: "I, the undersigned (....) testify that I live in the governorate of (....), in the section of (....), residence number (....), and I recognize that I will face the death penalty should the information indicated be false, or should I alter my address without notifying the appropriate administration and authorities.   To this I affirm my support."[6]

The refugees were granted only until 6:00 p.m. on October 9, barely a month, to "return to the national ranks."   Anyone who surrendered to the government after this grace period had expired would be taken into military custody and handed over to the Ba'ath Party's Northern Bureau Command--for what purpose it was not stated.[7]

A flurry of other decrees followed, for although the regime spoke of a "general" amnesty, it by no means intended that all Kurds should escape further punishment. First, on September 8, the Revolutionary Command Council decreed that any amnestied Iraqi Kurds who had been affiliated with the armed forces, the domestic security services or the *jahsh*

---

[5] Letter no. Q/1509, dated September 7, 1988, from the Presidential Office of the Iraqi Republic to "[illegible] Deputy Commander in Chief of the Armed Forces, Respected Defense Minister, Respected Interior Minister and Ali Hassan al-Majid, Respected Secretary General of the Northern Bureau."

[6] Middle East Watch has examined many files of these sworn statements, duly filled in by returnees and dated at various times in September and October 1988. The documents also bear the signatures of representatives of the civil administration, the police, security and intelligence agencies and the local Ba'ath Party branch.

[7] This procedure is spelled out in two documents, both issued by the local office of *Amn* in Shaqlawa.   One is a letter to the Ba'ath Party's Returnee Reception Committee, dated October 7, 1988; the other is a letter (#5823) to all police stations, dated October 11, 1988.

were henceforth discharged and barred from re-enlisting as volunteers.[8]
The authorities were also worried that those "returning to the national
ranks" would offer fertile soil for any attempt at reorganization by the
peshmerga--even if the "saboteurs" seemed, for the time being, to present
no further threat. Accordingly, Ali Hassan al-Majid resolved that it was
necessary for those who benefited from the amnesty to have their civil
rights radically curtailed and their activities strictly monitored. "Kurdish
citizens shall be treated by the same standards applied to any other Iraqi
citizen in so far as their rights and duties are concerned," the Northern
Bureau ordered, "with the exception of those Kurds who benefited from
the amnesty decree no. 736 of September 8, 1988."

> These shall not be treated on an equal footing with other
> Iraqis in terms of rights and duties, unless they can
> effectively match good intentions with proper conduct
> and demonstrate that they have ended all collaboration
> with the saboteurs, and that they are more loyal to Iraq
> than their peers who have benefited from the above-
> mentioned amnesty decree.
>
> In dealing with such cases, the following parameters shall
> apply:
>
> 1: These Kurds shall not be entitled to be nominated for
> membership in the National Assembly (*Al-Majlis al-*
> *Watani*), the Legislature (*Al-Majlis al-Tashri'i*), the People's
> Councils (*Majlis al-Sha'ab*), the Municipal Councils (*Majlis*
> *al-Baladiya*) or mass organizations.

---

[8] The reader might imagine that this would hardly constitute punishment
for a Kurd. However, entry into the military, the *jahsh* or the security forces had
always been seen as an option that offered economic benefits as well as immunity
from the regime's anti-Kurdish activities. The prohibition was therefore a blow
to Kurdish aspirations as well as a further erosion of the civil rights of the Iraqi
Kurdish minority. These modifications to the amnesty were set forth in
Revolutionary Command Council decrees nos. 737 (September 8, 1988) and 785
(September 29, 1988).

2: Those Kurds who took advantage of the Amnesty Decree shall not be entitled to sell, buy or lease state lands or concerns for which ownership is attributed to the state. Nor shall they be entitled to enter into any contract with any state organ or to engage in private business, whether as professionals or workers, until a period of two years has elapsed since their return to the national ranks.

3: The competent authorities will monitor the behavior of those who benefited from the amnesty decree, and will determine their inclinations through the placement of thorough and diligent informers in their midst.[9]

In its attempt to understand the thinking of the few "saboteurs" who survived, *Amn* scrutinized a communique in which the Kurdish opposition-in-exile gave its response to the general amnesty decree.[10] Kurdish propagandists were presenting the decree as a victory, *Amn* reported; it had been issued "to try and absorb part of the resentment inside the country, and to ease the worldwide campaign of protest." In the wake of its crushing of the Kurds, the regime no doubt found this show of bravado amusing. "The subject has been brought to the attention of the Struggling Comrade Ali Hassan al-Majid, Secretary General of the Northern Bureau," the *Amn* report concluded, "and his excellency's view of the matter was this: that those who betray Iraq or remain abroad should no longer be entitled to keep their nationality."[11]

---

[9] Letter no.14951, dated November 23, 1988 and classified "Secret and Confidential" from the Secretariat of *Amn* for the Autonomous Region to *Amn* Suleimaniyeh, citing instructions of the Northern Bureau Command.

[10] The organization in question here is the Political Command of the Iraqi Kurdistan Front (*Al-Qiyadeh al-Siyasiyeh lil-Jabha al-Kurdistaniyeh al-Iraqiyeh*), a seven-party body (later eight) dominated by the PUK and the KDP.

[11] "Reactions to the General Amnesty for the Kurds." Letter no. Sh.S Sh 3/5089, dated October 18, 1988 and classified "Secret and Confidential," from *Amn* Chamchamal to all security directorates.

* * *

Guards broke the news of the amnesty to the women and children at the Dibs army base and the Salamiyeh prison, to the old people who had survived the summer in Nugra Salman, and to the last groups of prisoners who remained at the Popular Army camp of Topzawa. Refugees in Iran and Turkey learned of the amnesty from Baghdad Radio and reported by the thousand to army border posts. According to former field officers in Badinan, the order came down instructing them no longer to kill their prisoners.[12] Even fighters returning from Iran were not mistreated at the border. One group of former *peshmerga* who turned themselves in at the military base at Piramagroun, close to the destroyed PUK headquarters at Sergalou, was briefly questioned before being released. "We were asked about the size of our forces, the kinds of weapons we used, and our reasons for fleeing to Iran. They asked us what we wanted. I answered that we were Kurds and that we wanted our rights. The government gave us one document to get us through the checkpoints, and another that gave us permission to be in the new *mujamma'at* where we had been assigned to live."[13]

One group, however, seems to have been singled out for a harsher welcome. These were the draft dodgers and deserters who had eluded capture in the mountains, warding off starvation by eating wild grasses and the crops that had been left in the fields outside abandoned and bulldozed villages. Some of these Kurds were returned to their old units and detained for as long as five months--in the custody, ironically, of the same army that had "Anfalized" their families and destroyed their homes. One group of sixty deserters from the Shwan area surrendered to the army in Kirkuk after four months on the run. Each man was given a letter to his old military unit and detained at that unit's base. "We were put in small overcrowded rooms with no space to sleep and very little food, and soldiers and officers beat me with cables," said Rezgar, a young man who was imprisoned at the army's Khaled camp, outside Erbil. From here, he was transferred to a training camp in the city, where he spent weeks being drilled and listening to lectures from a Kurdish officer on the virtues of the Ba'ath Party. "'What good is the

---

[12] Middle East Watch interview, Zakho, June 24, 1992.

[13] Middle East Watch interview, Taqtaq, April 24, 1992.

Ba'ath Party?' we asked. 'If the Ba'ath Party is so good, where are our families and our villages?' They had no answer to this." After two months the men were released, but not before the army confiscated ten dinars (then $30) from each of them--"for the rebuilding of Fao," scene of the costliest battle of the Iran-Iraq War.[14]

DISPERSAL OF THE CAMP SURVIVORS

For the inmates of Topzawa, Dibs and Nugra Salman, the regime used two principal dispersal points, and a number of secondary ones. Most of the detainees were abandoned either in Suleimaniyeh city or in nearby Arbat. A few were taken on as far as Chamchamal, where they were eventually resettled in the new Shoresh complex, or to Kalar, where their final home would be the complex of Sumoud. One old woman from the Taqtaq area reported being left off a little closer to her former home, at a government building in Dukan. Officials there asked her only a few questions. Had her sons been *peshmerga*? they wanted to know:

"No," she replied, "they are with the government."
Al-hamdu lillah," the men replied. Thanks be to God.

* * *

"Stand in line, you criminals," a guard snapped at the several thousand elderly inmates who had survived the rigors of Nugra Salman. "You must remember this experience forever, and you shall never think of doing anything against our leader, Saddam Hussein. You have been granted amnesty." The *Amn* guards registered their names once more and began to sort everyone out into different groups. It was time to get rid of these useless people by dumping them in the cities, the loathsome Lt. Hajjaj was heard to remark.[15]

The prisoners were released from Nugra Salman at weekly intervals. Convoys of vehicles arrived every Saturday, and took them away in fearful and crying groups of about five hundred at a time.

---

[14] Middle East Watch interview, Taqtaq, April 24, 1992.

[15] Middle East Watch interview, Erbil, April 23, 1992.

Occasionally army IFAs were used, sometimes windowless military transports of the kind used for the mass execution victims, but more often large civilian buses--"open and pleasant" vehicles with seats, accommodating fifty or sixty people each. The lame, the blind and the infirm were the first to be allowed to leave. If a person was sick or ailing, then his or her entire family was let go from Nugra Salman at the same time.

The final releases from "the pit of Salman" were not complete until well into November. One woman who left at the end of October said that many of those who remained were originally from the Qara Dagh or Halabja areas.[16] But the greatest mystery surrounds the two large groups of women and children from southern Germian, who had been brought here from Dibs--the first after about six weeks, and the second not until August. Numbering about five hundred in all, they were held in separate quarters at Nugra Salman and forbidden to have any contact with the elderly prisoners. During their detention, dozens reportedly died of starvation and disease.

The survivors of this group were the last to be released from Nugra Salman, with the exception of three old men from the Kifri area of southern Germian who refused to go until their daughters went too. "When I was released [in November]," said a teenage girl from Omerbel, "there was no one left there. We were the last ones."[17] Yet some of the group were never accounted for, such as two adult women and four children from the village of Benaka (*nahya* of Tilako). Their disappearances added to the already immense weight of tragedy that struck this part of southern Germian in the wake of the Third Anfal.

After release from Nugra Salman, the first stop was sometimes Topzawa, sometimes Samawa. Sometimes the buses and their *Amn* guards travelled north in dog-legged fashion, stopping in both places. Many of those who were processed through Topzawa had the unnerving experience of passing once more through the same building--even in some cases spending a night in the same cell--that had housed them on their outward journey several months earlier. Others had their names

---

[16] Middle East Watch interview, Zarayen complex, July 28, 1992.

[17] Middle East Watch interview, Kifri, March 30, 1993. This account of the southern Germian women in Nugra Salman also draws on interviews in Basirma complex, March 24, 1993; Suleimaniyeh, April 1, 1993; and Zakho, April 8, 1993.

taken one more time at the Kirkuk office of the Ba'ath Party. Some of
the deportees were issued with new ID papers that bore the words
"Affected by Anfal Operations."[18]

At Samawa, the nearest town to Nugra Salman, the newly
released prisoners spent anywhere from an hour to a week. The fittest
of them paused only briefly to have their names registered yet again.
Those who were sick were "treated very kindly" by army personnel in an
empty school or in the wards of an old military hospital. Everyone was
cleaned up; the old men were shaved. "We looked like monsters,"
commented an old man from the *nahya* of Aghjalar, "we had to be made
presentable."[19] After the privations of Nugra Salman, the diet was
almost too rich. There was meat, fruit and rice. "They wanted to show
that the government was treating us well," remembered a middle-aged
man from the Qara Dagh region. "We were given medicine and good
food, like chicken and fish. The guards told us we had to sing and enjoy
ourselves. The government is nice, they told us; it is going to set you
free."[20]

On arrival at Suleimaniyeh and Arbat, there was one final name
check. Fingerprints were taken, release papers signed. In the provincial
capital some of the prisoners were taken to a security building "like a big
hospital," where friendly city residents tossed food in over the high walls.
Others ended up at the Suleimaniyeh soccer stadium, where the huge
crowds were divided into groups according to their *nahya* of origin and
told that they were free to go--anywhere but to their home villages
(which, in any case, no longer existed). Anyone who strayed into the
prohibited areas, one group was warned, "will be taken in a helicopter to
heaven and dropped to the ground, or executed without trial."[21]

At the Ba'ath Party office in Arbat, the message was the same.
Here, a few prisoners were asked to fill in questionnaires about their
family members and issued with new papers. "Do you know why you were
released?" one Ba'ath "comrade" asked a man from the Kalar area.

---

[18] Middle East Watch interview, Benaslawa complex, April 20, 1992.

[19] Middle East Watch interview, Erbil, April 23, 1992.

[20] Middle East Watch interview, Ja'faran, Qara Dagh, May 11, 1992.

[21] Middle East Watch interview, Erbil, April 23, 1992.

"Because God saved me," the man answered. After some brief ritual questioning of this sort, the deportees were told that they should now proceed to "modern villages"--*mujamma'at*--such as Sumoud and Bayinjan, where they would be given good housing.

The few who were driven on to Chamchamal had a somewhat different experience. Here, the newcomers were received by the *qaym maqam*, the civilian head of the *qadha* of Chamchamal. There were the usual harsh warnings: "They told us not to go to the villages, it was forbidden. We could not go beyond the paved highway. If they found us out there, we would be punished."[22]   New housing would be made available in local complexes such as Shoresh and Benaslawa. But more significantly, the prisoners could not go free until local citizens vouched for them and agreed to take them temporarily into their homes. In some cases these guarantees were demanded for prisoners in groups of four. There was no shortage of guarantors: the residents of Chamchamal distinguished themselves once more, as they had during the April protest to free the Anfal prisoners, by their spontaneous display of generosity toward their fellow Kurds.

* * *

THE MUJAMMA'A DUMPING OPERATION

The survivors of Anfal ended up in more than a dozen complexes, according to their place of origin. Those from the southern part of Germian gravitated above all to Sumoud ("Steadfastness"), the large complex outside the town of Kalar. Most people from northern Germian found their way to Shoresh ("Revolution"), on the outskirts of Chamchamal. Those from the Lesser Zab Valley were mainly relocated in Benaslawa and Daratou, on the plain south of Erbil. But the harshest fate of all awaited the survivors of the Final Anfal in Badinan, who were dumped in their tens of thousands on the barren earth north of Erbil.

Sumoud and Shoresh had both existed in rudimentary form since a year before Anfal, having been laid out originally to house the relocated inhabitants of the 1987 program of village clearances in Germian and the Erbil plain. As Anfal swept through these areas in 1988, many fleeing

---

22   Middle East Watch interview, Taqtaq, April 24, 1992.

villagers found refuge in the two complexes, though without official permission. After the September amnesty, both were enormously expanded to house the survivors. According to estimates of the Kurdish administration, the population of Sumoud had grown by 1992 to 50,000, 85 percent of whom were *Anfalakan*. Shoresh was even larger. Subdivided into four geographical areas, it housed 60,000 people, including the entire population of the former district center of Qader Karam, who were brought here after the town was bulldozed in May 1988. Fully seventy percent of those housed in Shoresh were Anfal survivors.[23]

The word "housed" may give a misleading impression, for all that the new arrivals ever received from the Ba'ath government was a piece of paper giving them nominal title (subject to good behavior) to a small plot of land and, in a few cases, a bare cement floor. "Build your house," a former inmate of Nugra Salman was told when he was released in Kalar. "But how could I build?" he asked Middle East Watch rhetorically. "I had no children, no son, no food, no money, no mats."[24] Gradually, however, two squalid townships came into existence, with rough cinderblock homes and eventually electric power lines and running water. The complexes were controlled by police and army posts, and no one could venture beyond the perimeter without an official pass.

To this arrangement there was no alternative. The villages and their adjoining farmlands were prohibited, on pain of death, and Iraqi government files contain many references to individuals and groups of people executed after being found in "prohibited" areas in the post-Anfal period as residents of the towns left standing after Anfal were warned over loudspeakers that anyone sheltering *Anfalakan* would be punished. The sweeps even went into the cities, especially Suleimaniyeh; most, if not all, of the families in the complexes had lost their male breadwinners, and there was no question of compensation for the lives, homes and property that had been destroyed and pillaged. There was also no food

---

[23] These figures were provided by Jawhar Nameq, speaker of the new Kurdish Parliament, elected in May 1992. Middle East Watch interview, Erbil, June 18, 1992.

[24] This man last saw his two sons, aged eleven and thirteen, in detention in Tikrit. He also lost fifteen other members of his family in Anfal. Middle East Watch interview, Suleimaniyeh, May 12, 1992.

without ration cards. Entitlement to these had been based on the 1987 census; each person's card, stamped with the seal of the Ba'ath Party, was marked with the village and *nahya* of residence. Now they could only be obtained by registering as a resident of one of the complexes--or by the time-honored means of bribery. Some residents of the *mujamma'a* of Ber Hoshter were reportedly told by Ba'ath officials that they would receive food and other privileges if they joined the ruling Party.[25] Those who did so found that the promise was an empty one.

Many *Anfalakan* also found it impossible to obtain new identity documents, without which there could be no public sector employment, no education for the children, no access to health care, or other government services. According to one Anfal widow who was shuttled between the complexes of Shoresh and Jedideh Zab:

> When I went to look for a job, I was told that Anfal families were not allowed to work. At the school, I was told that Anfal families could not register their children. At the hospital, we were denied treatment for the same reason. I wanted to get IDs for my children, but the authorities were not allowed to issue them. At the school they told me I needed a citizenship card for the children. They sent me to Chamchamal and Erbil, and from there to Baghdad, to the Secretary General of *Amn*. I finally got a letter saying my husband was lost in Anfal, but this was less of a help than a hindrance. It marked me. The police station at the Jedideh Zab complex told me this letter should make things easier for me, but when people saw it I was always turned down.[26]

* * *

A half-dozen camps--for want of a better word--straggled across the barren, windswept scrubland northeast of the city of Erbil. At a Northern Bureau meeting on September 7, Ali Hassan al-Majid decided

---

[25] Middle East Watch interview with former resident of Ber Hoshter, Zarayen complex, July 28, 1992.

[26] Middle East Watch interview, Jedideh Zab complex, May 2, 1992.

to have the survivors of the Badinan campaign trucked to this inhospitable area from the prison at Salamiyeh, from the fort at Dohuk, from the smaller army posts at Atrush and Aqra, and from the Turkish border, where they had now begun to arrive in response to the previous day's amnesty. The largest single contingent was to be dumped, in many cases at dead of night, on a patch of wasteland near the complex of Baharka. The site came to be known as Jezhnikan, after a nearby Kurdish village destroyed in an earlier army campaign. Over time, the twin settlements of Baharka-Jezhnikan, housing 4,241 families, effectively merged into one single, huge complex.[27]

There was nothing here to welcome the new arrivals: just bare earth, thorn bushes and guard towers with machine guns. It was September, and while the days still brought fierce heat, the nighttime chill heralded the approach of winter. There was no protection from the elements. "They gave us nothing, we had to sleep on the ground, we were starving," said one man who came to Baharka.[28] With no infrastructure, no food or water, no housing or shelter, it was clearly a matter of complete indifference to the planners of Anfal whether these deportees lived or died, and the camp guards frequently told them as much.

Yet most of them survived as the result of a prodigious private voluntary relief effort. The Kurdish citizens of Erbil were the first to help, bringing food, water, tea, sugar and blankets to the *Anfalakan*, often at great personal risk. In time they were helped by relatives of the camp inmates--those who had survived Anfal because their place of residence was a town or a *mujamma'a*. The first volunteers were fired on as they tried to approach Baharka and Jezhnikan across the open scrub; later

---

[27] The decisions of the Northern Bureau meeting are reported in an *Amn* Erbil letter dated September 16, 1988. It reads, "It is possible to house the families returning to the national ranks in the new towns of our governorate, up to a maximum of 12,714 families, to be distributed among the following new towns:

Jezhnikan	4,241
Girdachal	2,794
Ber Hoshter	2,314
Shakholan	2,387"

[28] Middle East Watch interview, Dohuk, June 2, 1992.

they were detained by soldiers, questioned and beaten. But in the end the authorities turned a blind eye to the relief operation, perhaps because they feared the spread of disease from the camps.[29]

By the end of the year, epidemics were rife. There were outbreaks of typhoid and hepatitis, as well as the more routine--but still deadly--scourges of influenza and dysentery. Despite the best efforts of the people of Erbil, many of the camp residents failed to make it through that first autumn and winter.[30] The great majority of those who died were children, many of them from villages in Dohuk governorate that had been exposed to chemical weapons. Villagers from Tilakru, Warmilleh and Warakhal all reported burying many of their infants in Baharka, and one elderly woman from Gizeh, herself injured in a poison gas attack, lost three small grandchildren in Jezhnikan. They were Zana Muhammad Sharif (age two), Nahida (age two) and her brother Saman Abd-al-Rahman (age four).[31]

For the first few months the deportees lived in makeshift "shades" of blankets or plastic sheeting on a crude framework of wooden stakes or poles. During this time the only solid structures were the guard towers, and the offices of *Amn* and *Istikhbarat*. Although the camp residents--having been victims of Anfal--were not able to obtain building loans from the state Real Estate Bank, after a year or so they had begun to build more substantial homes, thanks to the cheap sale or outright donation of

---

[29] This at least was the view expressed to Middle East Watch by a number of Kurdish doctors in Erbil who had entered Baharka and Jezhnikan clandestinely at the end of 1988, by which time epidemics were a serious threat.

[30] A Middle East Watch-Physicians for Human Rights forensic team investigated the Baharka-Jezhnikan cemetery in June, 1992, and took measurements of eighty-five graves of camp inmates. Of these, seventy-one were judged to be of sub-adult age. For a full discussion of the team's methodology, see *The Destruction of Koreme*, pp.65-70, 92-95.

[31] Several survivors said that twenty children from Tilakru died in the camps, as well as thirty from Warmilleh and between thirty-three and forty from Warakhal. In the first two cases, the effects of exposure to chemical weapons may well have been a contributing factor. The MEW-PHR forensic team exhumed the remains of three infant girls in the Baharka-Jezhnikan cemetery; each showed signs of severe malnutrition and/or disease stress. See *The Destruction of Koreme*, p.68.

cinderblocks from a local factory. Gradually, the complexes began to take on the semi-permanent appearance of the dozens of others that the Iraqi regime had built during earlier waves of Kurdish resettlement. At first no one was allowed to leave the camps for more than an hour a day, and then only with a permit. But after three months or so these rules were relaxed, and the Ba'ath Party issued passes that allowed people to travel to Erbil to shop and, eventually, to work. Some of the able-bodied teenage boys and elderly men managed to find jobs as laborers on construction sites, although most families remained without any significant source of income.

Free now to move outside the camp, many of the women journeyed to Erbil to inquire after their missing husbands and brothers. The police and officials at the governorate gave them the runaround: "We have no information...perhaps in a couple of days...don't worry, they are on their way." The more persistent women were referred to the authorities in Dohuk, or Mosul, or Baghdad. But there was never any news, and none of their men were ever seen again.

By the summer of 1990, with government control of Iraqi Kurdistan fully restored, the inmates of Baharka-Jezhnikan were told that they were free to leave. There was no question of their being allowed to return to their home villages, which were now rubble. But many accepted the alternative of resettlement in one of the smaller complexes in Dohuk governorate--Hizawa, Gri Gowr, Telkabber and others--that were closer to their former homes in a Kurmanji-speaking area. Others stayed where they were, and two years after they arrived the government finally supplied the complex with water and electricity and opened primary and secondary schools. And there some 15,000 of the Badinan deportees remained until the spring of 1991, the Gulf War and the failed Kurdish uprising (*raparin*) that followed. As the uprising spread to the bleak camps on the Erbil plain, their inmates tore down the *Amn* post and the police station and took control of their own affairs for a few short days. But then the Republican Guard retook the complexes and drove the *Anfalakan* of Baharka-Jezhnikan into exile in Iran, leaving them homeless and destitute once more.

* * *

THE FATE OF THE CHRISTIANS AND YEZIDIS

Barely two weeks after the arrival of the first deportees at Baharka--a number of testimonies suggest that the exact date was September 23 or 24, 1988--the official loudspeakers announced that a number of the camp's inmates should present themselves at the police station without delay. Those who were singled out in this way were either Assyrian and Chaldean Christians or members of the Yezidi sect of ethnic Kurds. What happened to these two groups remains one of the great unexplained mysteries of Anfal: a brutal sideshow, as it were, to the Kurdish genocide.

Despite Kurdish demands for autonomy, Iraqi Kurdistan is far from ethnically homogenous. Although its minority populations have declined sharply in number in the course of the 20th century, as the result of massacre, flight and religious conversion, the region is still home to three important groups. In addition to the Yezidis and the Assyrians (and their Catholic subgroup, the Chaldeans), there is an important Turkoman concentration in the mixed city of Kirkuk and several neighboring towns. With the exception of male deserters and draft dodgers, the Turkomans have long lived in government-controlled areas and have sometimes had tense relations with the Kurds. The Assyrians and the Yezidis are quite different cases, and despite violent conflicts with the Kurds earlier this century, the two groups have made common cause with them since the 1960s, sharing a common legacy of oppression by the regime in Baghdad.

The Assyrians, who number more than a million, are one of the oldest Christian communities in the Middle East. Most of them now live in the cities--Mosul, Dohuk and Erbil all have large Christian populations, as does the resort town of Shaqlawa. By the time of Anfal their once large rural presence had dwindled to a handful of villages in the mountains of Badinan. These were attractive places, with pretty churches, neatly laid out gardens and orchards, and sophisticated irrigation systems. Those Christians who live in Iraqi Kurdistan speak Kurmanji as well as their own Aramaic dialects. Although they are not ethnic Kurds, they also wear Kurdish clothes. Yet the regime officially classified them as Arabs in the 1977 census, a designation that many Assyrians and Chaldeans indignantly reject. "Saddam Hussein calls us Arabs unfairly," one Chaldean Christian told Middle East Watch, pointing indignantly to the headscarf that he wore as any Muslim Kurd would.[32] Having taken an active part in the Kurdish movement for years, they are sometimes referred to in everyday parlance as "Christian Kurds."[33]

The Yezidis are a quite different matter. Kurmanji-speaking ethnic Kurds, they belong to a syncretist sect that worships the Peacock Angel (*Malak Tawus*), and are sometimes incorrectly spoken of as "devil worshippers."[34] In northern Iraq, the Yezidis are mainly concentrated in the hilly plains that stretch from the southern edge of the Badinan mountains as far as the Tigris river, to the north of the city of Mosul-- areas that are also home to a number of Assyrian Christians.

This pattern of settlement had left the Yezidis and Christians prey to a number of earlier campaigns of village destruction by the Iraqi regime, and it left them prey to Anfal too. Several thousand Yezidis were displaced from their homes in Jabal Sinjar, west of Mosul, in early 1973. Along with their Muslim Kurdish neighbors, many Yezidis and Christians in the Sleivani and Sheikhan areas were removed from their villages during the Arabization campaign of the mid-1970s. The border clearances of 1977 destroyed a dozen Christian churches in Badinan, some of them more than a thousand years old.[35] Yet more Yezidis were removed from their homes and resettled in complexes to make way for the construction of the gigantic Saddam Dam on the Tigris in 1985.

---

[32] Middle East Watch interview, Erbil, July 7, 1992.

[33] The Iraqi Christians had their own *peshmerga* organization, the Assyrian Democratic Movement--a full member of the Kurdistan Front. According to one PUK commander interviewed by Middle East Watch, the ADM had some 100-150 men under arms. Christians also had five seats reserved for them in the 105-seat Kurdish parliament elected in 1992.

[34] The Peacock Angel is a divinity who may be associated with the Christian Satan, although he shares none of Satan's evil attributes. See Martin van Bruinessen, "Kurdish Society, Ethnicity, Nationalism and Refugee Problems," in Kreyenbroek and Sperl, *op. cit.*, p.37, citing T. Menzel, "Ein Beitrag zur Kenntnis der Jeziden," in H. Grothe, ed., *Meine Vorderasienexpedition, 1906, 1907*, Volume 1 (Leipzig: Hiersemann, 1911). See also the chapter on religion in Izady's *The Kurds*, pp.131-166.

[35] According to a list prepared by Shorsh Resool and published as an appendix to his 1990 report, *Destruction of a Nation*.

It is apparent that Ali Hassan al-Majid had nothing but contempt for the Yezidis. "We must Arabize your area," he snaps at an unnamed official from Mosul in one taperecorded meeting during the Anfal campaign. "And only real Arabs--not Yezidis who one day say that they are Kurds and the next that they are Arabs. We turned a blind eye to the Yezidi people joining the *jahsh* in the beginning, in order to stop the saboteurs from growing. But apart from that, what use are the Yezidis? No use."[36]

Al-Majid seems to have little more regard for the Assyrians, and the "first stage" of his 1987 program of village clearances leveled a number of Christian villages in the north. The death of the village of Bakhtoma that April was vividly described to Middle East Watch by an Assyrian priest in Dohuk:

> I had been told that they would destroy Bakhtoma because they had already destroyed most of the surrounding villages. It was around noon when I went to the church of St. George to remove the furniture, but Iraqi Army tanks and bulldozers were already beginning to roll into the village. I was the last one to pray in the church. After finishing my prayers, I removed the furniture to take it with me to Dohuk. It was a very sad day. The Iraqi soldiers and army engineers put the equivalent of one kilo of TNT at each corner of the church. After five minutes they blew up the building, and then went on to demolish every house in the village. Later they paid me compensation of 3,000 dinars. I went to the head of the Ba'ath Party in Dohuk, to ask why they were destroying our villages. He replied, "You are Arabs and we decide what you should do. That is all there is to it." I left his office then; what could I say?[37]

* * *

---

[36] Ali Hassan al-Majid, taperecorded conversation with unnamed Ba'ath officials, Kirkuk, August 1, 1988.

[37] Middle East Watch interview, Dohuk, June 19, 1992.

In Anfal there was not even the hope of compensation, and Assyrian villages like Kani Balaf (in the *nahya* of Berwari Bala), Mezeh (Sarseng) and Gund Kosa (Al-Doski) were burned and bulldozed along with those of their Muslim Kurdish neighbors. Some of the people from these villages took to the mountains together with the fleeing Kurds. Hundreds more sought refuge in Turkey. All of them waited where they were until they heard news of the September 6 amnesty, at which point they surrendered. A few days after the amnesty a large contingent of Christian and Yezidi refugees crossed the Khabour river in Turkish buses and gave themselves up to the Iraqi Army at the border post of Ibrahim Khalil. The *Istikhbarat* officers monitoring the repatriation asked the Yezidis and Christians to identify themselves and then ordered them to form a separate line off to one side. They said only that the men were to be returned to their army units if they were deserters, and that the women and children would be sent back to their homes. The Muslim Kurds who were present were given a piece of paper, marked "To be sent to Erbil"; the Assyrians and Yezidis left empty-handed. The Kurds were at a loss to explain this, but assumed that their neighbors were being shown some special favor.[38]

After surrendering under the amnesty, the Christians and Yezidis were sent to Dohuk, like everyone else. The majority of the group were Yezidis, according to a witness who saw them there, and they occupied six rooms on the second floor of the fort, segregated from the Muslim Kurdish prisoners. Word of the new arrivals spread rapidly, and relatives who heard the news rushed to Dohuk in an attempt to visit them. Isho, an elderly Chaldean Catholic from the village of Mezeh, came to inquire after his four sons. None of them was a *peshmerga*, although three were deserters and the other a draft dodger. But it was a fruitless visit; Isho learned that all the Christian and Yezidi men had been taken away the day before in nine sealed vehicles. It was the last time they were seen alive. The women and children and the elderly, meanwhile, after a single night in Dohuk, were bussed to the barren camps of Baharka and Jezhnikan.

And there, after two weeks or so, came the curious call that the Christians and Yezidis should all report to the police station or the camp's

---

[38] This separation procedure at the Ibrahim Khalil bridge was described by a number of witnesses. Middle East Watch interviews, Dohuk, September 3 and 5, 1992.

Ba'ath Party office. *Istikhbarat* officers drove through the complexes in a Toyota Landcruiser to broadcast the announcement. The agents were thorough: later, they went around the camps to deliver the message individually to each family in turn, as they huddled beneath their temporary "shades." But there seemed nothing to fear, especially when an Assyrian priest repeated the request. "You are going to be taken back to the places where we took you from," one *Istikhbarat* agent said. "We are going to take you to your men," said another--a choice of phrasing that may have euphemistically conveyed the brutal truth.

At the police station, names were read out and checked off against a master list. One witness recalled that *Istikhbarat* then ordered the prisoners to divide themselves up into three groups: Christians; Yezidis who had surrendered in Dohuk governorate; and Yezidis who had turned themselves in to the army at Aqra, in the neighboring governorate of Nineveh. This last distinction made some people suspicious, and several of them lied about their place of capture, lining up with those who had surrendered in Aqra.[39]

Other residents of the camp said they watched enviously as the Yezidi prisoners waited by the main gate for the minibuses that they believed would take them to their homes in the Sheikhan area. A few days later, a single khaki-colored military bus arrived, accompanied by an army officer and nine or ten soldiers, to pick up twenty-six people from the Assyrian Christian village of Gund Kosa. Now only a handful of Christians remained, along with the Yezidis who had surrendered in Aqra--and these people stayed in Baharka-Jezhnikan until the summer of 1990, when the restrictions on movement were lifted. None of those who were bussed away from the camps ever reached their homes, and none was ever seen in the complexes, like Mansuriya (Masirik) and Khaneq,

---

[39] The lie was a judicious one, for the separation of the Yezidis suggests that the regime's intent was to disappear only those who had been captured within the theater of operations covered by Anfal, which ended at the edge of Nineveh governorate. This same logic--which reflects bureaucratic rigidity rather than clemency--is evident in Iraqi government documents dealing with the treatment of captured civilians. For example, a secret letter from *Amn* headquarters in the governorate of Erbil, no. Sh 2/12809, dated August 26, 1988, says that two named individuals detained in the Anfal theater have been "returned by the Northern Bureau Command, due to the fact that they are *not residents of areas that were included in the Anfal operations.*" (emphasis added)

that were set aside for relocated Christians and Yezidis. The inescapable conclusion is that all of them were murdered. An Assyrian priest interviewed by Middle East Watch said that he had assembled a list of some 250 Christians disappeared during Anfal and its immediate aftermath.[40]

Isho, the elderly Chaldean man from Mezeh village, embarked on a long and anguished search for his four missing sons. He wrote a petition to President Saddam Hussein, but received no reply. He begged *Amn* and *Istikhbarat* agents at the Baharka camp to tell him what could have happened to his sons. They answered that the four would not have been covered by the September 6 amnesty, since it only applied to ethnic Kurds (although evidently not to Yezidis). "If we had known that," the old man replied bitterly, "we would never have surrendered." At some risk to his own life, he even visited the fort at Dohuk, only to be told that the Christian and Yezidi men had already been taken away to an unknown destination.

Although the old man's petititon to the president went unanswered, it did trigger--unknown to him--an internal inquiry by military intelligence. The results of that *Istikhbarat* investigation came to light during Middle East Watch's analysis of the captured Iraqi documents. Detailed below at pp.340-342, they shed important light on the chain of command of the Anfal operation. But they do not explain why the Christians and Yezidis should have been disappeared en masse, even after an amnesty was in force.

One plausible explanation is this: These obstinate minorities had refused to be part of the "national ranks" as defined by the Iraqi authorities. To aggravate their crime, they also refused to accept the regime's designation of their ethnicity. Not only did they want to be treated like Kurds, they also acted like bad Arabs. Accordingly, they were to be considered traitors on two counts, and punished accordingly.

---

[40] Middle East Watch interview, Dohuk, June 10, 1992. In the course of a dozen interviews with Christians, Yezidis and other survivors of Baharka-Jezhnikan, Middle East Watch assembled a total of ninety-eight names of people who had disappeared. This list consisted of sixty-four Christians (twenty-five men, eighteen women, twelve children under the age of sixteen, and nine of unknown age and sex), and thirty-four Yezidis (four men, nine women and twenty-one children). Several of those who disappeared were infants of less than one year; the oldest was a woman of eighty-five.

12
AFTERMATH

"With God's help, we have managed to eliminate from our beloved North the saboteur factions and collaborators with the enemy. The situation in the Northern Region now calls for certain measures commensurate with this new phase."
   -- Communique from Ali Hassan al-Majid's Northern Bureau, November 1988.

As the experience of the Yezidis and Christians suggested, the general amnesty of September 6 was not the end of the Anfal story. As we shall see, there were continued mass executions of prisoners captured before the amnesty. The Ba'ath Party's Returnee Reception Committee (*Lajnet Istiqbal al-A'idin*) continued to function until at least February 1989, relocating the families of "saboteurs" to complexes on the Erbil plain.[1] In addition to the sworn residence statements mentioned earlier, "returnees to the national ranks" were also to undertake: (a) to live in housing assigned to them and not to change their address; (b) not to take part in any "saboteur" activity; and (c) to "stand for their country"--on pain of punishment as stipulated by the law.[2]

---

[1] The minutes of the Ba'ath Party's Returnee Reception Committee meeting on February 1, 1989 refers to the relocation of a saboteur's family in the Ber Hoshter complex. The minutes of another meeting of the committee, dated September 13, 1988--a week after the declaration of the general amnesty--resolve that "people who used to live in areas controlled by the saboteurs are to be treated as saboteurs," and notes that returnees are to be transferred to the complexes by the Iraqi Police and the [Erbil governorate's] Committee to Fight Hostile Activity.

[2] A number of sworn statements to this effect, bearing various dates in late 1988, were found among files recovered from Ba'ath Party offices in Erbil.

The new *mujamma'a* of Ber Hoshter, to the north of the city of Erbil, was opened for returnees on November 27, 1988,[3] and the resettlement of the families of suspected *peshmerga* in nearby Girdachal went on for at least another six or seven months after that.[4]   The regime appears to have set up a special Pursuit (or "Follow-Up") Committee (*Lajnet al-Mutaba'a*) to enforce the terms of the returnee program, and a flurry of orders from *Amn* and other agencies exhorted the security forces to greater vigilance of the complexes. *Amn* also issued arrest warrants for anyone who left the *mujamma'at* without permission or otherwise infringed the terms of their resettlement.   In at least one case, the Erbil governorate's Committee to Fight Hostile Activity (*Lajnet Mukafahat al-Nashat al-Mu'adi*) also appears to have revived a pattern more characteristic of the 1970s, relocating individual Kurdish families in the south of Iraq.[5]

By the end of the year, the note of urgency in government documents had somewhat diminished, to be replaced by a tone of wary confidence. "With God's help," began an order from Ali Hassan al-Majid's

---

[3] According to an undated Ba'ath Party letter found in Iraqi government files in Erbil.

[4] This was reported to us by a family from the village of Gelnaski, one of the principal KDP headquarters in Badinan, whose son was reportedly executed after surrendering under the amnesty.   Middle East Watch was shown a grave at Dohuk that supposedly contained the young man's body.   It lay in an unmarked area outside the Dohuk municipal cemetery that appeared to contain approximately forty-five other graves. Middle East Watch interview, Dohuk, June 4, 1992.

[5] A series of instructions from the local Committee to Fight Hostile Activity in Shaqlawa indicates that five families from the Harir area, totalling thirty-seven people, were deported to the marshy southern governorate of Thiqar (formerly Nasiriya) on January 2, 1989, in vehicles supplied by the Traffic Directorate (*Mudiriyat al-Murour*) of the Erbil governorate.   These people were accompanied by a regular Iraqi Police officer, indicating that there was nothing secretive about the transfer.

An *Amn* Shaqlawa memorandum, dated May 16, 1989, also notes that the former residents of the destroyed village of Khirkhawa, who now live in complexes, will be deported to the south if the "saboteurs" attempt to make contact with them.

Northern Bureau, "we have managed to eliminate from our beloved North the saboteur factions and collaborators with the enemy."

> The situation in the Northern Region now calls for certain measures commensurate with this new phase, taking precautions against any new method to which the remaining saboteurs may turn--those who will try to create pockets of sabotage from which to carry out acts that will inspire their sympathizers, and give the impression to their masters abroad that they still possess footholds in our nation's soil and are capable of undertaking acts of sabotage. There is no doubt that, from now on, we will not find a group of saboteurs that is large in size, or that operates out of fixed bases, or that launches large-scale operations. Instead what we may find are small mobile groups of saboteur elements numbering no more than ten or fifteen. These groups would then wait to gauge the level of our response to their acts. If the reaction is normal and routine, then they will redouble their activities, broaden their base and undertake larger operations in graduated phases. They would also organize their internal structures in such a way as to keep in touch with some of their friendly elements who may have benefited from the amnesty decree.[6]

Al-Majid clearly felt that he faced a delicate dilemma. On the one hand, he could not afford to appear lax, in case this emboldened the *peshmerga*. To prevent this, he ordered draconian measures by the security apparatus. "Force and just harshness" must be used in the struggle. "There shall be a prompt and decisive response to any incidents that may occur, with the scale of the response being out of proportion to the scale of the incident, no matter how trivial the latter may be."

---

[6] These are extracts from the decisions taken at a meeting held on November 8, 1988, and relayed to *Amn* chiefs in the Autonomous Region by a set of instructions from the region's Security Director, no.14951, dated November 21, 1988 and classified "Secret and Confidential."

On the other hand, as far as the economic life of Iraqi Kurdistan was concerned, "what is called for is a departure from emergency measures, because the continuation of the economic siege gives the impression that we are still nervous about the situation." The blockade of the north would be relaxed slightly, the document concluded, although there would still be restrictions on the sale of gasoline, a blockade on the sale of certain foodstuffs and a continued ban on any sale of food outside the complexes. Any *mujamma'a* found to be involved in smuggling food to "the seats of sabotage" would immediately have its food rations terminated.[7]

Now that the rural population had been removed, there would also be a new census, or "sub-census," to determine and count the numbers of those who were not registered in the 1987 census in the Autonomous Region.[8] By the following spring planting season, the regime was even prepared to countenance the resumption of some modest farming activities in the Kurdish countryside. On April 9, 1989, the Northern Bureau Command issued order no.3335, which modified the ban on farming in the prohibited areas. At least in principle, these lands could now be worked once more by their owners (although not by amnestied returnees), or leased for agricultural use if they were the property of the state.

In practice, however, little changed. There would be no rebuilding of what had been destroyed. "The prohibited areas have been demarcated, and agriculture may not be pursued there," *Amn* reminded its branches. "Nor shall there be [any] human presence in them, due to their effect in the military and security sphere and their location in the Third Phase [of village clearances]."[9] Clause 5 of Northern Bureau

---

[7] ibid.

[8] Plans for the sub-census are outlined in a communique from the Office of the Presidency, no. K/2/1/45508, dated December 2, 1988. These in turn are conveyed to the Ministry of Planning in letter no. 548 from the Northern Affairs Committee of the RCC, dated January 25, 1989.

[9] The "Third Phase," in other words, clearly refers to the period since June 22, 1987 and continuing after the Anfal operation. This order is conveyed in letter no.6271 from *Amn* Erbil to *Amn* Shaqlawa, dated April 26, 1989 and apparently classified.

Command directive SF/4008, ordering the summary killing of anyone found in the prohibited areas, remained in force.[10] Having eradicated much of its Kurdistan bread basket, Iraq would be more reliant then ever on food imports and generous agricultural credit from abroad, notably the U.S. and Australia.[11]

Farmers would only be allowed to work their lands if they agreed to act as informers for *Amn* about any suspicious activities in their area. Indeed, in February 1990, *Amn* proposed to tighten these restrictions even further. Agriculture should only be permitted, the security agency suggested to the Fifth Army Corps, if the farmer in question was fully trusted by the authorities, and pledged in addition not to build any fixed structure and to refrain from working at night.

* * *

CONTINUED VILLAGE CLEARANCES

By now, only a few hundred villages remained intact in the three governorates that make up the Kurdistan Autonomous Region. According to a survey prepared by the Ministry of Reconstruction and Development of the new Kurdish government, 673 villages were still standing in the three governorates of Erbil, Suleimaniyeh and Dohuk;

---

[10] This was true until at least July 1989, several months after the derogation of al-Majid's exceptional powers. Erbil Committee to Fight Hostile Activity, "confidential" letter no. 3489 to Fifth Army Corps, dated July 5, 1989. The only exceptions to the rule were *Amn* informers and members of the *Mafarez Khaseh*, whose presence in the prohibited areas had to be coordinated in advance with the military. The exceptions are spelled out in an Erbil governorate *Amn* letter to the internal security section of Fifth Army Corps Command, no. Sh 3/1524, dated February 13, 1990.

[11] Between 1983 and 1988, Iraq acquired more than $2.8 billion in U.S. agricultural products under the Commodity Credit Corporation's (CCC) credit-guarantee program. In 1989, the Bush administration doubled the CCC program for Iraq, raising credits to a level exceeding one billion dollars in 1989. In addition to credit guarantees, the CCC program included interest-free loans and direct sales at prices subsidized by the U.S. government. See Middle East Watch, *Human Rights in Iraq*, New York, 1990, p.152.

4049 had been destroyed. Of those that remained, some two-thirds were concentrated in the environs of Erbil city, Makhmour and Aqra--areas that had been excluded altogether from Anfal.[12]

Yet there was no guarantee of lasting security for the minority of villages that had survived the Anfal campaign. On April 15, 1989, order No.3448 of the Northern Bureau authorized the "evacuation and rounding up" of an unspecified number of villages belonging to the Bradost and Dolamari tribes, in order to make way for a new dam on the Greater Zab river at Bakhma, an idea which had been in the works since the 1950s. The Bradost and Dolamari had been loyal to the government, but their location, in an area where the territory once controlled by the PUK abutted the traditional strongholds of the KDP, now became a liability. The Bakhma impoundment, in addition to its economic advantages, would drive a permanent strategic wedge between these two rebellious regions.[13]

Just a few miles to the south of the Bradost and Dolamari settlements, another fourteen villages were demolished in a joint army-*Amn* sweep in December 1988 and their inhabitants deported to the nearby complex of Basirma. This time the stated pretext was not the Bakhma Dam project but continuing counterinsurgency operations

---

[12] Resool's figures (*op. cit.*) closely parallel those of the Ministry. He cites a cumulative total of 3,839 villages destroyed since 1975. The villages that were spared include a hundred or so belonging to the loyalist Surchi tribe in the *qadha* of Aqra. On January 28, 1988, on the eve of Anfal, the Shaqlawa Security Committee "pointed out that it will not object to the lifting of the security prohibition regarding these villages, due to the fact that their population belongs to the Surchi tribe and that most of them are volunteer members of the National Defense Battalions. Furthermore, these villages have been beyond the reach of the saboteurs, their inhabitants have not collaborated with them, and no confrontations have occurred in the region." *Amn* Erbil to *Amn* Shaqlawa, letter no. S T/17922 of November 21, 1988.

[13] The Bakhma dam project was conceived originally as a small-scale irrigation and electricity-generating project. However, after the Ba'ath came to power in 1968 it grew more ambitious. Scheduled for completion in 1994, the dam remained only partially built by the time of the Kurdish uprising in March 1991, when its machinery was extensively looted and damaged. Middle East Watch interview with a former administrator in the Erbil headquarters of the *Jahafel al-Difa' al-Watani* (or *jahsh*), Erbil, July 7, 1992.

against any lingering pockets of *peshmerga* resistance.[14]   One of the villages affected was Serkand Khailani, a relatively large place of close to a thousand people. It had survived Anfal, but army troops now stormed it with artillery, helicopters and ground forces, as well as units of the *Mafarez Khaseh*.[15] In the wake of the assault, Serkand Khailani was razed to the ground and most of the villagers arrested. Everyone was taken to Shaqlawa, where they spent the night confined to IFAs at the army base, and from there to Basirma--everyone, that is, except for five people, who were taken off by *Amn* in a separate jeep. They included the wife, brother and teenage daughter of the village headman, or *ra'is*.

The headman himself was picked up by *Amn* in a separate incident early in 1989. He was detained for seven months at *Amn*'s Erbil headquarters and repeatedly tortured--beaten with a cable, suspended from a hook on the ceiling, soaked in water and given electric shocks to the earlobes. At frequent intervals, cellmates were taken out to be executed. Yet curiously, during the long sessions of interrogation that the *ra'is* endured, the five disappeared villagers of Serkand Khailani were mentioned only in passing. They were saboteurs, he was told, and he would never see them again. After seven months, without a word of explanation, the headman was released. At about the time he got back to the Basirma complex, he received two documents from the Census and Sanitary Department of the Ministry of Health in Erbil. They were death certificates for the two men who had disappeared. The date they bore was February 20, 1989; the cause of death was given as "execution by firing of bullets." No word was ever received about the fate of the three

---

[14] These fourteen villages lay between the town of Khalifan and the Greater Zab river. Their names are listed in an *Amn* Erbil report, dated December 11, 1988, as Faqian, Kulken Kolo, Madgerdan, Mingerdan, Daljar, Qalata Sin, Pir Marwa, Deremer, Serkand, Suka, Serkoz, Kuska, and upper and lower Jimkei. Resool, *op. cit.*, pp.65-67, lists nineteen villages in the *nahyas* of Salah al-Din and Harir destroyed during December 1988. Serkand Khailani is the only name that appears on both lists, and its story follows.

[15] On the *Mafarez Khaseh* and other special *jahsh* units, see above p. 22-24.

women, although documents describing their execution were reportedly found by the *peshmerga* during the 1991 uprising.[16]

* * *

CONTINUED MASS KILLINGS: YUNIS'S STORY

Murder, in other words--including mass execution--continued to be a fundamental tool of the regime in its dealings with the Kurds, even though Anfal was now over and most of the countryside was uninhabited. Anyone found in a "prohibited area" was likely to be killed, as was anyone suspected of *peshmerga* activity in the few villages that had been spared. Some of these killings were ordered by the Ba'ath Party's Northern Bureau, and Ali Hassan al-Majid appears to have kept a close personal eye on the elimination of prominent "saboteurs." (A handwritten note from September 1988, by the director of the Shaqlawa office of *Amn*, passes on al-Majid's compliments to the agents responsible for the liquidation of a Communist Party cadre and the burning of his body: "Well done!" the Northern Bureau chief writes. "May God bless them for their faith and loyalty.")

Other executions were decreed by Saddam Hussein himself; others by the Revolutionary Court (*Mahkamat al-Thawra*); and others still by special military tribunals.[17] A large number of individual death certificates and other official documents bear witness to these executions.

---

[16] Middle East Watch interview, Basirma complex, September 11, 1992. An internal *Istikhbarat* report on Serkand Khailani village, dated November 1, 1988, noted that a number of Kalashnikov rifles had been found in this man's home, concealed in a child's crib. Again, the match-up of documentary and testimonial evidence is striking.

[17] Letter No.25163 from the Security Director of the Suleimaniyeh governorate, dated October 29, 1988, mentions executions ordered by the Ba'ath Party's Northern Bureau and by the Revolutionary Court. One former prisoner was brought before Military Court No.23 in Erbil, a body with the power to impose the death sentence. In this particular case, the court's powers were superseded by "a special [execution] order from Baghdad." The man eventually escaped, and was interviewed by Middle East Watch in Khaneq complex on August 27, 1992.

An August 1989 report from *Amn* Suleimaniyeh, for example, enumerates eighty-seven executions since January 1 of that year. Many were people picked up in "prohibited" villages; one was a literature teacher executed for teaching his students the Kurdish language in Latin script.[18]

Most crucially, there continued to be mass executions of people who had been captured during the Anfal campaign *but remained alive in custody at the time of the September 6 amnesty*. Some were even killed after surrendering during the five-week amnesty grace period, their crime recorded in official documents as suspected membership in or collaboration with an illegal organization, such as the PUK, the KDP or the Islamic Party.[19] Middle East Watch was also able to find two survivors of these post-amnesty mass killings.

Yunis was a 19-year old *peshmerga* who had fought with the PUK in the battle of Sergalou and later in the Balisan Valley during the Sixth Anfal. Cut off from his main *peshmerga* force near Akoyan by Iraqi troops, he hid out for a while with relatives in the town of Khalifan. But he was persuaded by rumors of an amnesty to surrender to *Amn* in the town of Sadiq around the middle of August.[20] The local *Amn* office speedily transferred him to the agency's headquarters in Erbil, where he shared a large cell with about a hundred other prisoners--a mix of

---

[18] Secret and confidential letter no. 19727 from the director of *Amn* Suleimaniyeh to the director of *Amn* Autonomous Region headquarters, August 24, 1989.

[19] Handwritten documents found in an *Amn* Erbil file.

[20] Many Kurds in the Khalifan area surrendered prematurely as a result of these rumors. Another was a PUK *peshmerga* named Haydar Awla Ali Muhammad-Amin, whose arrest on September 15, 1988 is referred to in an *Amn* document of September 7, 1990. Haydar was persuaded to surrender to *Amn* by one Najma Grou, a leader of the *Amn*-controlled Kurdish *Mafarez Khaseh*. After this he disappeared. In response to his wife's persistent requests for news, Najma Grou told her, "Go home: your husband is no more." Middle East Watch interview, Galala complex, March 23, 1993.

In an earlier interview in Sadiq, July 18, 1992, Yunis told MEW that the only person he recognized in the group to be executed was a relative from Galala named "Haydar Abdullah." Since Awla is a shortened Kurdish form of the name Abdullah, this was almost certainly the same man.

peshmerga, deserters and *Anfalakan* from the Koysinjaq area. Yunis was interrogated and tortured off and on for another three weeks.

One day at the beginning of September, *Amn* guards assembled the prisoners, stripped them of their possessions and loaded them into a single large civilian bus. It was so crowded that the men had to sit on each other's laps. Their destination was the Popular Army camp on the outskirts of Dibs, which they reached at about 7:00 that evening. The prisoners received two daily rations of stale bread and water. Each day there were further rounds of questioning by plainclothes agents--also *Amn* men, Yunis guessed. Then, on September 6, guards told them that there had been a general amnesty and that they would be released.

But nothing changed. The daily interrogation sessions continued, together with brutal forms of torture. Beatings with a length of electrical cable were an everyday routine. The interrogators also devised two other standard torments. One was to fill a plastic bag with water and ice cubes, suspend it from the ceiling, pierce it with a pin, and allow the freezing liquid to drip on to the forehead of the prisoner, who was lashed to a bedframe beneath. This went on for up to twenty minutes each time; after ten, the pain was acute, and the prisoner would thrash around on the bed in a vain attempt to evade the icy drip. The ice-water treatment alternated with the application of extreme heat. The interrogators would slide a hot electric stove under the prisoner's bed for four or five minutes at a stretch, causing painful burns to the lower back.

These torments were the worst that Yunis personally had to endure. But one day, just before the amnesty was announced, he and the other prisoners from Erbil watched through the windows of their cell as three men accused of being "internal *peshmerga*"--that is to say, active in the cities--were brought into the courtyard below. The men were blindfolded, made to stand on chairs and tied to posts in the yard, arms raised above their heads. The chairs were then kicked away, leaving the prisoners' feet dangling a couple of feet from the ground. Next, guards attached one end of a string to an empty Butagaz container and the other to each prisoner's scrotum. When the signal was given, the guard would drop the gas cylinder, ripping out the man's testicles. Within half an hour, all three were dead.

A few days later the guards entered Yunis's cell, carried out a head count of the prisoners and told them that they were to be transferred. By now their numbers had swelled to about 180, including new arrivals--as before, a motley assortment of *peshmerga*, deserters and ordinary civilians. Each man was blindfolded and stripped of his IDs and had his hands tied behind his back. The prisoners were then loaded into six windowless vehicles, with benches in the rear and a separate driver's compartment--of the same sort, in other words, as those described by survivors of the earlier mass executions near Ramadi. They left Dibs at about 7:30 p.m. just before sunset. It was the evening of September 14, according to Yunis, and the general amnesty had been in force for eight days.

The buses turned left out of the camp gate, drove along a paved surface for a few minutes and then turned right on to a dirt road. As the bus bumped along this track, Yunis managed to work his hands free and loosen his blindfold. After an hour or so the convoy came to a halt, and the guards began to pull the prisoners out through the rear door. When it came to Yunis's turn, they saw that his hands were no longer tied. The guards pushed him to the ground and kicked him viciously. Over the top of his blindfold, Yunis could see a uniformed officer walk over and raise his hand. There was a sharp blow to the base of his skull with a heavy metal object, and Yunis felt himself falling forward. The last thing he knew before he lost consciousness was the touch of his fingers on another human face.

When he came to, he found that his lower body was covered with sand. He saw now that he was in a narrow trench--twenty yards long, one yard across and two deep--apparently dug by a backhoe. As he took stock of his surroundings, he heard the sound of a bulldozer approaching, and a fresh load of dirt was dumped into the trench next to him, throwing up a large cloud of dust. In the dust and darkness, Yunis scrambled free, away from the buses, the bulldozer and the voices of the guards. In the distance, to the east, he could see fires, which he guessed were the oilfields of Kirkuk.

He ran in the direction of Kirkuk until he reached a paved road. Hearing the sound of an engine, he jumped out to flag it down, but as the sound grew nearer he realized that it was an army IFA truck accompanied by a jeep, and he flung himself down by the roadside before the drivers could spot him in their headlights. Before long a civilian car stopped. The driver, a fellow Kurd, was wearing the uniform of the Popular Army, but Yunis was too exhausted to care, and to his relief the man drove him to Dibs without asking too many questions. From there, Yunis eventually rejoined his fellow *peshmerga* in Iran.[21]

* * *

CONTINUED MASS KILLINGS: HUSSEIN'S STORY

"Hussein" presents a very different case. A year younger than Yunis, he was sympathetic to the *peshmerga* cause, as indeed most Kurds were, but was not politically active himself. At the time of Anfal, he and four companions had found work as carpenters in a number of towns and complexes around Erbil. On November 26, 1988, they were working on a house in the village of Shiwarash, which had escaped destruction during the 1987 campaign on the Erbil plain, when four or five pick-ups and Landcruisers pulled up, filled with members of "security and the organization"--in other words, *Amn* and the Ba'ath Party. The five young men were bundled into the vehicles and driven first to Party headquarters in Khabat. As they approached their next destination, Hussein heard church bells ring. From this he concluded that they were in Einkawa, a Christian suburb of Erbil.[22]

Here they stayed for three days, handcuffed and blindfolded with their cummerbunds (*pishtend*). They were given no food or water and forbidden to leave their cell, even to urinate. An electric light burned day and night, while a team of interrogators, headed by a man whom his colleagues referred to as *Amn* Lieutenant Ghassan, tried to get the five to admit to their connection to the PUK. The Lieutenant played "good cop"; when his gentler methods failed, he transferred the prisoners to harsher colleagues. Each denial of PUK links brought a fresh round of torture. Hussein endured the *faiaka*, in which the prisoner is beaten on the soles of the feet while seated with his legs in the air; he was hung from the ceiling by a rope tied to his handcuffs; if he passed out, he was revived by being burned with a lighted cigarette.

After three days of this, Hussein and his companions were taken to *Amn* headquarters in Erbil, where Yunis had been held three months

---

[21] ibid.

[22] Middle East Watch interview. Erbil, July 14, 1992.

earlier. There, each man was placed in an isolation cell that measured less than ten square feet.[23] Hussein counted the passage of nine days, the first seven filled with interrogation and torture. Again, there was the *falaka*; again, suspension from the ceiling. But there were new tortures as well--the application of burning irons to his legs and neck; electric shocks to the tongue and penis. The interrogators told him that if he confessed to his PUK ties, he would be released; if he denied them, he would be executed. He told them that he knew nothing.

On the seventh day, Hussein was forced to put his thumbprint to a piece of paper. He was still blindfolded, and the contents of the document were not read out to him. With this, the questioning and the torture ceased, and two days later a guard opened the door of Hussein's cell to tell him that Saddam Hussein had decreed another general amnesty.[24] All the prisoners were to be freed. Hussein and his four friends were again placed in a common cell, handcuffed once more, and taken to a waiting vehicle. As they drove--between an hour and two hours on a paved road, then another half-hour on dirt--they could hear the guards discussing their fate. "Where are we taking them?" asked the first. "To the south," answered another. And then a third voice joined in: "They cannot live in the south." At that, the five men knew what was going to happen to them.

When they stopped, it was twilight and cold. "Sit down and don't move," the guards told the prisoners. "We are going to take your photographs." They sat crosslegged in a line, and almost at once the guards opened fire with automatic weapons. The first volley of shots missed Hussein and he instinctively threw his head into his lap for protection. As he did so, a bullet from a second round of firing struck him in the right shoulder, passing right through the flesh. The impact

---

[23] Middle East Watch accompanied Hussein to the former *Amn* building in Erbil on July 14, 1992, where he identified the room in which he had been detained.

[24] The Revolutionary Command Council did in fact issue an amnesty decree on December 14. Yet Hussein was convinced--and his chronology bears this out--that the date of his attempted execution was December 8. Amnesties, as noted elsewhere, are a regular feature of life under the Ba'athist regime, and yet another was decreed on February 29, 1989, this one for all those who had fled to Iran, with the exception of PUK leader Jalal Talabani.

knocked him forward into a deep ditch, and he could hear the bodies of the other four men tumbling in beside him. There was another burst of gunfire. When it was over, the executioners shovelled earth roughly on top of their five victims and went on their way.

Hussein, semi-conscious, pushed aside the dirt, which had not fully covered him. He lay where he was for two hours as darkness fell. The grave, he saw now, was an abandoned and derelict well, its walls eroded by rainfall. He touched his friends to see if they were alive, but there was no response. Clawing his way upward over their bodies, he managed to pull himself out of the pit, leaving only his Adidas track shoes behind. It was cold and raining, and in the distance he could see two separate clusters of city lights. Closer at hand, perhaps two miles away, he saw the glow of a fire and struck out in that direction. Shoeless, and with his feet bruised and swollen from the *falaka* torture, it took Hussein all night to reach the house.

He guessed--wrongly, as it turned out--that he was somewhere near Kirkuk, and called out in Arabic, "Family of the house!" (*ahl al-beit*). A man's voice answered, "Come on in!" (*tfaddal*). He knocked, and a woman opened the door. Seeing a young man barefoot and covered in blood, she started back in fear and beat her breast in pity. But the couple brought him a meal of water and tea and sheep's fat (*samneh*), and he told them the outlines of his story. As he talked, the woman fetched Arab clothing and a heavy Popular Army greatcoat to conceal the bloodstains from the wound in Hussein's shoulder. And at daybreak the man took him to the door to show him where he was. The nearby highway, where Hussein could see electricity pylons and passing trucks, led in one direction to Mosul and in the other to Al-Qayyara. The man explained that the lights that Hussein had seen in the night belonged to the Arab towns of Tharthar and al-Hadhar.[25]

---

[25] And thus of particular interest, since the archaeological site of Al-Hadhar, south of Mosul, was mentioned several times as a mass execution site during Anfal. See above p.253. Hussein's story is based on a Middle East Watch interview, Erbil, July 14, 1992.

Eventually, like Yunis, Hussein escaped to Iran. Some time later, *Amn* presented his mother with the young man's death certificate.[26]

* * *

THE END OF THE "EXCEPTIONAL SITUATION"

When did Anfal reach its conclusion? The question can be answered in a number of different ways. In a strict military sense, it ended with the victory over the KDP in Badinan and the announcement of the September 6 amnesty. From the point of view of the Iraqi public, it may be said to have ended on October 1, when ritual celebrations of the victory were organized by the ruling Ba'athist Party.[27] As far as the logic of Anfal as a campaign of extermination is concerned, it certainly went on for several more months, at least until well into 1988.

Some might even argue that Anfal lasted until June 1989, for it was then that Iraqi troops destroyed Qala Dizeh, a large town of some 70,000 people to the east of Dukan Lake. Qala Dizeh is an ancient settlement and a celebrated name in Kurdish history, for it was the target of a notorious bombing raid by the Iraqi Air Force on April 24, 1974, which left hundreds dead.[28] As a city, Qala Dizeh itself was exempt from the narrow logic of Anfal, but certainly not from reprisals or punitive action. Although parts of the city center had been demolished

---

[26] A third reported example of post-amnesty killings involves Omar and Rahman, the two brothers from the Sheikh Bzeini area whose flight during the Fourth Anfal is recounted above at pp.185-188, and who were captured by the army in mid-June, 1988. Another prisoner who was released under the September 6 amnesty saw them in jail at that time, still alive, but that is the last that was ever seen of them. Middle East Watch interview, Daratou complex, July 15, 1992.

[27] Yusef Rahim Rashid, a lawyer with the Kurdish Human Rights Organization (KHRO) told Middle East Watch that he attended one such ceremony in Erbil.

[28] The motive for the 1974 bombing was apparently the KDP's decision to reopen the University of Suleimaniyeh in Qala Dizeh. The university had been closed down by the regime that March.

in 1987, Ba'ath Party officials repeatedly assured the residents that they had nothing further to fear. The area around Qala Dizeh, which included the nearby town of Sengaser and the complexes of Pemalek, Tuwasuran and Jarawa--built for evacuees from the border clearances of the late 1970s--was also spared by Anfal. Although some villages were destroyed here in mid-1988, their population had not been "Anfalized."

Sandwiched between the depopulated Iranian border area and Dukan Lake, and in relatively flat terrain, the Qala Dizeh area had not harbored any significant *peshmerga* threat during Anfal, and the regime had been content to leave it alone. But by the spring of 1989, it had become a glaring anomaly, the only sizeable population center that remained so close to the Iranian border. Worse, the mountains to the east had become the principal regrouping point for the PUK as it struggled to reassert a presence inside Iraq, and on March 22, 1989, the RCC's Northern Affairs Committee ordered "maximum measures" against the area east of Dukan lake.[29]

In late May, troops surrounded Qala Dizeh with tanks and heavy artillery and gave the townspeople a month to leave. They were to be moved "in the public interest," to "modern villages."[30] A number of choices were offered: trucks would take them either to Bazian, on the road to Suleimaniyeh, or to three new complexes on the Erbil plain-- Khabat, Kawar Gosek and Daratou. It took the army engineers three weeks, beginning June 1, to demolish Qala Dizeh, and they left nothing standing, not even the new electrical power substation and the water-pumping station that the regime itself had built in 1987. On June 24, 1989, Qala Dizeh was officially declared a "prohibited area."

Yet Qala Dizeh may best be seen, perhaps, as a postscript to Anfal--a return to the same logic of anti-Kurdish activities that had gone on for years. The best answer to our question may be that the logic of

---

[29] RCC Northern Affairs Committee directive no. 1925 of March 22, 1989, signed by Abd-al-Rahman Aziz Hassan. These measures were to include the temporary deportation to the south of families who had contact with the "saboteurs." The directive also insists that the "clear instructions" of Northern Bureau Command directive no. SF/4008 of June 20, 1987 should continue to be observed.

[30] Middle East Watch interviews with former residents, Qala Dizeh, May 23, 1992.

Anfal ended when the behavior of the Iraqi bureaucracy shifted into a perceptibly different gear. This is not the same as saying "when the killing stopped," or "when the deportations ended," or "when the last village had been burned and bulldozed." For killings and deportations and scorched earth policies have been a feature of life under the Ba'ath Party for many years, and they continue to this day. But, by the spring of 1989, it is safe to say that the Iraqi regime felt that all the goals of Anfal had been met, and on April 23, the Revolutionary Command Council issued its decree No.271, in which the special powers conferred upon Ali Hassan al-Majid were revoked.[31] The sense that the Kurdish problem was now fully under control is further reinforced by Saddam Hussein's December 1989 decision to abolish even the Northern Affairs Committee of the RCC, which had been in existence for more than ten years.[32]

With his task in Kurdistan complete, other duties now awaited Ali Hassan al-Majid's singular talents--notably, after the August 1990 invasion, as Governor of occupied Kuwait.

"I would like to admit," he told Ba'ath officials gathered to welcome Hassan Ali al-Amiri, his successor as General Secretary of the Northern Bureau, "that I am not the right person for the current stable situation.... I hope that the comrades in the North will not ask Comrade Hassan Ali to do things that he cannot do. Because that stage is over. It will no longer be allowed for a member of the Party to have power over the army, because the exceptional situation has come to an end. These powers are not being withdrawn from Comrade Hassan Ali because he is not capable of the task, but because that stage has finished."[33]

---

[31] The RCC decree is conveyed in a circular from *Amn* Erbil to all Section Security Directors, no. Sh 3/7604, classified "secret and confidential" and dated May 17, 1989. The circular reads, "By virtue of the Revolutionary Command Council's decree no. 271 of April 23, 1989, it has been decided to abrogate RCC decree no. 160 of March 24, 1987 granting special authority to the Comrade Secretary General of the Northern Bureau."

[32] RCC decree no. 771 of December 3, 1989, signed by Saddam Hussein, revoking RCC decree no. 997 of August 2, 1979.

[33] Audiotape of a meeting between Ali Hassan al-Majid and unnamed officials, Kirkuk, April 15, 1989.

Al-Majid was evidently well-pleased with his efforts--not, he added, that the humanity of his motives should be doubted. "I cry when I see a tragic show or movie," he told his audience that day. "One day I cried when I saw a woman in a movie who was lost and without a family. But I would like to tell you that I did what I did and what I was supposed to do. I don't think you could do more than what I could do."

During another meeting with Party officials, al-Majid is heard to remark that, "What we have managed to do is something which the Party and the leadership never achieved until 1987. Some of it was just the result of help and mercy from God. Nothing else." An unnamed party member chimes in to offer praise. "Only God can do more than you did. Otherwise you can do anything. This Ba'ath Party can do anything."[34]

_____

[34] Audiotape of meeting between Ali Hassan al-Majid and unnamed officials, Kirkuk, May 26, 1988.

13
THE VANISHING TRAIL

"These measures will have a deterrent effect because
(a) the prisoners will vanish without leaving a trace;
(b) no information may be given as to their whereabouts or their fate."
     -- Nacht und Nebel Erlass (Nazi Germany's Night
     and Fog Decree), modified version, February 1942.

"They have sunk into deep water. They were lost. We have no
information about them."
     -- elderly female survivor from Goktapa.

Forced disappearance is the distinctive act of terror of the modern state. It immobilizes the survivor with doubt and fear, with unconsummated grief and mourning that is permitted none of the rituals of closure. The washing and clothing of the dead, the placing of the body with its face turned toward Mecca that is required of the devout Muslim-- these acts were not possible for the disappeared of Anfal. In the case of those who were executed in captivity under the routine terror of the Ba'ath regime, a punctilious bureaucracy at least furnished the family with the legal proof of death. But for most of the Kurds who disappeared during Anfal, there was not even this.

Once the campaign was over, most of the survivors inhabited a netherworld of uncertainty. Women had lost their breadwinners, and Islamic law forbade them to remarry until seven years had passed since their husbands went missing. Although the stories of the firing squads were known and repeated, the Kurds' squalid resettlement complexes were still swept by rumors of *Anfalakan* kept alive in secret jails in the desert, held as bargaining chips in some future round of negotiations between the regime and the *peshmerga*, taken off to other countries-- Sudan, Yemen or Jordan--to be used as slave labor.

Before the uprising of March 1991, while the Ba'ath Party still controlled Iraqi Kurdistan, few had the temerity to inquire after their lost ones, fearing that the same fate might await them or their surviving relatives. Even leaving aside questions of security, few would have known how or where to start an inquiry into the labyrinth of the state bureaucracy: with the district head, the *qaym maqam*? the governor's office? the local police station? the *mustashar*? the Ba'ath Party? the Army base? the dreaded *Amn*? But some did take the risk, and their searches-- when pieced together with Iraqi government documents and the testimony of those who survived the camps--shed important light on how Anfal worked. It appears to have been a highly compartmentalized operation, with each of the agencies involved knowing only what it needed to know. Only a tiny circle at the heart of the Ba'ath Party machine was ever privy to the whole story about what happened to those who were "Anfalized."

* * *

Some survivors came to learn the truth, but only in the most bald and unadorned terms. Rashid, a young shepherd from Chircha Qala, at the foot of Zerda Mountain, had managed to live through Anfal by walking past the troops on the main road with his farm animals. But he lost his mother, ten-year old sister, six-year old brother and two aunts. Later he was drafted into the same army that had captured his family. A sympathetic Christian officer took a liking to Rashid and told him candidly to stop thinking about his relatives: "All the people from Anfal have been buried with bulldozers."[1]

Most, however, did not even discover this much. Nuri, an elderly man from the devastated village of Jelamort, in the Lesser Zab valley, went to the office of the *qaym maqam* of Chamchamal to inquire after his missing son, daughter-in-law and two-year old granddaughter. The authorities registered their names and told him to come back after three days. When he returned, they said that the governorate could do nothing to help in this case. In fact, the official told Nuri, "I can do even less than you. You asked, but I am afraid to ask."[2]

Salim, a younger man from the Sheikh Bzeini tribal area, had been away from his village when the army came. But the troops had captured his wife and eight children--the eldest a boy of fifteen, the youngest a year-old girl. Some sympathetic *jahsh* from Salim's own tribe

---

[1] Middle East Watch interview, Naser complex, March 26, 1993.

[2] Middle East Watch interview, Erbil, April 23, 1992.

had tried bribing the soldiers, offering them 1,000 dinars ($3,000) for the freedom of each child. It was too late for this, the soldiers answered; the children had already been loaded into the trucks. After Anfal, Salim went on the track of every rumor; he went to Kirkuk, to Topzawa, and even to Nugra Salman. *Amn* arrested him three times for his persistence. On the last occasion they blindfolded him and warned him never to ask about his family again.[3]

Mahmoud Tawfiq Muhammad, the elderly head of the Jaff-Roghzayi tribe in one of the worst hit areas of southern Germian, refused to take no for an answer. Twenty members of his immediate family had vanished, most of them small children; Mahmoud had been with them in the fort at Qoratu, but had lost track of them when the sexes were separated at Topzawa. After his own release from Nugra Salman, Mahmoud traveled to the home of Haji Ahmad Fatah, the Kurdish village elder (*mukhtar*) who had been in charge of the Dibs camp. "I kissed his shoes and begged him. But I was told not to ask. 'You have nothing to do with it,' they told me. 'Go to Nugra Salman.'" All that the *mukhtar* would tell the old man was that the Dibs prisoners had been transferred--but he did not know, or would not say, where.

From Dibs, Mahmoud went up to Erbil, where his personal connections enabled him to arrange a meeting with the head of *Amn* in that city. The security boss told him that the missing had been sent to a place called Ar'ar, an important border crossing point to Saudi Arabia and a resting place for pilgrims on their way to Mecca.[4] It was forbidden for anyone to visit or communicate with them. Mahmoud pleaded with the *Amn* chief, offering him 1,000 dinars for each person freed, but the man said this was impossible: "Only Saddam Hussein or Ali Hassan al-Majid could free them."

The civilian governor of Erbil said that he, too, was powerless. Despite Mahmoud's deferential gift of a number of sheep, the Kurdish governor of Suleimaniyeh, Sheikh Ja'far Barzinji,[5] told much the same

---

[3] Middle East Watch interview, Daratou complex, April 20, 1992.

[4] On Ar'ar as a possible mass execution site, see above p.253, footnote 10.

[5] Sheikh Ja'far, it should be recalled, was the brother of the notorious Qader Karam *mustashar*, Sheikh Mu'tassem Barzinji. Sheikh Ja'far was also reportedly the main point of liaison between Ali Hassan al-Majid and the *mustashars* during

story: many prisoners, both men and women, were being held in Ar'ar in a facility that was serviced by Egyptian truck drivers in the interests of secrecy. Personally, he could do no more than Mahmoud. The affair rested in the hands of the president and his cousin. But in Kirkuk, the information department of the Ba'ath Party's Northern Bureau told Mahmoud that Majid "had no time to meet me." In despair, he went back to Suleimaniyeh, where he approached a certain powerful Kurd who was known to be close to al-Majid and frequently entertained him in his home. The man agreed to intercede personally. "But Majid swore by the Holy Koran that only Saddam Hussein and God could save the disappeared." Exhausted and dispirited, Mahmoud abandoned his search.[6]

* * *

THE BA'ATH PARTY:
ALPHA AND OMEGA OF THE ANFAL CAMPAIGN

A number of captured Iraqi documents corroborate this kind of anecdotal evidence about the extreme degree to which power was concentrated during the Anfal campaign. Perhaps the most revealing case is that of four brothers, Chaldean Catholics, who disappeared from a Christian village near Gara Mountain in the *nahya* of Sarseng, in the wake of the Final Anfal.[7] Their father "Isho," an influential local figure, was interviewed by Middle East Watch in Erbil in July 1992. (see also above p.317) He explained that the family had fled their village before Anfal reached them. His sons--three of them deserters and one a draft-dodger--had surrendered to the army during the five-week grace period that followed the September 6 amnesty; they had last been seen by relatives who were able to visit them in the Nizarkeh fort outside Dohuk. After this sighting, Isho himself tried to visit the fort, but when he arrived

---

the Anfal campaign.

[6] Middle East Watch interview, Sumoud complex, May 20, 1992.

[7] All names and locations in this account have been altered or omitted to protect the witnesses.

a guard told him that all the Christians and Yezidis had been removed the previous day in sealed buses. In Baharka, Isho made inquiries with both *Amn* and *Istikhbarat*, demanding to know why his sons had not been brought to the complex with the rest of their family. As non-Kurds, he was told, they were not covered by the September 6 amnesty. They had no information about the young men's present whereabouts. Finally, the family wrote to Saddam Hussein himself, but they never received an answer.[8]

Six months after this interview, Middle East Watch researchers happened upon the family's file in a box of documents from the Erbil regional office of *Istikhbarat*. The disappearance of Isho's four sons is the subject of a sequence of a dozen separate "secret and urgent" documents, beginning with a petition from Isho's sister-in-law to Saddam Hussein, dated January 7, 1989. She writes:

> "Mr. President, Commander-in-Chief (May God Protect and Guide Him): My heartiest greetings and great admiration for the builder of Iraq's glory and the realizer of victories over its despicable enemies:
>
> I am the citizen M. ... The four sons of my husband's brother are soldiers enlisted in the Southern Division. Upon your announcement of a general amnesty, they turned themselves in at Dohuk. Since that time, we have heard nothing of their fate.
>
> Victorious and respected sir, please grace me with some knowledge of their fate.
>
> Just as one knocks on the door of your justice, it opens on to the sweet smell of your compassion."

The petition is signed with the woman's fingerprint.

---

[8] Middle East Watch interview, Erbil, July 7, 1992. Further information on this case was provided by additional interviews with former residents of the village.

Since the case involved army deserters and draft dodgers, the presidential office referred it to military intelligence. It appears that *Istikhbarat* conducted a serious internal investigation into the affair, and that it was genuinely unaware of what had happened to the four men. Although *Istikhbarat*'s Northern Region headquarters complains angrily about the sloppiness of its Mosul and Dohuk offices, and the contradictory quality of their reports, the initial facts of the case are quickly established. The four brothers are known to have surrendered to military units in Atrush on September 10, 1988, four days into the amnesty period, and Mosul *Isitikhbarat* can find no evidence that they "bore arms with the saboteurs." From there the prisoners were transferred to the Party-run Returnee Reception Committee of Dohuk and detained--as their father already knew--in the Nizarkeh fort. Mosul reports that the Dohuk detainees were subsequently split up into two groups. One was sent to a fort in the Daraman area, on the highway between Altun Kupri and Kirkuk. The other was transferred to Topzawa--the only reference so far found to indicate that this Popular Army camp being used for prisoners from the Final Anfal in Badinan.

After this, the trail goes cold. Northern Region *Istikhbarat* dispatches agents to the Baharka-Jezhnikan complex to interview the family, as well as to each of the army forts along the Kirkuk-Erbil road. But these inquiries yield no fresh information. The Dohuk office might be more helpful, an *Istikhbarat* captain comments pointedly in his report to the Northern Region director, if it were prodded by the ruling Party. Three days later, however, on March 14, 1989, the director makes his final report to *Istikhbarat* headquarters. The four men, he writes, "were handed over to the [Returnee] Reception Committee of Dohuk governorate, which in turn handed them over to the Northern Bureau Command in Ta'mim [Kirkuk] governorate. We have no further information on their fate."[9]

* * *

---

[9] Classified correspondence between *Istikhbarat* national headquarters, Northern Regional headquarters, and Dohuk and Mosul offices, February 12 to March 14, 1989.

It should be recalled that the September 6 amnesty decree stipulated that anyone surrendering *after October 9*--not the case here--was to be taken into military custody and then handed over to the Northern Bureau Command.

While *Istikhbarat* was clearly kept in the dark, it seems that even *Amn*, which wielded such enormous power over the lives of all Iraqis, was unaware of the final destination of those who disappeared during Anfal or surrendered to the authorities under the various amnesty decrees of 1988 and 1989. The archives of *Amn* headquarters in the governorate of Erbil, for example, are full of requests to local branches for information about hundreds of men, women and children whose relatives have come inquiring about their whereabouts.[10] Eventually, as the survivors continued to knock on the door of the powerful security agency seeking "the sweet smell of compassion," *Amn* ordered a change in how its standard response to them would be worded. A handwritten *Amn* letter notes:

> On September 25, 1990, the honorable director issued the following directive: The phrase 'We do not have any information about their fate' will replace the phrase 'They were arrested during the victorious Anfal operation and remain in detention.' The purpose of this is to be accurate in dealing with such an eventuality."[11]

Both *Amn* and *Istikhbarat* had to defer to the final authority of the Ba'ath Party's Northern Bureau on the matter of those who vanished. Evidence for this can be found, for example, in a communication from *Amn* Erbil that appears insignificant at first glance. Dated August 26, 1988, this is a brief note informing the agency's municipal office that two women "have been returned [to *Amn*] by the Northern Bureau Command, due to the fact that they are not residents of areas that were included in the Anfal operations." While both women are former residents of villages in the *nahya* of Taqtaq, which was decimated by Anfal, one had previously been relocated with her family to the city of Erbil and the other to the Qushtapa complex--and were thus not liable to be "Anfalized." Conversely, it is clear, it would have been up to the Northern Bureau

---

[10] The *Amn* requests examined by Middle East Watch were issued between June and August 1989. They refer, however, to detentions and surrenders as far back as the Second Anfal in April 1988.

[11] Handwritten internal memo from the "Person in Charge of Political Affairs," *Amn* Erbil, October 18, 1990.

Command to dispose finally of anyone who *was* a resident of an area affected by Anfal.[12]

* * *

Decree no. 160 of March 29, 1987 had made it quite clear that Ali Hassan al-Majid was to enjoy the full authority of the Revolutionary Command Council to orchestrate the efforts of the whole pyramid of other state and party agencies--military, civilian and security--which played a role in Anfal. (see Appendix B, pp. 355-357) And as the captured Iraqi documents and survivor testimonies indicate, it was the Ba'ath Party apparatus in the north, headed by al-Majid, which weighed in its hands the fate of each individual captured in the course of the campaign.

There remain many unsolved mysteries about the Anfal campaign, some of which may be answered by future study of the captured Iraqi documents.[13] The identity of the uniformed men who made up the Anfal firing squads may remain forever a secret. Were they *Amn* agents? Members of the Republican Guard? Or were they, as seems more likely, "comrades" of the Ba'ath Party itself?[14]

---

[12] *Amn* Erbil to *Amn* municipal command, letter no. Sh2/12809, classified "secret" and dated August 26, 1988. This document is also an excellent illustration of both the meticulous bureaucratic procedures and the rigid logic of Anfal. Individual detainees were evidently evaluated on a case-by-case basis before a decision was made about their fate. Although it is noted that one of these two women is "politically independent" and the other a "housewife," it is not this which saves them, but their place of residence. This appears to be the key to the logic of the whole Anfal operation.

[13] By the time of the publication of this report, Middle East Watch had scrutinized only a small proportion of the Iraqi documents captured by the Patriotic Union of Kurdistan. The results of MEW's continuing research into these unique materials will be detailed in future reports.

[14] This tentative conclusion is supported by two factors. One is the known subordination of *Amn*, *Istikhbarat* and other agencies to the Ba'ath Party in all aspects of the Anfal campaign. The other is the frequent reference, in Revolutionary Command Council decrees and other documents, to the Party as the agency responsible for executing draft dodgers and deserters--terms which

Why were the women and children only killed in certain areas? Did their execution reflect patterns of combat and resistance, or was some other criterion used? Where are the graves of all those who died, and how many bodies do they hold? The answer cannot conceivably be less than 50,000, and it may well be twice that number. When Kurdish leaders met with Iraqi government officials in the wake of the spring 1991 uprising, they raised the question of the Anfal dead and mentioned a figure of 182,000--a rough extrapolation based on the number of destroyed villages. Ali Hassan al-Majid reportedly jumped to his feet in a rage when the discussion took this turn. "What is this exaggerated figure of 182,000?" he is said to have asked. "It couldn't have been more than 100,000"--as if this somehow mitigated the catastrophe that he and his subordinates had visited on the Iraqi Kurds.[15]

The identity of the executioners, and the precise number of their victims, may never be known--or at least not until the files in Baghdad can be opened. But whatever the answers to these lingering questions, there can be no doubt that the Northern Bureau of the ruling Ba'ath Party, and its parallel Command, headed by RCC member Taher Tawfiq, functioned as both the Alpha and the Omega of the Anfal operation. And it was Ali Hassan al-Majid--"Ali Anfal," "Ali Chemical," Iraqi's present Minister of Defense--who gave the killers their orders.

Al-Majid appears almost defensive in talking about the Anfal operation with unnamed Northern Bureau officials in January 1989. "How were we supposed to convince them to solve the Kurdish problem and slaughter the saboteurs?" he asks them, alluding to the misgivings of senior military officers about the Anfal operation. In addition, he adds, what was to be done with so many captured civilians? "Am I supposed to keep them in good shape?" al-Majid asks. "What am I supposed to do with them, these goats?....[T]ake good care of them? No, I will bury them with bulldozers." And that is what he did.

---

became virtually synonymous, as we have seen, with anyone living in the "prohibited areas" of the Kurdish countryside.

[15] This remark was reported to Middle East Watch by Kurdish officials present at the meeting, and has appeared in a number of press reports. See, *inter alia*, Makiya, "The Anfal," *Harper's Magazine*, May, 1992, pp.58-59.

APPENDIX A
THE ALI HASSAN AL-MAJID TAPES

The following are selected remarks by Ali Hassan al-Majid, Secretary General of the Ba'ath Party's Northern Bureau, from a number of meetings with senior Ba'ath officials in 1988 and 1989. Audiotapes of more than a dozen of these meetings were recovered from Iraqi government offices and from al-Majid's home in Kirkuk during the failed Kurdish uprising in March 1991.

1. *Meeting with members of the Northern Bureau and governors of the Autonomous Region of Iraqi Kurdistan, April 15, 1988.*

By next summer there will be no more villages remaining spread out here and there, but only complexes. It'll be just like the hen when she puts the chicks under her wing. We'll put the people in the complexes and keep an eye on them. We'll no longer let them live in the villages where the saboteurs can go and visit them. Emigration from the villages to the city is necessary in the north of Iraq.

From now on I won't give the villagers flour, sugar, kerosene, water or electricity as long as they continue living there. Let them come closer to me to hear me, so that I can tell them the things I believe and want in ideology, education and common sense. Why should I let them live there like donkeys who don't know anything? For the wheat? I don't want their wheat. We've been importing wheat for the last twenty years. Let's increase it for another five years.

I will prohibit large areas; I will prohibit any presence in them. What if we prohibit the whole basin from Qara Dagh to Kifri to Diyala to Darbandikhan to Suleimaniyeh? What is this basin? What good is this basin? What did we ever get from them? Imagine how much we paid out and lost on those areas. How many good citizens are there among those people, and how many bad ones?

What went wrong? What happened? Thirty, twenty, twenty-five years of saboteur activity. Imagine how many martyrs we have!.... Now you can't go from Kirkuk to Erbil any more without an armored vehicle. All of this basin, from Koysinjaq to here [Kirkuk]...I'm going to evacuate it. I will evacuate it as far as Gweir and Mosul. No human beings except on the main roads. For five years I won't allow any human existence there. I don't want their agriculture. I don't want tomatoes; I don't want okra and cucumbers. If we don't act in this way the saboteurs' activities will never end, not for a million years. These are all just notes, but with the help of God we will apply them very soon, not more than a month from now. In the summer nothing will be left.

2.   *Meeting with Northern Bureau members and directors of the Ba'ath Party headquarters in the northern governorates: tape is dated May 26, 1988, but from context appears to be 1987.*

(Response to a question about the success of the deportation campaign):

As a matter of fact what we have achieved is something that the party and the leadership never managed to do until 1987. Some of it was just the help and mercy of God. Nothing else. Otherwise if you just go and conduct military exercises for the troops who were used in the campaign you will have more casualties than we had. Imagine in such an exercise how many martyrs and casualties there will be!....

What happened? Are these the saboteurs? Are these the people you were afraid of? This is the reality of the saboteurs, and you have all these facilities and this capacity. They could not confront you. In the past they were confronting a division with just a few machine guns. This time they were just shelling us from far away with light artillery.

Some of you who were working here at the time when I arrived, so motivated with this duty, perhaps you said in your hearts, "OK, wait a minute! Wait a minute! The people who were here before you said the same things and then didn't do anything!" You will be forced to take action. All those years and the saboteurs still existed. At a time when we had this huge military! I swear to God it was not done in that way. All the Iraqi troops couldn't have done what we did. But this [deportation] hurt them. It kills them.

(voice identified as Abu Muhammad: Only God can do more than you. Otherwise you can do anything. This Ba'ath Party can do anything.)

The saboteurs watch the orders and directives. The orders are not that strong. The previous ones were a hundred times stronger. But they were not combined with a belief on the part of those executing them. Now that exists. We said that at that date we will start to implement the deportation campaign. And we did it everywhere, with the help of God. The same day [in 1987] they captured Qara Dagh in retaliation.

Jalal Talabani asked me to open a special channel of communication with him. That evening I went to Suleimaniyeh and hit them with the special ammunition.[1] That was my answer. We continued the deportations. I told the *mustashars* that they might say that they like their villages and that they won't leave. I said I cannot let your village stay because I will attack it with chemical weapons. Then you and your family will die. You must leave right now. Because I cannot tell you the same day that I am going to attack with chemical weapons. I will kill them all with chemical weapons! Who is going to say anything? The international community? Fuck them! The international community and those who listen to them.

Even if the war with Iran stops and the Iranians withdraw from all occupied lands, I will not negotiate with him [Talabani] and I will not stop the deportations.

This is my intention, and I want you to take serious note of it. As soon as we complete the deportations, we will start attacking them everywhere according to a systematic military plan. Even their strongholds. In our attacks we will take back one third or one half of what is under their control. If we can try to take two-thirds, then we will surround them in a small pocket and attack them with chemical weapons. I will not attack them with chemicals just one day, but I will continue to attack them with chemicals for fifteen days. Then I will announce that anyone who wishes to surrender with his gun will be allowed to do so. I will publish one million copies of this leaflet and distribute it in the North, in Kurdish, Sorani, Badinani and Arabic. I will not say it is from the Iraqi government. I will not let the government get involved. I will say it is from here [the Northern Bureau]. Anyone willing to come back is welcome, and those who do not return will be attacked again with new, destructive chemicals. I will not mention the name of the chemical

---

[1] This presumably refers to the April 1987 chemical attack on the PUK headquarters in the Jafati Valley.

because that is classified information. But I will say with new destructive weapons that will destroy you. So I will threaten them and motivate them to surrender. Then you will see that all the vehicles of God Himself will not be enough to carry them all. I think and expect that they will be defeated. I swear that I am sure we will defeat them.

I told the expert comrades that I need guerrilla groups in Europe to kill whoever they see from them [the saboteurs]. I will do it, with the help of God. I will defeat them and follow them to Iran. Then I will ask the *mujaheddin* to attack them there.[2]

3.   *Meeting with unnamed officials, August 1, 1988.*

...Any Arab who changes his ethnicity to Kurdish is doing so to avoid serving in the army. This is a big problem. What shall we do about it?.... Why did Mosul [governorate] register them as Kurds? We asked them to deport every Kurd who lives there and send them to the mountains to live like goats. Fuck them! Why do you feel embarrassed by them?

We deported them from Mosul without any compensation. We razed their houses. We said come on, go, go! But those who are already fighters, we tell them from the beginning that they must go and settle in the complexes. After that we will tell them to go to the Autonomous Region. We will not get into any arguments with them. I read the pledge for them and they must sign it. Then wherever I find [passage unclear], I will smash their heads. These kind of dogs, we will crush their heads. We will read the pledge for them: I the undersigned admit that I must live and settle in the Autonomous Region. Otherwise I am ready to accept any kind of punishment including the death penalty. Then I will put the pledge in my pocket and tell the *Amn* director to let him go wherever he wants. After a period of time, I will ask where is he? They will tell me, here he is. The Ba'ath Party director must write to me saying that the following people are living in that place. Immediately I will say blow him away, cut him open like a cucumber.

Do you want to increase the Arab population with these bloody people?.... We must Arabize your area [Mosul]--and only real Arabs, not

---

2 Following their expulsion from France in 1986, the People's Mujaheddin of Iran relocated to Iraq and came under the patronage of the Ba'ath Party.

Yezidis who say one day that they are Kurds and the next that they are Arabs. We turned a blind eye to the Yezidi people joining the *jahsh* in the beginning, in order to stop the saboteurs from increasing. But apart from that, what use are the Yezidis? No use.

4.   *Northern Bureau meeting to review the campaigns of 1987 and 1988; the tape is undated, but is in a batch dated January 21 and 22, 1989.*

The most dangerous stage of the threat to Iraq was between August 1987 and April 1988. It was a dangerous situation. We started to do serious work on the military front from February 18 to September 4, 1988.

All the successive commanders of the First Corps and the Fifth Corps: Lt. Gen. Nazar [al-Khazraji] and Sultan Hashem of the First Corps and Tali'a al-Durri, the martyr al-Hadithi, Muhammad and Ne'ama Fares and Ayad of the Fifth Corps... All these men that I mentioned are commanders who have been serving in the north of Iraq since they were lieutenants. The first one among them to join the Ba'ath Party was Tali'a al-Durri.

When we made the decision to destroy and collectivize the villages and draw a dividing line [i.e. the so-called "red line"] between us and the saboteurs, the first one to express his doubts to me and before the President was Tali'a al-Durri. The first one who alarmed me was Tali'a al-Durri. To this day the impact of Tali'a is evident. He didn't destroy all the villages that I asked him to at that time. And this is the longest-standing member of the Ba'ath Party. What about the other people then? How were we to convince them to solve the Kurdish problem and slaughter the saboteurs?

So we started to show these senior commanders on TV that [the saboteurs] had surrendered. Am I supposed to keep them in good shape? What am I supposed to do with them, these goats? Then a message reaches me from that great man, the father [i.e. Saddam Hussein], saying take good care of the families of the saboteurs and this and that. The general command brings it to me. I put his message to my head.[3]

---

[3] The sense conveyed in the Arabic phrase is that Saddam Hussein's wish is always al-Majid's command--but not, he goes on to say defensively, in this instance.

But take good care of them? No, I will bury them with bulldozers. Then they ask me for the names of all the prisoners in order to publish them. I said, "Weren't you satisfied by what you saw on television and read in the newspaper?" Where am I supposed to put all this enormous number of people? I started to distribute them among the governorates. I had to send bulldozers hither and thither...[4]

5.   *Meeting to welcome Hassan Ali al-Amiri, his successor as Secretary General of the Northern Bureau, April 15, 1989.*

I would like to admit that I am not and will not be the right person for the current stable situation in the North....For this current peaceful and stable situation, Comrade Hassan Ali is the right person. I am ready to come back and do whatever you think is necessary, though I would like to remain a member of the Northern Bureau.

I hope that the comrades in the North will not ask Comrade Hassan Ali to take administrative measures and do other things that he cannot do. Because that stage is finished. It will no longer be allowed for a member of the leadership to have power over the army, because the exceptional situation is over. These powers are not being withdrawn from Comrade Hassan Ali because he is not up to the task, but because that stage has now finished.

In my first meeting in April 1987 with the army corps commanders, *Amn* and police directors, governors and Ba'ath Party directors, we decided to deport all the villagers in order to isolate the saboteurs. We made it in two stages. The first stage started on April 21 and ran until May 21. The second stage ran from May 21 to June 21. From June 22 anyone who was arrested in those areas was to be killed immediately without any hesitation, according to the directives which are still in force.

In one of the meetings with the army chiefs of staff I was asked to postpone the campaign for a month by one of our best commanders. I said no, not even for one day. From now on our slogan will be to wipe out saboteur activity. That is our objective. That is the objective of this stage. Anyone who thinks he is not capable of implementing this must tell me now, One of the best commanders, the commander of the Fifth

---

[4] The tape is cut off in mid-sentence at this point.

Corps, was reluctant, despite me providing him with more facilities than the First Corps. The result now is that the saboteurs are finished, and they had frozen 40 percent of Iraqi power.

When the [September 1988] amnesty was announced, I was about to get mad. But as a responsible party member I said OK. I said probably we will find some good ones among them [the Kurds], since they are our people too. But we didn't find any, never. If you ask me about the senior officials of the Kurds, which ones are good and loyal, I will say only the governors of Erbil and Suleimaniyeh. Apart from those two there are no loyal or good ones.

I cry when I see a tragic show or movie. One day I cried when I saw a woman who was lost and without a family in a movie. But I would like to tell you that I did what I did and what I was supposed to do. I don't think you could do more than what I could do.

I would like to speak about two points: one, arabization; and two, the shared zones between the Arab lands and the Autonomous Region. The point that we are talking about is Kirkuk. When I came, the Arabs and Turkomans were not more than fifty-one percent of the total population of Kirkuk.[5] Despite everything, I spent sixty million dinars until we reached the present situation. Now it is clear. For your information, the Arabs who were brought to Kirkuk didn't raise the percentage to sixty percent. Then we issued directives. I prohibited the Kurds from working in Kirkuk, the neighborhoods and the villages around it, outside the Autonomous Region....

Kirkuk is a mixture of nations, religions and doctrines. The people we deported from May 21 to June 21, not one of them was from the prohibited areas. But they were under the control of the saboteurs, whether they were for them or against them.

---

[5]   It is unclear here whether al-Majid is referring to the city or the governorate of Kirkuk.

APPENDIX B
THE PERPETRATORS OF ANFAL:
A ROAD-MAP TO THE PRINCIPAL AGENCIES AND
INDIVIDUALS

• **THE REVOLUTIONARY COMMAND COUNCIL:**
The highest formal authority in Iraq is the ruling Revolutionary Command Council (RCC), headed by President SADDAM HUSSEIN. While Saddam involved himself personally in operational aspects of Anfal through the Office of the Presidency of the Republic, supreme powers for handling Kurdish affairs between 1987-1989 were vested in his cousin, ALI HASSAN AL-MAJID.

• **THE BA'ATH ARAB SOCIALIST PARTY:**
Anfal was a Ba'ath Party operation, commanded by the party's Northern Bureau, buttressed administratively by the Northern Bureau Command and the Northern Affairs Committee of the RCC. Under RCC decree no.160 of March 29, 1987, the Northern Bureau's Secretary General, Ali Hassan al-Majid, was given extraordinary powers over all other state, party, military and security agencies. Al-Majid's co-signatory on Northern Bureau Command orders was TAHER TAWFIQ AL-ANI, secretary of the RCC's Northern Affairs Committee. Deputy Secretary of the Northern Bureau Command was RADHI HASSAN SALMAN.

Under al-Majid's command, the following were the other main agencies involved in Anfal.

• **THE IRAQI ARMY AND AIR FORCE** (including commandos, special forces, chemical weapons units, engineering corps): all field combat operations; village burnings and destruction; mass transportation of detainees. The Iraqi Defense Minister at the time of Anfal was Gen. ADNAN KHAIRALLAH (later deceased). The Army Chief of Staff was Brig. Gen. NIZAR ABD-AL-KARIM AL-KHAZRAJI. Most Anfal operations were handled by the Kirkuk-based First Corps (commander Lt. Gen. SULTAN HASHEM) and the Erbil-based Fifth Corps (commander Brig. Gen. YUNIS MOHAMMED AL-ZAREB).

355

Lt. Gen. Hashem was also the field commander of the First Anfal operation; Brig. Gen. AYAD KHALIL ZAKI and Brig. Gen. BAREQ ABDULLAH AL-HAJ HUNTA commanded the Second and Third Anfals respectively. The field commanders of other Anfals are not known.

• **REPUBLICAN GUARD:** elite combat operations during the First and Second Anfals.

• **GENERAL MILITARY INTELLIGENCE DIRECTORATE** (*MUDIRIYAT AL-ISTIKHBARAT AL-ASKARIYEH AL-AMEH*): supervision of initial holding facilities such as the Qoratu and Nizarkeh forts; some interrogation; matters affecting draft dodgers and deserters; field command of the *jahsh*. Two of *Istikhbarat*'s four regional commands played key roles in Anfal. The commander of Eastern Sector *Istikhbarat* was KHALED MUHAMMAD ABBAS; the commander of Northern Sector *Istikhbarat* was FARHAN MUTLAQ SALEH.

• **GENERAL SECURITY DIRECTORATE** (*MUDIRIYAT AL-AMN AL-AMEH*) (including the special units of Kurdish agents known as *Mafarez Khaseh*): case-by-case intelligence-gathering and surveillance of the population; interrogation of prisoners at Topzawa and other detention camps; supervision of informers; tracking down escapees and those sheltering them; monitoring of complexes. The director of *Amn* for the Kurdistan Autonomous Region was ABD-AL-RAHMAN AZIZ HUSSEIN.

• **EMERGENCY FORCES** (*QUWAT AL-TAWARE'*): Units under Ba'ath Party command, including members of the *jahsh* and *Amn* and police agents, in charge of urban intelligence and counter-terrorism and supervision of initial detention facilities in the city of Suleimaniyeh, and perhaps other locations.

• **NATIONAL DEFENSE BATTALIONS** (*JAHAFEL AL-DIFA' AL-WATANI*, or *jahsh*): auxiliary role in combat operations; roundups and surrender of prisoners; guard duty at collection points.

• **POPULAR ARMY** (*JAYSH AL-SHA'ABI*): guard duties at principal transit facilities (Topzawa, Dibs etc.)

• **INTER-AGENCY COMMITTEES:** a number of inter-agency groups were in charge of discrete aspects of the Anfal operation and associated anti-Kurdish campaigns during the 1987-1989 period. Normally chaired by a Ba'ath Party official, most included representatives of *Amn*, the Army's First and Fifth Corps and/or *Istikhbarat*, the Iraqi Police, and civilian authorities. The most notable were the following:

• **RETURNEE RECEPTION COMMITTEES** (*LAJNET ISTIQBAL AL-A'IDIN*): responsible for those "returning to the national ranks" under the General Amnesty between September 6 and October 9, 1988 and other later amnesties;

• **SECURITY COMMITTEES** (*LAJNET AL-AMNIYEH*) **and COMMITTEES TO FIGHT HOSTILE ACTIVITY** (*LAJNET MUKAFAHAT AL-NASHAT AL-MU'ADI*): organized to combat the *peshmerga* at the governorate and local level respectively; and a number of ad hoc committees which monitored the economic blockade of the "prohibited areas," controlled food rationing and attempted to prevent smuggling;

• **FOLLOW-UP COMMITTEES** (*LAJNET AL-MUTABA'A*): charged with ensuring compliance with laws governing returnees, tracking down escapees and otherwise tying up the loose ends of the campaign.

In addition, a number of civilian ministries played supportive roles in Anfal: For example, the Agriculture Ministry harvested and disposed of the abandoned 1988 crop; the Finance Ministry administered the confiscated property of "saboteurs" and oversaw house demolitions; while the Real Estate Bank arranged loans for new housing in the complexes.

APPENDIX C
KNOWN CHEMICAL ATTACKS
IN IRAQI KURDISTAN, 1987-1988

This table includes only those attacks that Middle East Watch has been able to document through eyewitness testimony. The true figure may be considerably higher, since we have received many other unconfirmed reports and allegations of chemical weapons attacks during 1987-1988. Based on our field interviews, at least sixty villages, as well as the town of Halabja, were attacked with mustard gas, nerve gas, or a combination of the two;

The Iraqi regime appears to have used chemical weapons for at least four complementary purposes:

(a) To attack base camps and main-force concentrations of Kurdish *peshmerga*. This logic accounts for many of the attacks on the Jafati valley (First Anfal), the Qara Dagh area (Second Anfal), the Balisan and Smaquli valleys (Fifth, Sixth and Seventh Anfals) and Zewa Shkan (Final Anfal);

(b) To harass and kill retreating *peshmerga* as Anfal progressed. Attacks of this sort include those on Shanakhseh (#14 in the accompanying table), Zerda mountain (#19), Tazashar (#20) and the Shaqlawa-Rawanduz area (#26 and 27);

(c) To inflict exemplary collective punishment on civilians for their support for the *peshmerga*. The most dramatic case is the bombing of Halabja after the seizure of the town by *peshmerga* and Iranian revolutionary guards. Others include the 1987 attacks on Sheikh Wasan and Balisan (#4), and the Anfal attacks on Sayw Senan (#15) and Goktapa (#22);

(d) To spread terror amongst the civilian population as a whole, flushing villagers out of their homes to facilitate their capture, relocation and killing. The opening of almost every phase of the Anfal campaign was marked by attacks of this sort, but they are most apparent in the Final Anfal (*Khatimat al-Anfal*) in the Badinan region, where more than thirty villages were bombed simultaneously along an east-west strip on the morning of August 25, 1988.

While a distinction between these different kinds of targets is helpful in understanding the tactical thinking behind the Iraqi campaign, it is without meaning in legal terms. Chemical weapons are by their nature indiscriminate, and their use is outlawed under any circumstances.

DATE (M/D/Y)	LOCATION	MEANS	DEATHS
1. 4/15/87	Sergalou-Bergalou	air	not known
2. 4/15/87	Gojar mountain, Mawat	rajima*	not known
3. 4/15/87	Zewa Shkan	air	not known
4. 4/16/87	Sheikh Wasan, Balisan	air	225-400**
5. 5/?/87	Ja'faran (Qara Dagh)	rajima	--
6. 5/?/87	Serko (Qara Dagh)	air	--
7. 5/27/87	Bileh, Malakan (village and valley)	air	1+
8. 5-7/87	Bergalou, Haladin, Yakhsamar, Sekaniyan and surrounding areas (repeated attacks)	air + rajima	7+
9. 2/?/88	Sheikh Bzeini area	air	--
10. 2/?/88	Takiyeh, Balagjar	air	--
11. 3/16/88	Halabja	air	3,200-5,000

FIRST ANFAL (JAFATI VALLEY)

12. 2/23/88	Yakhsamar	*rajima*	5
13. 2/23-3/18/88	Sergalou, Bergalou, Haladin and neighboring villages and mountains (constant attacks)	air *rajima*	+ not known
14. 3/22/88	Shanakhseh	air	up to 28

SECOND ANFAL (QARA DAGH)

15. 3/22/88	Sayw Senan	*rajima*	78-87
16. 3/23/88	Dukan	*rajima*	not known
17. 3/24/88	Ja'faran	*rajima*	--
18. 3/24/88	Masoyi	helicopter	--
19. c.3/30/88	Zerda Mountain (Qara Dagh)	*rajima*	--

THIRD ANFAL (GERMIAN)

20. 4/10/88	Tazashar	air	15-25

FOURTH ANFAL (LESSER ZAB VALLEY)

21. 5/3/88	Askar	air	9
22. 5/3/88	Goktapa	air	154-300

FIFTH, SIXTH AND SEVENTH ANFAL (SHAQLAWA-RAWANDUZ)

23. 5/15/88	Wara	air	37
24. 5/23/88	Seran; Balisan, Hiran and Smaquli valleys	air	2+
25. 5/26/88	Akoyan, Faqian, Rashki Baneshan mountain	*rajima*	--
26. 7/31/88	Malakan, Seran, Garawan; Balisan, Hiran, Smaquli and Benmerd valleys	air	13+
27. 8/8-8/26/88	Balisan valley and adjacent areas (constant attacks)	air	not known

FINAL ANFAL (BADINAN)***

28. 8/24/88	Zewa Shkan	air + *rajima*	not known
29. 8/25/88	Birjinni	air	4
30. 8/25/88	Tilakru	air	not known
31. 8/25/88	Gelnaski	air	--
32. 8/25/88	Tuka, Barkavreh	air	14-15
33. 8/25/88	Warmilleh, Bilejaneh	air	--
34. 8/25/88	Ikmala, Heseh, Khrabeh	air	3-6
35. 8/25/88	Ruseh, Nazdureh	air	1+
36. 8/25/88	Berrabareh	air	--
37. 8/25/88	Swareh, Spindar, Avok, Sidara (south side of Gara Mountain)	air	2+

38. 8/25/88	Mergeti, Bawarkeh Kavri and other villages (north side of Gara Mountain)	air	not known
39. 8/25/88	Gizeh, Rodinya, Shirana and other villages (center of Gara Mountain)	air	9+
40. 8/25/88	Baluka	air	not known

* truck-mounted multiple barrel artillery.

** the dead include two busloads of adult men and teenage boys subsequently disappeared from *Amn* captivity.

*** Final Anfal fatality statistics refer only to on-site deaths; they exclude later deaths from the effects of chemicals.

APPENDIX D
SAMPLE MASS DISAPPEARANCES
DURING ANFAL, BY REGION

This table attempts to show the pattern, not the scale, of civilian disappearances and presumed mass killings during each successive phase of the Anfal campaign. Representing only a very small fraction of the total numbers lost during Anfal, it includes only those who were reported by name, or by precise numerical count, during more than 350 Middle East Watch field interviews with survivors.

FIRST ANFAL

No meaningful figures exist and there is no evidence to suggest mass disappearance of civilians. Recorded fatalities from four villages--Haladin, Sergalou, Qara Chatan (*nahya* Surdash) and Maluma (*nahya* Kareza)--seem to refer to deaths from bombing, shelling, chemical attacks, exposure and cold.

SECOND ANFAL

nahya	*villages*	*total disappeared*	*men*	*women*	*children*	*unspecified*
Qara Dagh/ Serchinar (a)	9	56	32	--	--	24
Qara Dagh/ Serchinar (b)	5	103	23	27	17	36
TOTAL:	14	159	55	27	17	60

(a) = villages whose inhabitants fled to Suleimaniyeh
(b) = villages whose inhabitants fled to Germian

THIRD ANFAL

nahya	villages	total disappeared	men	women	children	unspecified
Qader Karam (a)	13	148	129	--	--	19
Qader Karam (b)	8	208	110	6	27	65
Qara Hanjir	1	3	3	--	--	--
Qara Hassan	1	--	--	--	--	--
Altun Kupri	1	8	8	--	--	--
Sengaw[1]	9	196	60	11	21	104
Tilako	7	200	17	27	69	87
Kalar[2]	1	200	6	2	3	189
Serqala	2	82	6	3	10	63
Peibaz	5	273	24	22	54	173
TOTAL:	48	1318	363	71	184	700

(a) = areas where no combat is reported in army documents
(b) = areas of combat (Gulbagh Valley, Tazashar southward)

FOURTH ANFAL

nahya	villages	total disappeared	men	women	children	unspecified
Aghjalar	10	155	47	29	79	--
Shwan	7	68	43	9	16	--
Taqtaq	5	162	22	11	16	113
TOTAL:	22	385	112	49	111	113

---

[1] The heaviest pattern of mass disappearances from Sengaw appears to reflect paths of flight--either into southern Germian or toward Chamchamal through the Gulbagh Valley.

[2] The figure is an approximation, but the witness reported that almost all those who disappeared were women and children.

FIFTH, SIXTH, SEVENTH ANFALS
(*NAHYAS* KHALIFAN, RAWANDUZ, HARIR)

nahya	villages	total disappeared	men	women	children	unspecified
TOTAL:	5	123	59	7	6	51

FINAL ANFAL

(a) Kurdish villages
(b) Christian/Yezidi villages

nahya	villages	total disappeared	men	women	children	unspecified
Sarseng (a)	17	189	189	--	--	--
al-Doski (a)	7	175	175	--	--	--
Zawita (a)	1	1	1	--	--	--
al-Guli (a)	2	30	30	--	--	--
al-Sindi (a)	3	42	42	--	--	--
Berwari Bala (a)	2	40	40	--	--	--
Amadiya (a)	1	9	9	--	--	9
Nerwa Reikan (a)	3	155	155	--	--	--
Sarseng (b)	3	86	11	13	26	36
al-Doski (b)	1	34	11	11	3	9
Berwari Bala (b)	1	6	4	2	--	--
Deralouk (b)	1	17	6	2	9	--
Nerwa Reikan (b)	1	7	2	2	3	--
ALL (a)	36	632	632[3]	--	--	--
ALL (b)	7	150	34	30	41	45
TOTAL:	43	782	666	30	41	45

OVERALL

TOTAL:	132	2767	1255	184	359	969
AS PERCENTAGE		100.0	45.4	6.6	13.0	35.0

---

[3] Includes five boys aged 12 or 13.

APPENDIX E
GLOSSARY OF ARABIC AND KURDISH TERMS

Amn: Security (as in Mudiriyat al-Amn al-Ameh, General Security Directorate)

Chatta: Bandit or brigand; derogatory term for jahsh in Badinan region

Intifada: Uprising

Istikhbarat: Military Intelligence

Jahsh: Donkey foal; derogatory term for Kurdish National Defense Battalions

Lak: Peshmerga Branch Command (KDP)

Mafarez Khaseh: Special Unit (Kurdish section of *Amn*)

Maghawir: Commandos

Malband: Peshmerga Regional Command (PUK)

Mujamma'a: Complex or collective village used for Kurdish resettlement

Mukhabarat: Foreign Intelligence Agency

Mustashar: Adviser or consultant; Kurdish tribal commander of a *jahsh* unit

Nahya: Administrative unit; district center, and the villages within its jurisdiction

369

Peshmerga:	"Those who face death"; Kurdish guerrilla fighters
Qadha:	The largest administrative unit within a governorate
Rajima:	Truck-mounted multiple-barrel artillery, sometimes used to deliver chemical weapons
Sura:	Chapter of the Koran
Teep:	Division; basic PUK military unit within the malband